# JUST PRETEND

# JUST PRETEND

## TORI SHARP

Little, Brown and Company
New York  Boston

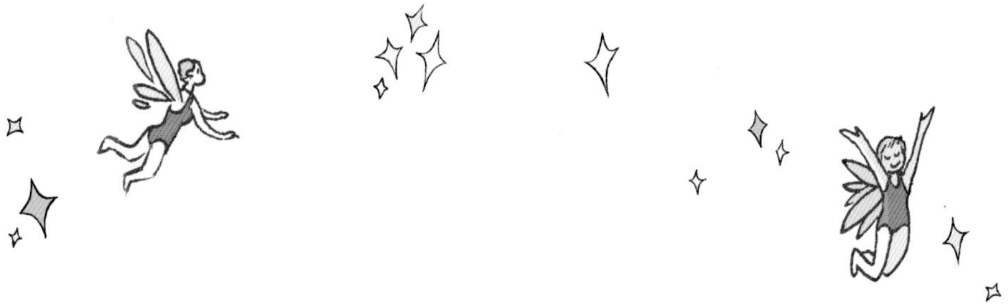

**ABOUT THIS BOOK**

This book was edited by Andrea Colvin and designed by Angelie Yap under the art direction of Sasha Illingworth. The production was supervised by Bernadette Flinn, and the production editor was Lindsay Walter-Greaney. The text was set in Anime Ace 2.0 BB, and the display type is Chin Up Buttercup Cutecaps.

 • Little, Brown and Company • Hachette Book Group • 1290 Avenue of the Americas, New York, NY 10104 • Visit us at LBYR.com • First Edition: May 2021 • Little, Brown and Company is a division of Hachette Book Group, Inc. • The Little, Brown name and logo are trademarks of Hachette Book Group, Inc. • The publisher is not responsible for websites (or their content) that are not owned by the publisher. • Library of Congress Cataloging-in-Publication Data • Names: Sharp, Tori, author, illustrator. • Title: Just pretend / Tori Sharp. • Description: First edition. | New York : Little, Brown and Company, 2021. | Summary: "Tori makes up stories all of the time, so she has never lived in just one world. Those stories might just save her when her world seems to crumble"–Provided by publisher. • Identifiers: LCCN 2020022102 (print) | LCCN 2020022103 (ebook) | ISBN 9780316538893 (hardcover) | ISBN 9780316538855 (paperback) | ISBN 9780316538862 (ebook) | ISBN 9780316538879 (ebook other) • Subjects: LCSH: Sharp, Tori–Childhood and youth–Juvenile literature. | Illustrators–United States–Biography–Juvenile literature. | Authors, American–21st century–Biography–Juvenile literature. | Graphic novels–Authorship–Juvenile literature. | Children of divorced parents–United States–Biography–Juvenile literature. | Graphic novels. • Classification: LCC PN6727.S488 Z46 2021 (print) | LCC PN6727.S488 (ebook) | DDC 741.5/973 [B]–dc23 • LC record available at https://lccn.loc.gov/2020022102 • LC ebook record available at https://lccn.loc.gov/2020022103 • ISBNs: 978-0-316-53889-3 (hardcover), 978-0-316-53885-5 (pbk.), 978-0-316-53886-2 (ebook), 978-0-316-59211-6 (ebook), 978-0-316-59212-3 (ebook) • PRINTED IN CHINA • APS • Hardcover: 10 9 8 7 6 5 4 3 2 1 • Paperback: 10 9 8 7 6 5 4 3

FOR TAYLOR.
I CAN'T IMAGINE A BETTER BFF.

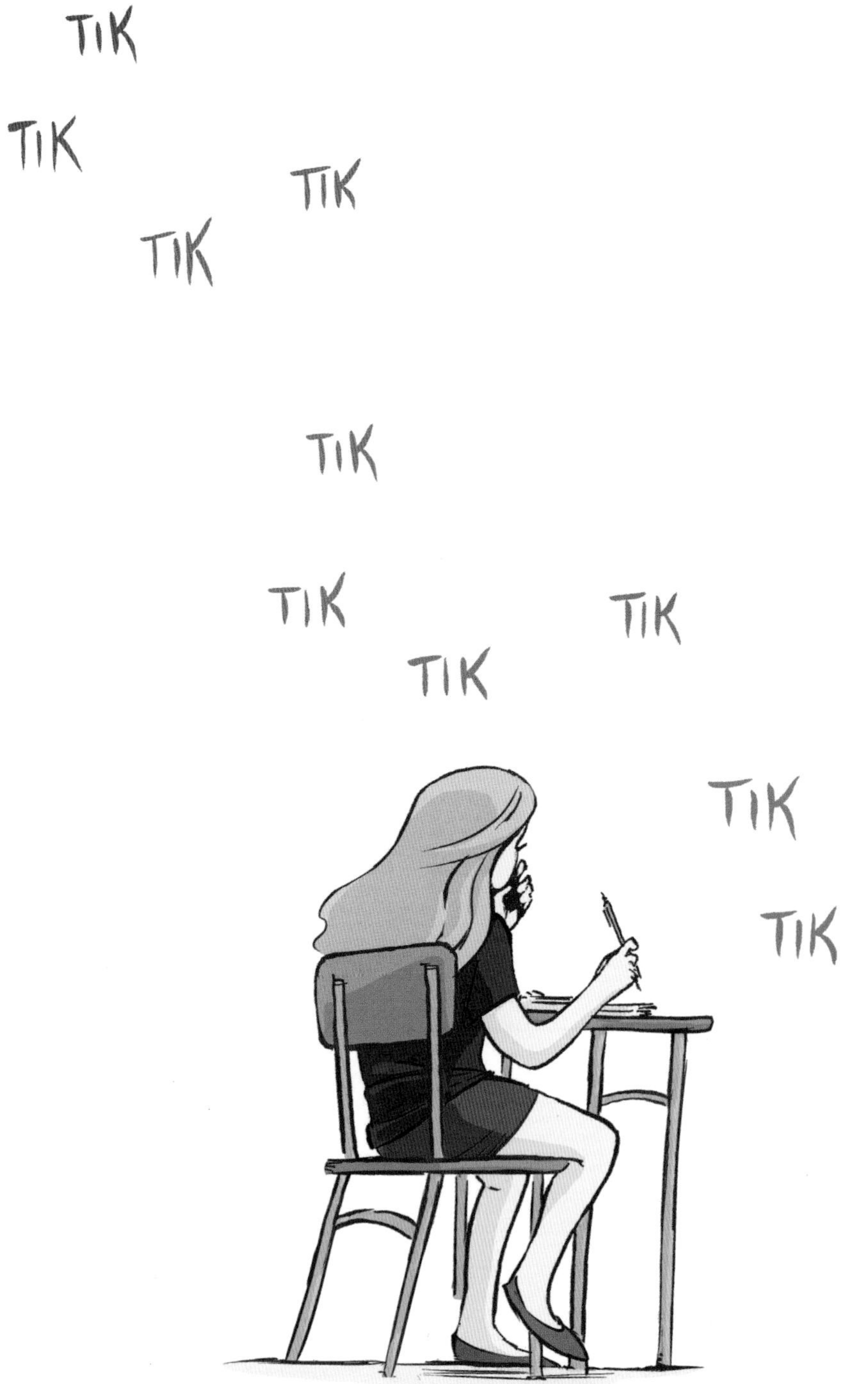
TIK
TIK
TIK
TIK
TIK
TIK
TIK
TIK
TIK
TIK

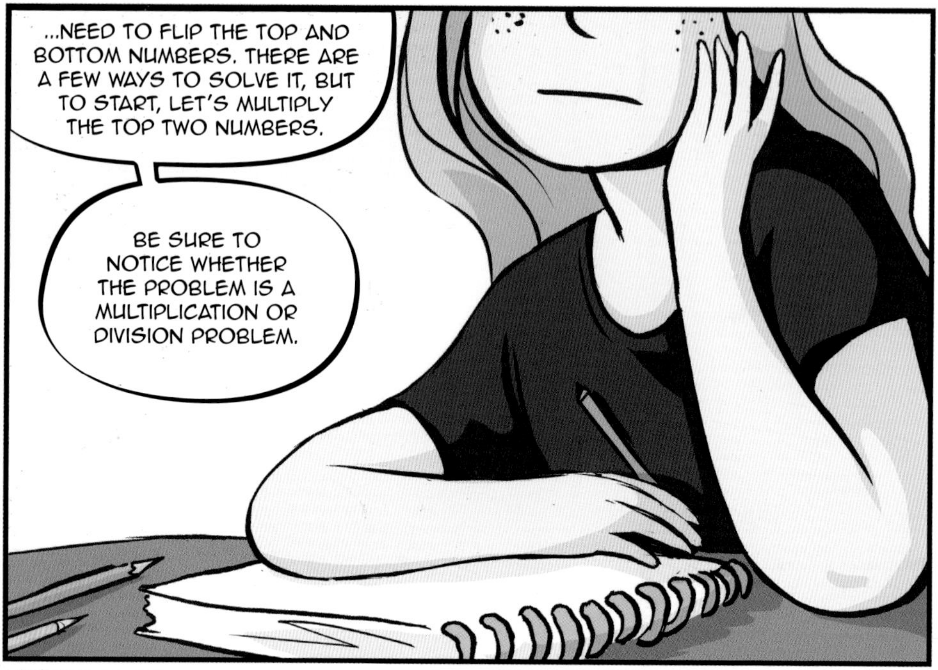
...NEED TO FLIP THE TOP AND BOTTOM NUMBERS. THERE ARE A FEW WAYS TO SOLVE IT, BUT TO START, LET'S MULTIPLY THE TOP TWO NUMBERS.
BE SURE TO NOTICE WHETHER THE PROBLEM IS A MULTIPLICATION OR DIVISION PROBLEM.

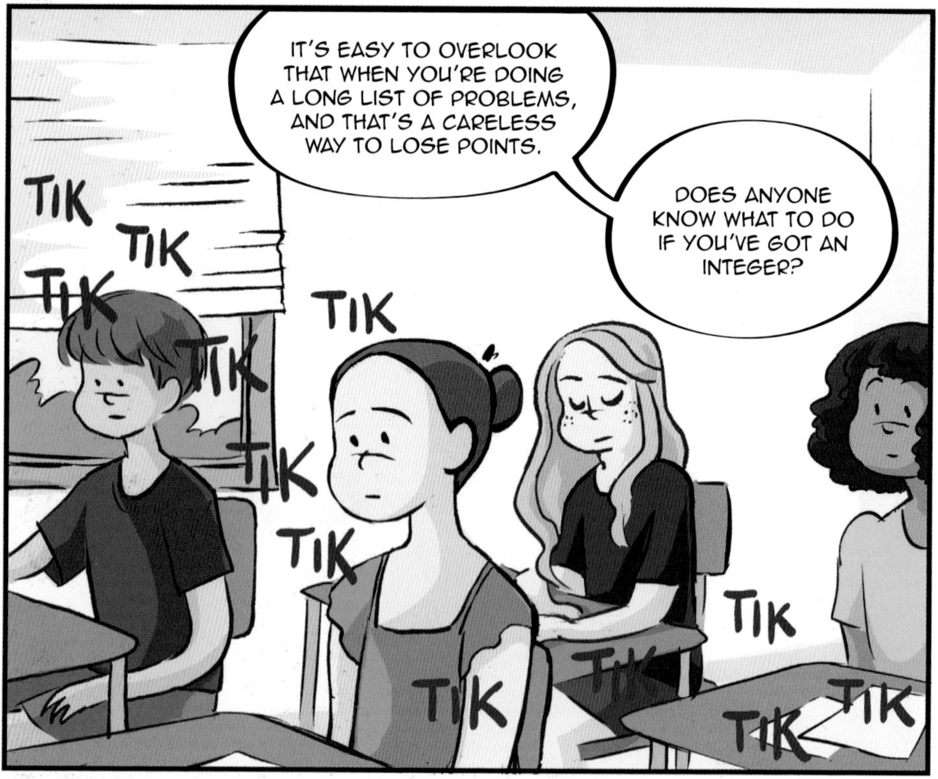
IT'S EASY TO OVERLOOK THAT WHEN YOU'RE DOING A LONG LIST OF PROBLEMS, AND THAT'S A CARELESS WAY TO LOSE POINTS.
DOES ANYONE KNOW WHAT TO DO IF YOU'VE GOT AN INTEGER?
TIK
TIK
TIK
TIK
TIK
TIK
TIK
TIK
TIK
TIK
TIK
TIK

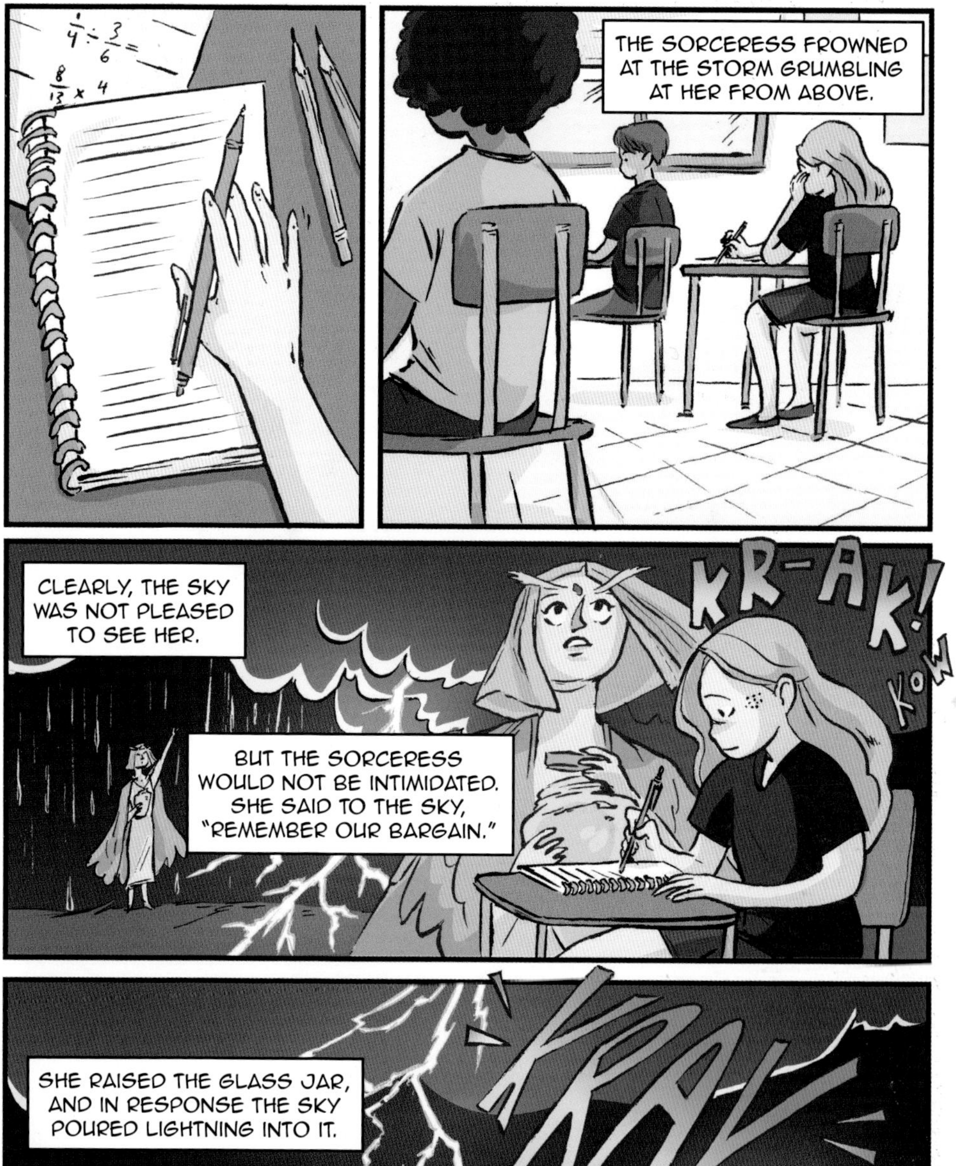

$\frac{1}{4} \div \frac{3}{6} =$
$\frac{8}{13} \times 4$
THE SORCERESS FROWNED AT THE STORM GRUMBLING AT HER FROM ABOVE.
CLEARLY, THE SKY WAS NOT PLEASED TO SEE HER.
KR-AK!
KOW
BUT THE SORCERESS WOULD NOT BE INTIMIDATED. SHE SAID TO THE SKY, "REMEMBER OUR BARGAIN."
KRAK
SHE RAISED THE GLASS JAR, AND IN RESPONSE THE SKY POURED LIGHTNING INTO IT.
THE SKY THUNDERED, "YOU OWE ME."

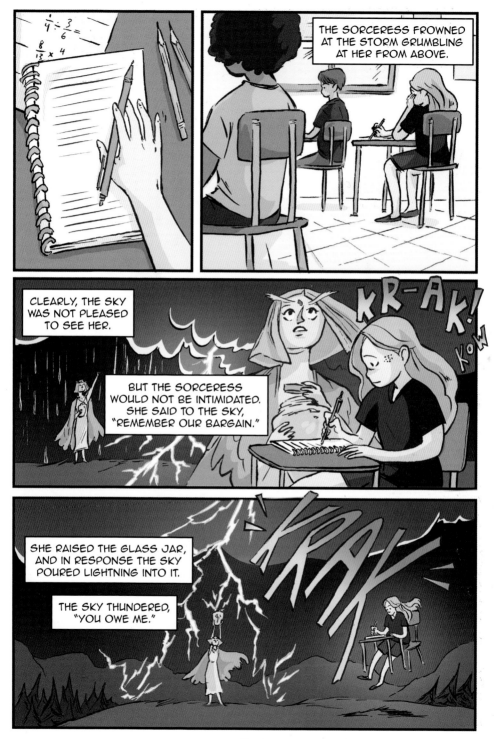

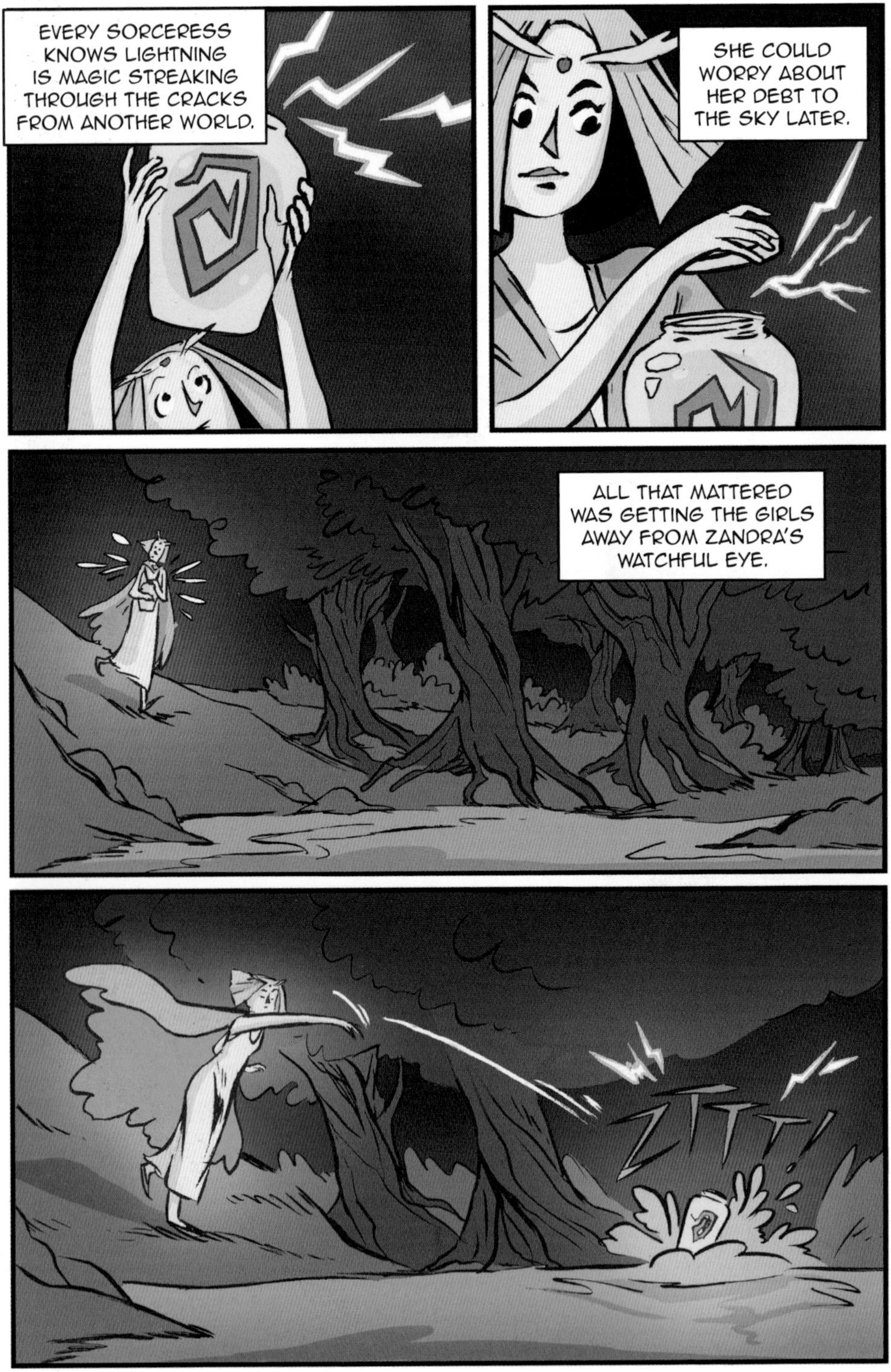
EVERY SORCERESS KNOWS LIGHTNING IS MAGIC STREAKING THROUGH THE CRACKS FROM ANOTHER WORLD.
SHE COULD WORRY ABOUT HER DEBT TO THE SKY LATER.
ALL THAT MATTERED WAS GETTING THE GIRLS AWAY FROM ZANDRA'S WATCHFUL EYE.
ZTTT!

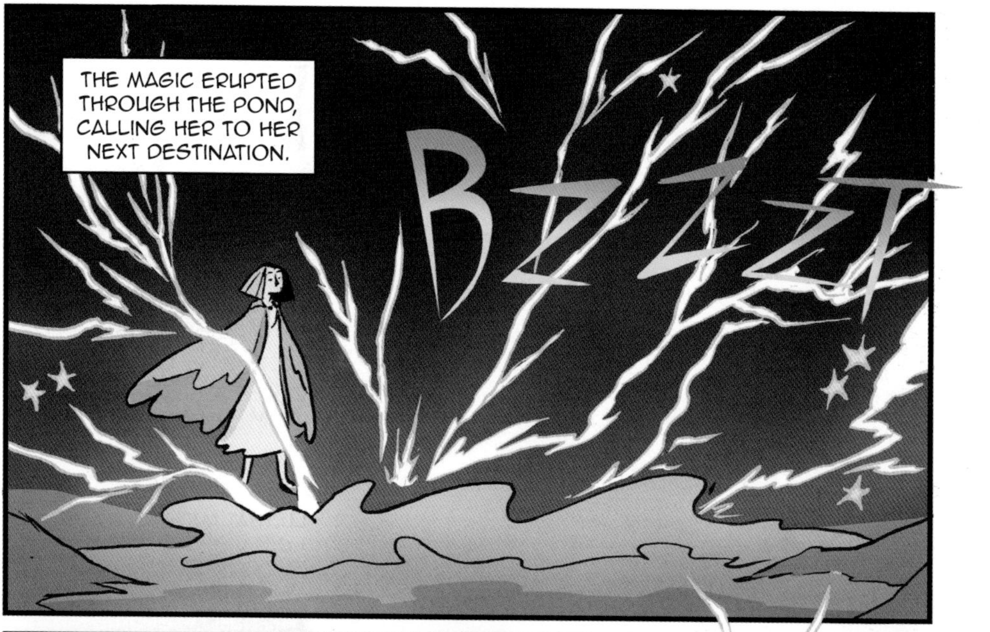
THE MAGIC ERUPTED THROUGH THE POND, CALLING HER TO HER NEXT DESTINATION.
BZZZT

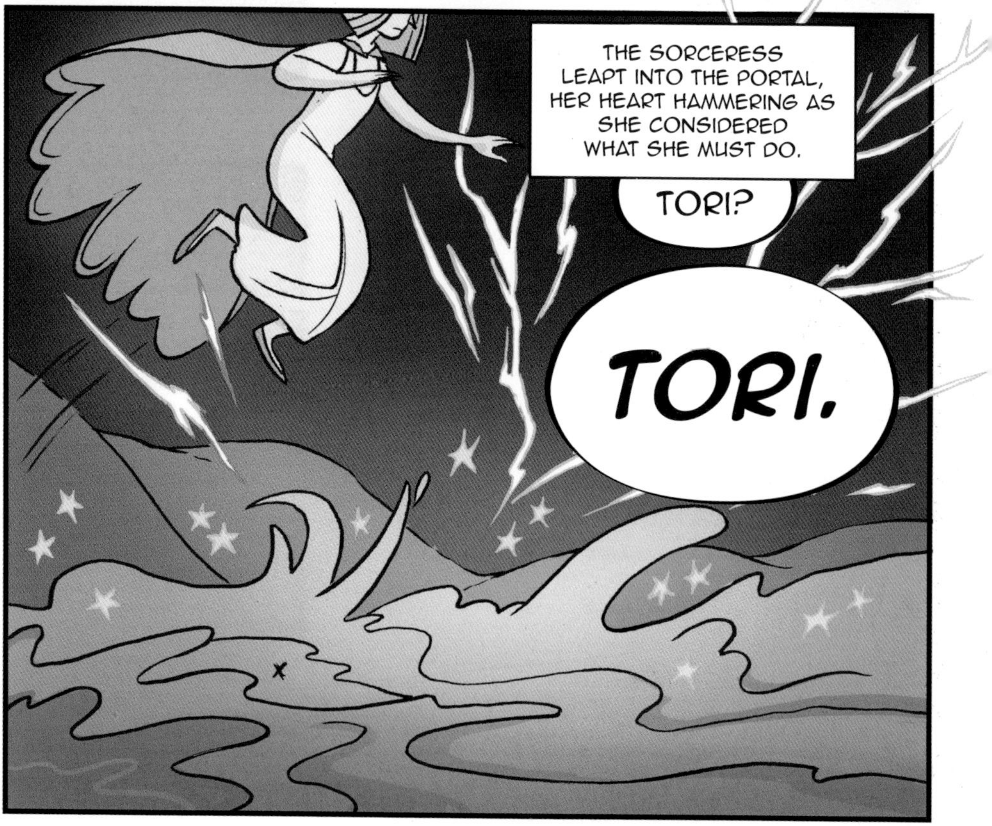
THE SORCERESS LEAPT INTO THE PORTAL, HER HEART HAMMERING AS SHE CONSIDERED WHAT SHE MUST DO.
TORI?
TORI.

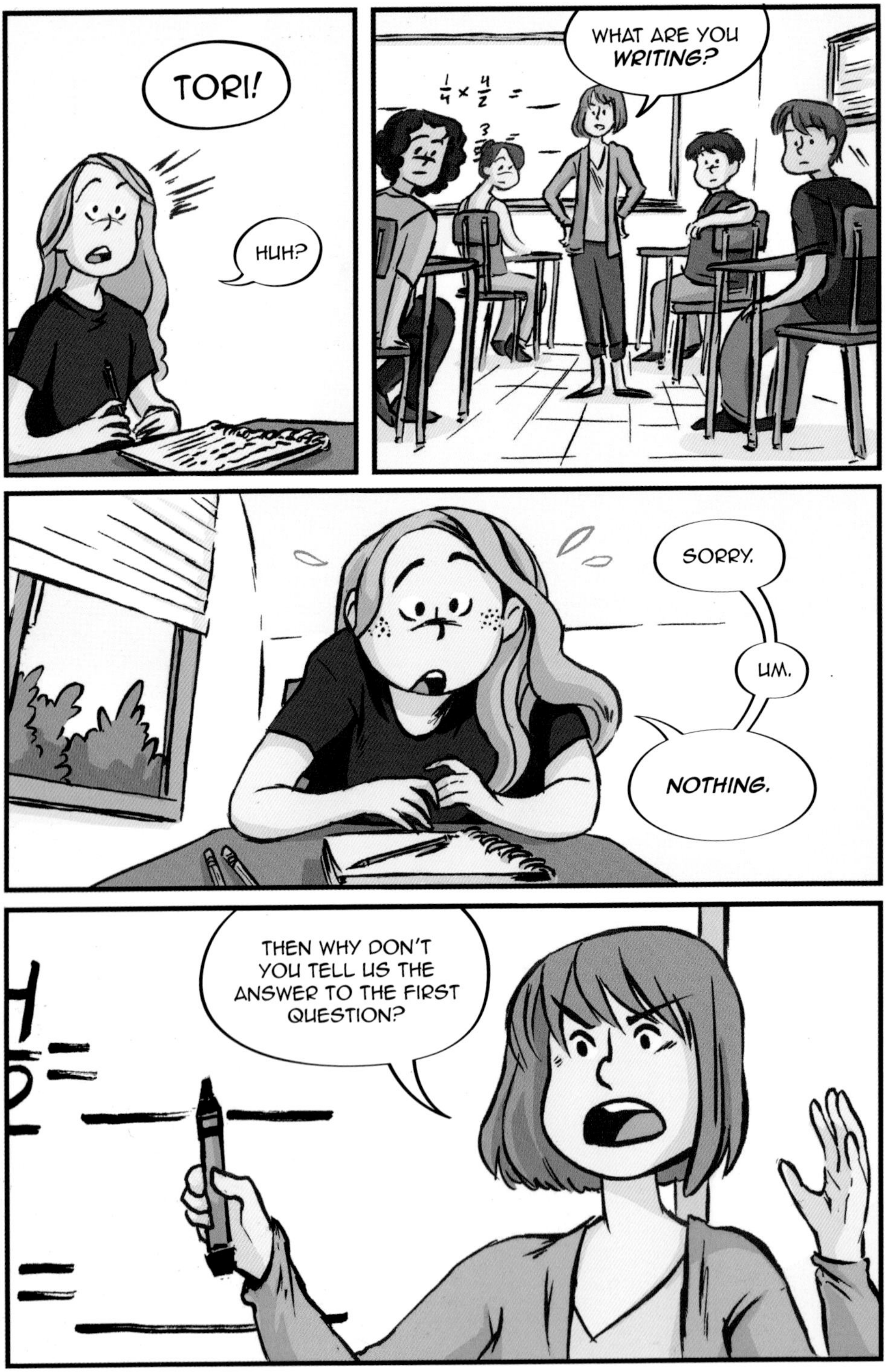
TORI!
HUH?
WHAT ARE YOU *WRITING?*
SORRY.
UM.
*NOTHING.*
THEN WHY DON'T YOU TELL US THE ANSWER TO THE FIRST QUESTION?

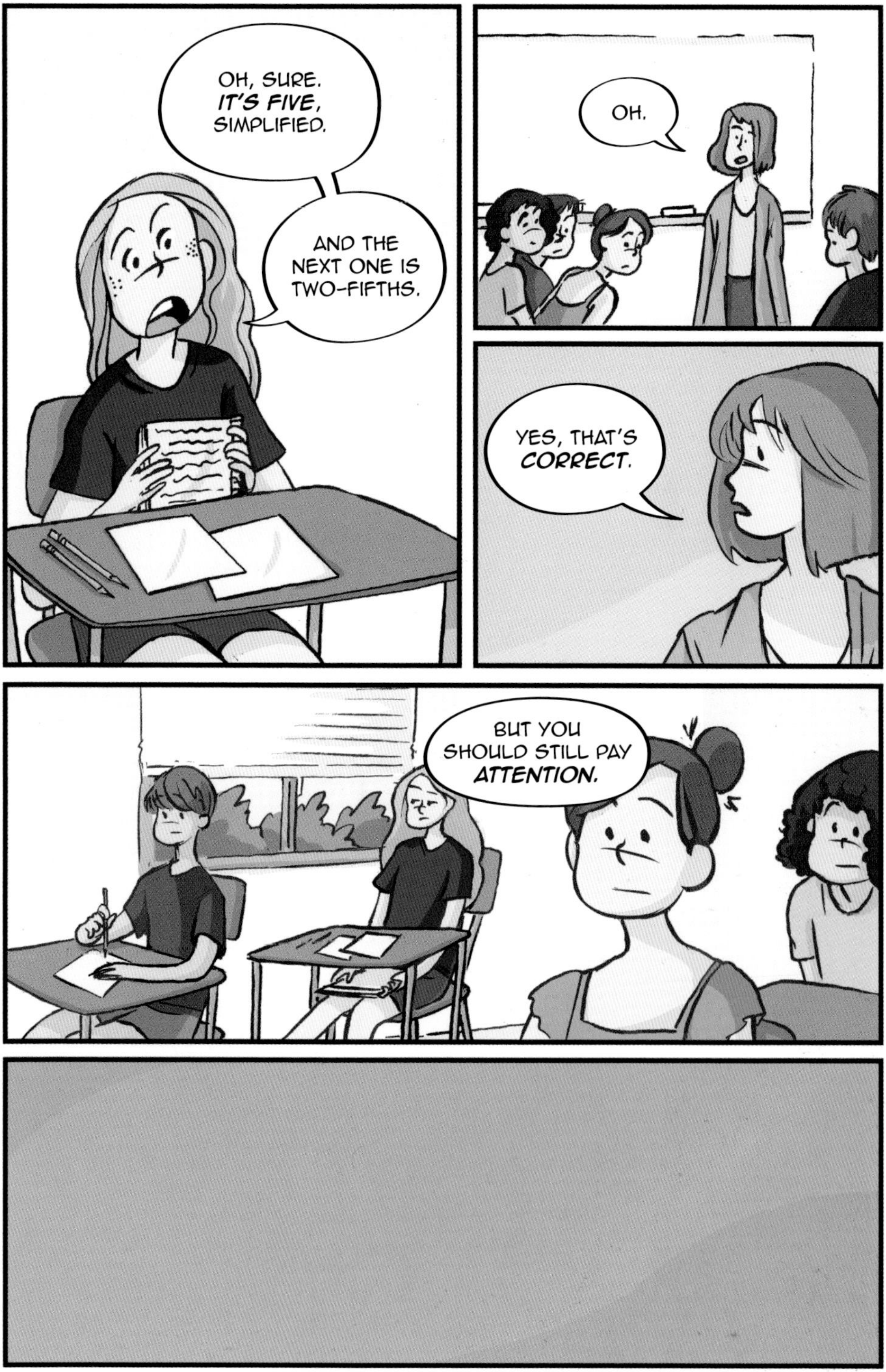
OH, SURE. IT'S FIVE, SIMPLIFIED.
AND THE NEXT ONE IS TWO-FIFTHS.
OH.
YES, THAT'S CORRECT.
BUT YOU SHOULD STILL PAY ATTENTION.

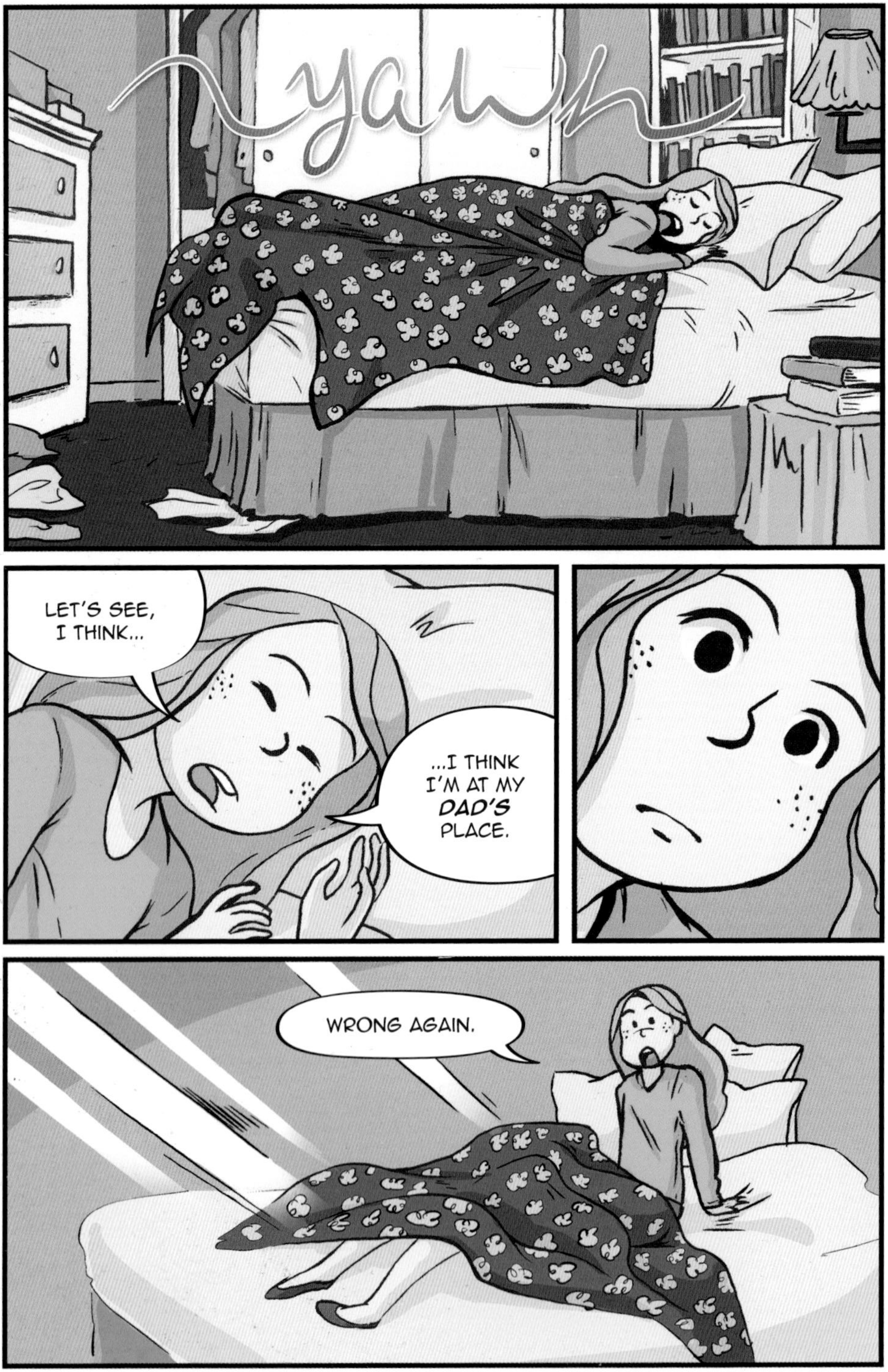
yawn
LET'S SEE, I THINK...
...I THINK I'M AT MY *DAD'S* PLACE.
WRONG AGAIN.

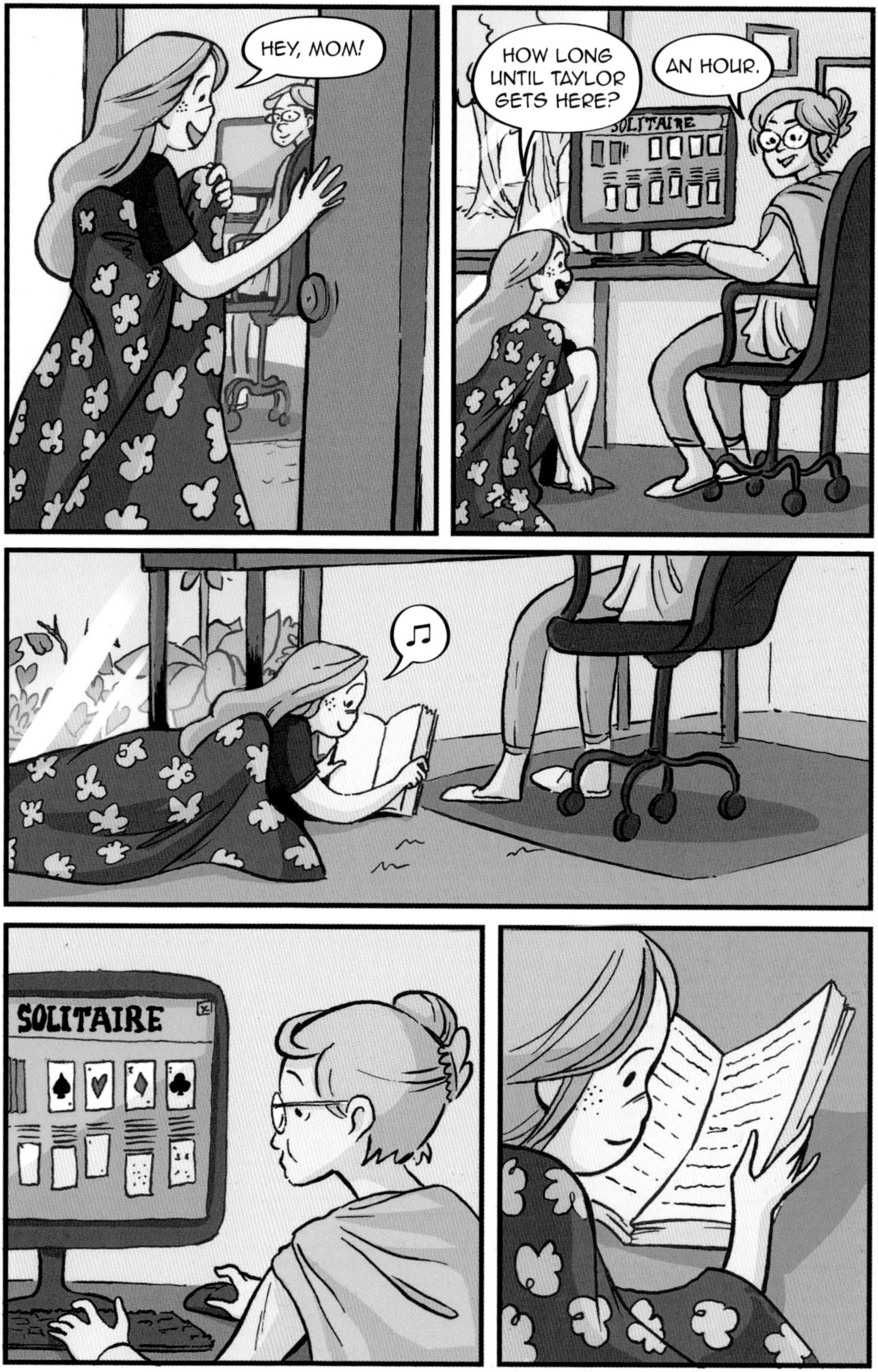
HEY, MOM!
HOW LONG UNTIL TAYLOR GETS HERE?
AN HOUR.
SOLITAIRE
♫
SOLITAIRE

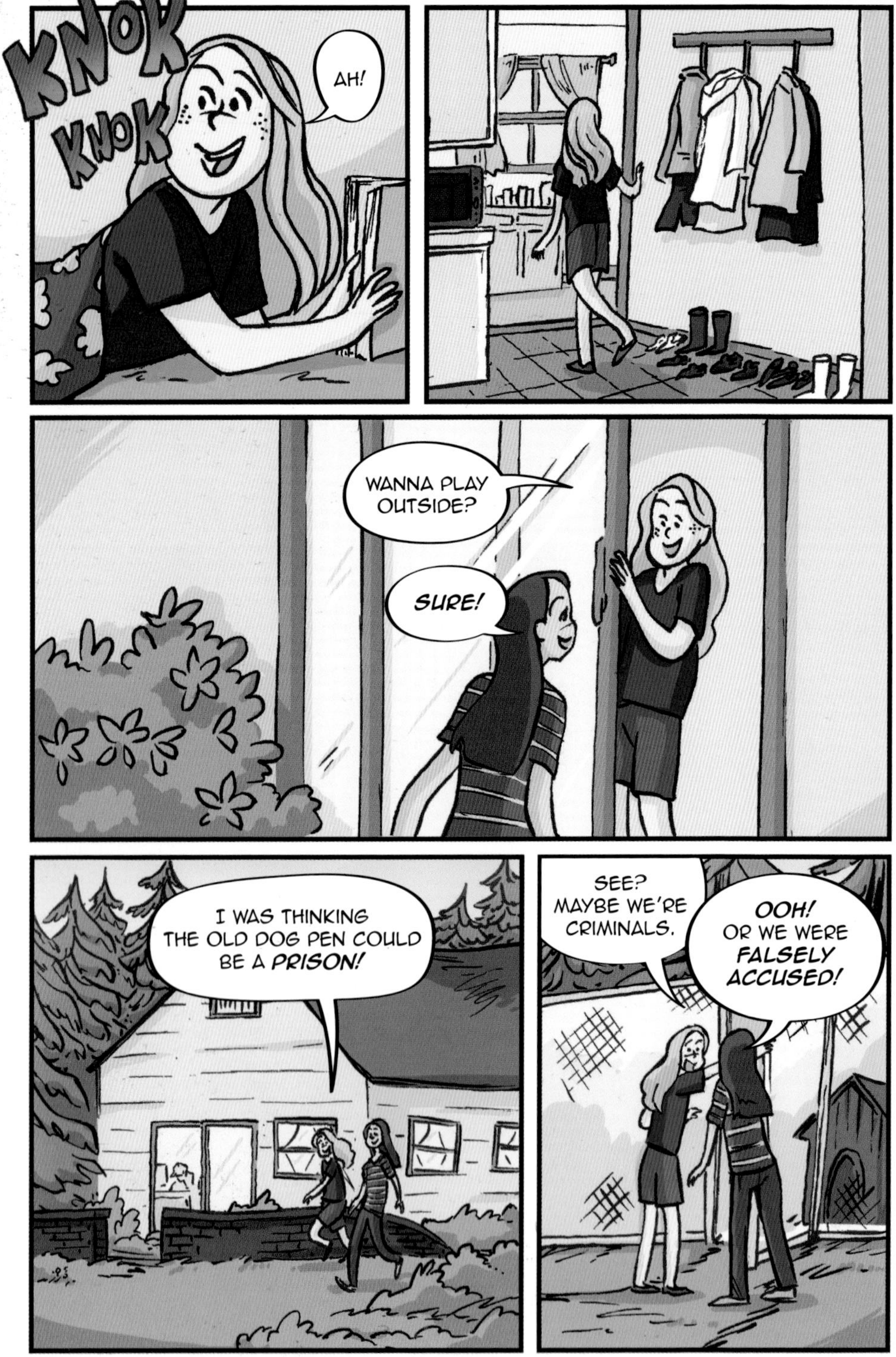
KNOK
KNOK
AH!
WANNA PLAY OUTSIDE?
SURE!
I WAS THINKING THE OLD DOG PEN COULD BE A PRISON!
SEE? MAYBE WE'RE CRIMINALS.
OOH! OR WE WERE FALSELY ACCUSED!

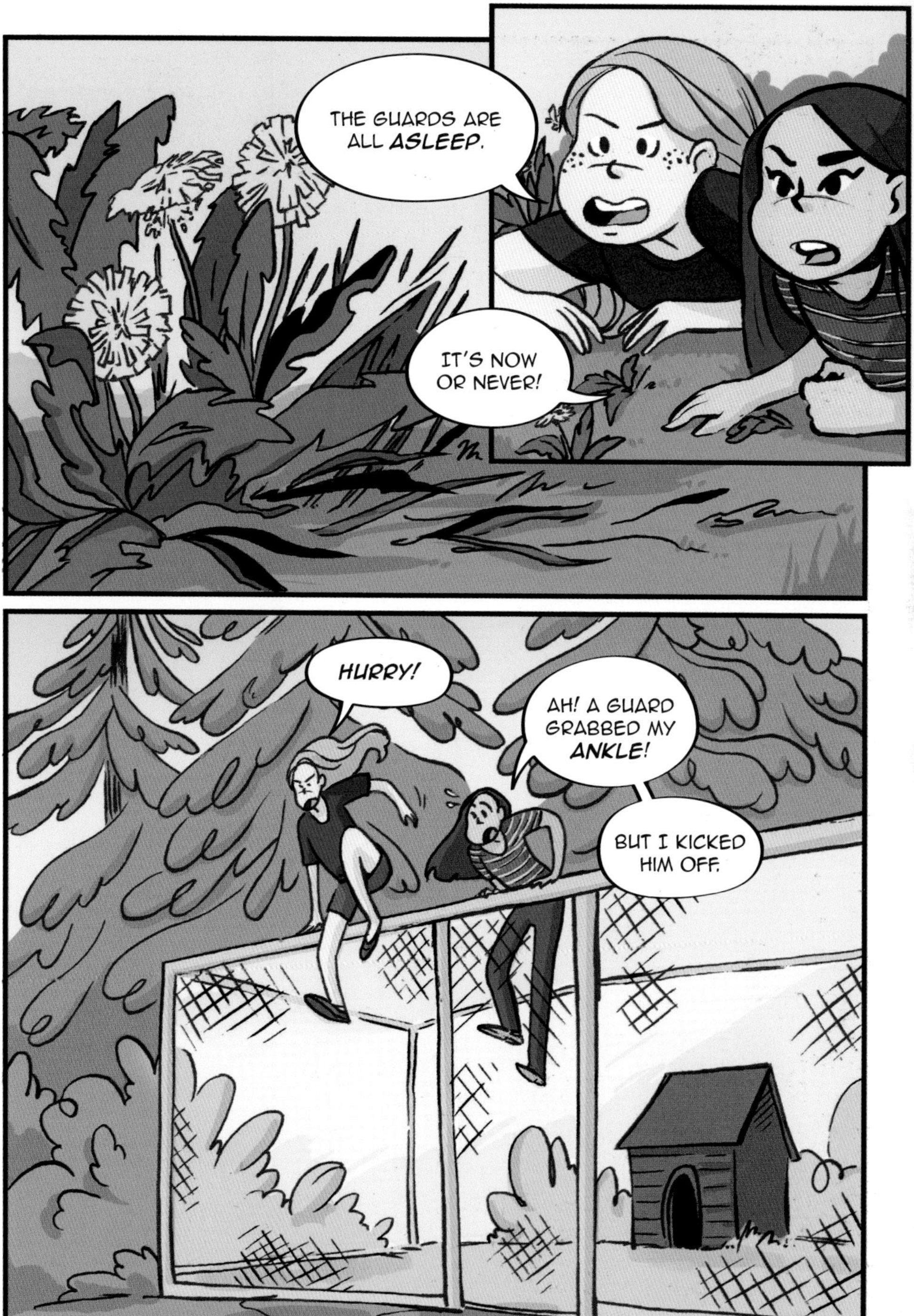
THE GUARDS ARE ALL ASLEEP.
IT'S NOW OR NEVER!
HURRY!
AH! A GUARD GRABBED MY ANKLE!
BUT I KICKED HIM OFF.

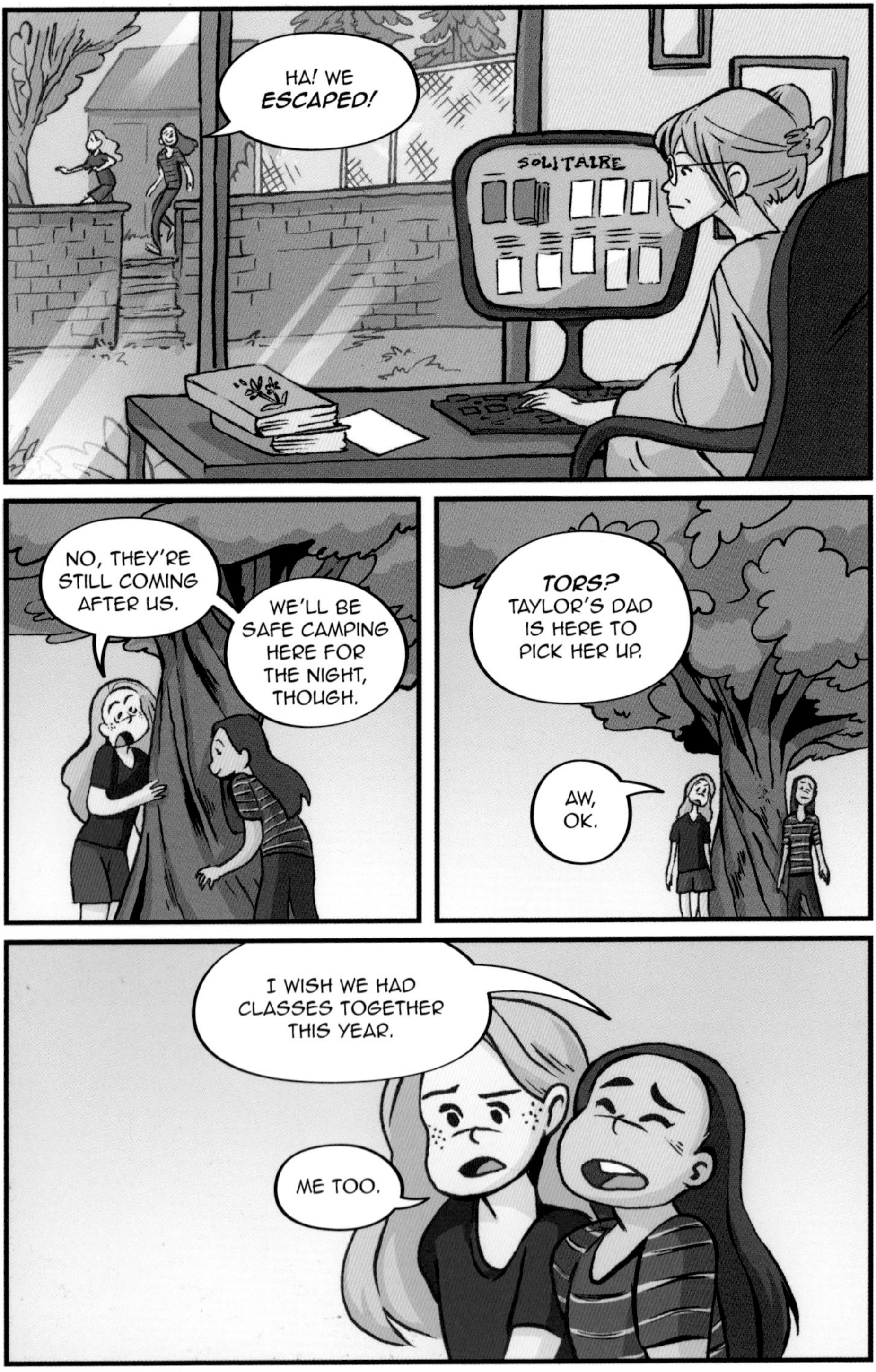
HA! WE ESCAPED!
SOLITAIRE
NO, THEY'RE STILL COMING AFTER US.
WE'LL BE SAFE CAMPING HERE FOR THE NIGHT, THOUGH.
TORS? TAYLOR'S DAD IS HERE TO PICK HER UP.
AW, OK.
I WISH WE HAD CLASSES TOGETHER THIS YEAR.
ME TOO.

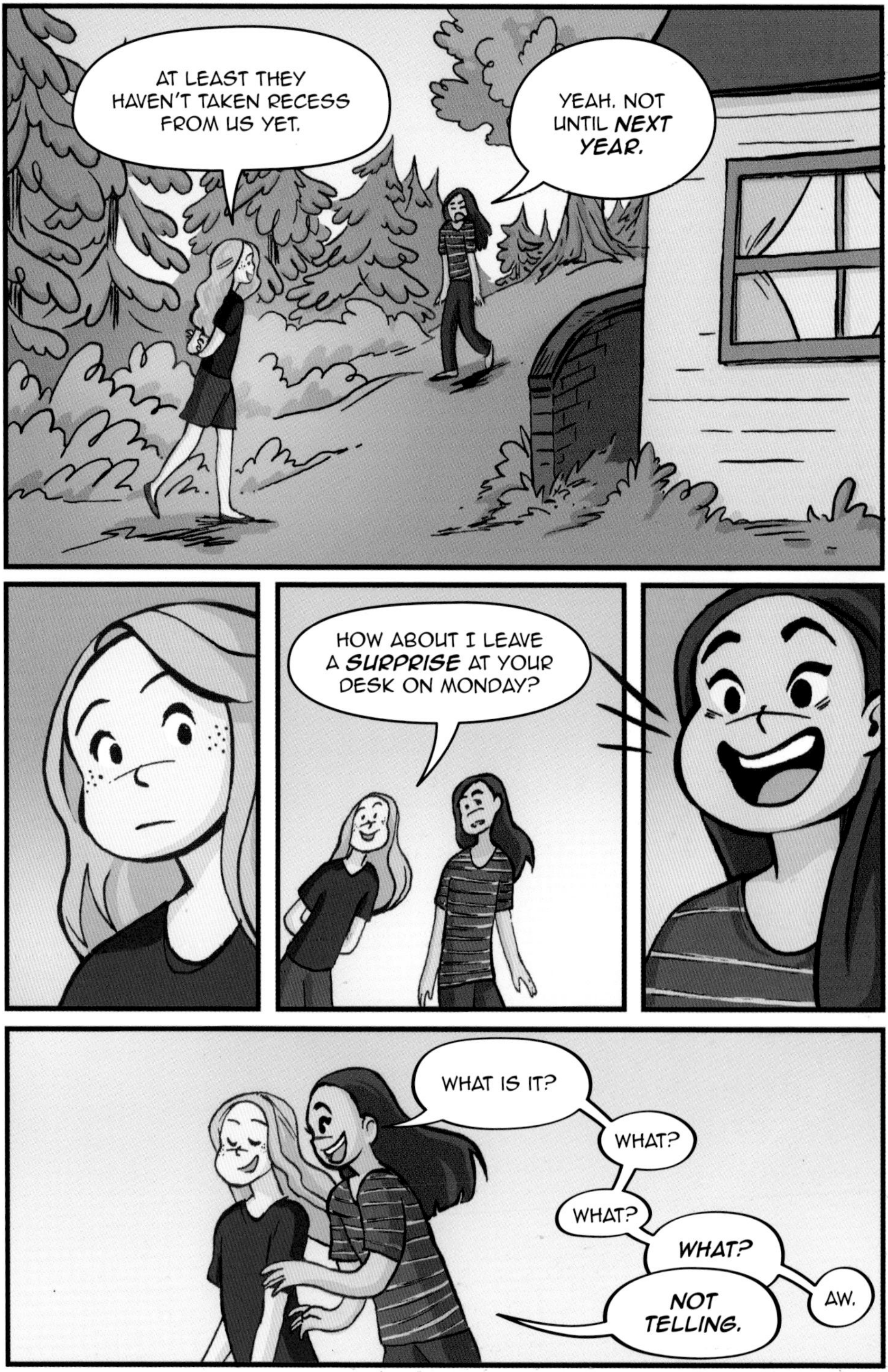
AT LEAST THEY HAVEN'T TAKEN RECESS FROM US YET.
YEAH. NOT UNTIL **NEXT YEAR.**
HOW ABOUT I LEAVE A **SURPRISE** AT YOUR DESK ON MONDAY?
WHAT IS IT?
WHAT?
WHAT?
**WHAT?**
**NOT TELLING.**
AW.

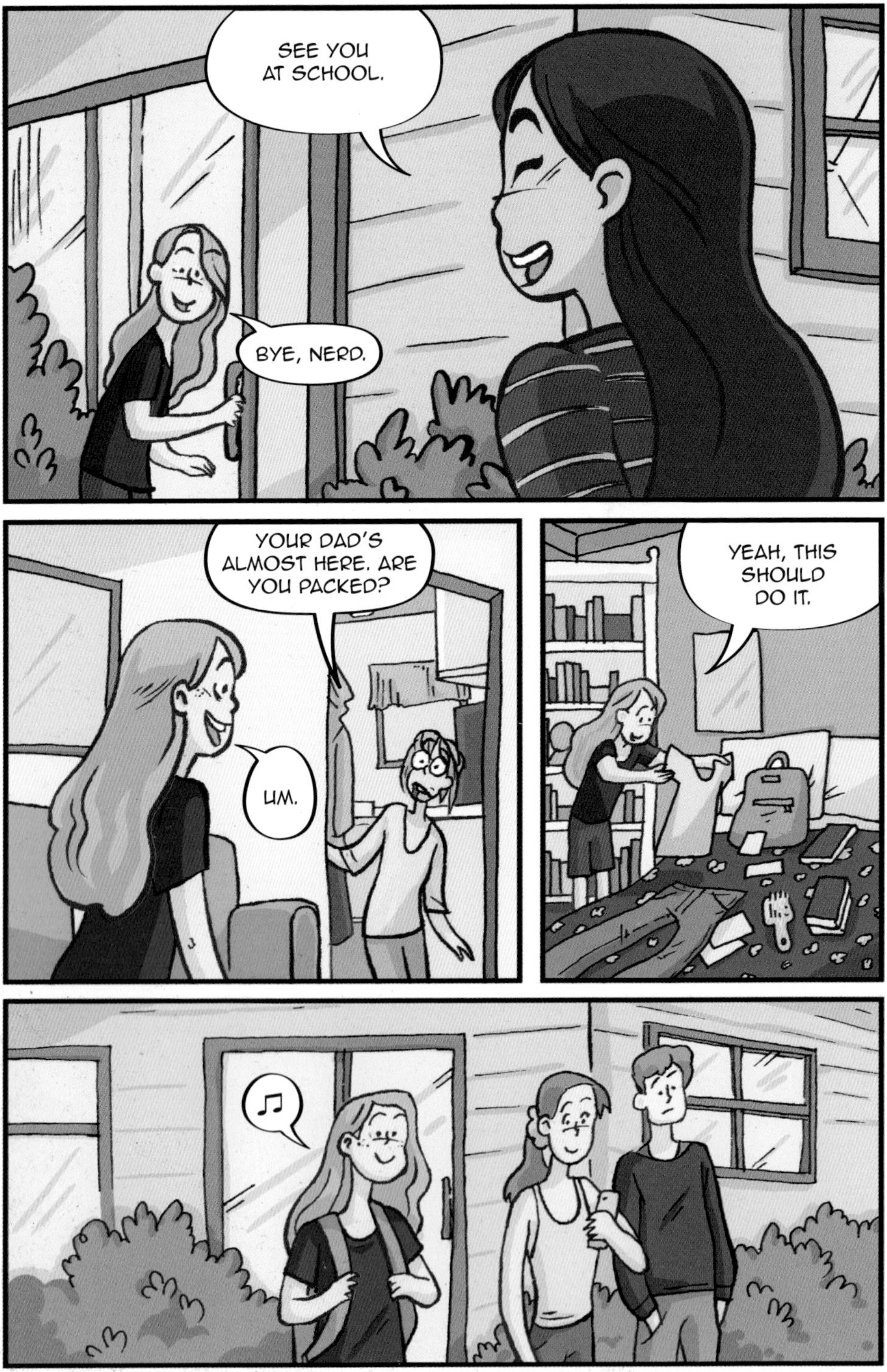
SEE YOU AT SCHOOL.
BYE, NERD.
YOUR DAD'S ALMOST HERE. ARE YOU PACKED?
UM.
YEAH, THIS SHOULD DO IT.
♫

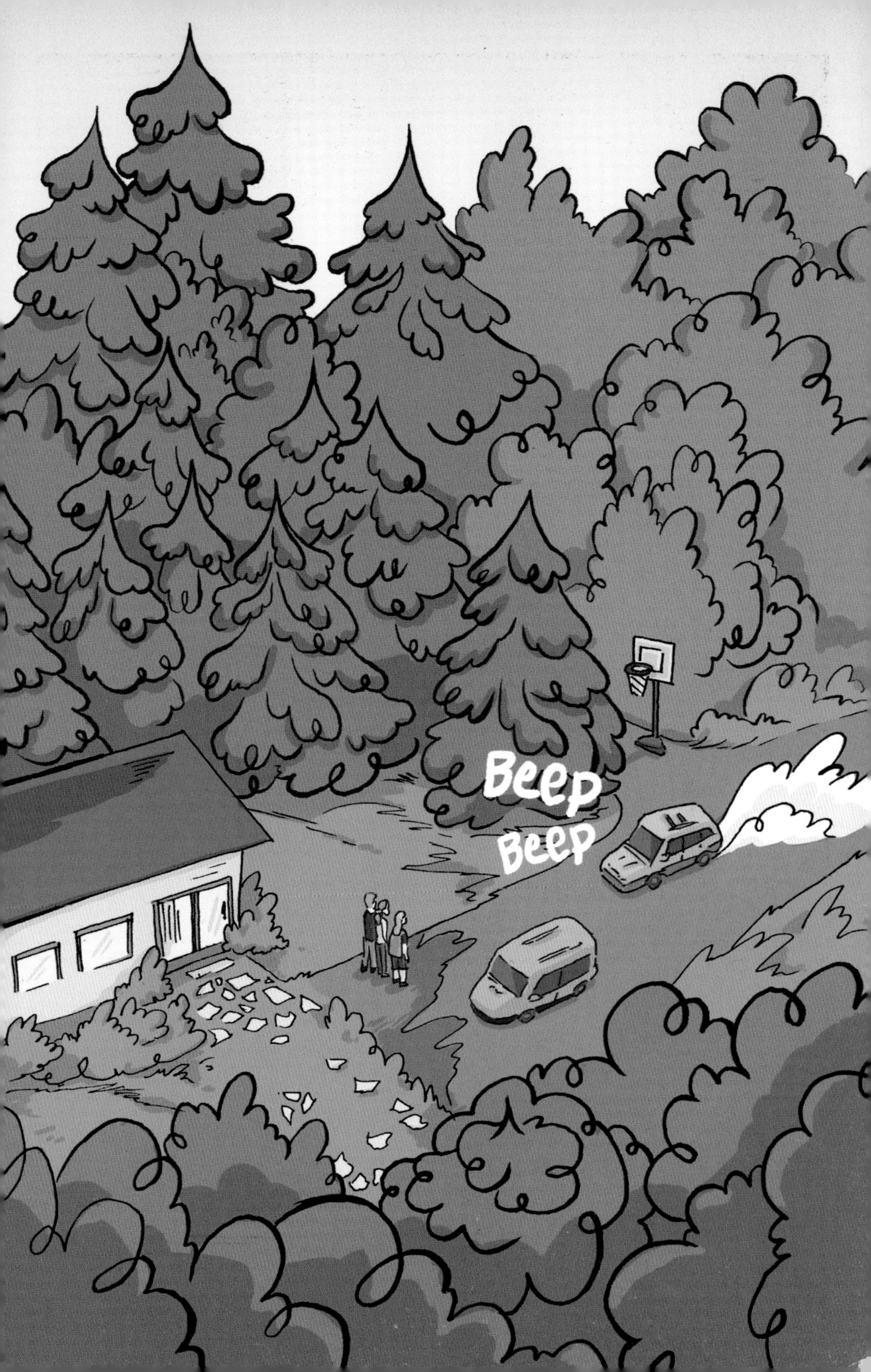
Beep
Beep

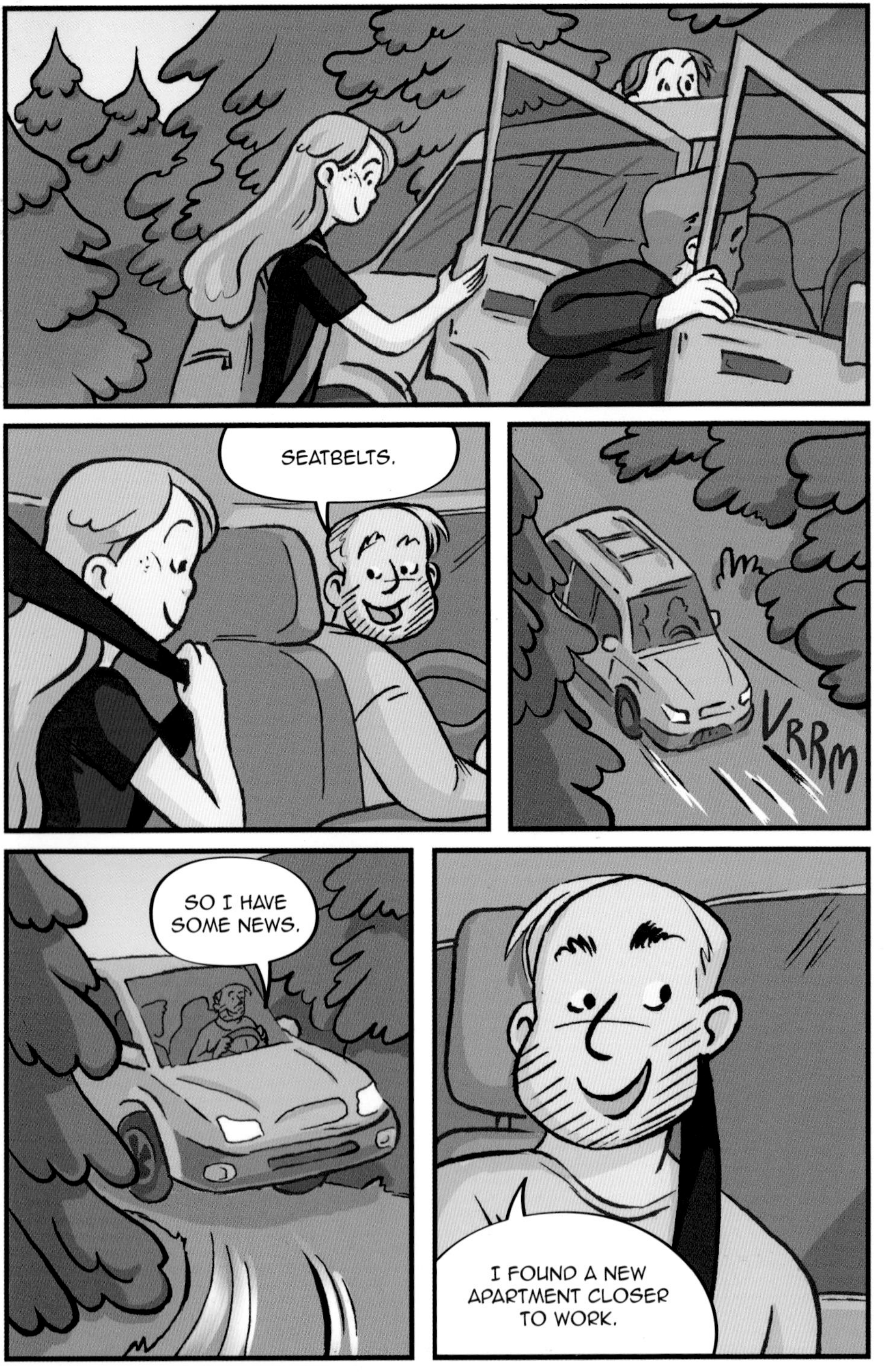
SEATBELTS.
VRRM
SO I HAVE SOME NEWS.
I FOUND A NEW APARTMENT CLOSER TO WORK.

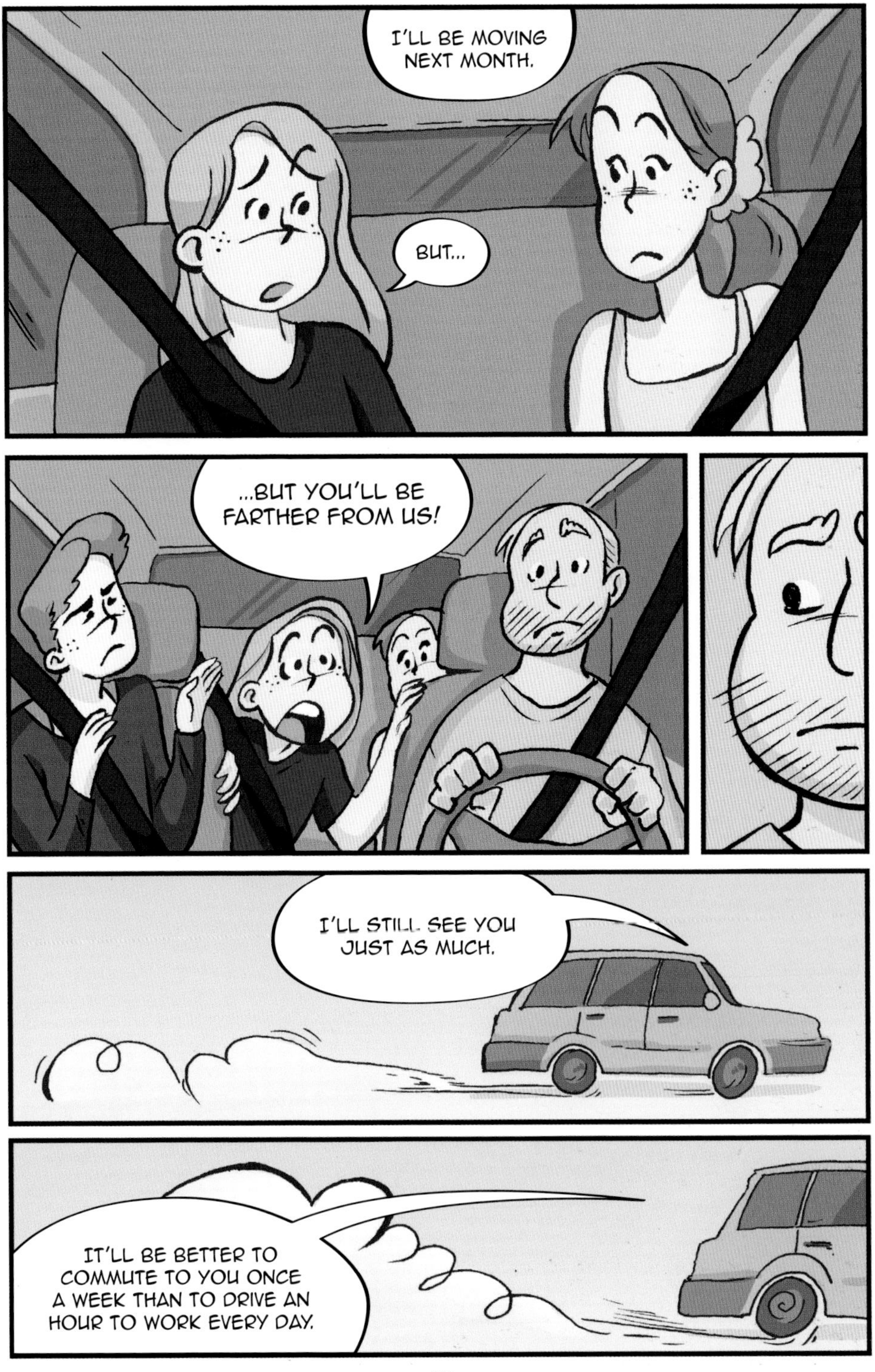
I'LL BE MOVING NEXT MONTH.
BUT...
...BUT YOU'LL BE FARTHER FROM US!
I'LL STILL SEE YOU JUST AS MUCH.
IT'LL BE BETTER TO COMMUTE TO YOU ONCE A WEEK THAN TO DRIVE AN HOUR TO WORK EVERY DAY.

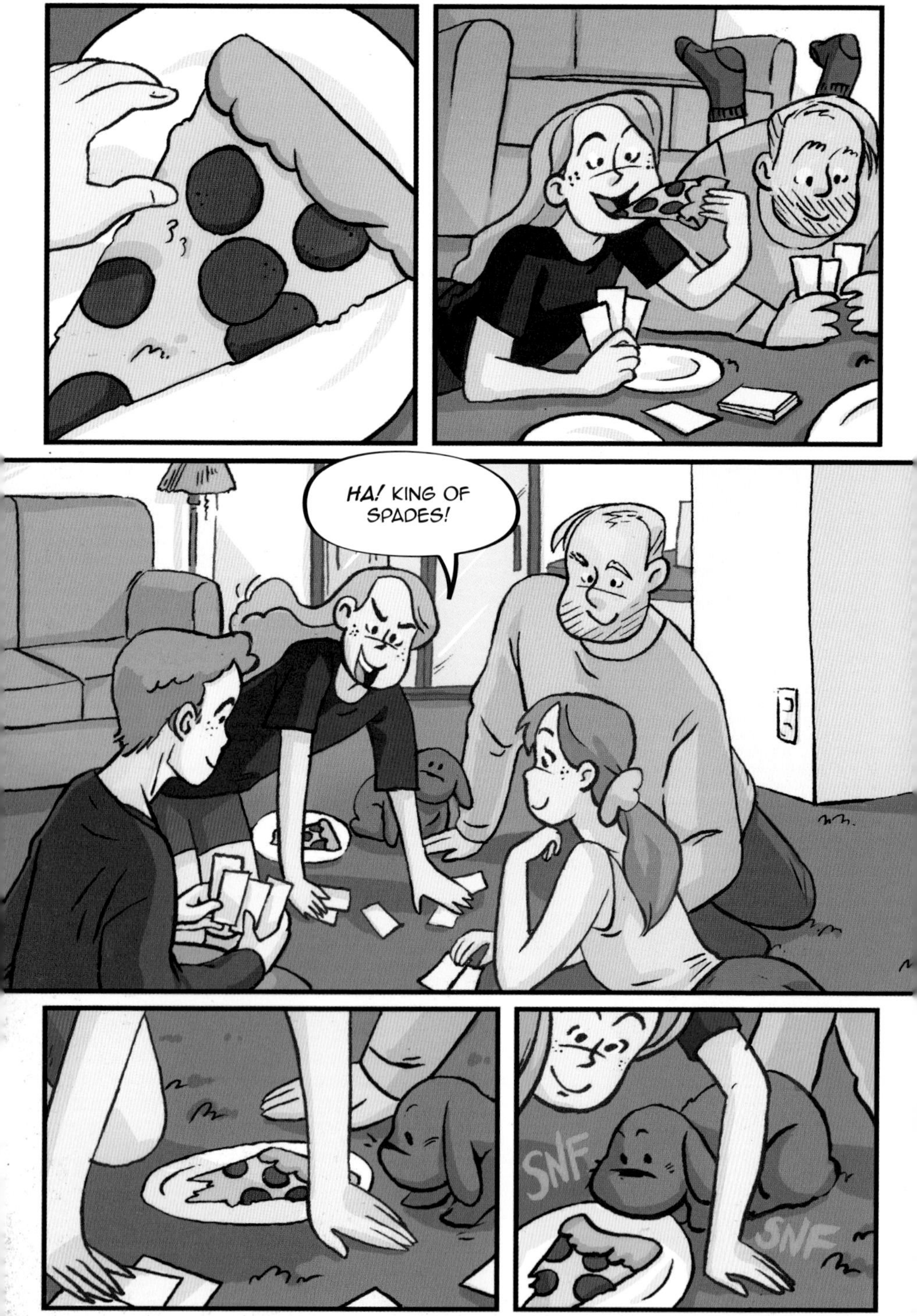
HA! KING OF SPADES!
SNF
SNF

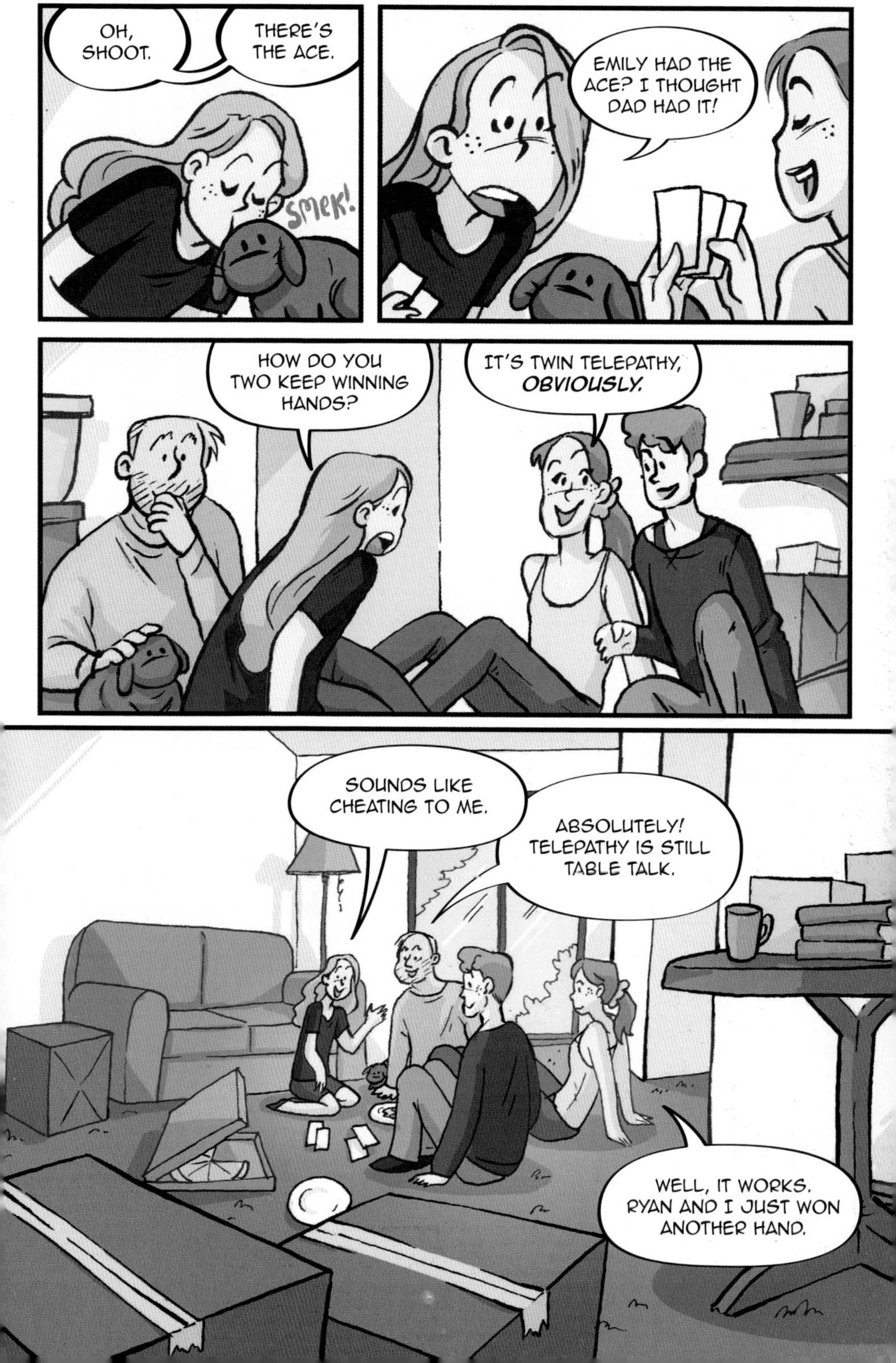
OH, SHOOT.
THERE'S THE ACE.
SMEK!
EMILY HAD THE ACE? I THOUGHT DAD HAD IT!
HOW DO YOU TWO KEEP WINNING HANDS?
IT'S TWIN TELEPATHY, *OBVIOUSLY.*
SOUNDS LIKE CHEATING TO ME.
ABSOLUTELY! TELEPATHY IS STILL TABLE TALK.
WELL, IT WORKS. RYAN AND I JUST WON ANOTHER HAND.

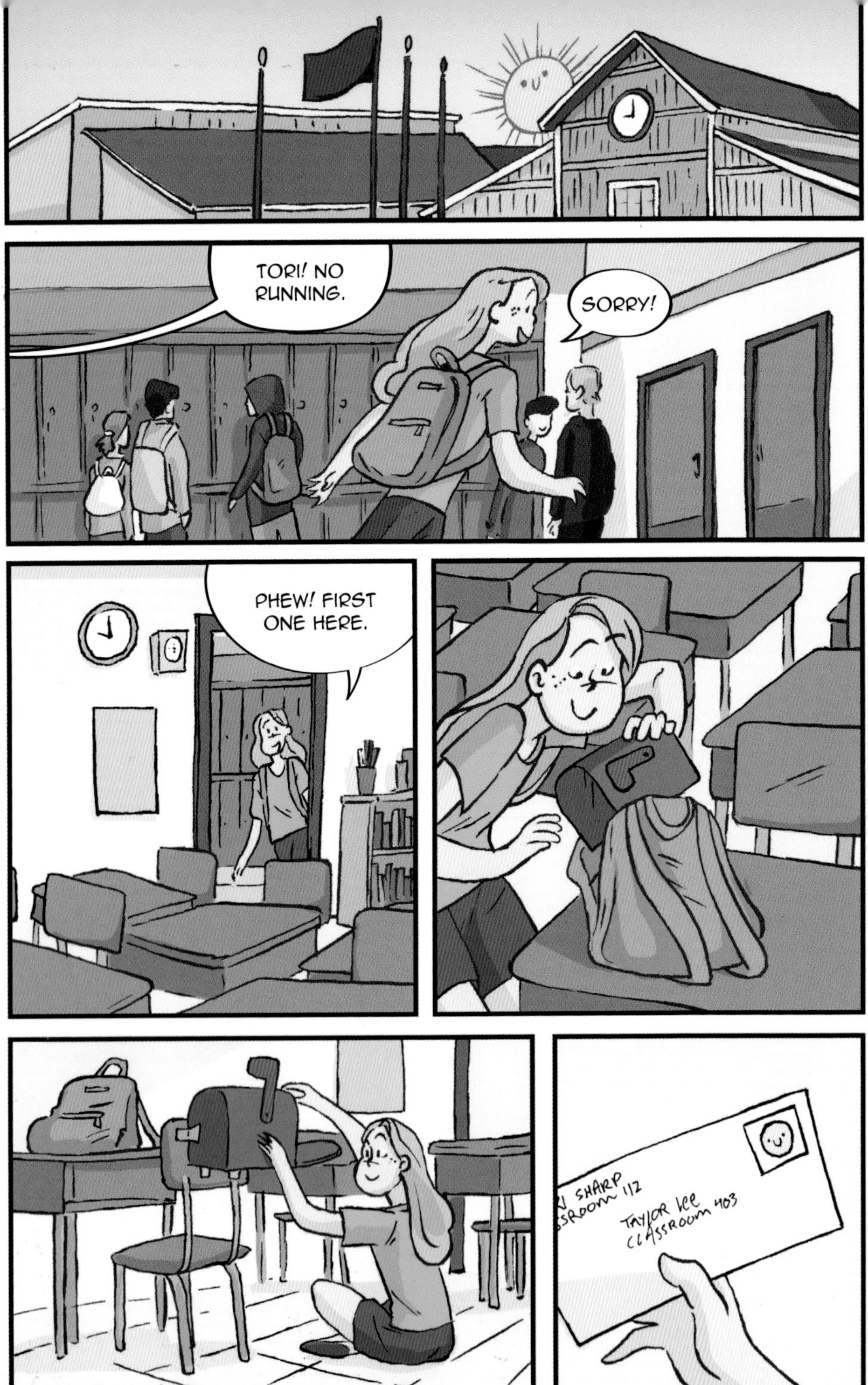
TORI! NO RUNNING.
SORRY!
PHEW! FIRST ONE HERE.
TAYLOR LEE
CLASSROOM 403

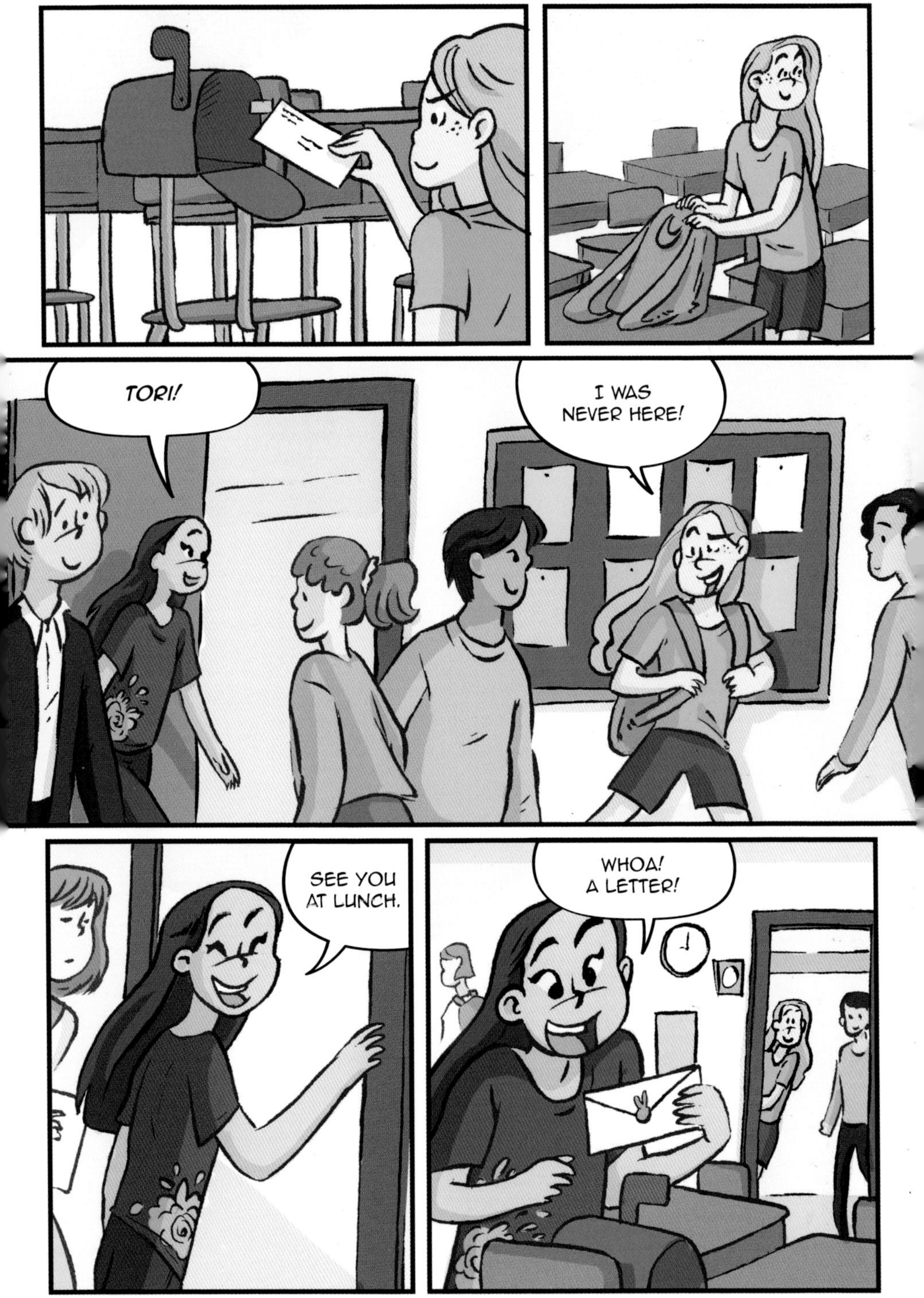
TORI!
I WAS NEVER HERE!
SEE YOU AT LUNCH.
WHOA! A LETTER!

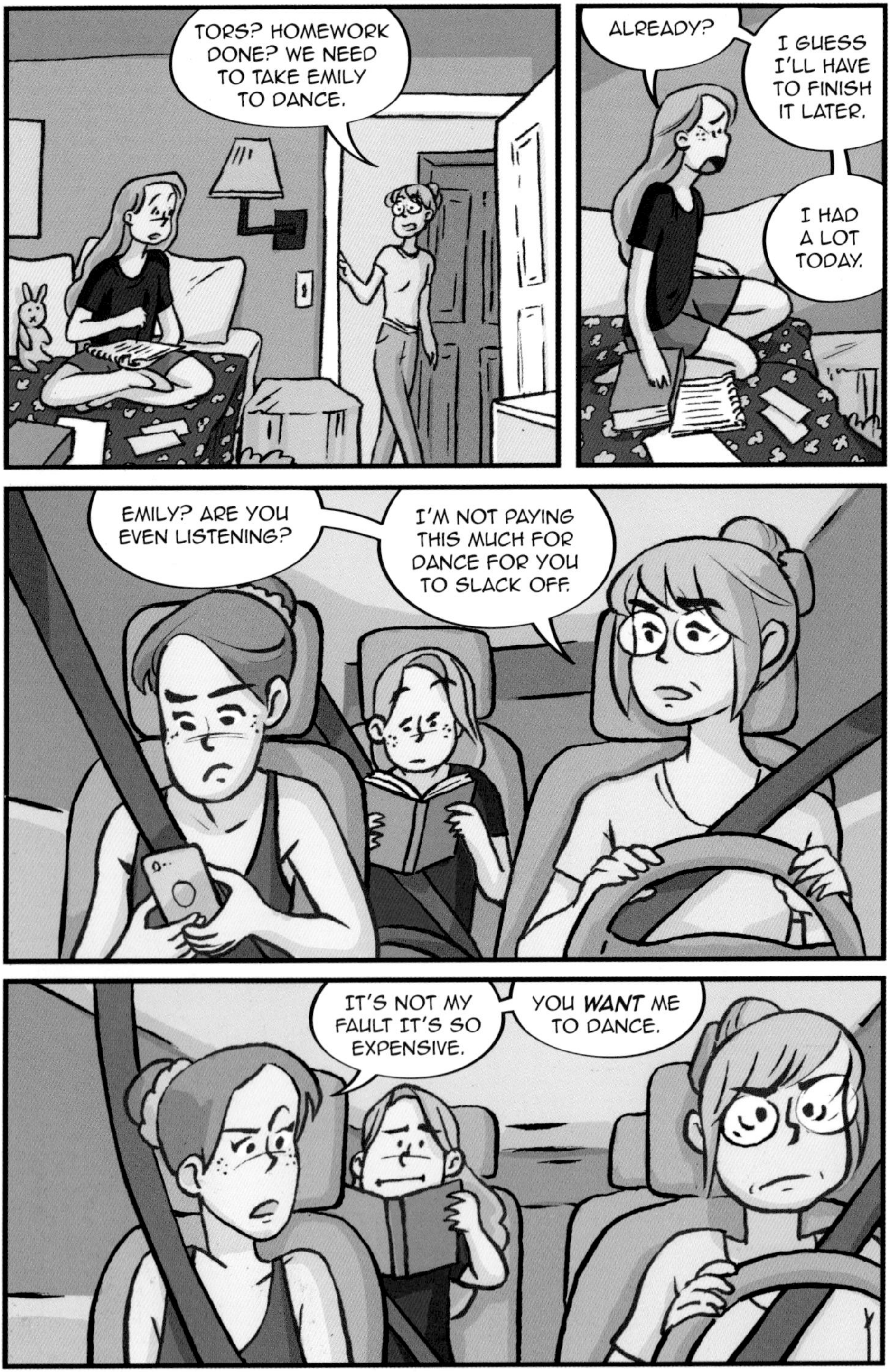
TORS? HOMEWORK DONE? WE NEED TO TAKE EMILY TO DANCE.
ALREADY?
I GUESS I'LL HAVE TO FINISH IT LATER.
I HAD A LOT TODAY.
EMILY? ARE YOU EVEN LISTENING?
I'M NOT PAYING THIS MUCH FOR DANCE FOR YOU TO SLACK OFF.
IT'S NOT MY FAULT IT'S SO EXPENSIVE.
YOU ***WANT*** ME TO DANCE.

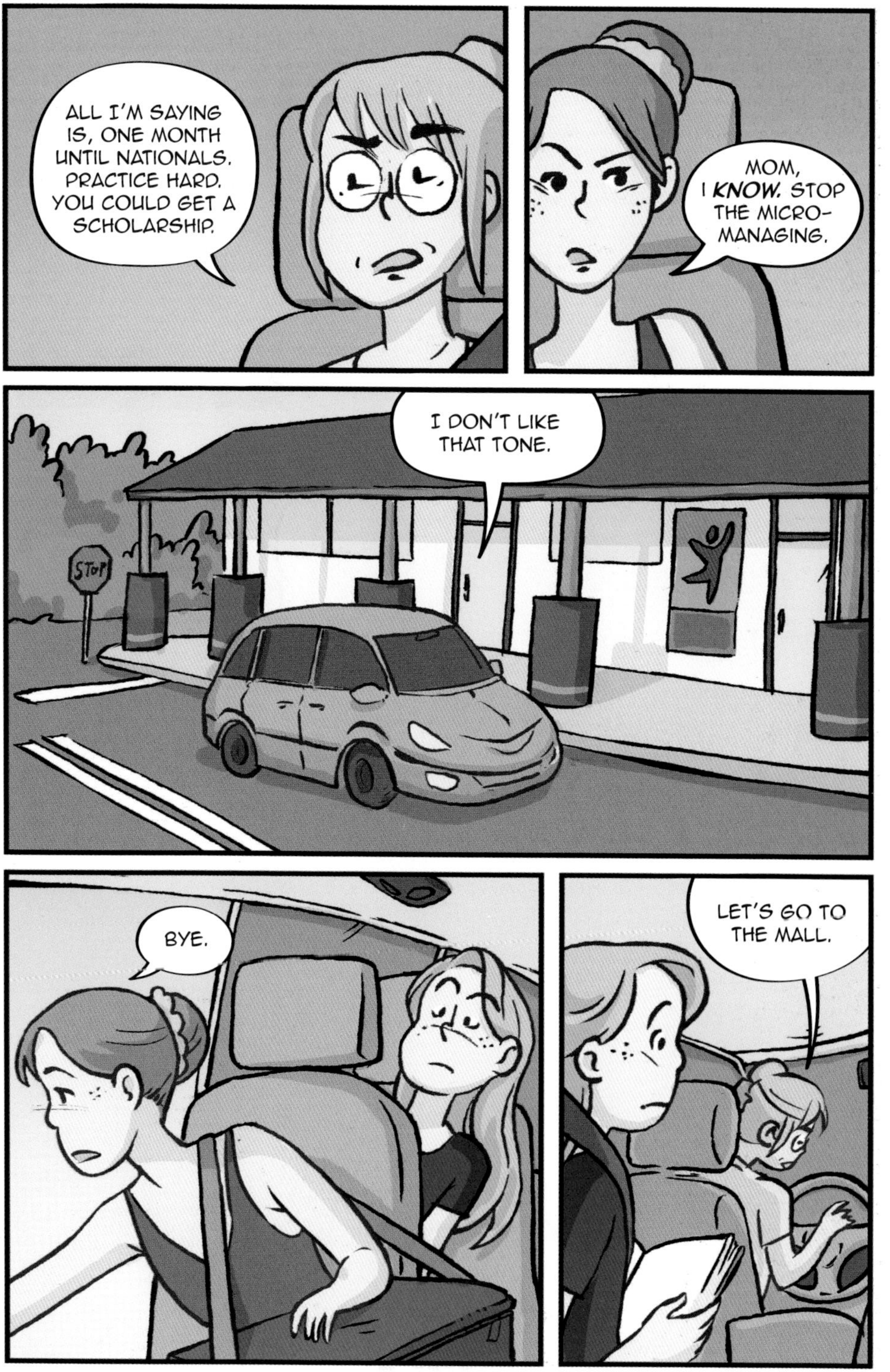
ALL I'M SAYING IS, ONE MONTH UNTIL NATIONALS. PRACTICE HARD. YOU COULD GET A SCHOLARSHIP.
MOM, I **KNOW.** STOP THE MICRO-MANAGING.
I DON'T LIKE THAT TONE.
STOP
BYE.
LET'S GO TO THE MALL.

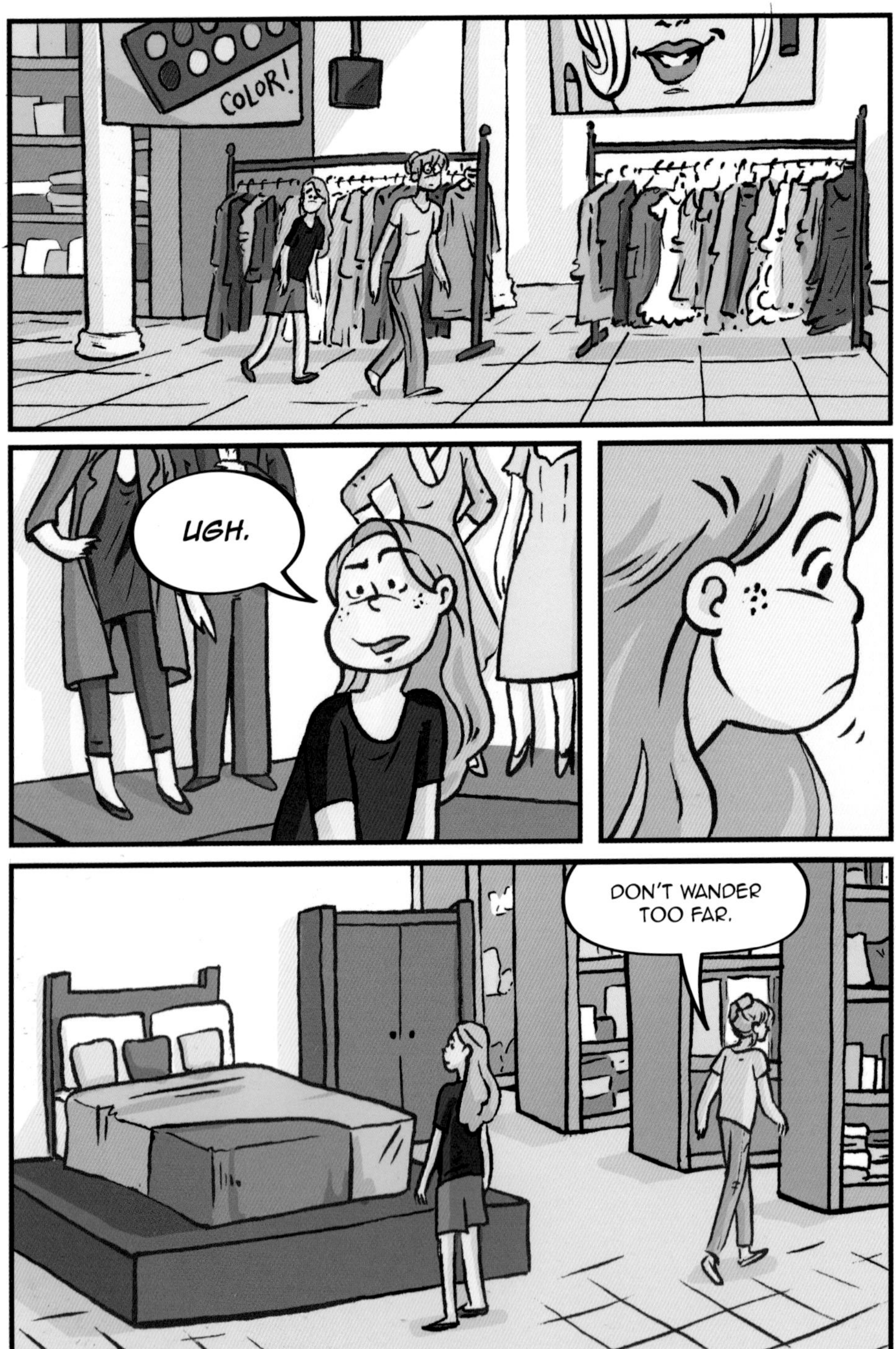
COLOR!
UGH.
DON'T WANDER TOO FAR.

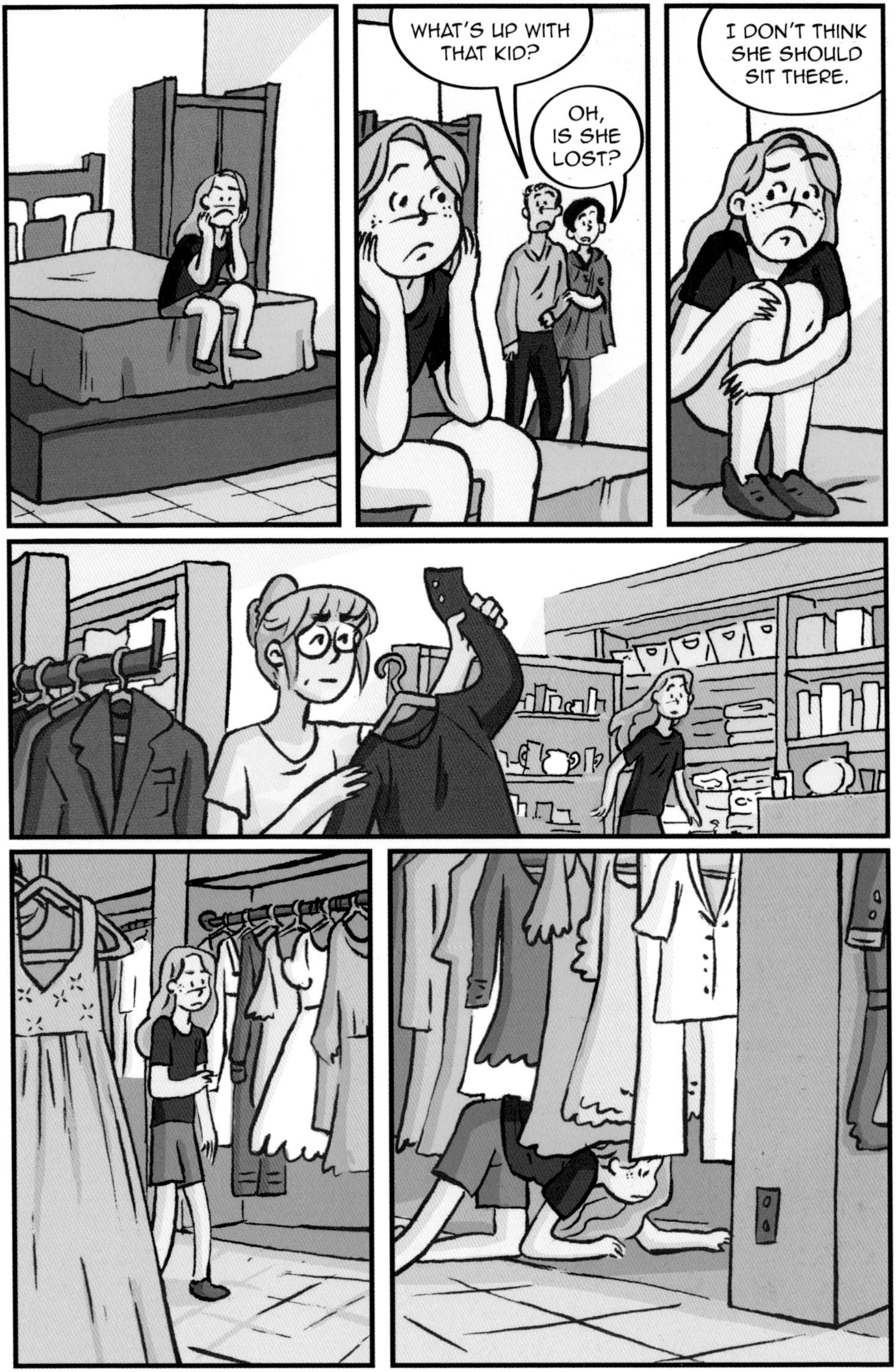
WHAT'S UP WITH THAT KID?
OH, IS SHE LOST?
I DON'T THINK SHE SHOULD SIT THERE.

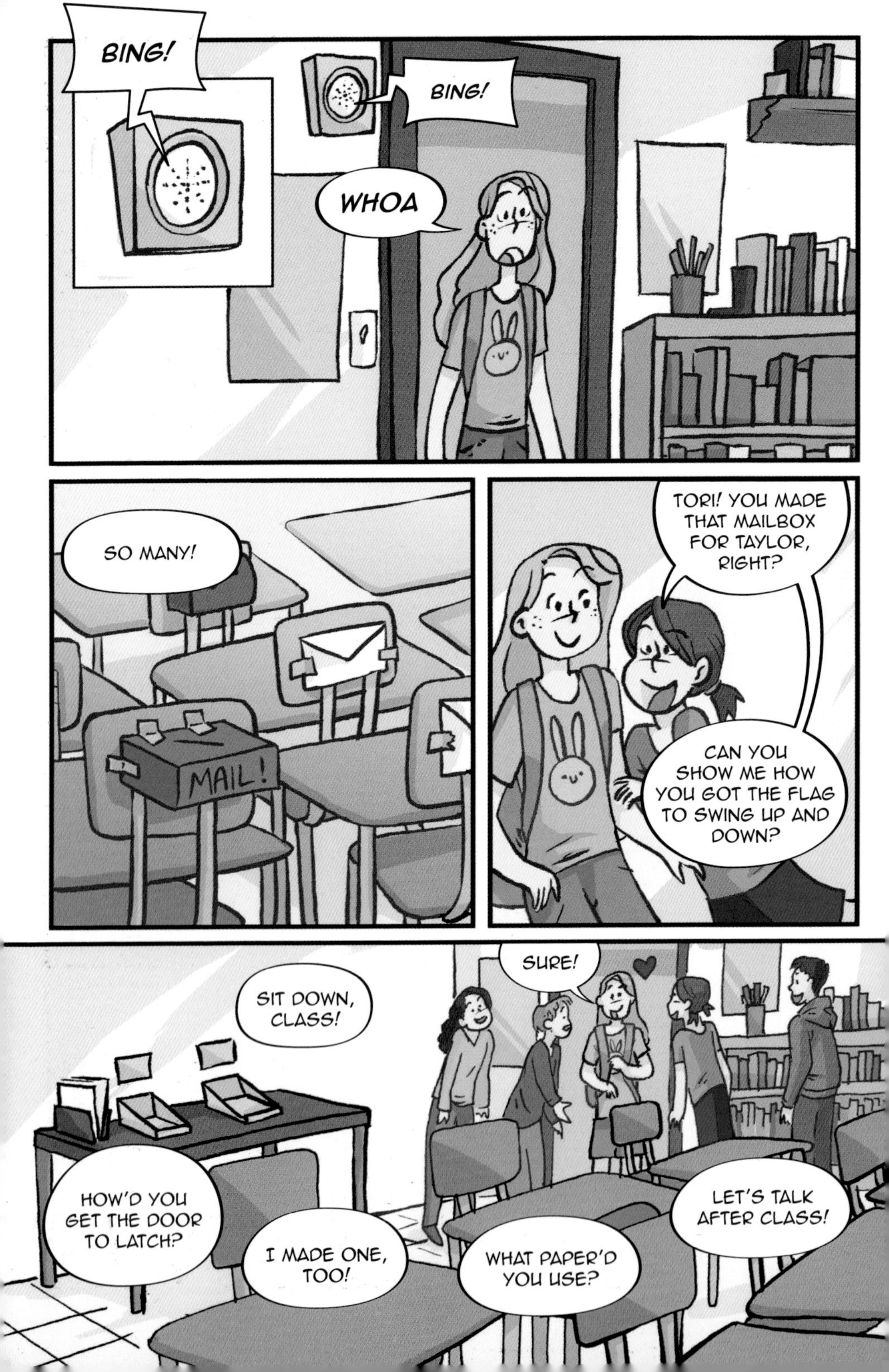
BING!
BING!
WHOA
SO MANY!
MAIL!
TORI! YOU MADE THAT MAILBOX FOR TAYLOR, RIGHT?
CAN YOU SHOW ME HOW YOU GOT THE FLAG TO SWING UP AND DOWN?
SIT DOWN, CLASS!
SURE!
HOW'D YOU GET THE DOOR TO LATCH?
I MADE ONE, TOO!
WHAT PAPER'D YOU USE?
LET'S TALK AFTER CLASS!

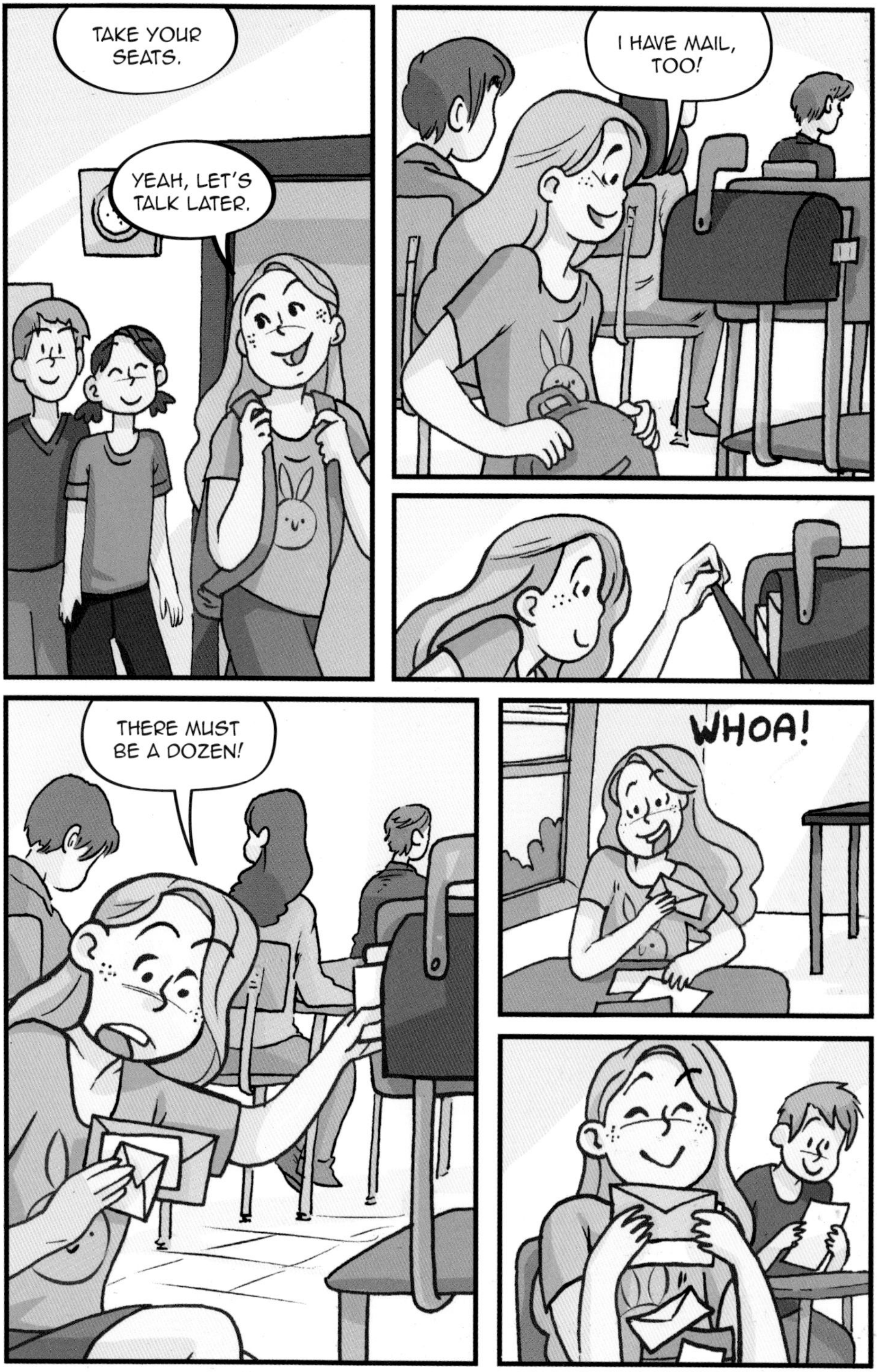
TAKE YOUR SEATS.
YEAH, LET'S TALK LATER.
I HAVE MAIL, TOO!
THERE MUST BE A DOZEN!
WHOA!

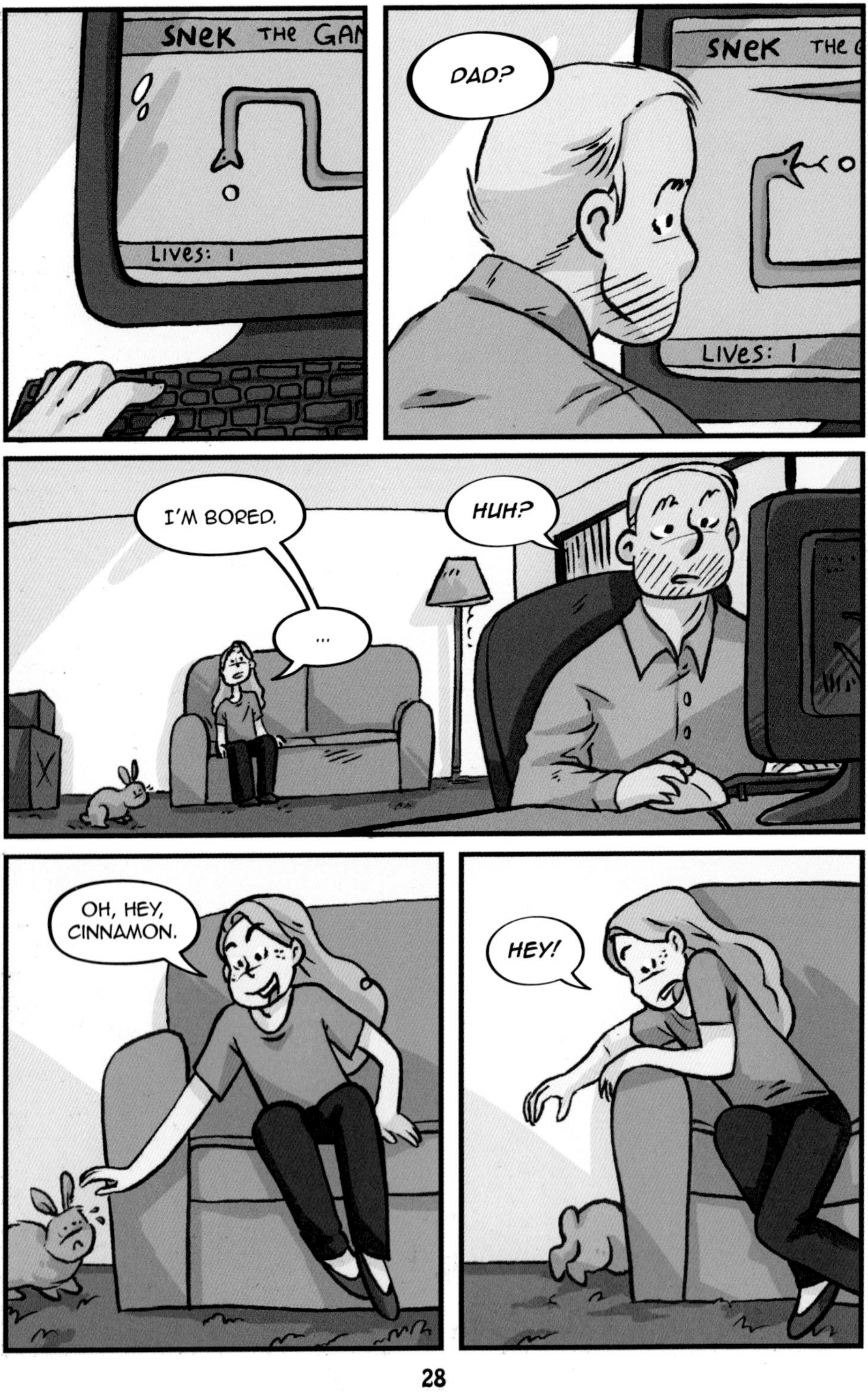
SNEK THE GAM
LIVES: 1
DAD?
SNEK THE G
LIVES: 1
I'M BORED.
HUH?
...
OH, HEY, CINNAMON.
HEY!

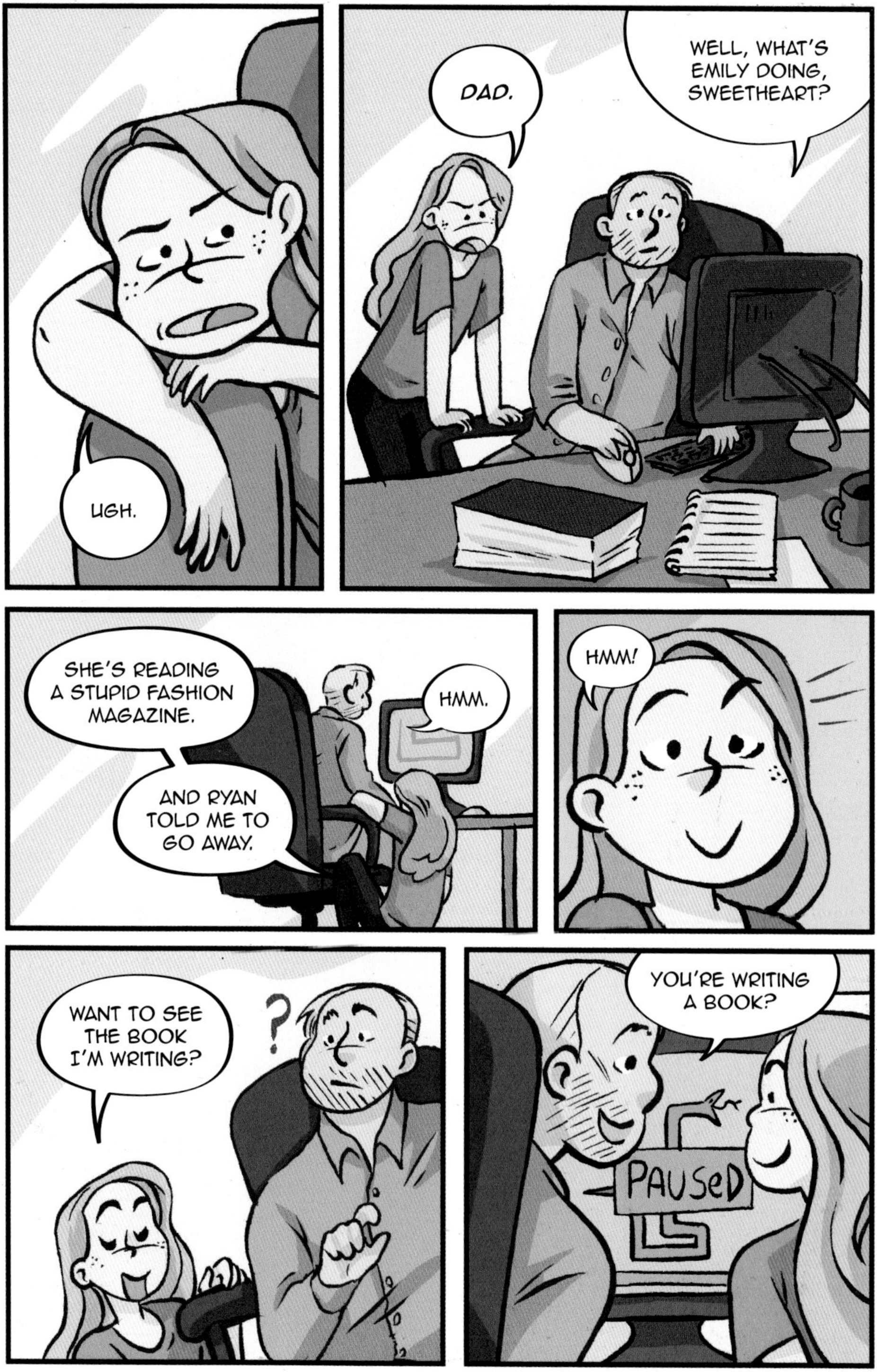
UGH.
DAD.
WELL, WHAT'S EMILY DOING, SWEETHEART?
SHE'S READING A STUPID FASHION MAGAZINE.
HMM.
AND RYAN TOLD ME TO GO AWAY.
HMM!
WANT TO SEE THE BOOK I'M WRITING?
?
YOU'RE WRITING A BOOK?
PAUSED

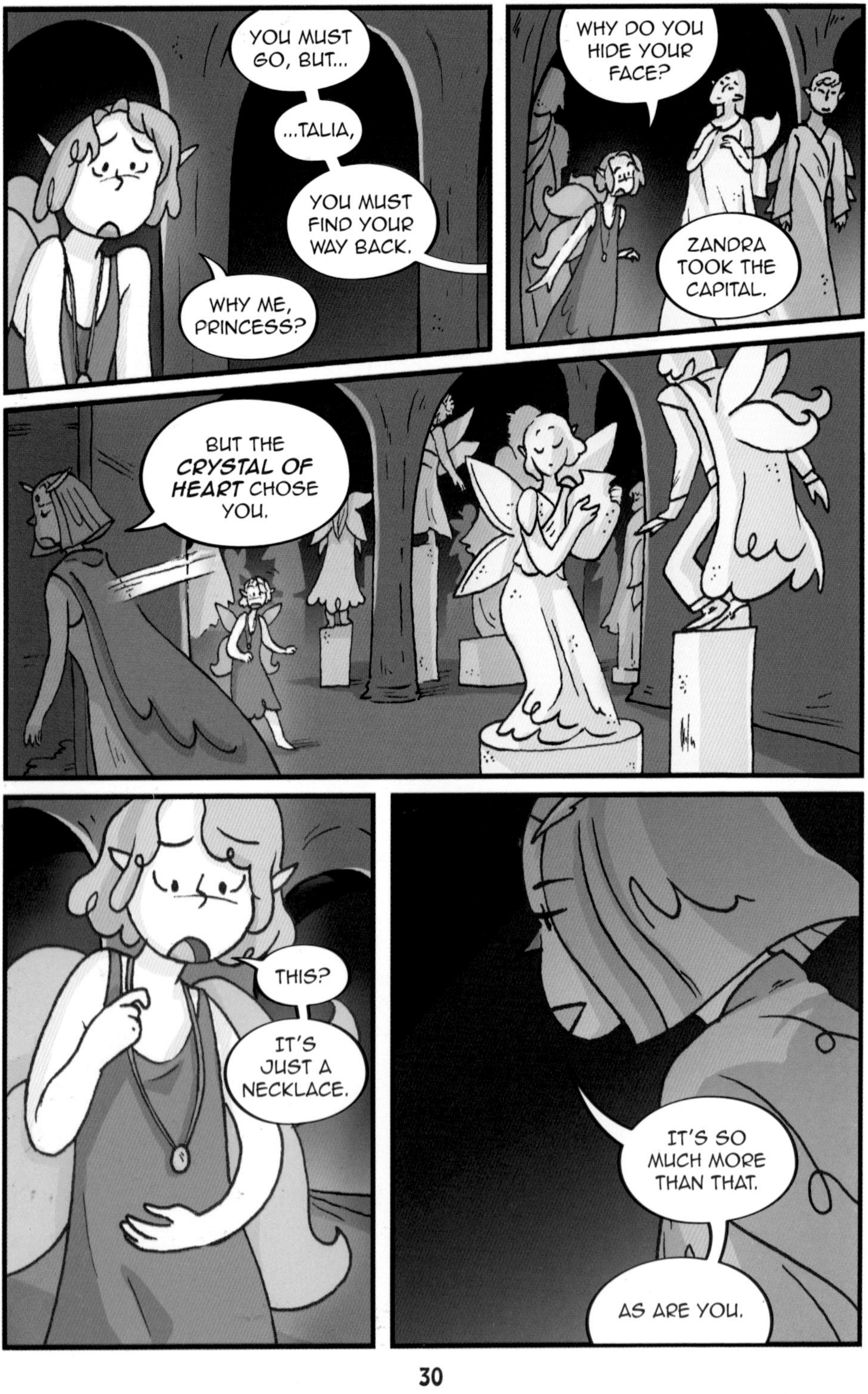
YOU MUST GO, BUT...
...TALIA,
YOU MUST FIND YOUR WAY BACK.
WHY ME, PRINCESS?
WHY DO YOU HIDE YOUR FACE?
ZANDRA TOOK THE CAPITAL.
BUT THE ***CRYSTAL OF HEART*** CHOSE YOU.
THIS?
IT'S JUST A NECKLACE.
IT'S SO MUCH MORE THAN THAT.
AS ARE YOU.

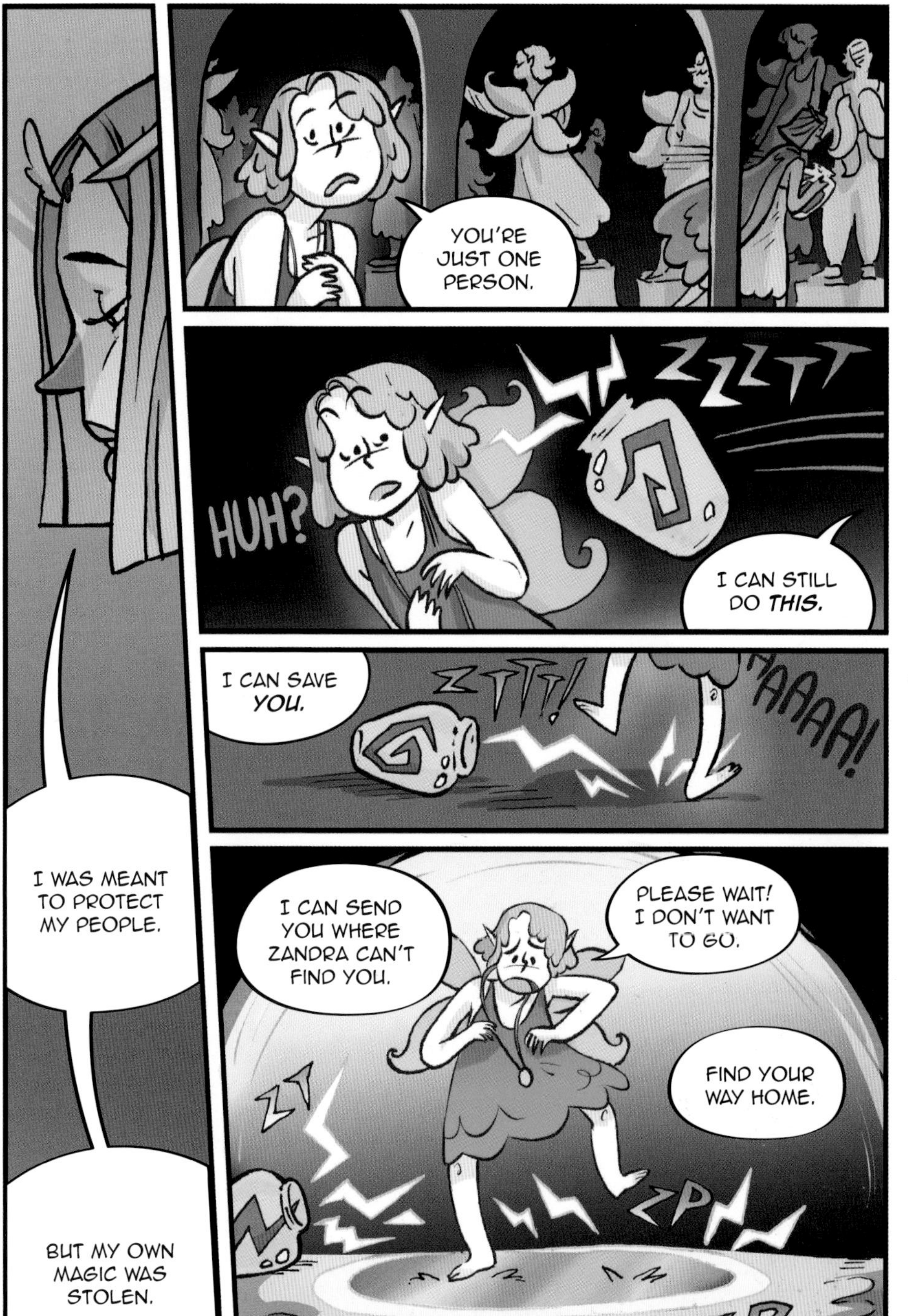
YOU'RE JUST ONE PERSON.
ZZZTT
HUH?
I CAN STILL DO THIS.
I CAN SAVE YOU.
ZTTT!
AAAAA!
I WAS MEANT TO PROTECT MY PEOPLE.
I CAN SEND YOU WHERE ZANDRA CAN'T FIND YOU.
PLEASE WAIT! I DON'T WANT TO GO.
FIND YOUR WAY HOME.
ZT
ZP
BUT MY OWN MAGIC WAS STOLEN.
ZP

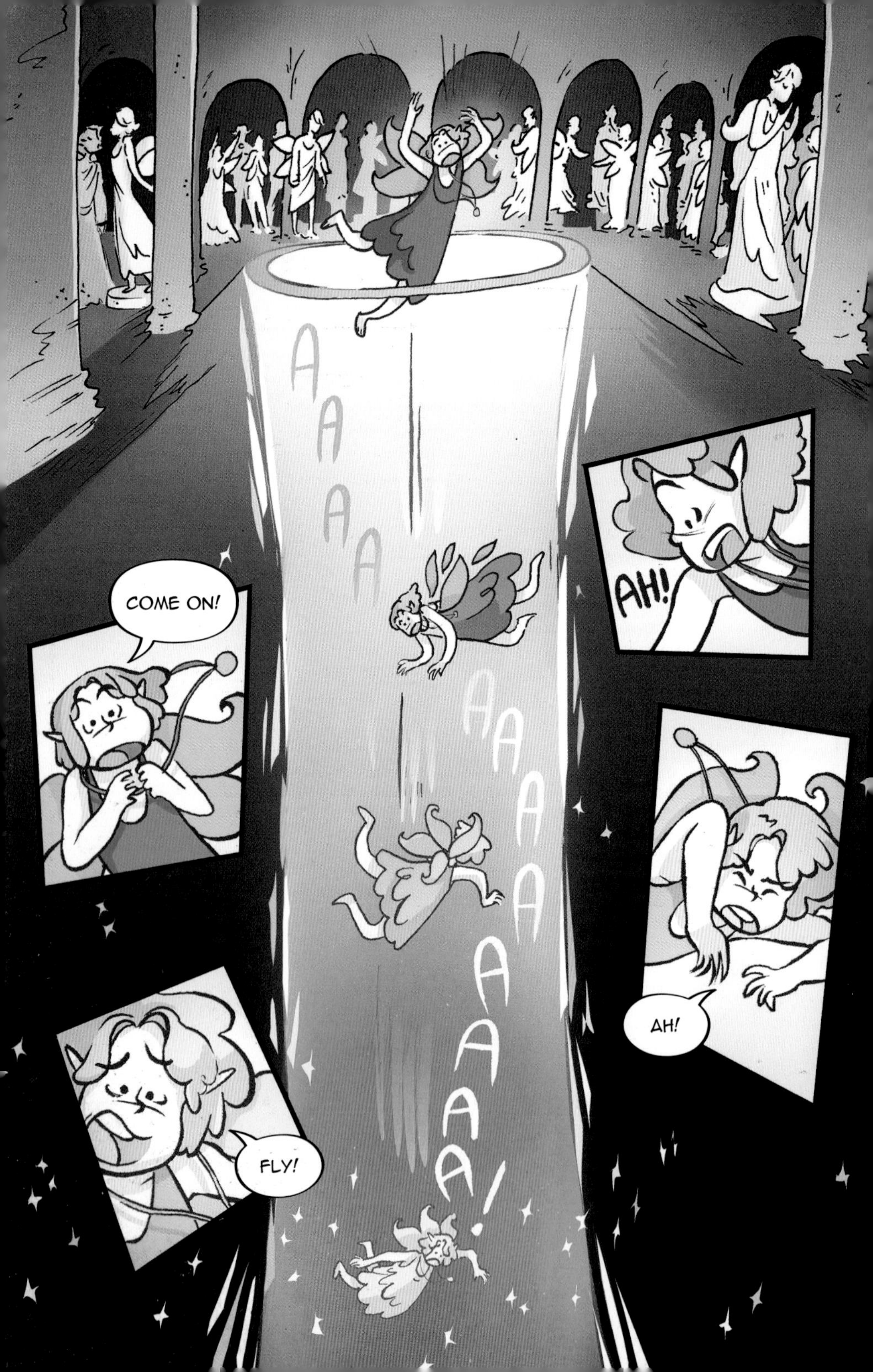

AAAAAA
COME ON!
AH!
AAAAAAAAAA!
AH!
FLY!

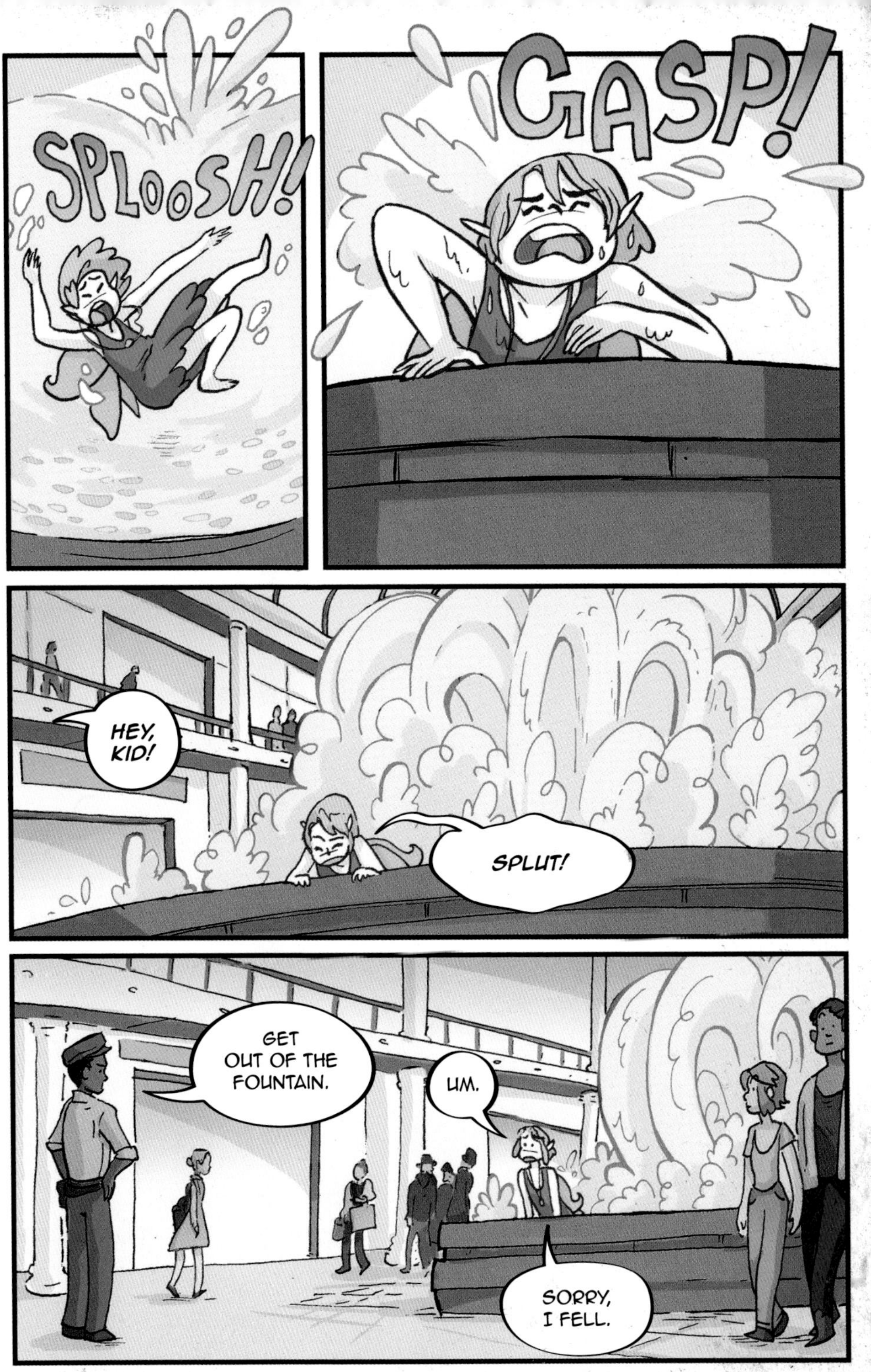
SPLOOSH!
GASP!
HEY, KID!
SPLUT!
GET OUT OF THE FOUNTAIN.
UM.
SORRY, I FELL.

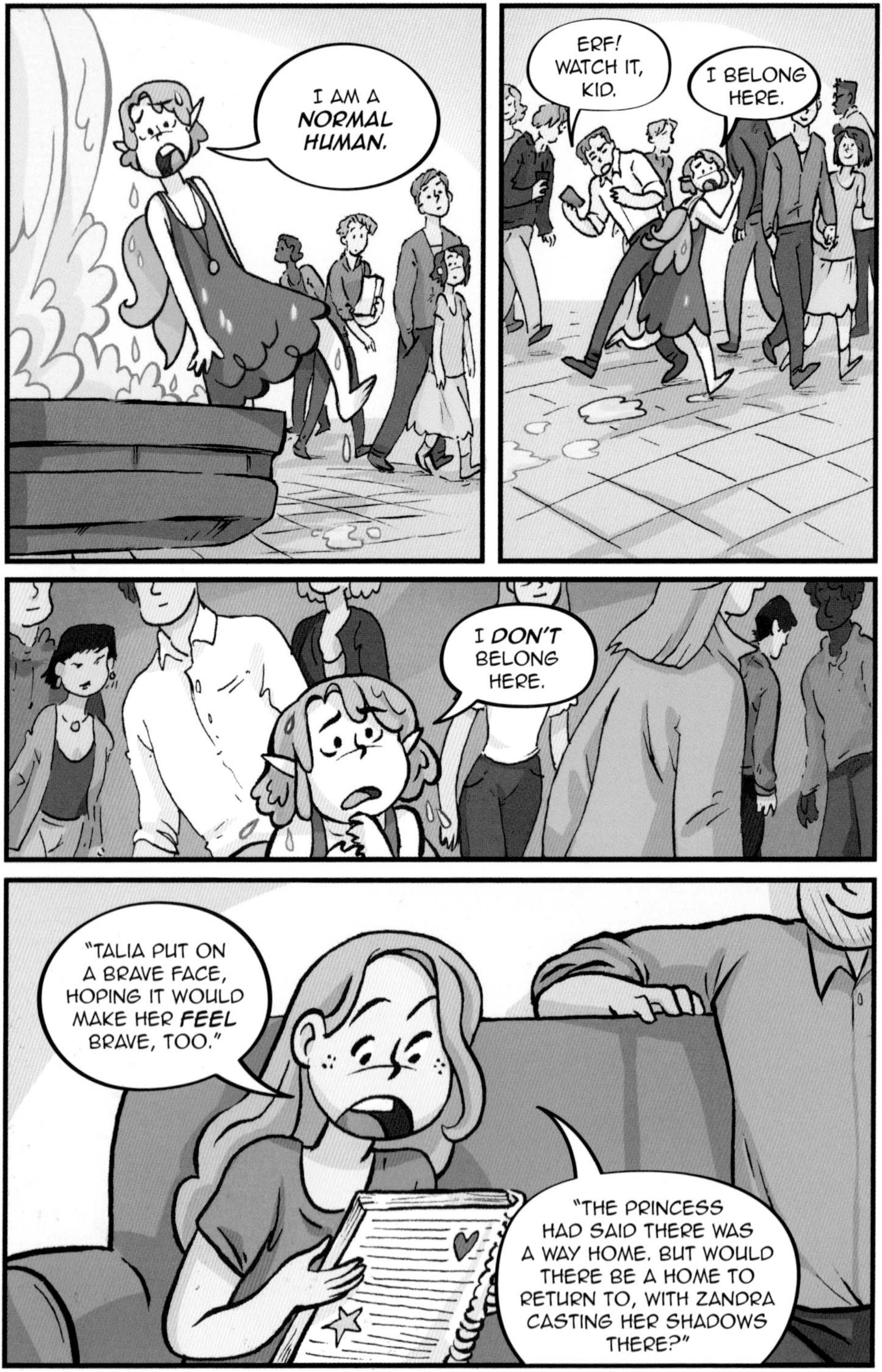
I AM A NORMAL HUMAN.
ERF! WATCH IT, KID.
I BELONG HERE.
I DON'T BELONG HERE.
"TALIA PUT ON A BRAVE FACE, HOPING IT WOULD MAKE HER FEEL BRAVE, TOO."
"THE PRINCESS HAD SAID THERE WAS A WAY HOME. BUT WOULD THERE BE A HOME TO RETURN TO, WITH ZANDRA CASTING HER SHADOWS THERE?"

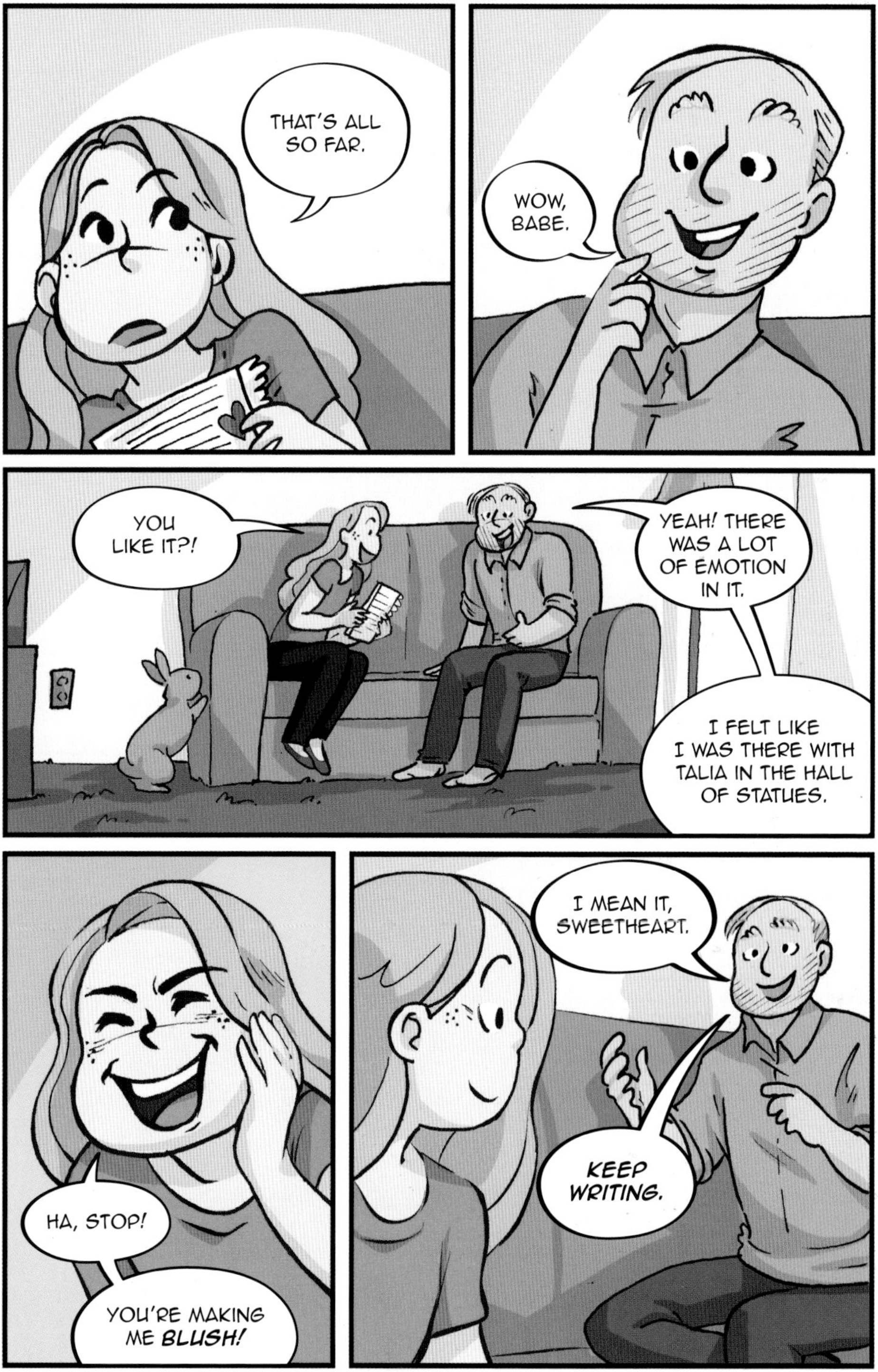
THAT'S ALL SO FAR.
WOW, BABE.
YOU LIKE IT?!
YEAH! THERE WAS A LOT OF EMOTION IN IT.
I FELT LIKE I WAS THERE WITH TALIA IN THE HALL OF STATUES.
HA, STOP!
YOU'RE MAKING ME *BLUSH!*
I MEAN IT, SWEETHEART.
*KEEP WRITING.*

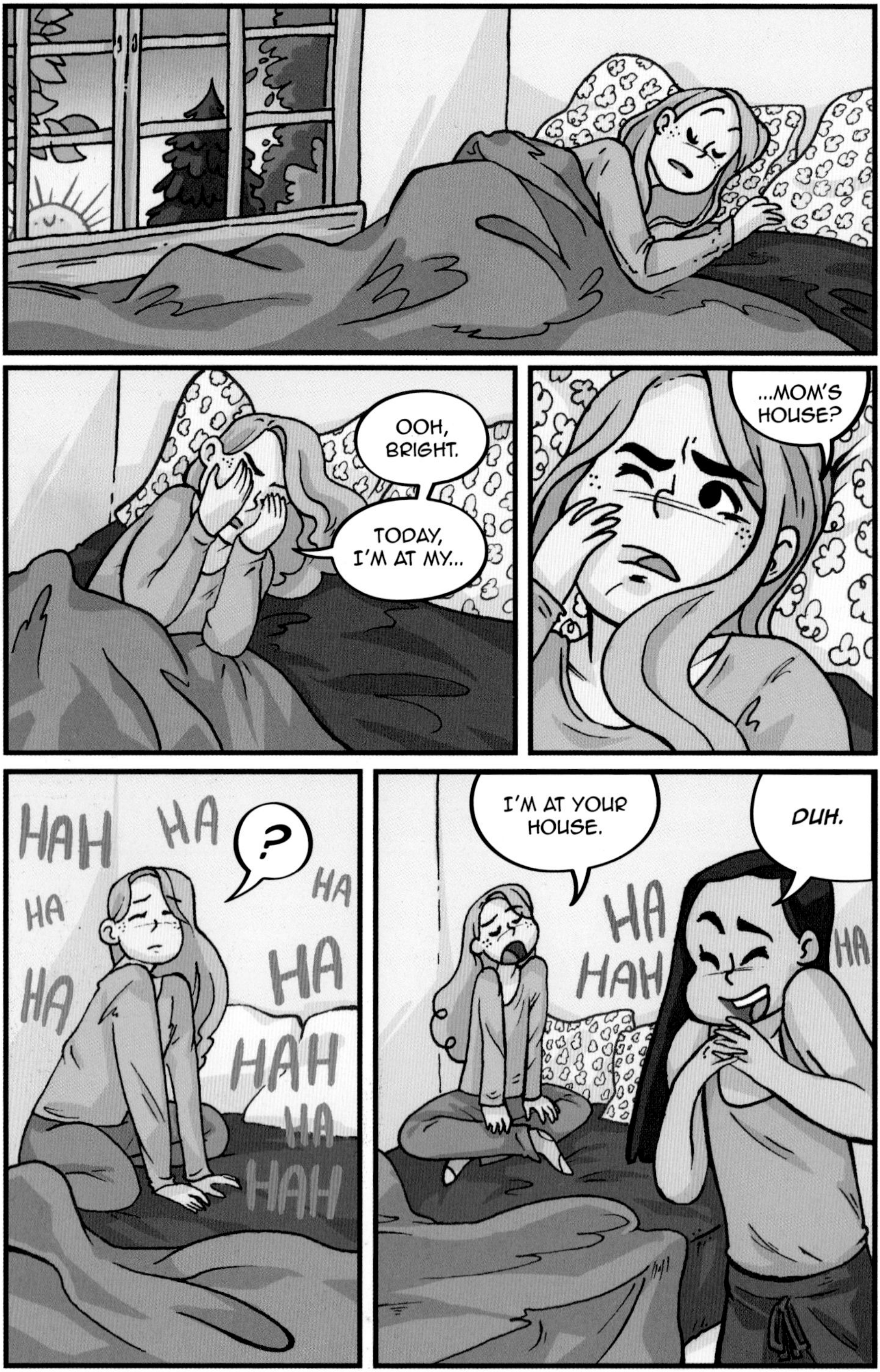
OOH, BRIGHT.
TODAY, I'M AT MY...
...MOM'S HOUSE?
HAH
HA
HA
HA
HA
HA
HAH
HA
HAH
?
I'M AT YOUR HOUSE.
DUH.
HA
HAH
HA

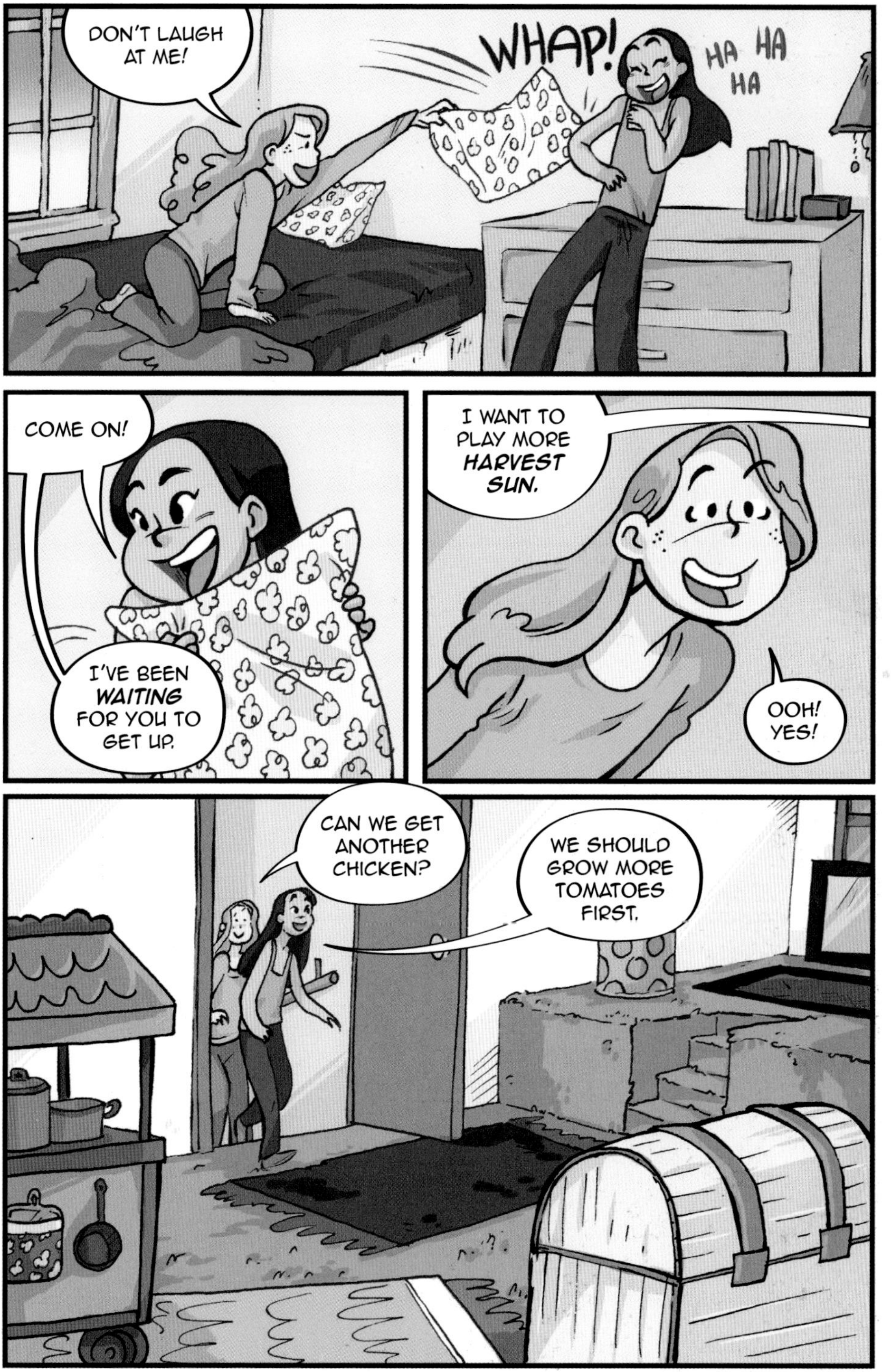
DON'T LAUGH AT ME!
WHAP!
HA HA HA
COME ON!
I'VE BEEN WAITING FOR YOU TO GET UP.
I WANT TO PLAY MORE HARVEST SUN.
OOH! YES!
CAN WE GET ANOTHER CHICKEN?
WE SHOULD GROW MORE TOMATOES FIRST.

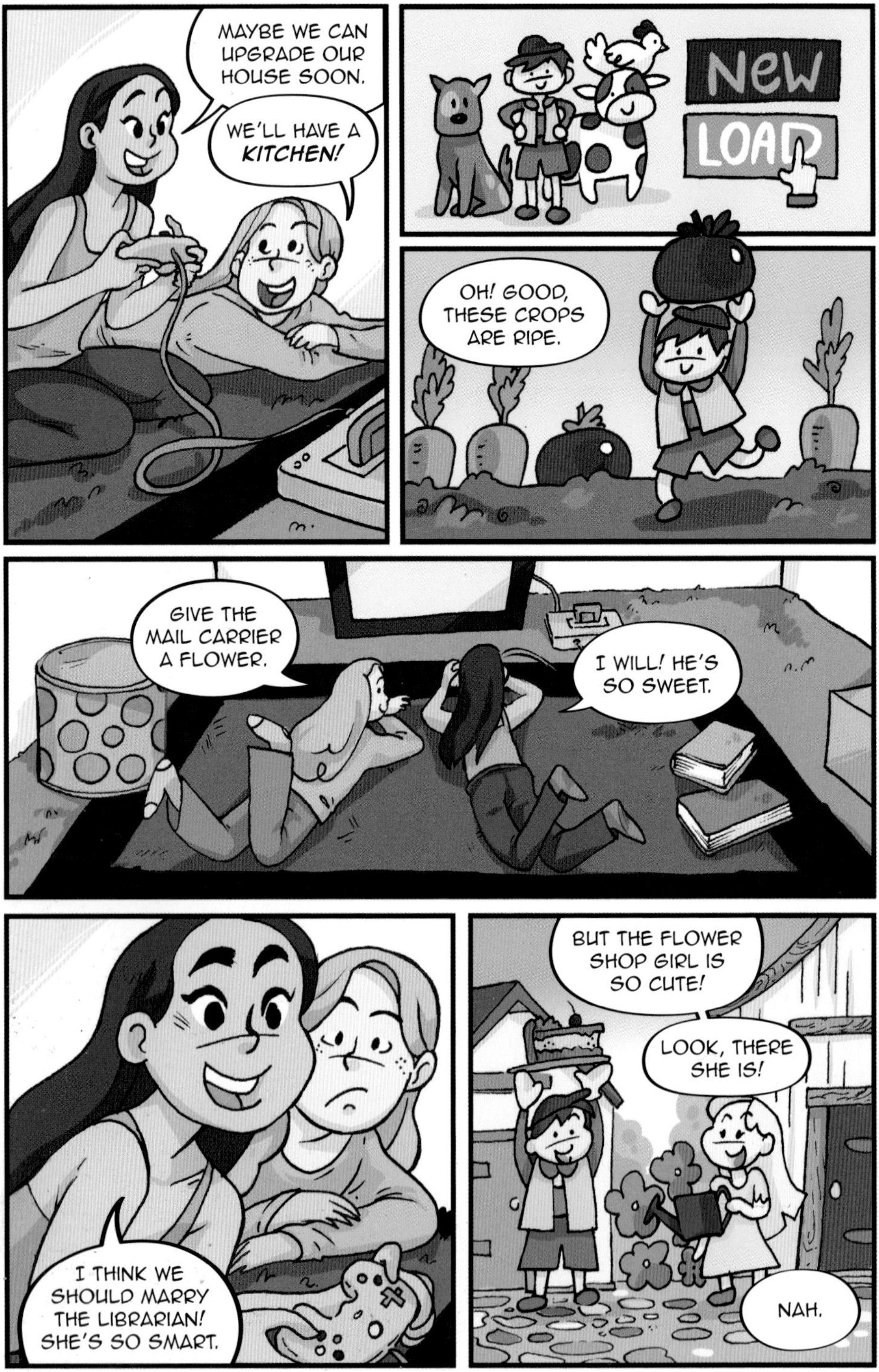
MAYBE WE CAN UPGRADE OUR HOUSE SOON.
WE'LL HAVE A *KITCHEN!*
New
LOAD
OH! GOOD, THESE CROPS ARE RIPE.
GIVE THE MAIL CARRIER A FLOWER.
I WILL! HE'S SO SWEET.
I THINK WE SHOULD MARRY THE LIBRARIAN! SHE'S SO SMART.
BUT THE FLOWER SHOP GIRL IS SO CUTE!
LOOK, THERE SHE IS!
NAH.

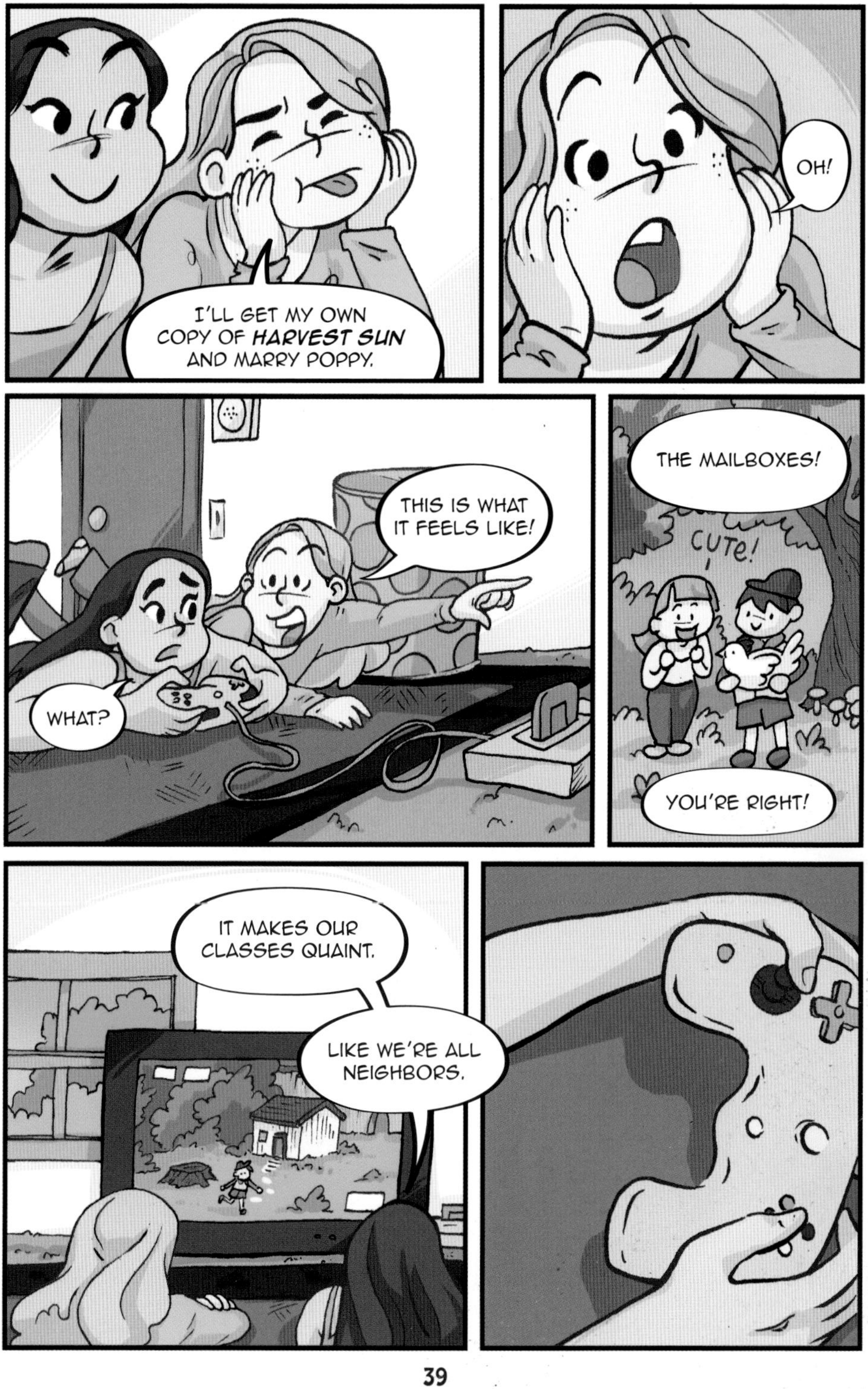
I'LL GET MY OWN
COPY OF ***HARVEST SUN***
AND MARRY POPPY.
OH!
THIS IS WHAT
IT FEELS LIKE!
WHAT?
THE MAILBOXES!
CUTE!
YOU'RE RIGHT!
IT MAKES OUR
CLASSES QUAINT.
LIKE WE'RE ALL
NEIGHBORS.

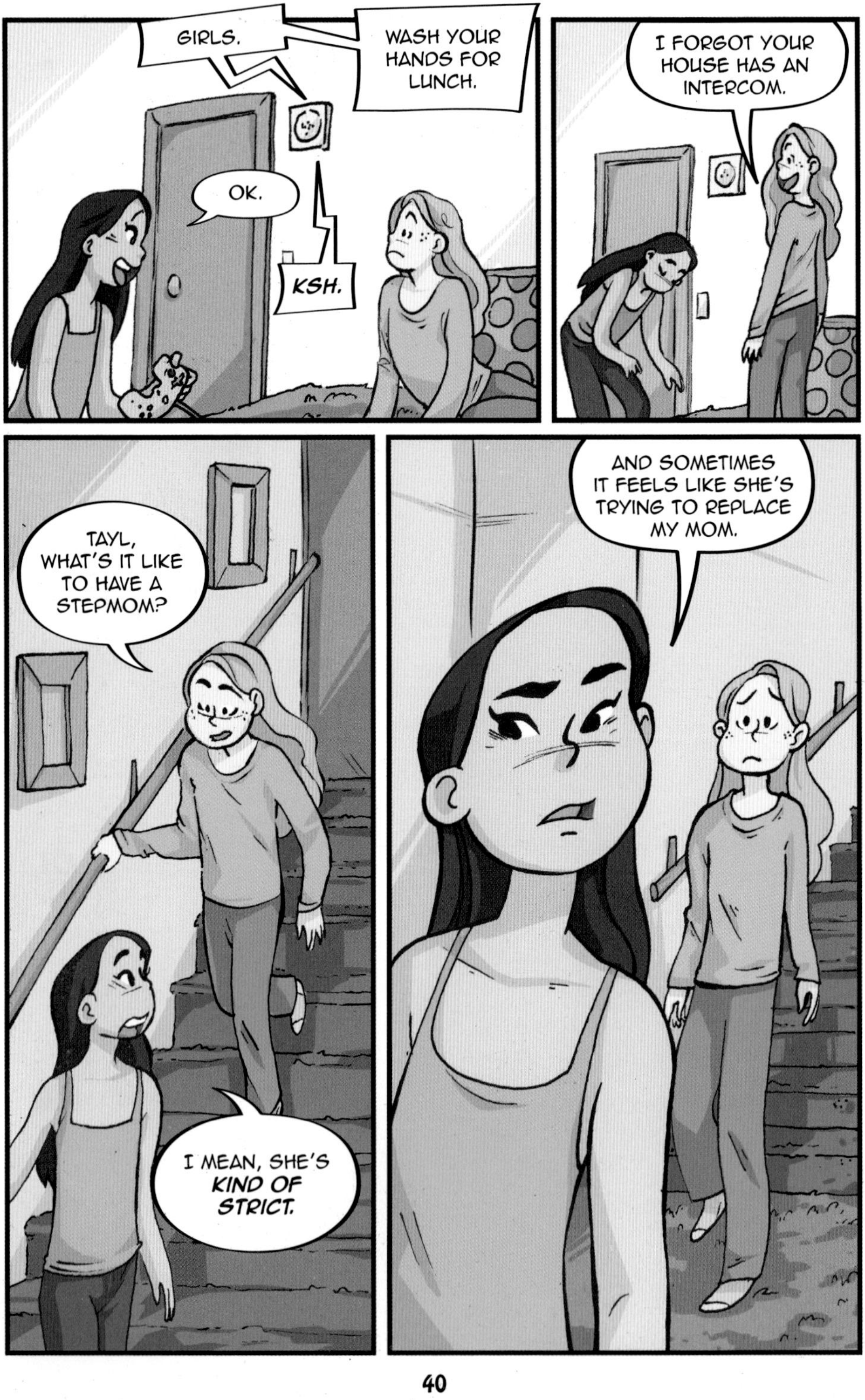
GIRLS.
WASH YOUR HANDS FOR LUNCH.
OK.
KSH.
I FORGOT YOUR HOUSE HAS AN INTERCOM.
TAYL, WHAT'S IT LIKE TO HAVE A STEPMOM?
I MEAN, SHE'S *KIND OF STRICT.*
AND SOMETIMES IT FEELS LIKE SHE'S TRYING TO REPLACE MY MOM.

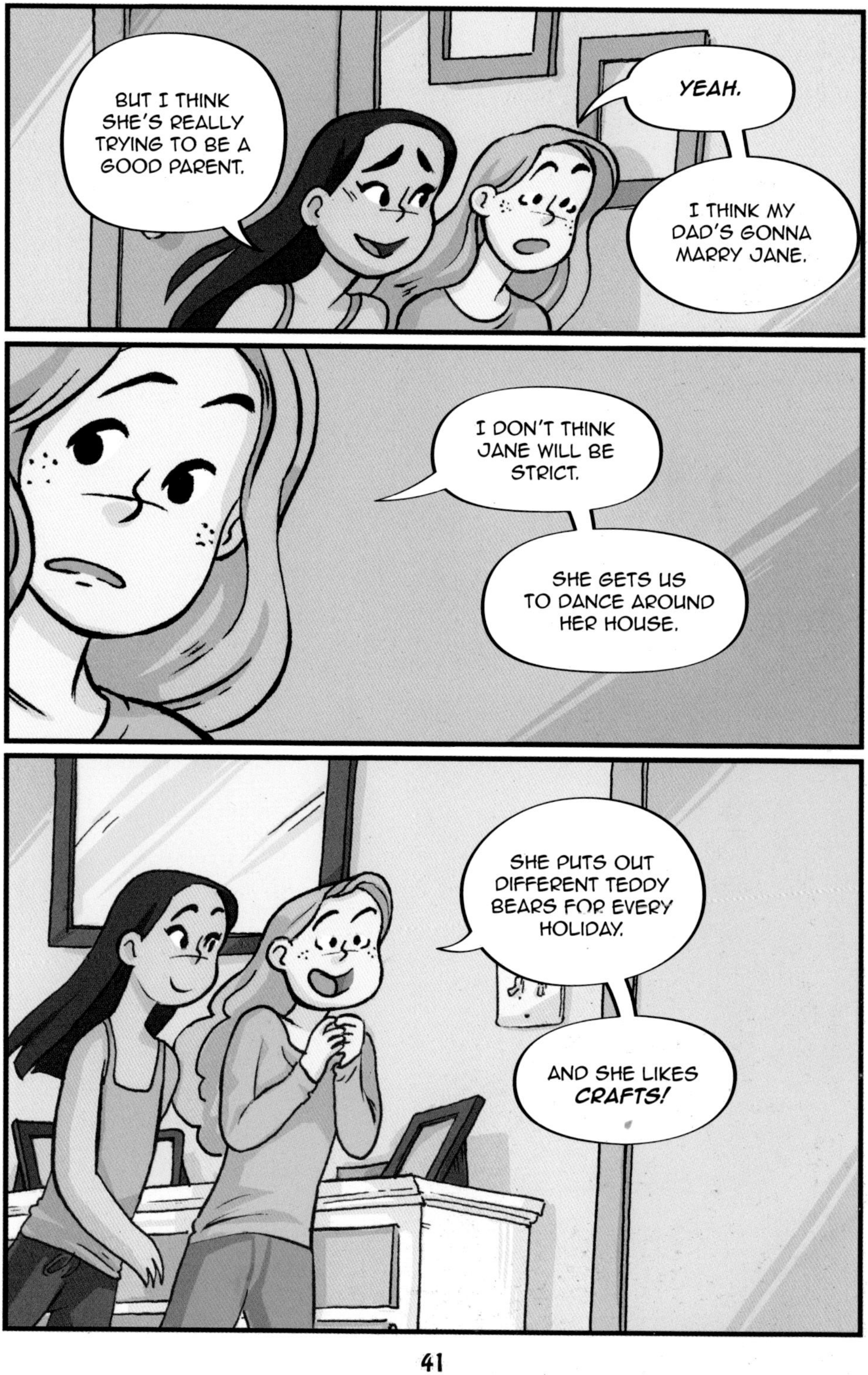
BUT I THINK SHE'S REALLY TRYING TO BE A GOOD PARENT.
YEAH.
I THINK MY DAD'S GONNA MARRY JANE.
I DON'T THINK JANE WILL BE STRICT.
SHE GETS US TO DANCE AROUND HER HOUSE.
SHE PUTS OUT DIFFERENT TEDDY BEARS FOR EVERY HOLIDAY.
AND SHE LIKES *CRAFTS!*

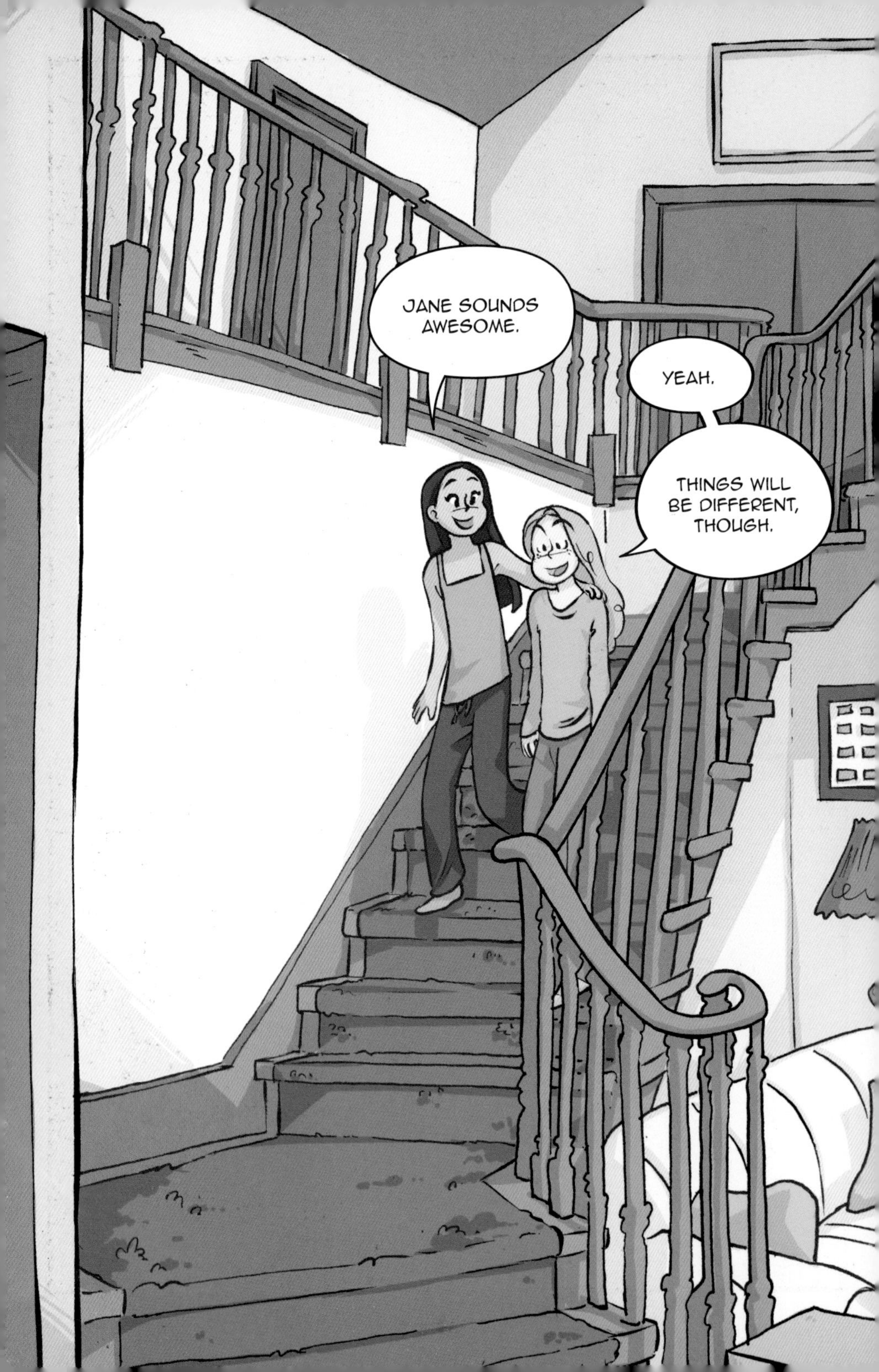
JANE SOUNDS AWESOME.
YEAH.
THINGS WILL BE DIFFERENT, THOUGH.

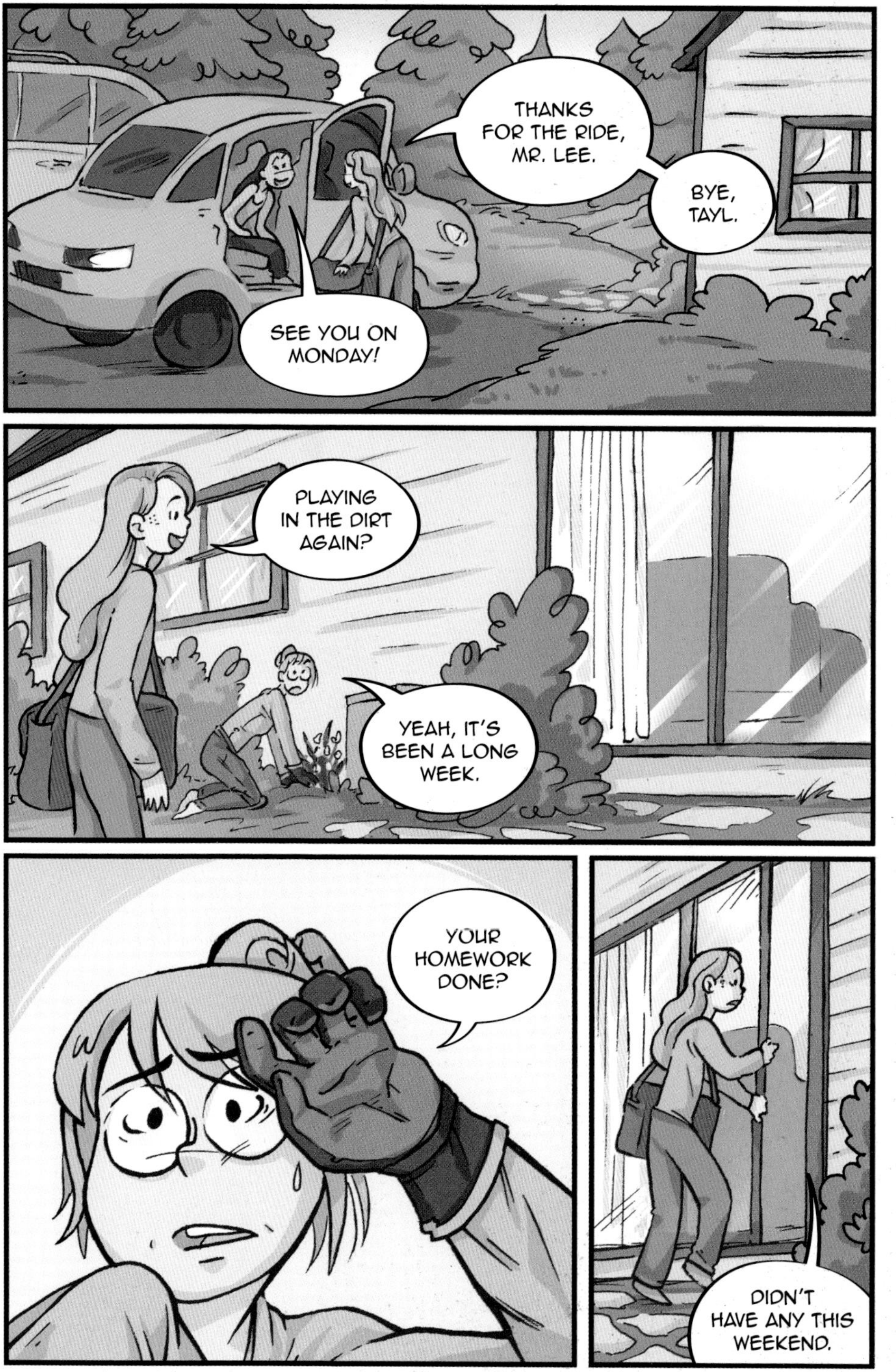
THANKS FOR THE RIDE, MR. LEE.
BYE, TAYL.
SEE YOU ON MONDAY!
PLAYING IN THE DIRT AGAIN?
YEAH, IT'S BEEN A LONG WEEK.
YOUR HOMEWORK DONE?
DIDN'T HAVE ANY THIS WEEKEND.

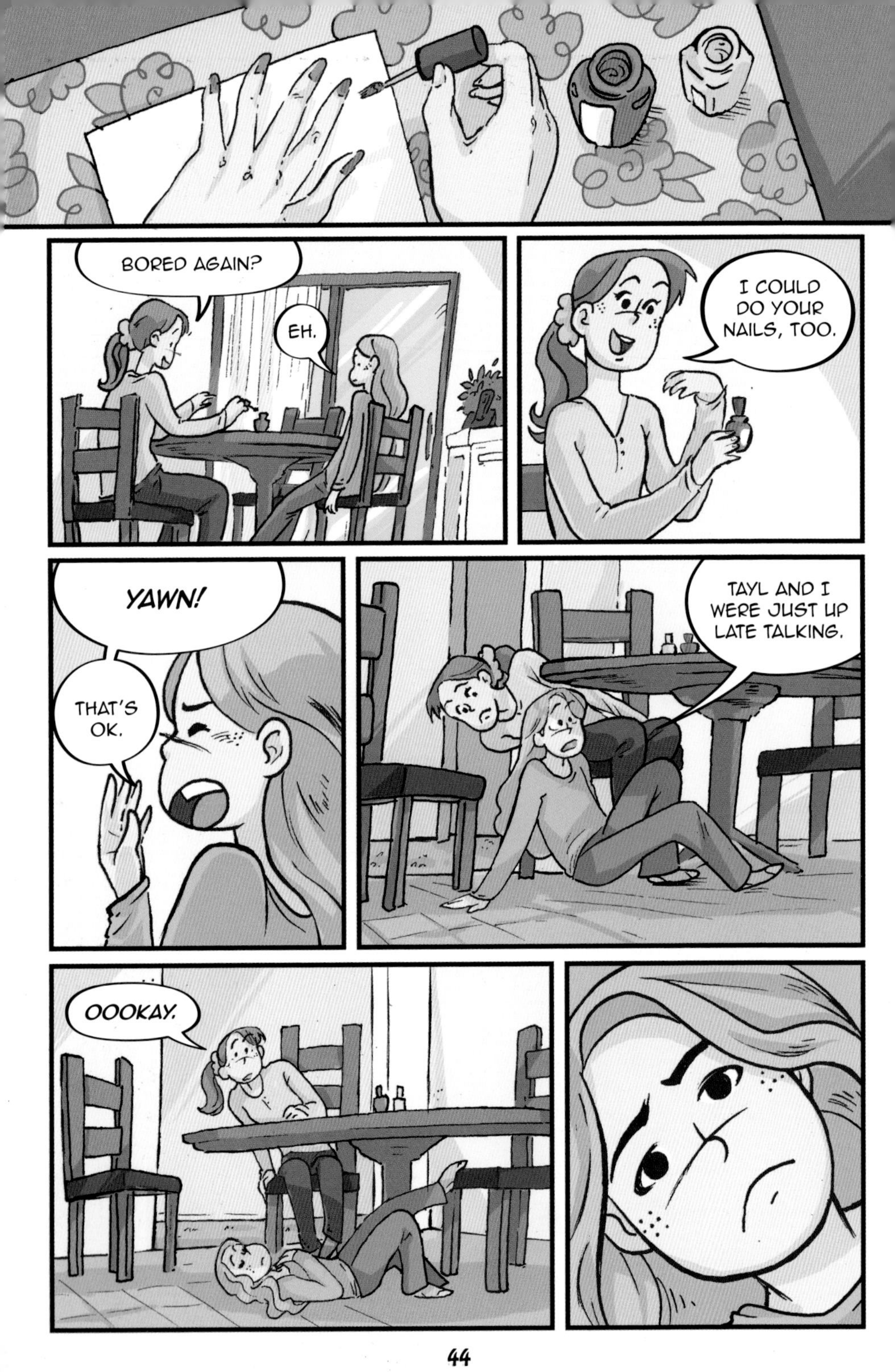
BORED AGAIN?
EH.
I COULD DO YOUR NAILS, TOO.
YAWN!
THAT'S OK.
TAYL AND I WERE JUST UP LATE TALKING.
OOOKAY.

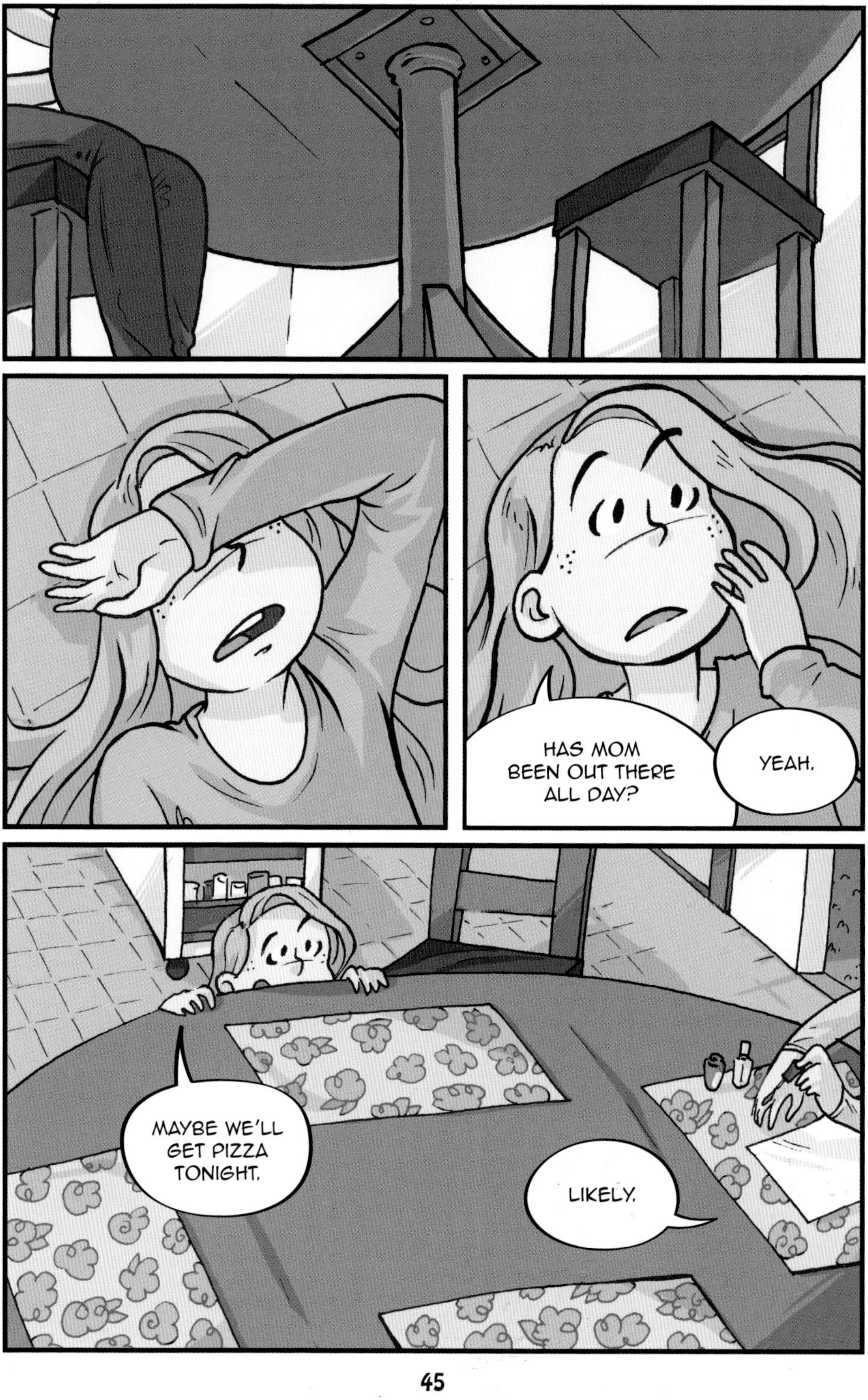
HAS MOM BEEN OUT THERE ALL DAY?
YEAH.
MAYBE WE'LL GET PIZZA TONIGHT.
LIKELY.

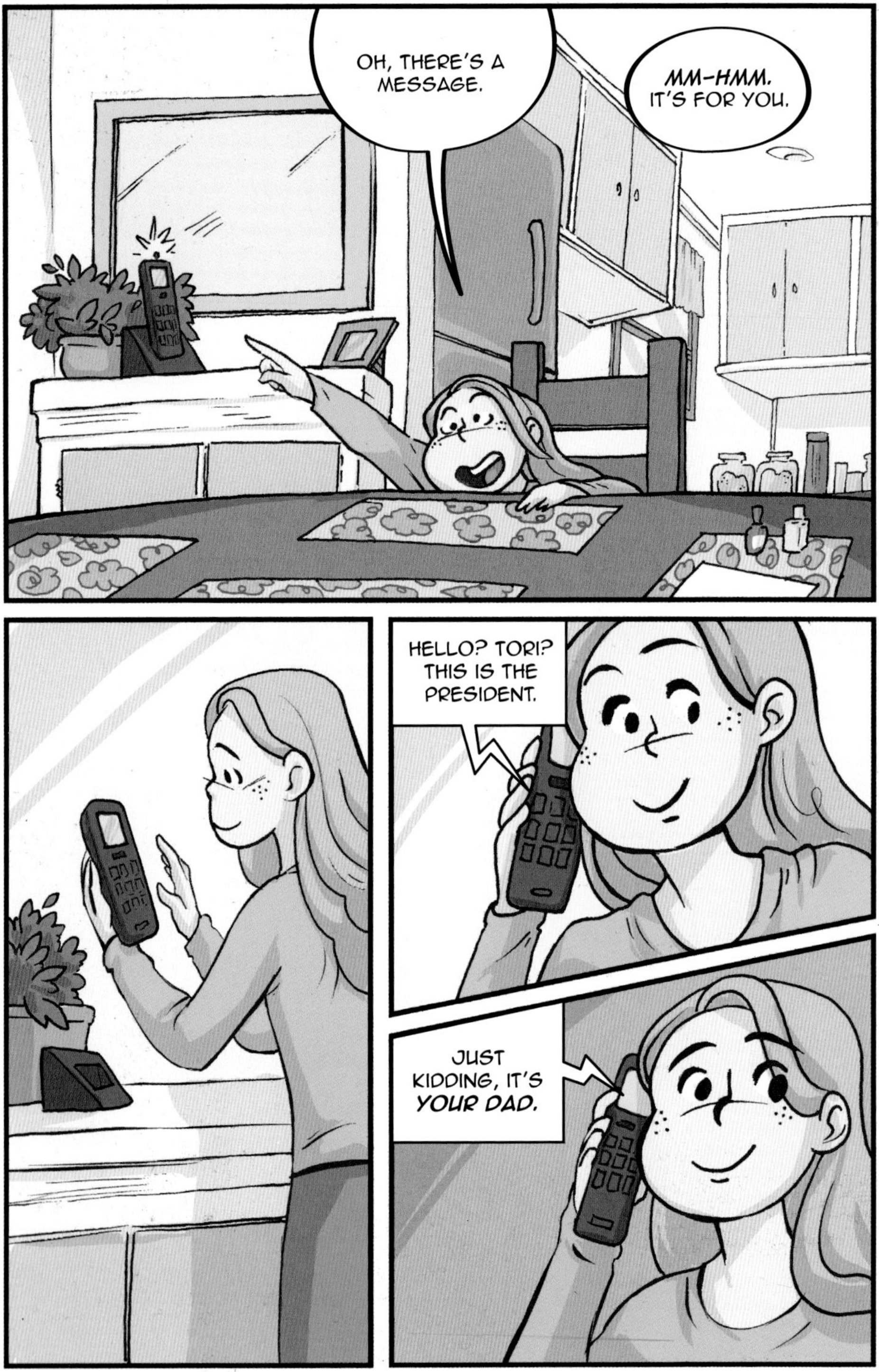
OH, THERE'S A MESSAGE.
*MM-HMM.* IT'S FOR YOU.
HELLO? TORI? THIS IS THE PRESIDENT.
JUST KIDDING, IT'S ***YOUR DAD.***

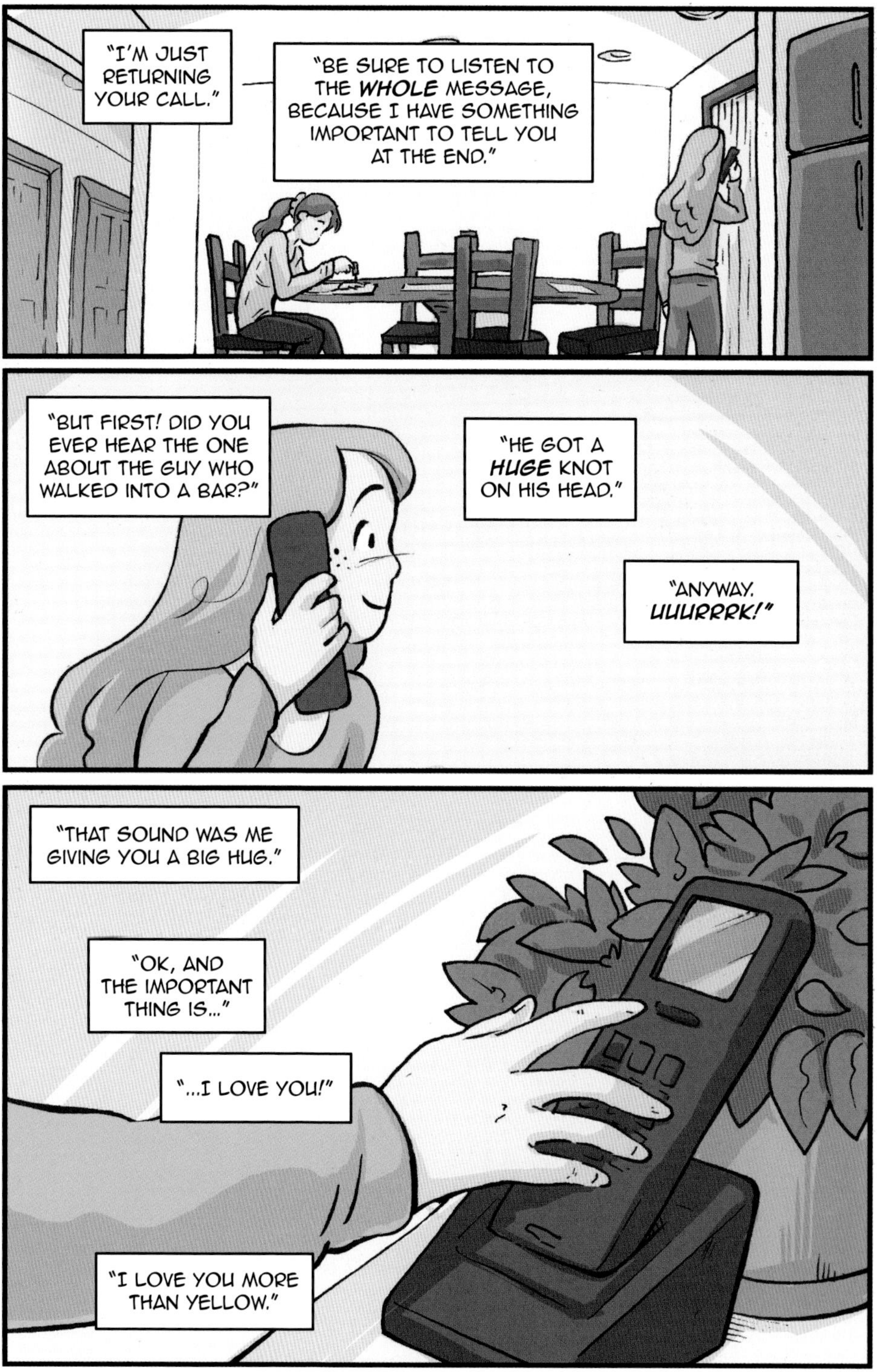
"I'M JUST RETURNING YOUR CALL."
"BE SURE TO LISTEN TO THE *WHOLE* MESSAGE, BECAUSE I HAVE SOMETHING IMPORTANT TO TELL YOU AT THE END."
"BUT FIRST! DID YOU EVER HEAR THE ONE ABOUT THE GUY WHO WALKED INTO A BAR?"
"HE GOT A *HUGE* KNOT ON HIS HEAD."
"ANYWAY. *UUURRRK!*"
"THAT SOUND WAS ME GIVING YOU A BIG HUG."
"OK, AND THE IMPORTANT THING IS..."
"...I LOVE YOU!"
"I LOVE YOU MORE THAN YELLOW."

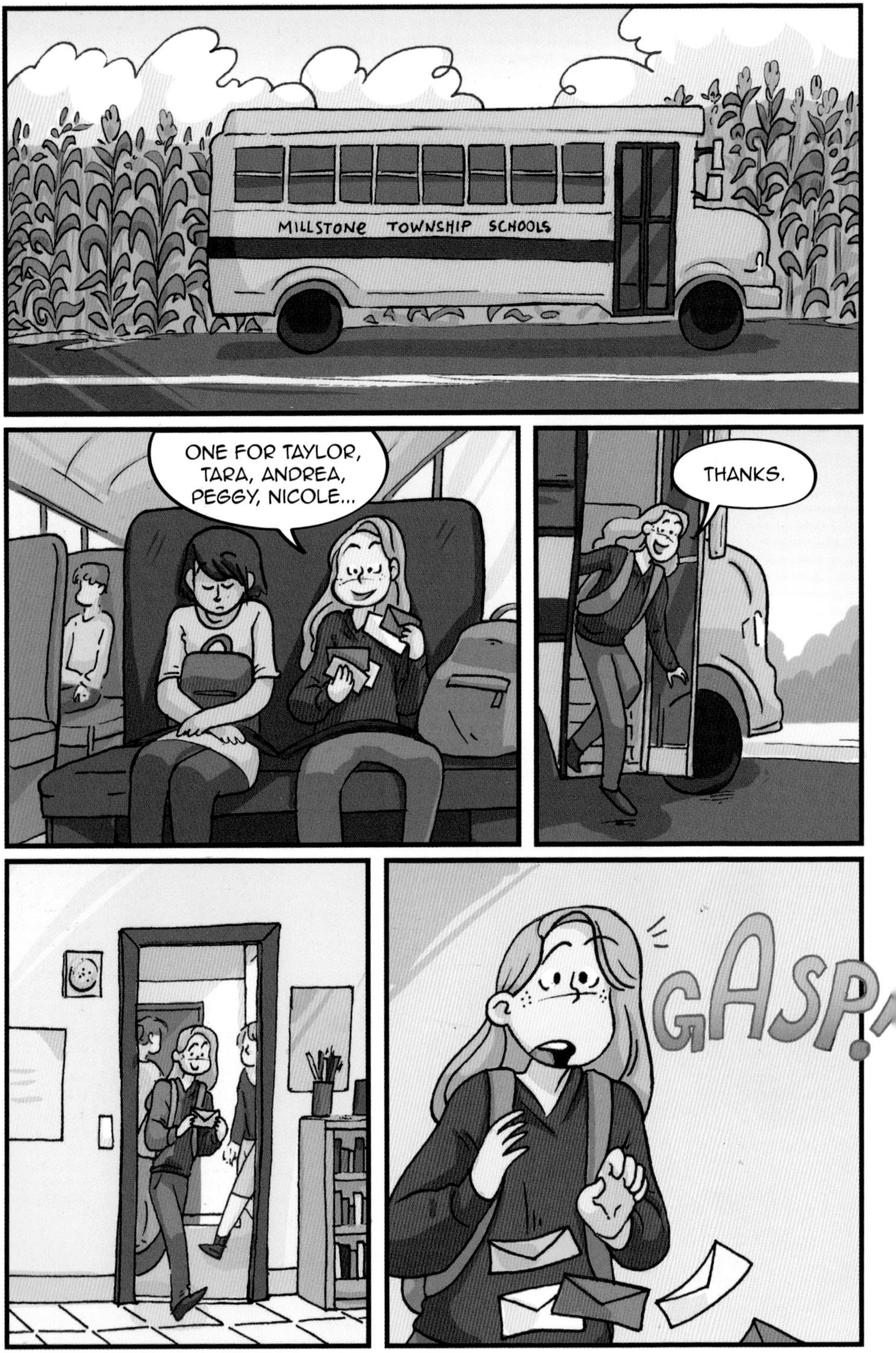
MILLSTONE TOWNSHIP SCHOOLS
ONE FOR TAYLOR, TARA, ANDREA, PEGGY, NICOLE...
THANKS.
GASP!

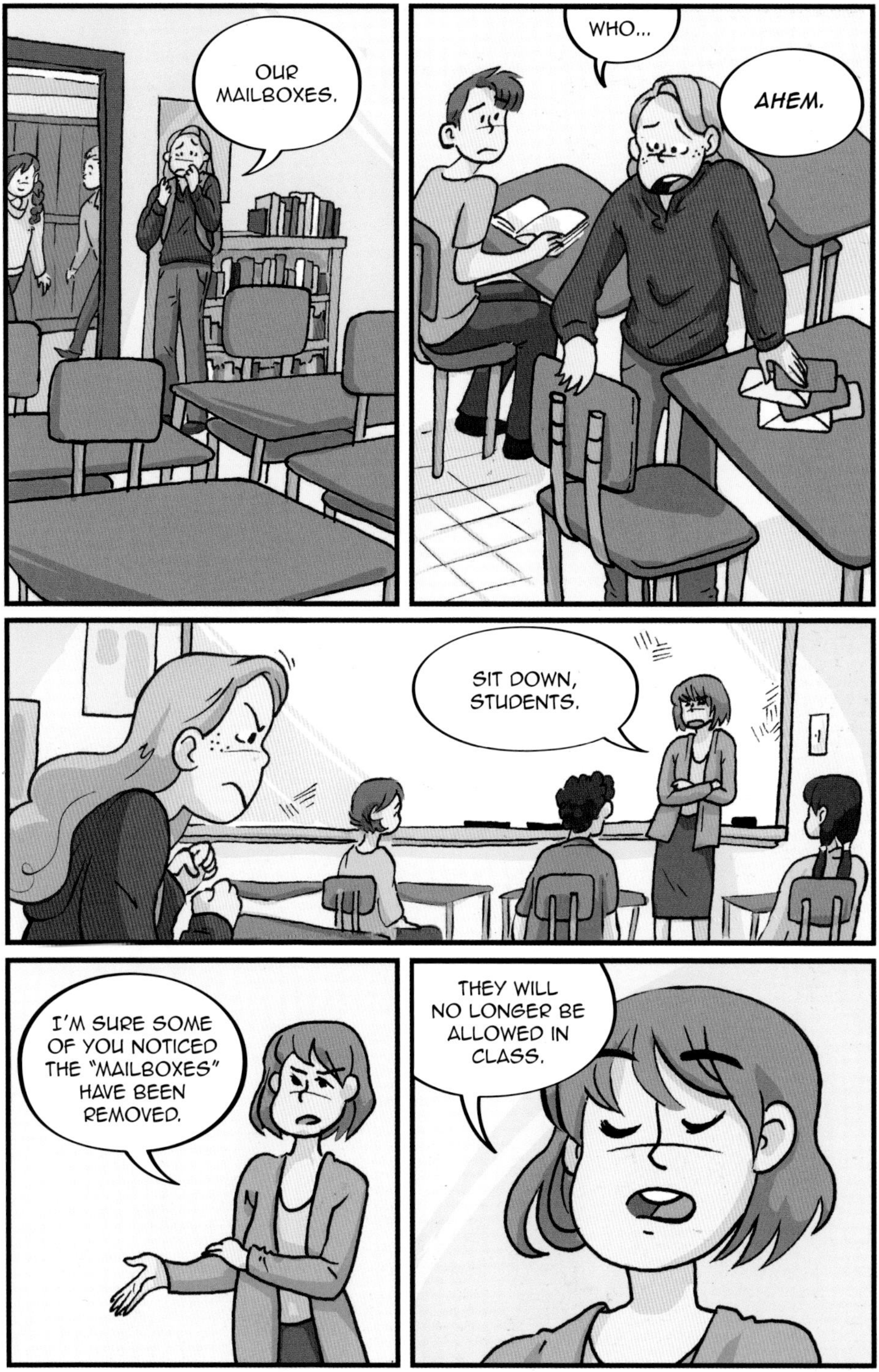
OUR MAILBOXES.
WHO...
AHEM.
SIT DOWN, STUDENTS.
I'M SURE SOME OF YOU NOTICED THE "MAILBOXES" HAVE BEEN REMOVED.
THEY WILL NO LONGER BE ALLOWED IN CLASS.

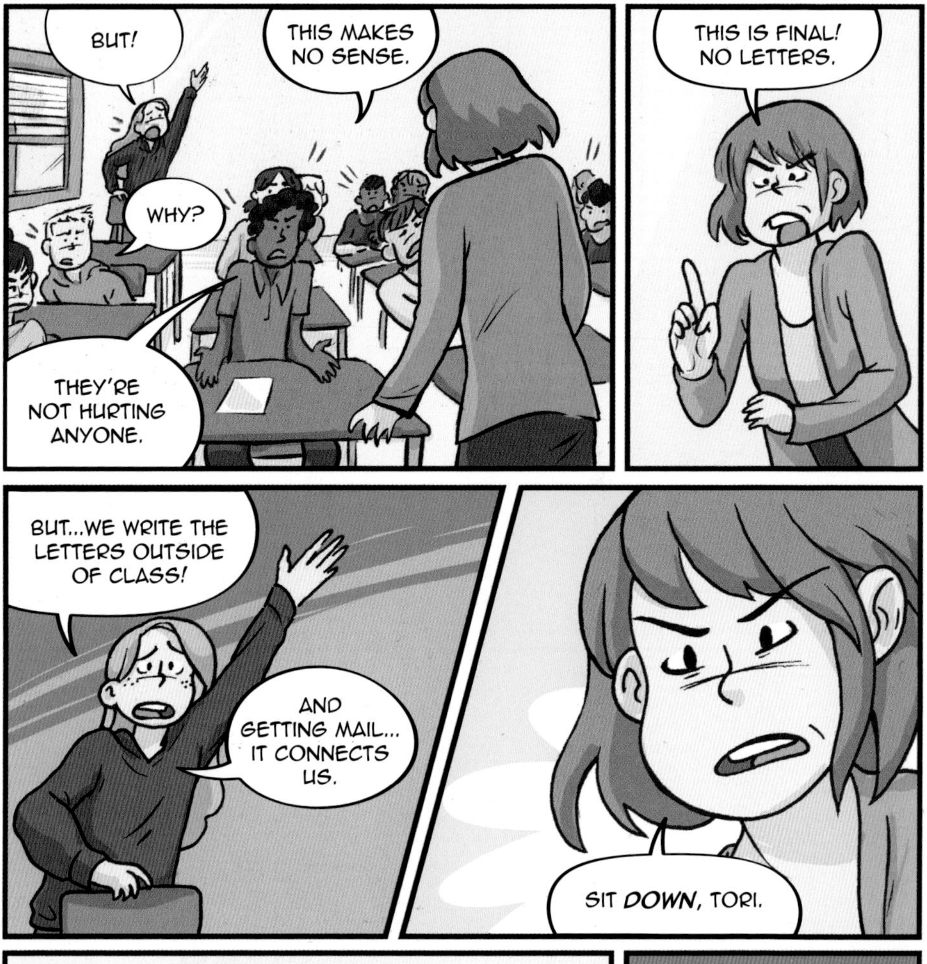
BUT!
THIS MAKES NO SENSE.
WHY?
THEY'RE NOT HURTING ANYONE.
THIS IS FINAL! NO LETTERS.
BUT...WE WRITE THE LETTERS OUTSIDE OF CLASS!
AND GETTING MAIL... IT CONNECTS US.
SIT *DOWN*, TORI.
WUMP
GIVING "MAIL" IS THE SAME AS PASSING NOTES.
TALK AT **LUNCH.**

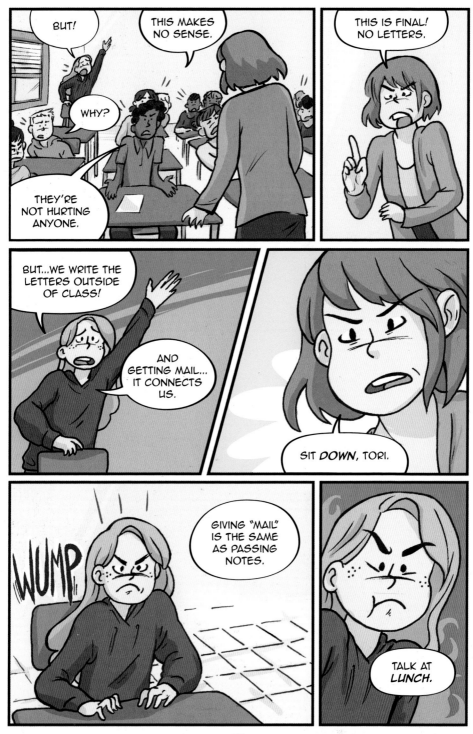

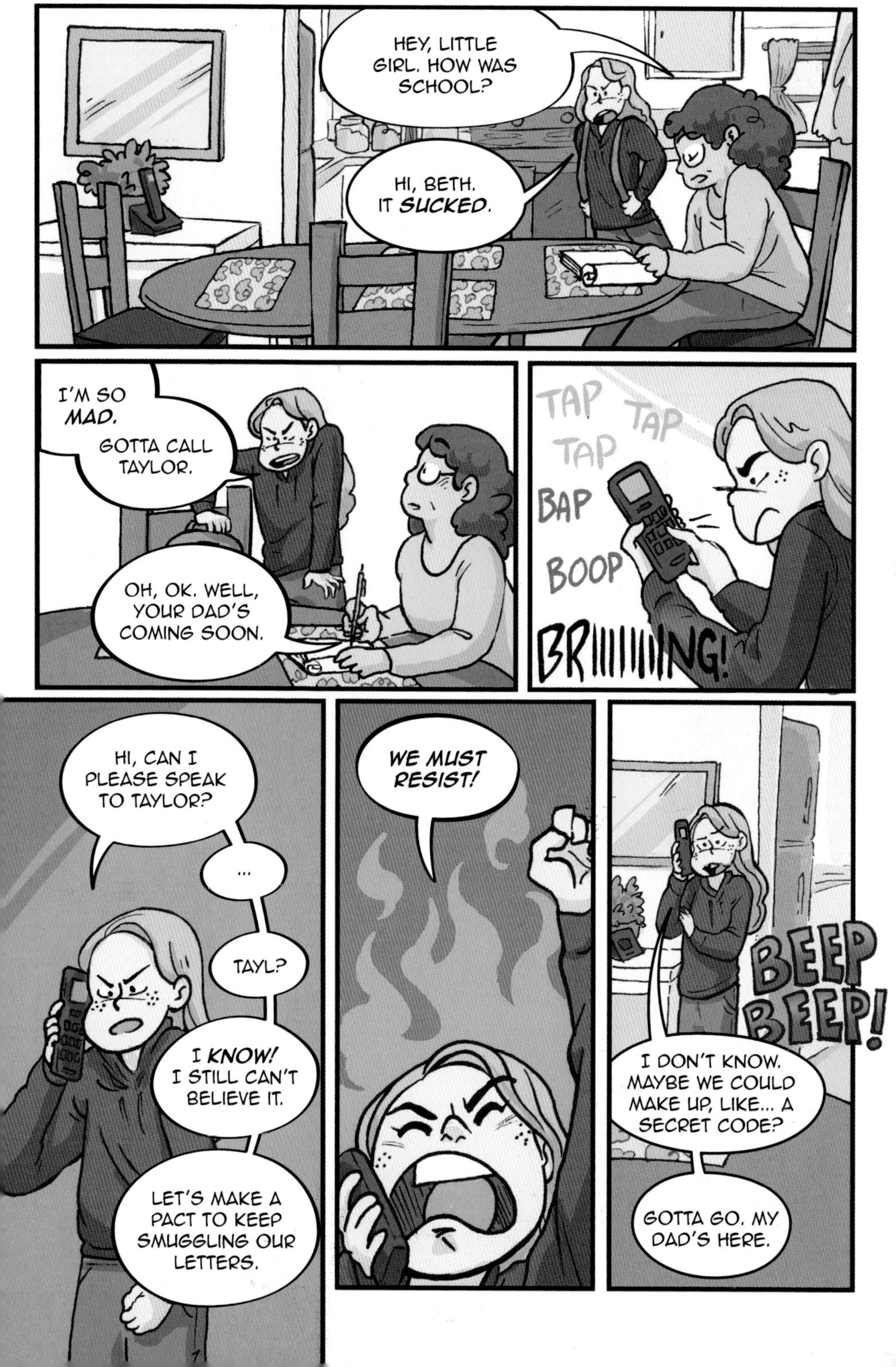
HEY, LITTLE GIRL. HOW WAS SCHOOL?
HI, BETH. IT SUCKED.
I'M SO MAD.
GOTTA CALL TAYLOR.
OH, OK. WELL, YOUR DAD'S COMING SOON.
TAP TAP
TAP
BAP
BOOP
BRIIIIIIIING!
HI, CAN I PLEASE SPEAK TO TAYLOR?
...
TAYL?
I KNOW! I STILL CAN'T BELIEVE IT.
LET'S MAKE A PACT TO KEEP SMUGGLING OUR LETTERS.
WE MUST RESIST!
BEEP BEEP!
I DON'T KNOW. MAYBE WE COULD MAKE UP, LIKE... A SECRET CODE?
GOTTA GO. MY DAD'S HERE.

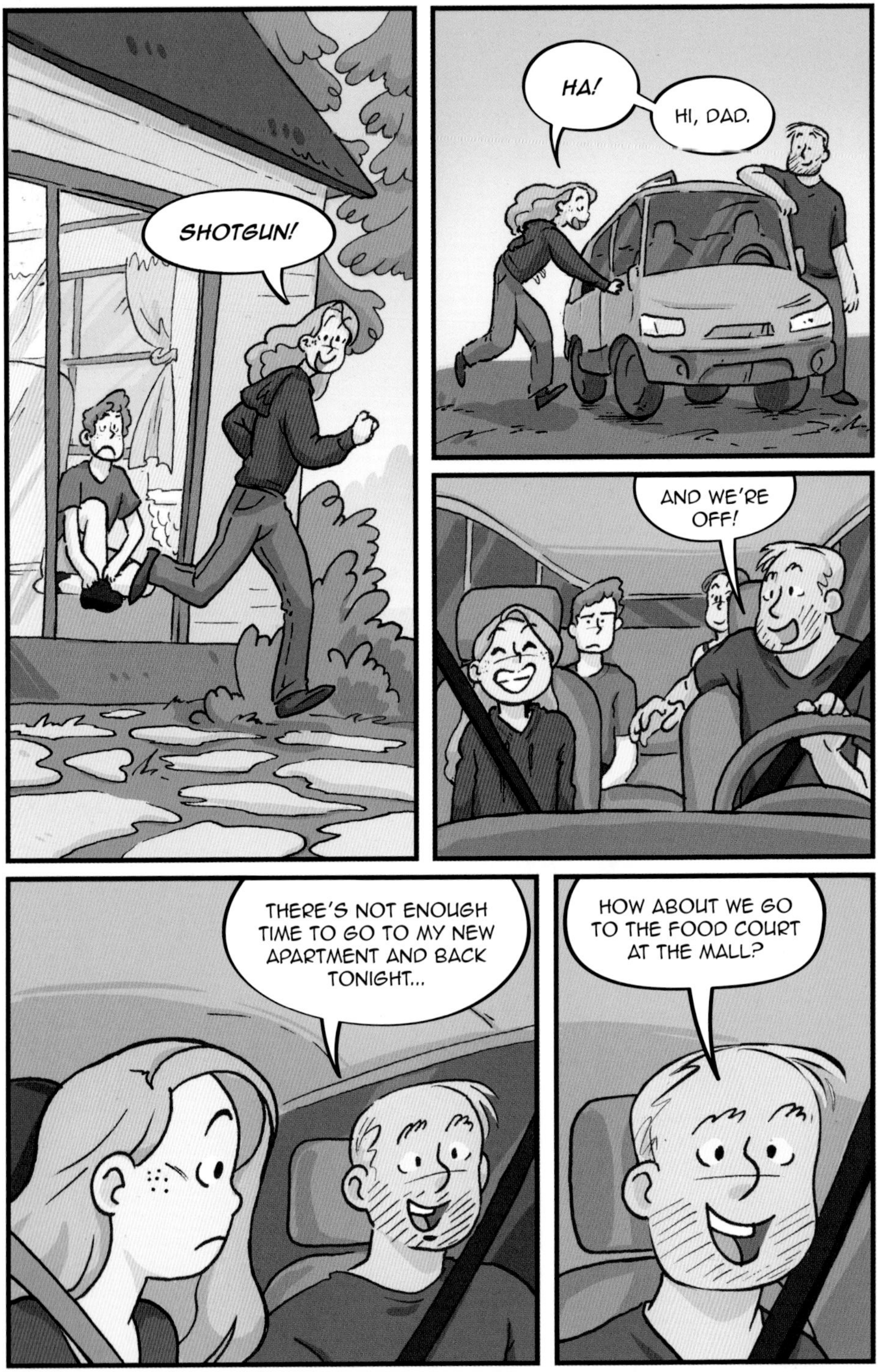
SHOTGUN!
HA!
HI, DAD.
AND WE'RE OFF!
THERE'S NOT ENOUGH TIME TO GO TO MY NEW APARTMENT AND BACK TONIGHT...
HOW ABOUT WE GO TO THE FOOD COURT AT THE MALL?

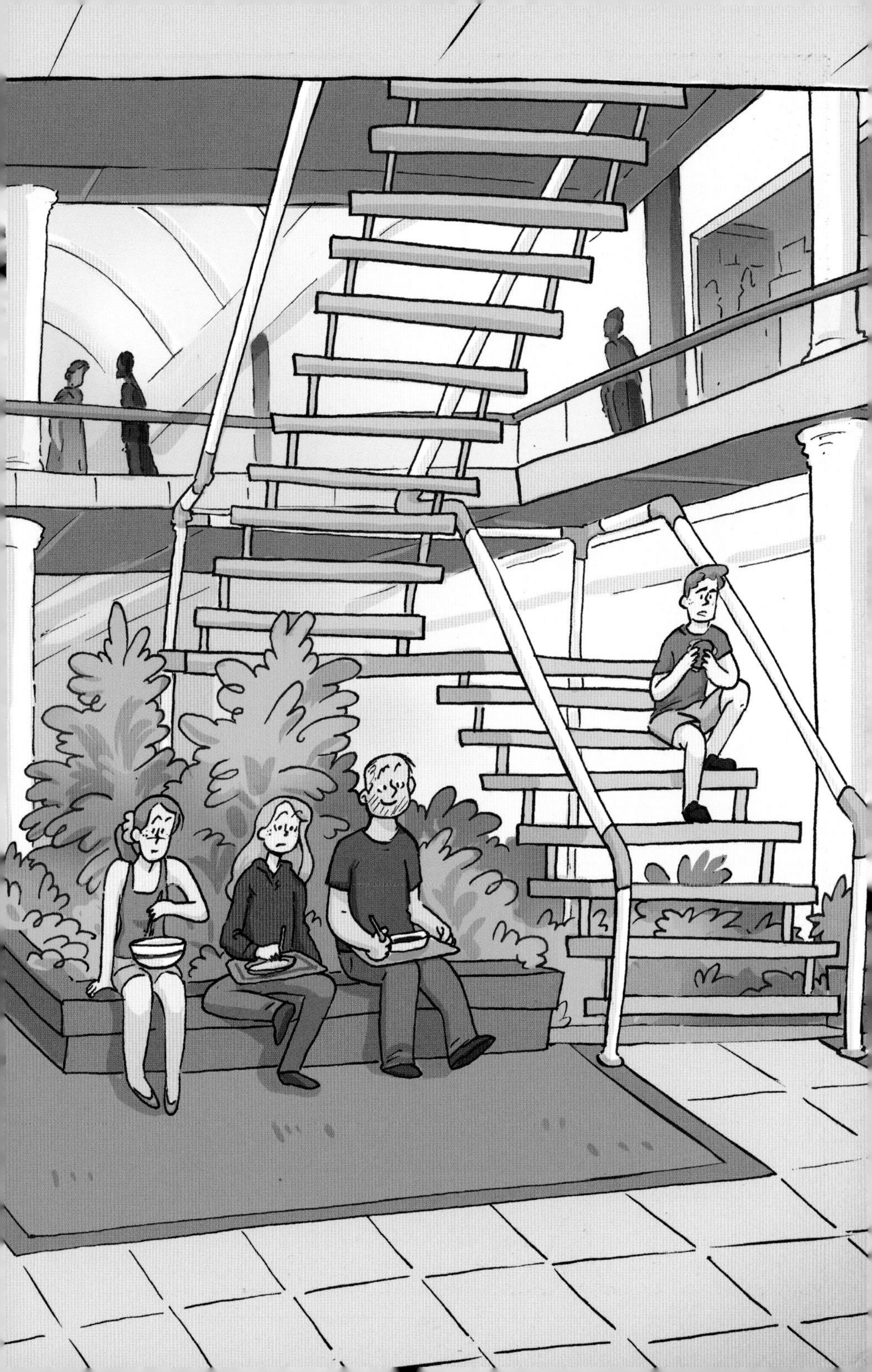

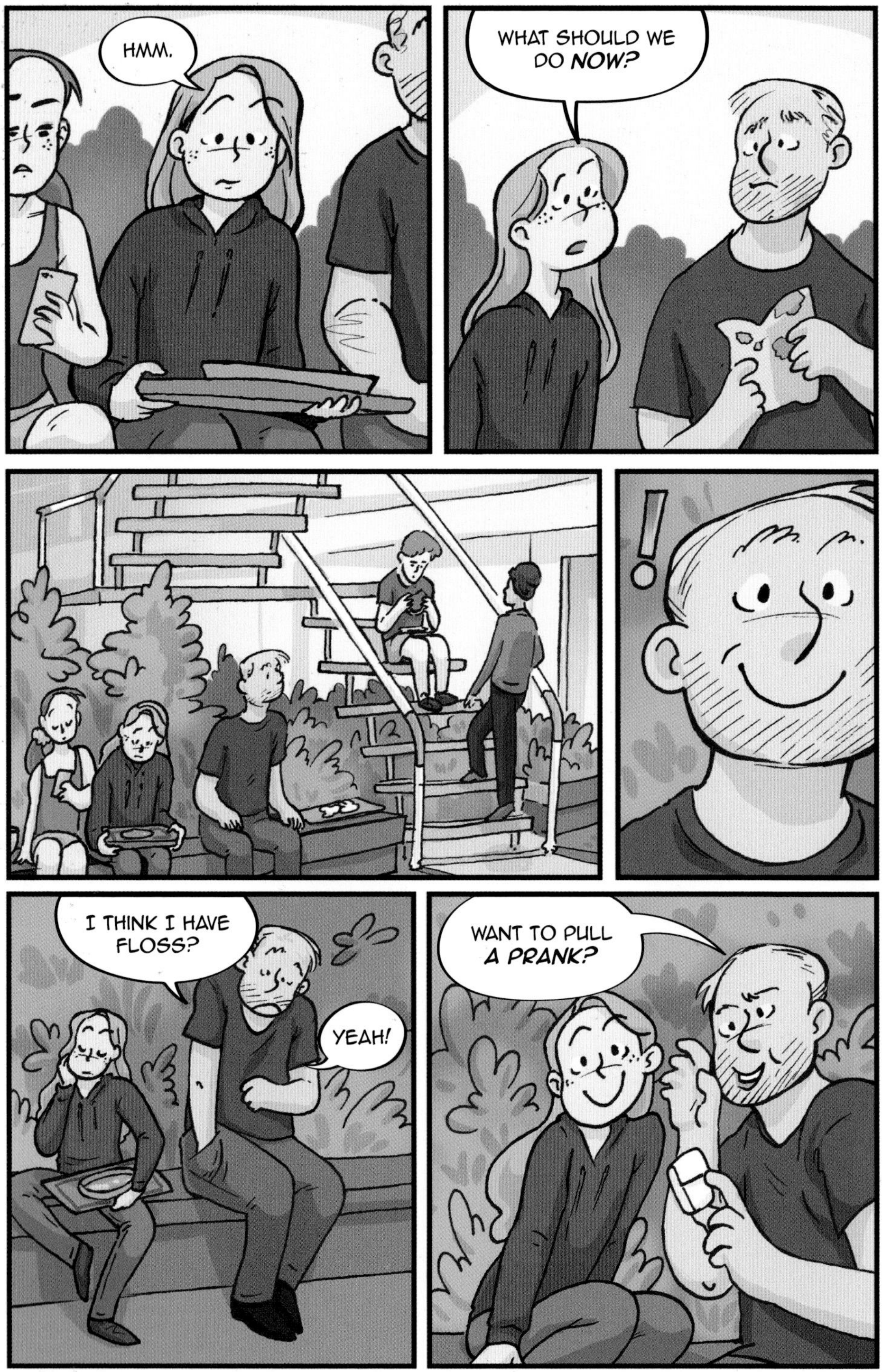
HMM.
WHAT SHOULD WE DO NOW?
!
I THINK I HAVE FLOSS?
YEAH!
WANT TO PULL A PRANK?

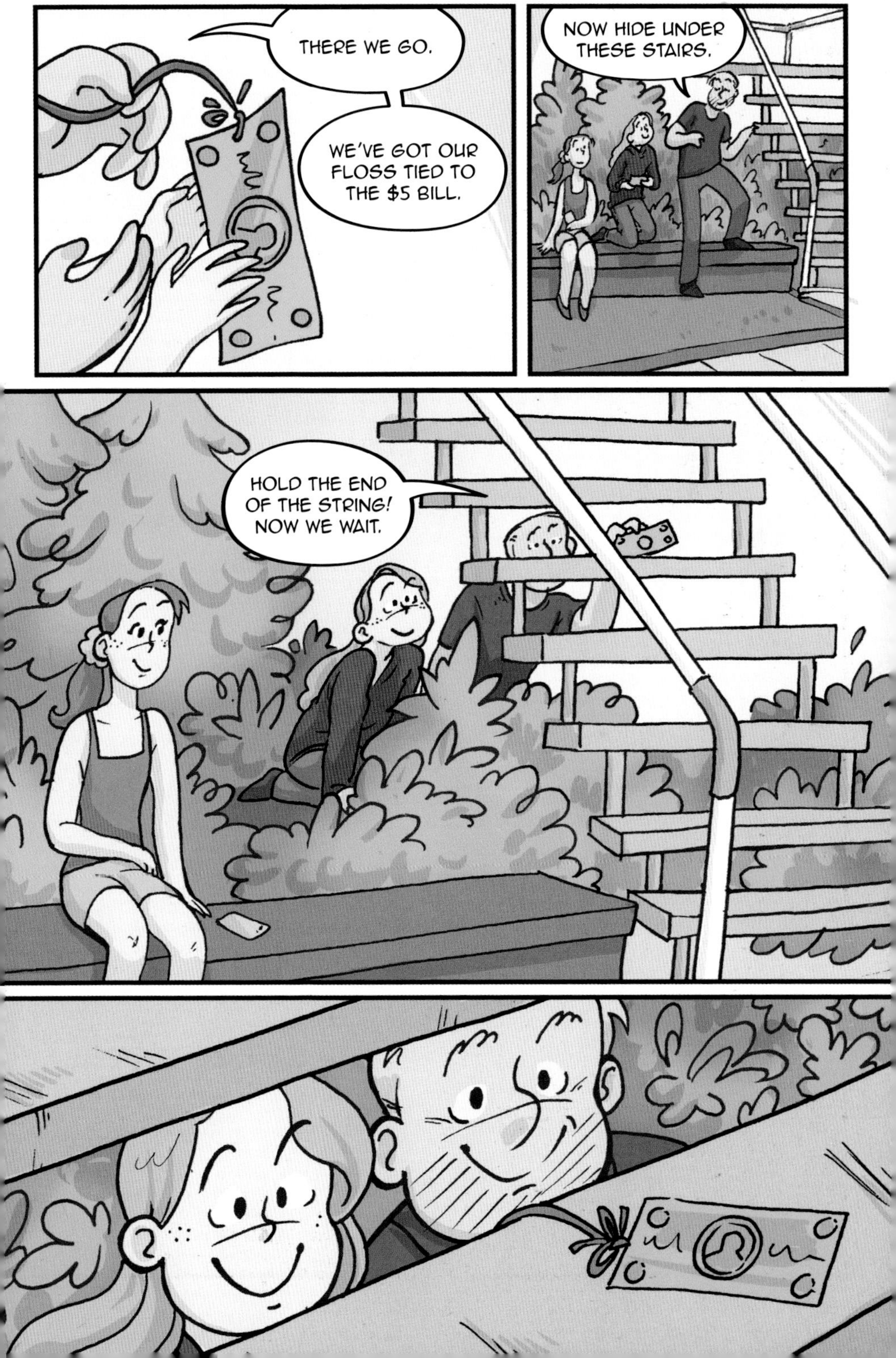
THERE WE GO.
WE'VE GOT OUR FLOSS TIED TO THE $5 BILL.
NOW HIDE UNDER THESE STAIRS.
HOLD THE END OF THE STRING! NOW WE WAIT.

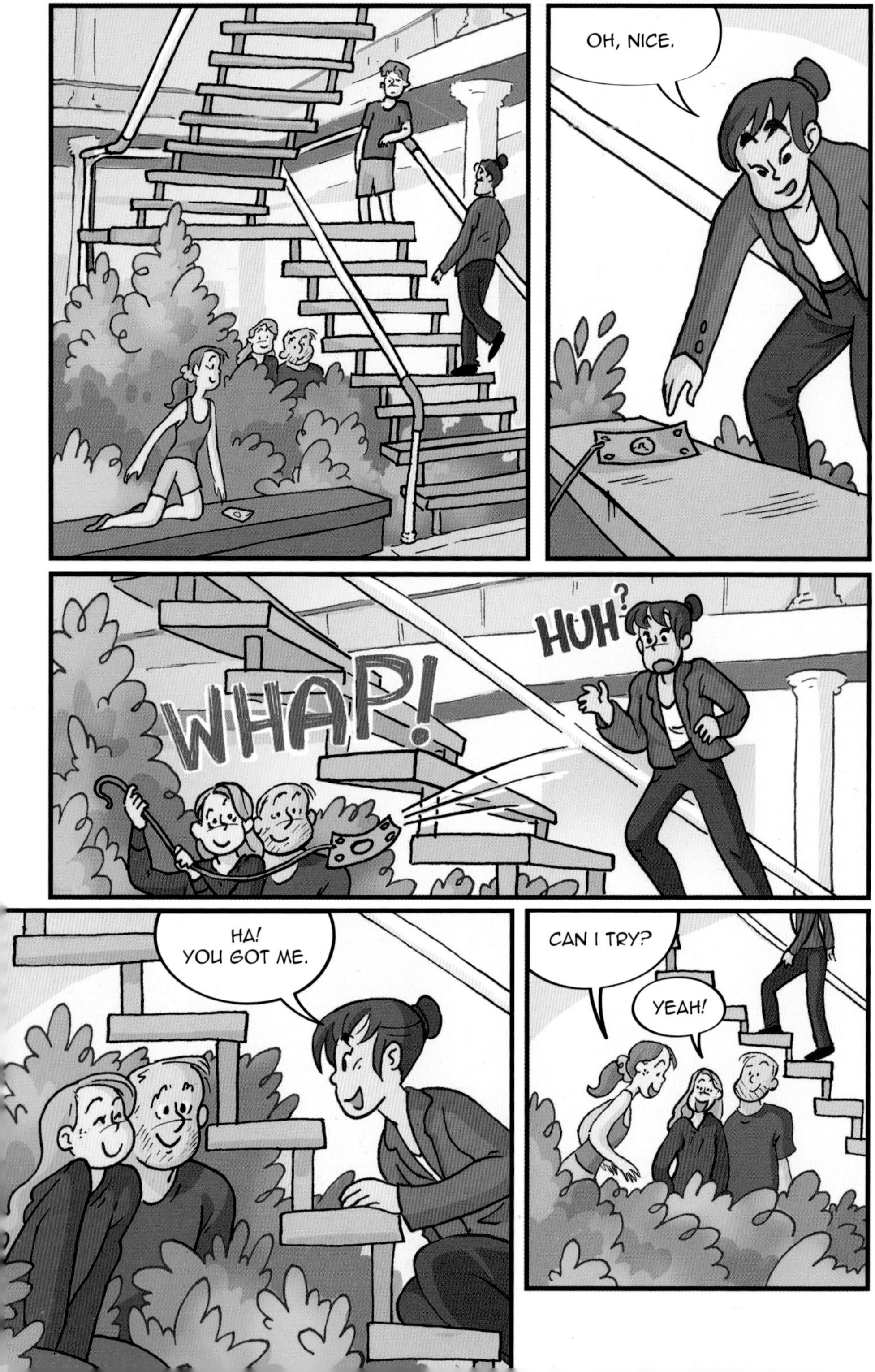
OH, NICE.
HUH?
WHAP!
HA!
YOU GOT ME.
CAN I TRY?
YEAH!

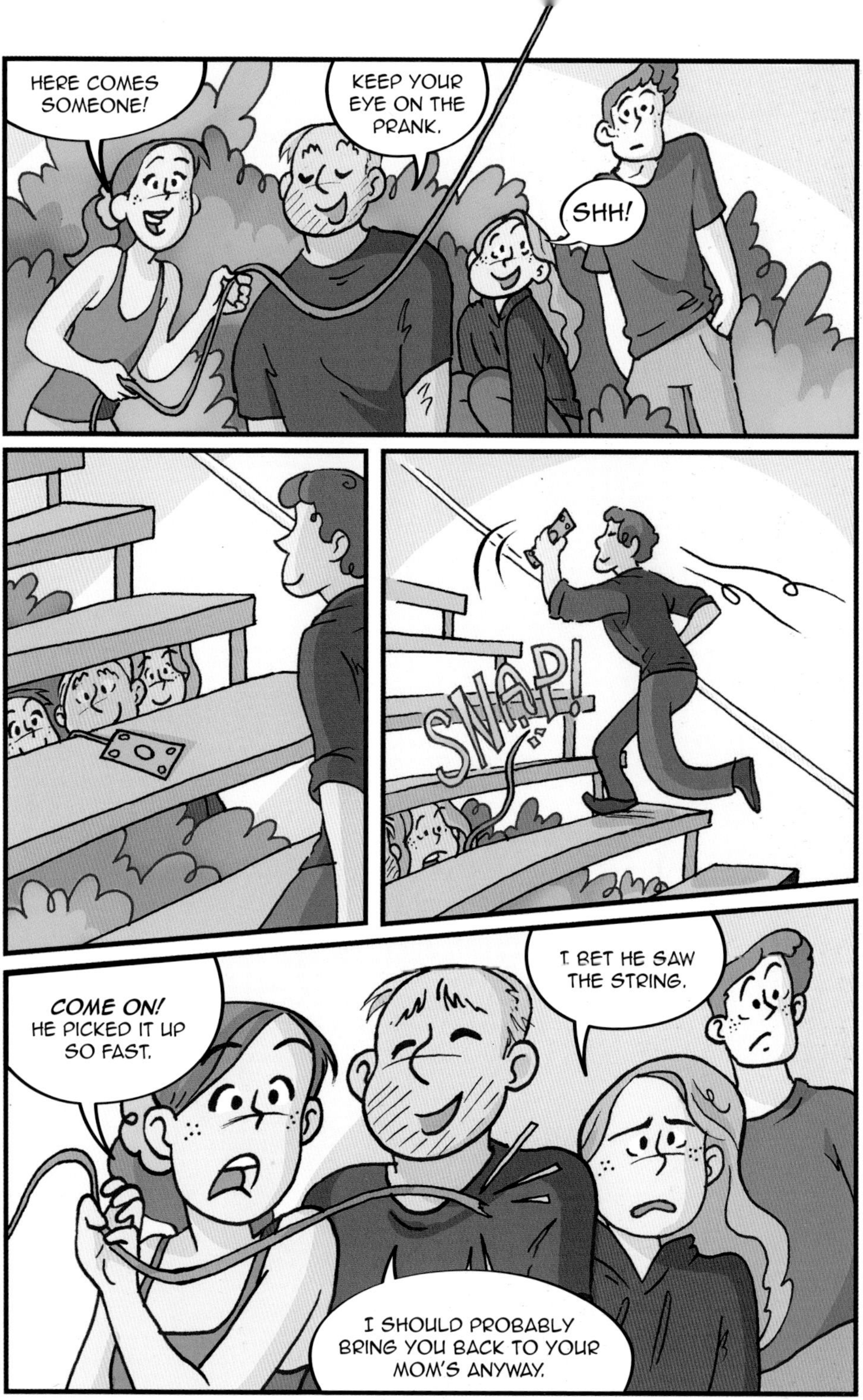
HERE COMES SOMEONE!
KEEP YOUR EYE ON THE PRANK.
SHH!
SNAP!
COME ON! HE PICKED IT UP SO FAST.
I BET HE SAW THE STRING.
I SHOULD PROBABLY BRING YOU BACK TO YOUR MOM'S ANYWAY.

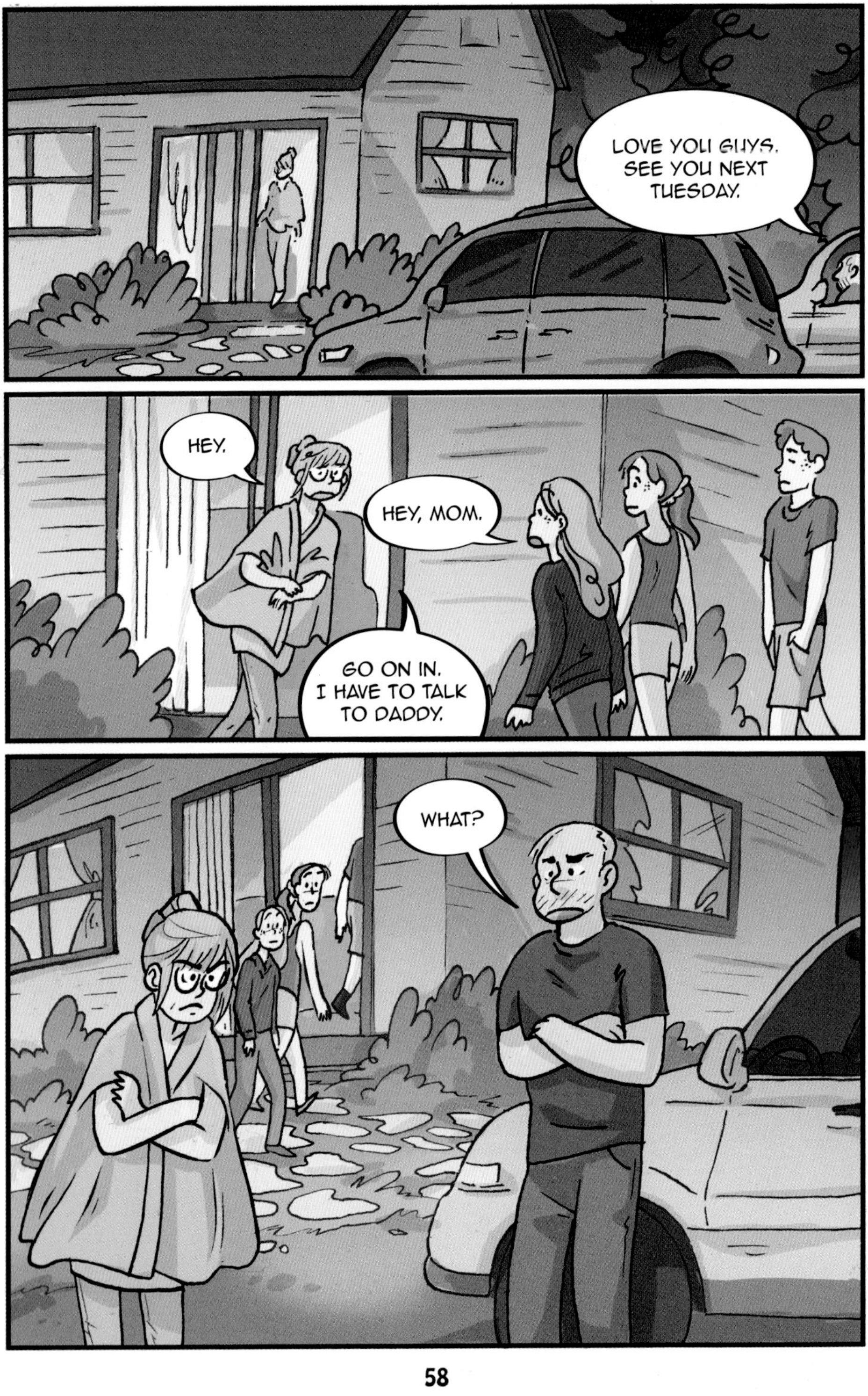
LOVE YOU GUYS. SEE YOU NEXT TUESDAY.
HEY.
HEY, MOM.
GO ON IN. I HAVE TO TALK TO DADDY.
WHAT?

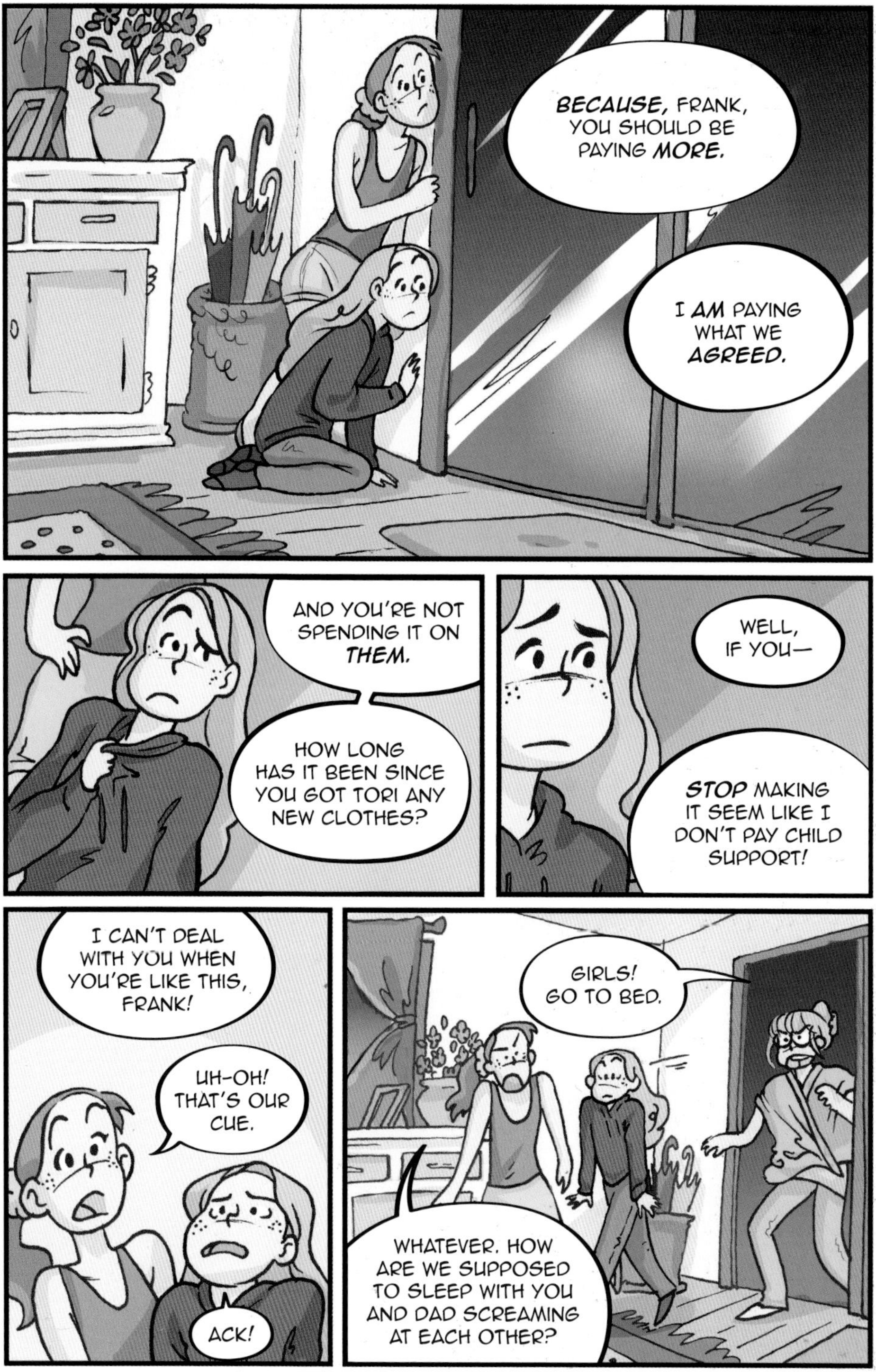
BECAUSE, FRANK, YOU SHOULD BE PAYING MORE.
I AM PAYING WHAT WE AGREED.
AND YOU'RE NOT SPENDING IT ON THEM.
HOW LONG HAS IT BEEN SINCE YOU GOT TORI ANY NEW CLOTHES?
WELL, IF YOU—
STOP MAKING IT SEEM LIKE I DON'T PAY CHILD SUPPORT!
I CAN'T DEAL WITH YOU WHEN YOU'RE LIKE THIS, FRANK!
UH-OH! THAT'S OUR CUE.
ACK!
GIRLS! GO TO BED.
WHATEVER. HOW ARE WE SUPPOSED TO SLEEP WITH YOU AND DAD SCREAMING AT EACH OTHER?

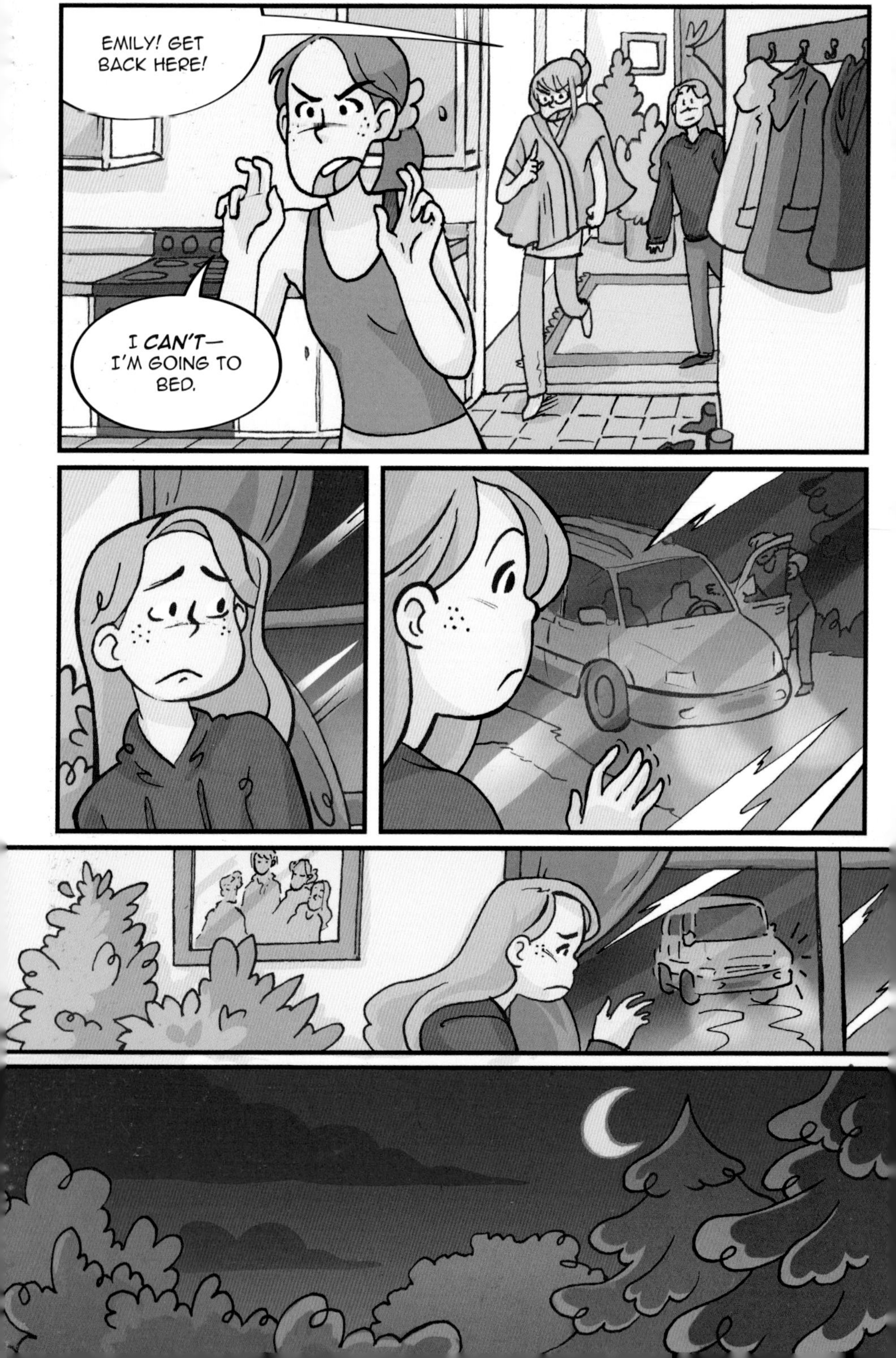
EMILY! GET BACK HERE!
I CAN'T— I'M GOING TO BED.

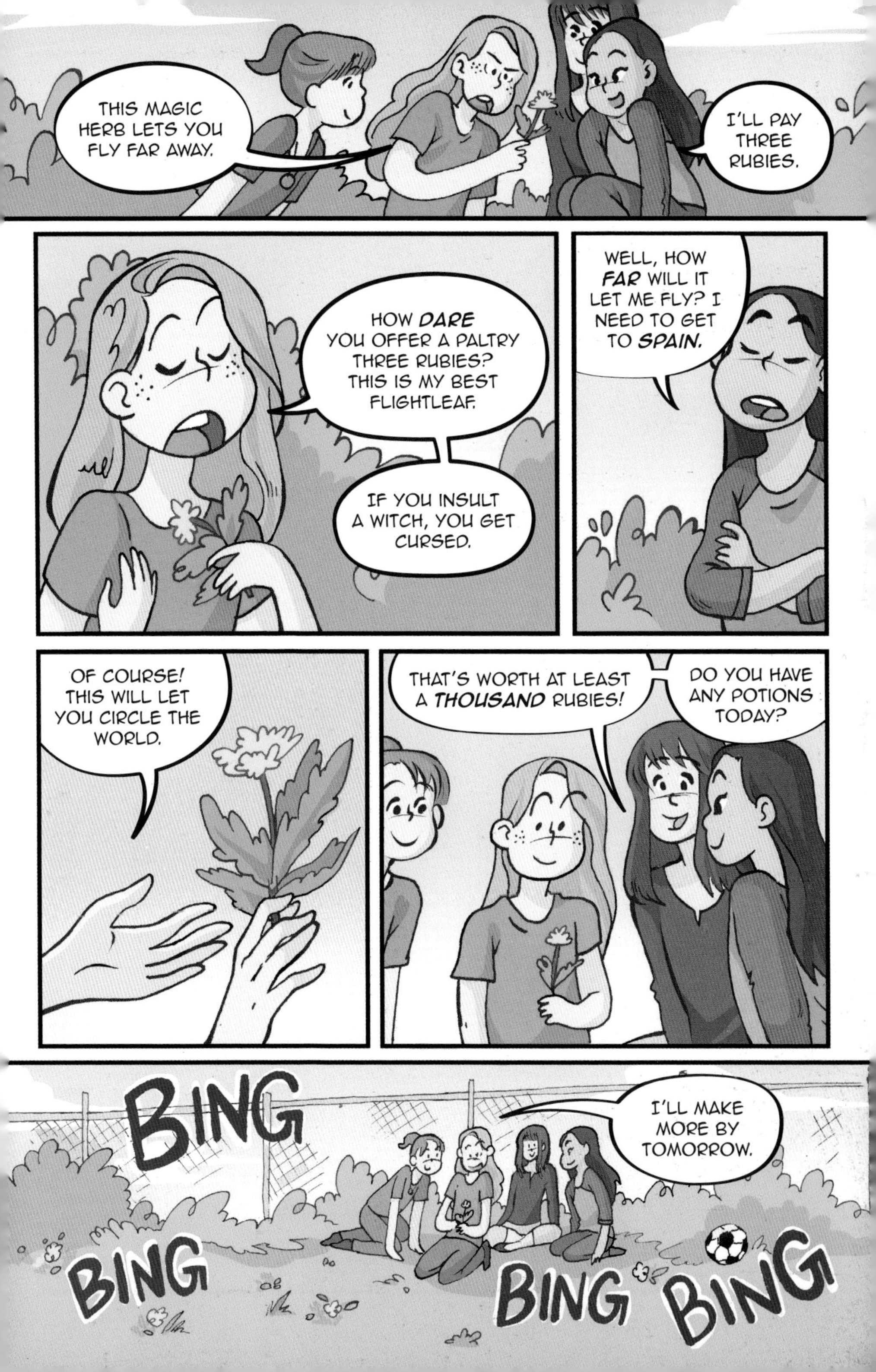
THIS MAGIC HERB LETS YOU FLY FAR AWAY.
I'LL PAY THREE RUBIES.
HOW *DARE* YOU OFFER A PALTRY THREE RUBIES? THIS IS MY BEST FLIGHTLEAF.
IF YOU INSULT A WITCH, YOU GET CURSED.
WELL, HOW *FAR* WILL IT LET ME FLY? I NEED TO GET TO *SPAIN.*
OF COURSE! THIS WILL LET YOU CIRCLE THE WORLD.
THAT'S WORTH AT LEAST A *THOUSAND* RUBIES!
DO YOU HAVE ANY POTIONS TODAY?
BING
I'LL MAKE MORE BY TOMORROW.
BING
BING BING

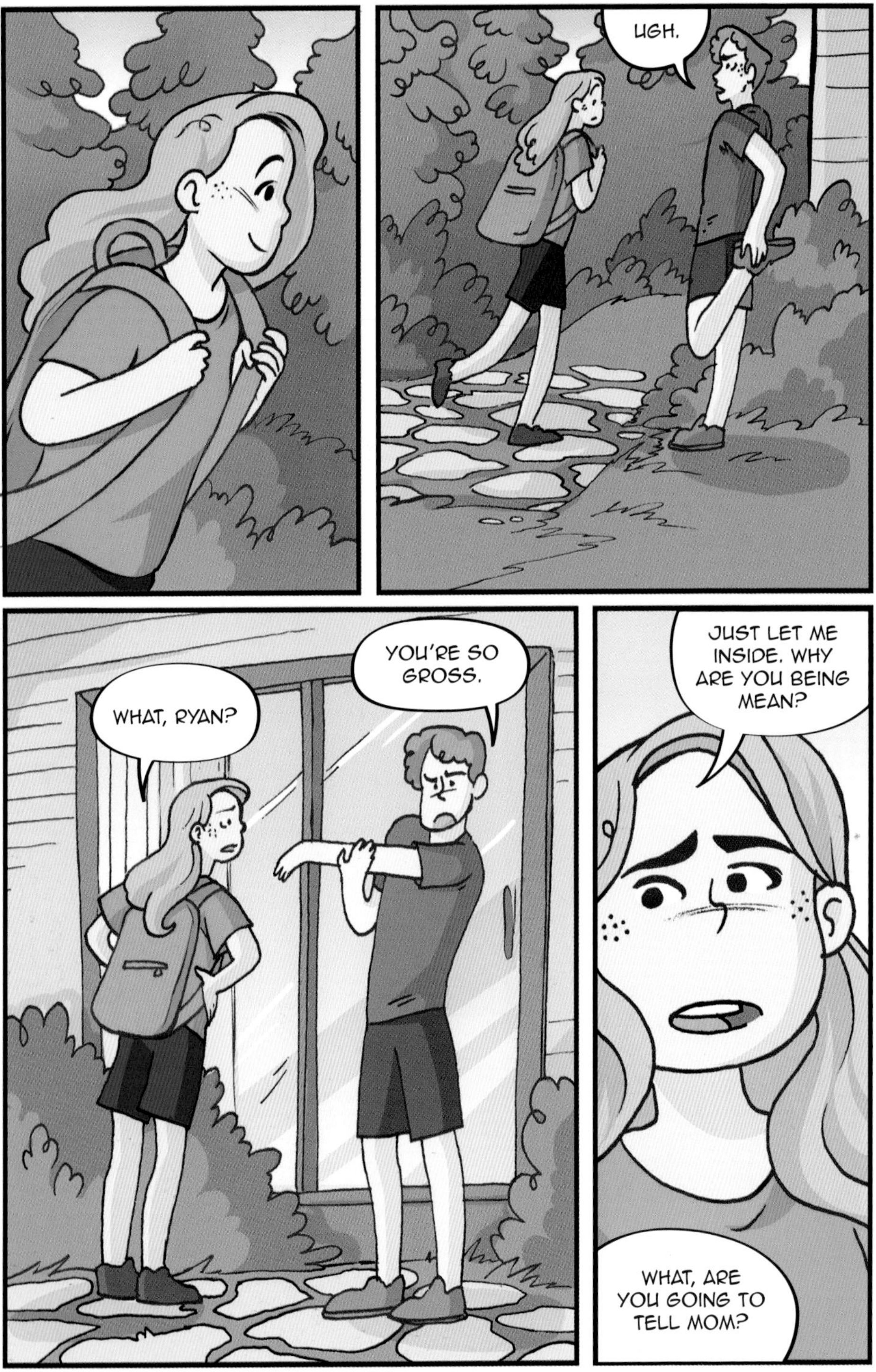
UGH.
WHAT, RYAN?
YOU'RE SO GROSS.
JUST LET ME INSIDE. WHY ARE YOU BEING MEAN?
WHAT, ARE YOU GOING TO TELL MOM?

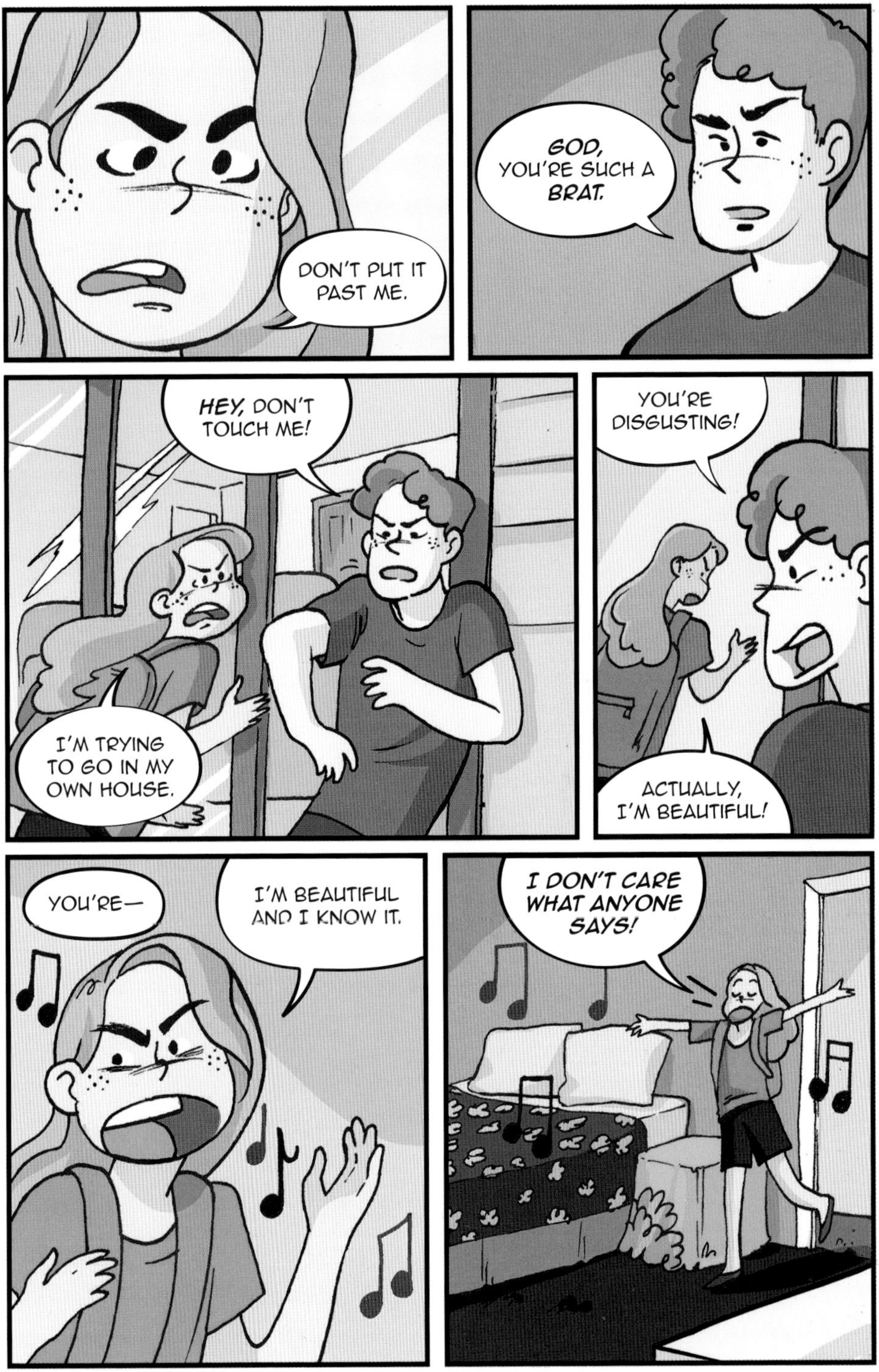
DON'T PUT IT PAST ME.
GOD, YOU'RE SUCH A BRAT.
HEY, DON'T TOUCH ME!
I'M TRYING TO GO IN MY OWN HOUSE.
YOU'RE DISGUSTING!
ACTUALLY, I'M BEAUTIFUL!
YOU'RE—
I'M BEAUTIFUL AND I KNOW IT.
I DON'T CARE WHAT ANYONE SAYS!

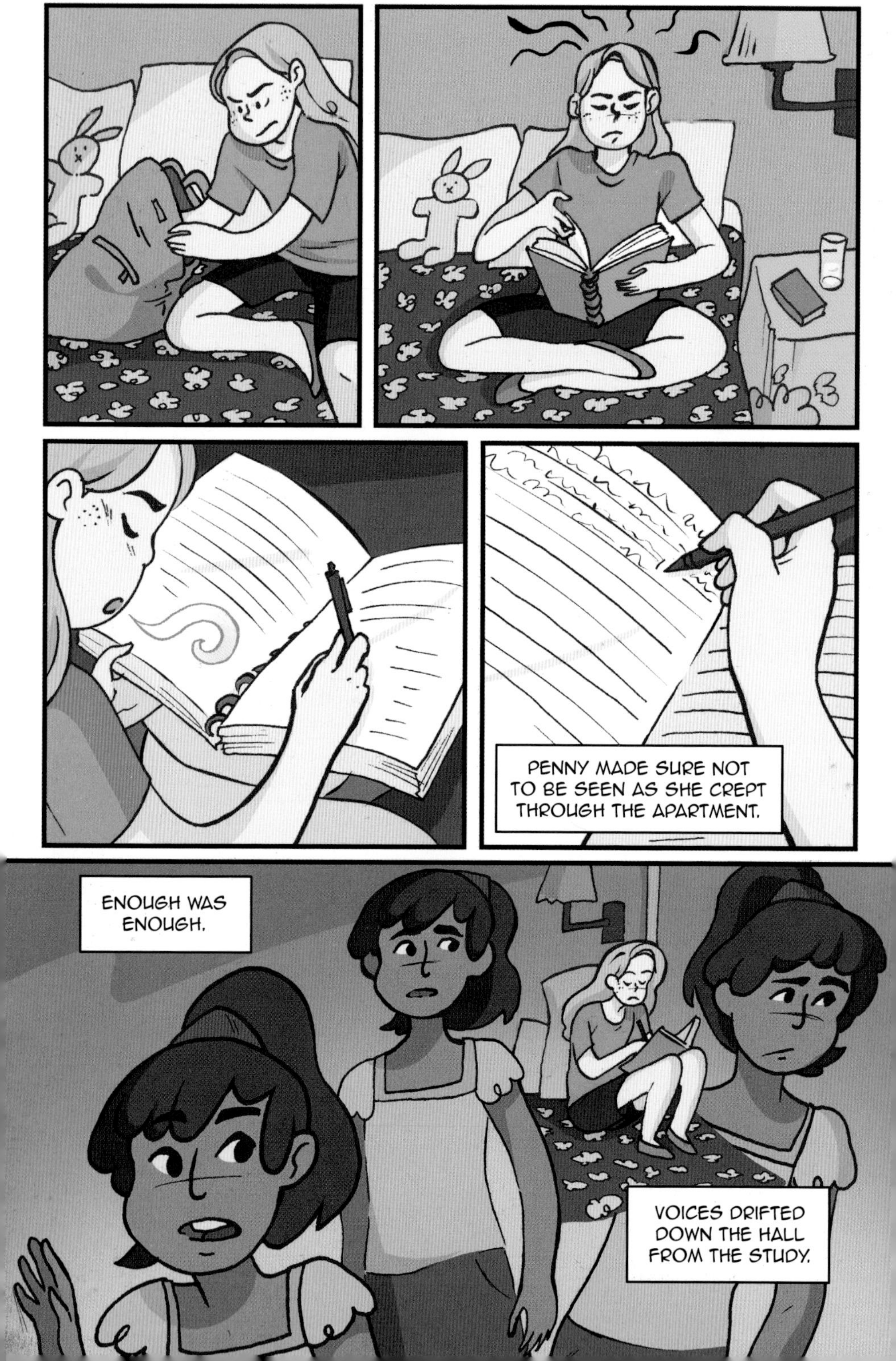
PENNY MADE SURE NOT TO BE SEEN AS SHE CREPT THROUGH THE APARTMENT.
ENOUGH WAS ENOUGH.
VOICES DRIFTED DOWN THE HALL FROM THE STUDY.

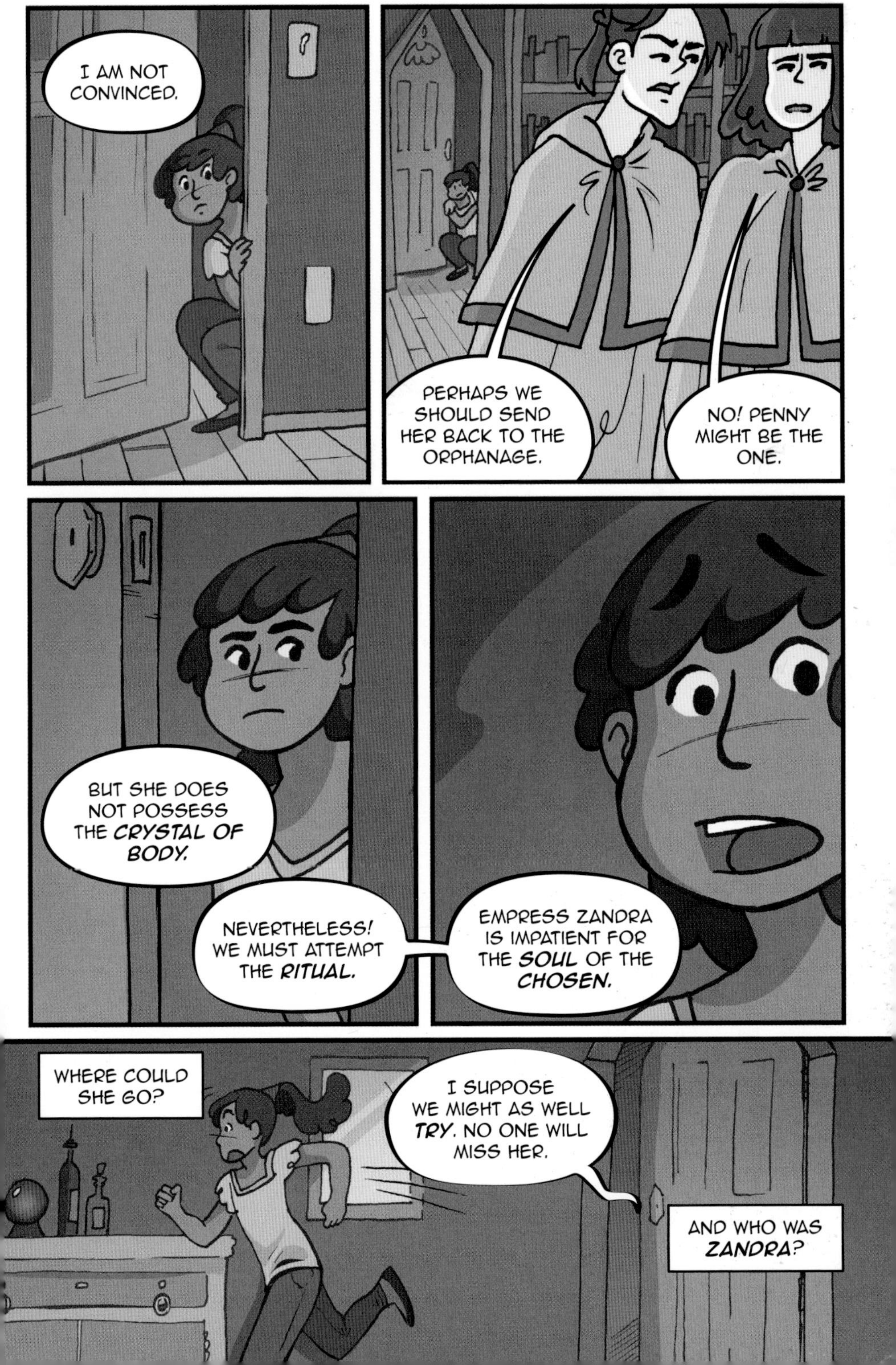
I AM NOT CONVINCED.
PERHAPS WE SHOULD SEND HER BACK TO THE ORPHANAGE.
NO! PENNY MIGHT BE THE ONE.
BUT SHE DOES NOT POSSESS THE *CRYSTAL OF BODY.*
NEVERTHELESS! WE MUST ATTEMPT THE *RITUAL.*
EMPRESS ZANDRA IS IMPATIENT FOR THE *SOUL* OF THE *CHOSEN.*
WHERE COULD SHE GO?
I SUPPOSE WE MIGHT AS WELL *TRY*. NO ONE WILL MISS HER.
AND WHO WAS *ZANDRA*?

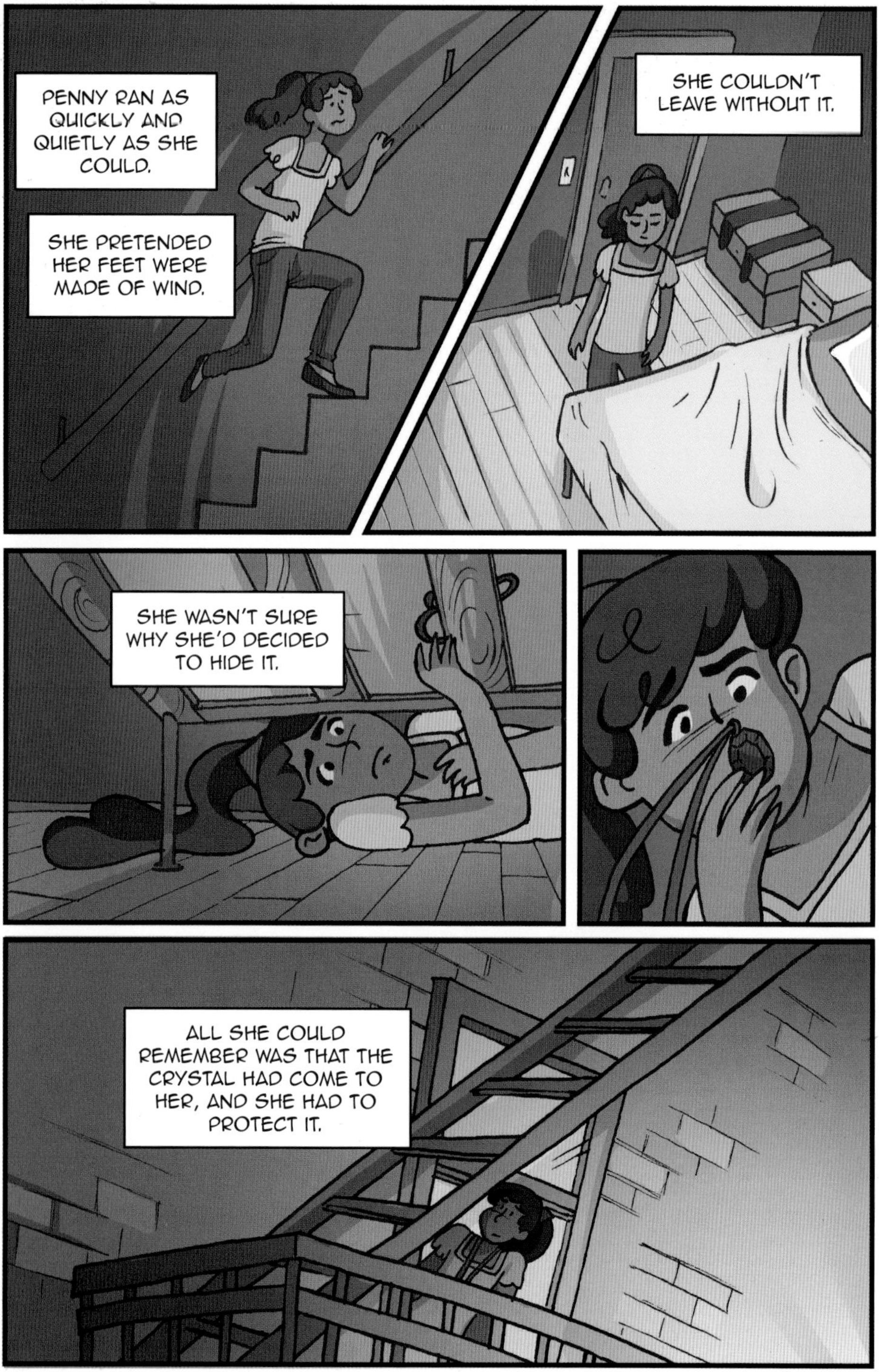
PENNY RAN AS QUICKLY AND QUIETLY AS SHE COULD.
SHE PRETENDED HER FEET WERE MADE OF WIND.
SHE COULDN'T LEAVE WITHOUT IT.
SHE WASN'T SURE WHY SHE'D DECIDED TO HIDE IT.
ALL SHE COULD REMEMBER WAS THAT THE CRYSTAL HAD COME TO HER, AND SHE HAD TO PROTECT IT.

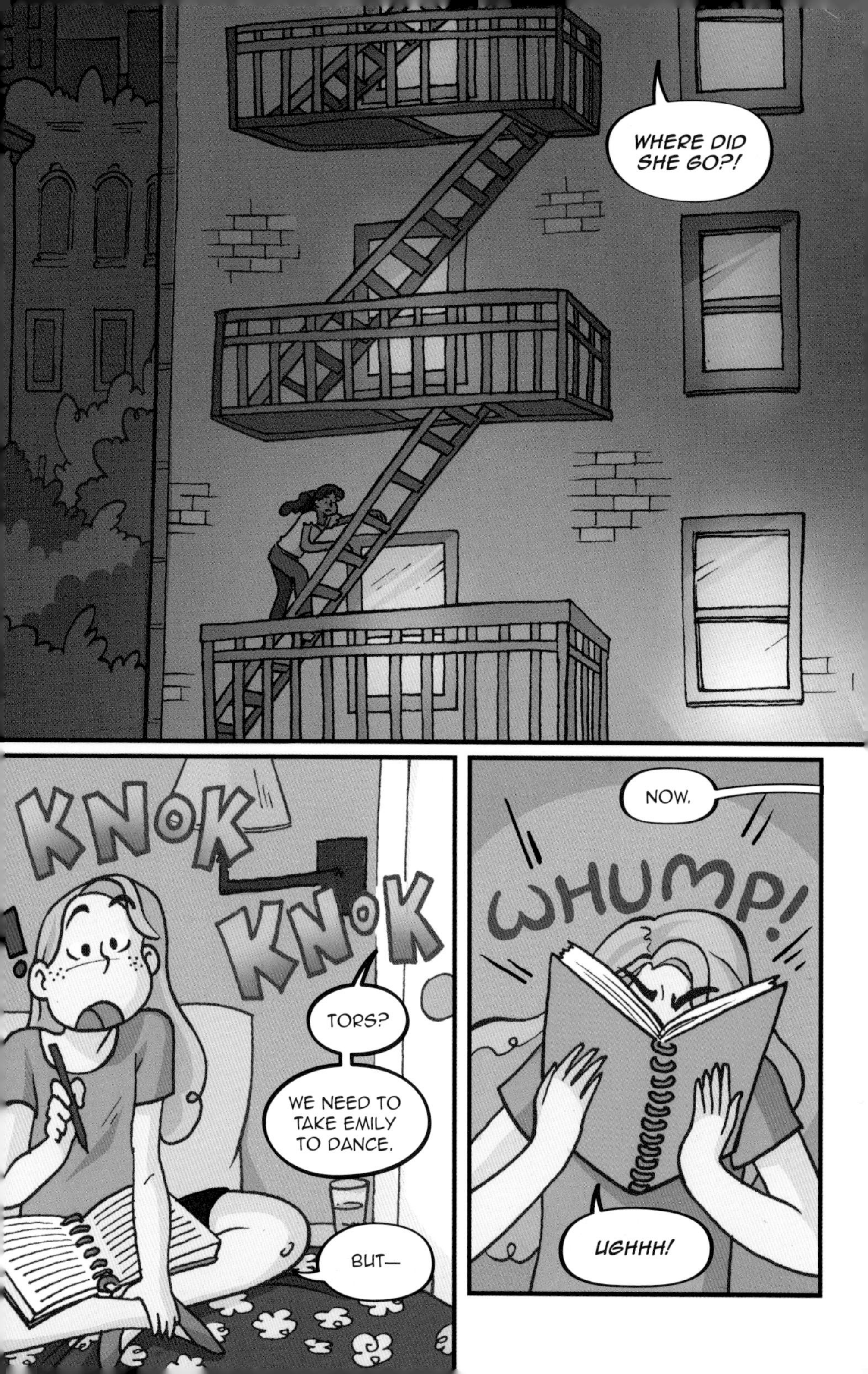

WHERE DID SHE GO?!
KNOK KNOK
TORS?
WE NEED TO TAKE EMILY TO DANCE.
BUT—
NOW.
WHUMP!
UGHHH!

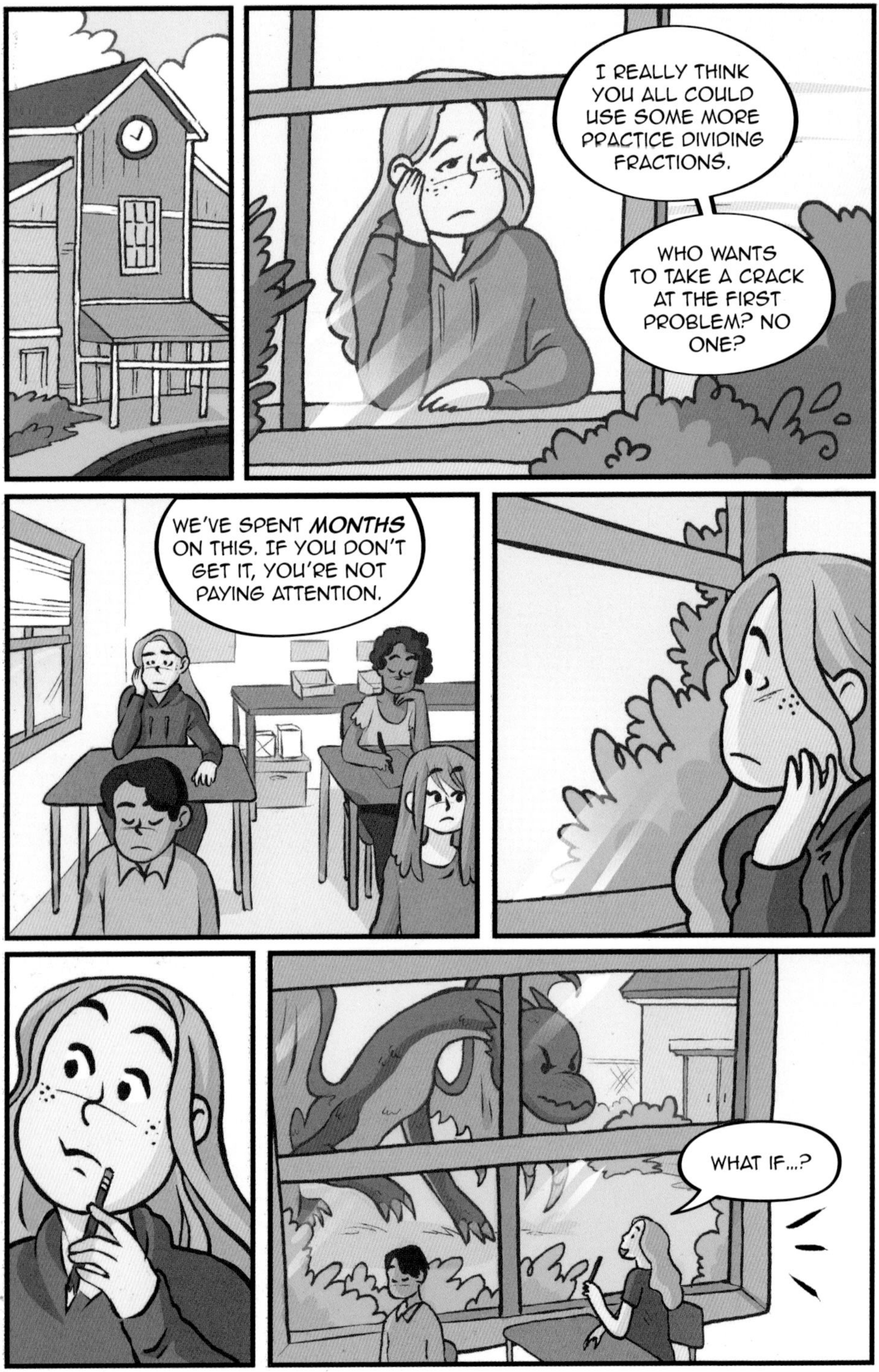

I REALLY THINK YOU ALL COULD USE SOME MORE PRACTICE DIVIDING FRACTIONS.
WHO WANTS TO TAKE A CRACK AT THE FIRST PROBLEM? NO ONE?
WE'VE SPENT MONTHS ON THIS. IF YOU DON'T GET IT, YOU'RE NOT PAYING ATTENTION.
WHAT IF...?

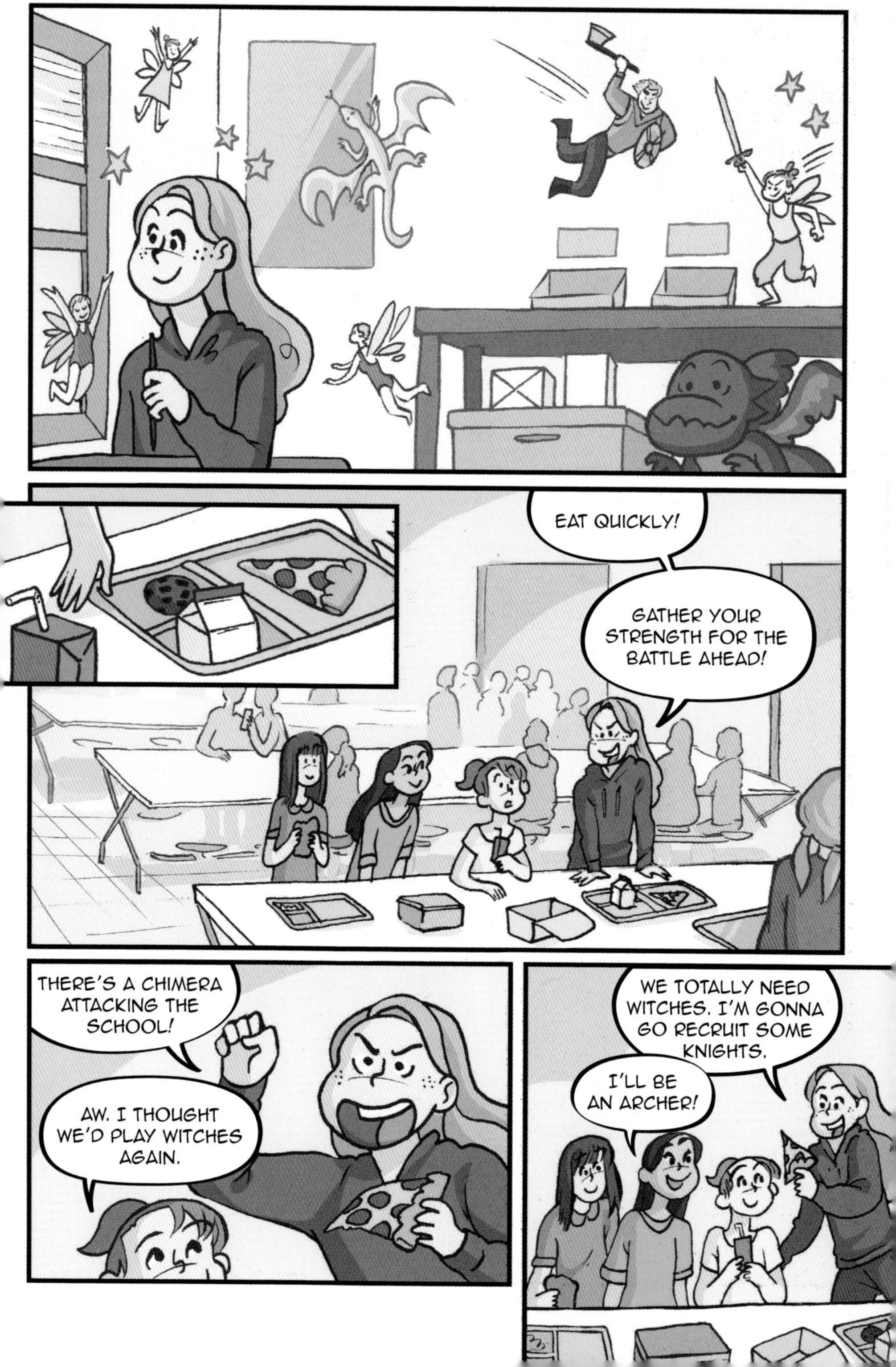
EAT QUICKLY!
GATHER YOUR STRENGTH FOR THE BATTLE AHEAD!
THERE'S A CHIMERA ATTACKING THE SCHOOL!
AW. I THOUGHT WE'D PLAY WITCHES AGAIN.
WE TOTALLY NEED WITCHES. I'M GONNA GO RECRUIT SOME KNIGHTS.
I'LL BE AN ARCHER!

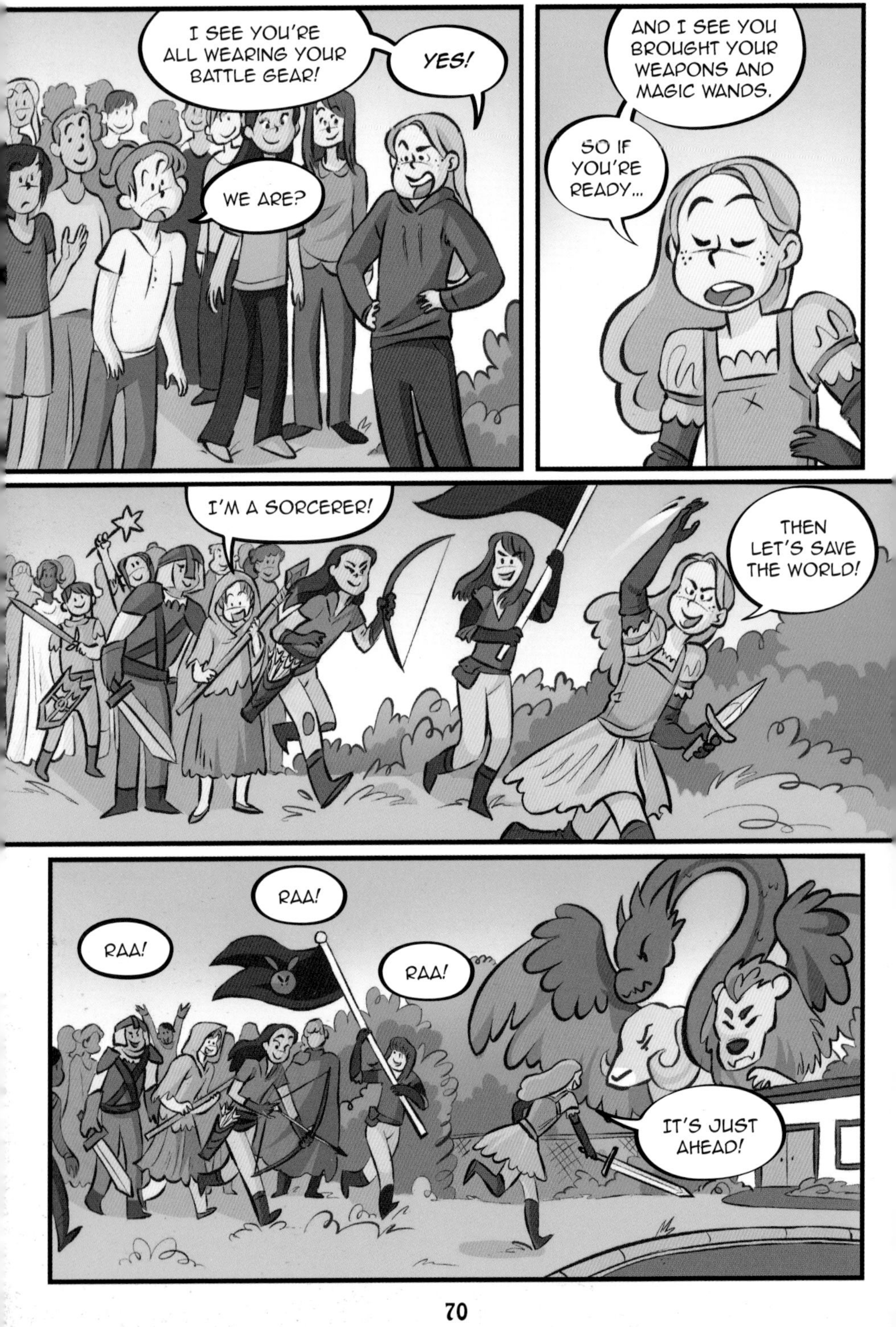
I SEE YOU'RE ALL WEARING YOUR BATTLE GEAR!
YES!
WE ARE?
AND I SEE YOU BROUGHT YOUR WEAPONS AND MAGIC WANDS.
SO IF YOU'RE READY...
I'M A SORCERER!
THEN LET'S SAVE THE WORLD!
RAA!
RAA!
RAA!
IT'S JUST AHEAD!

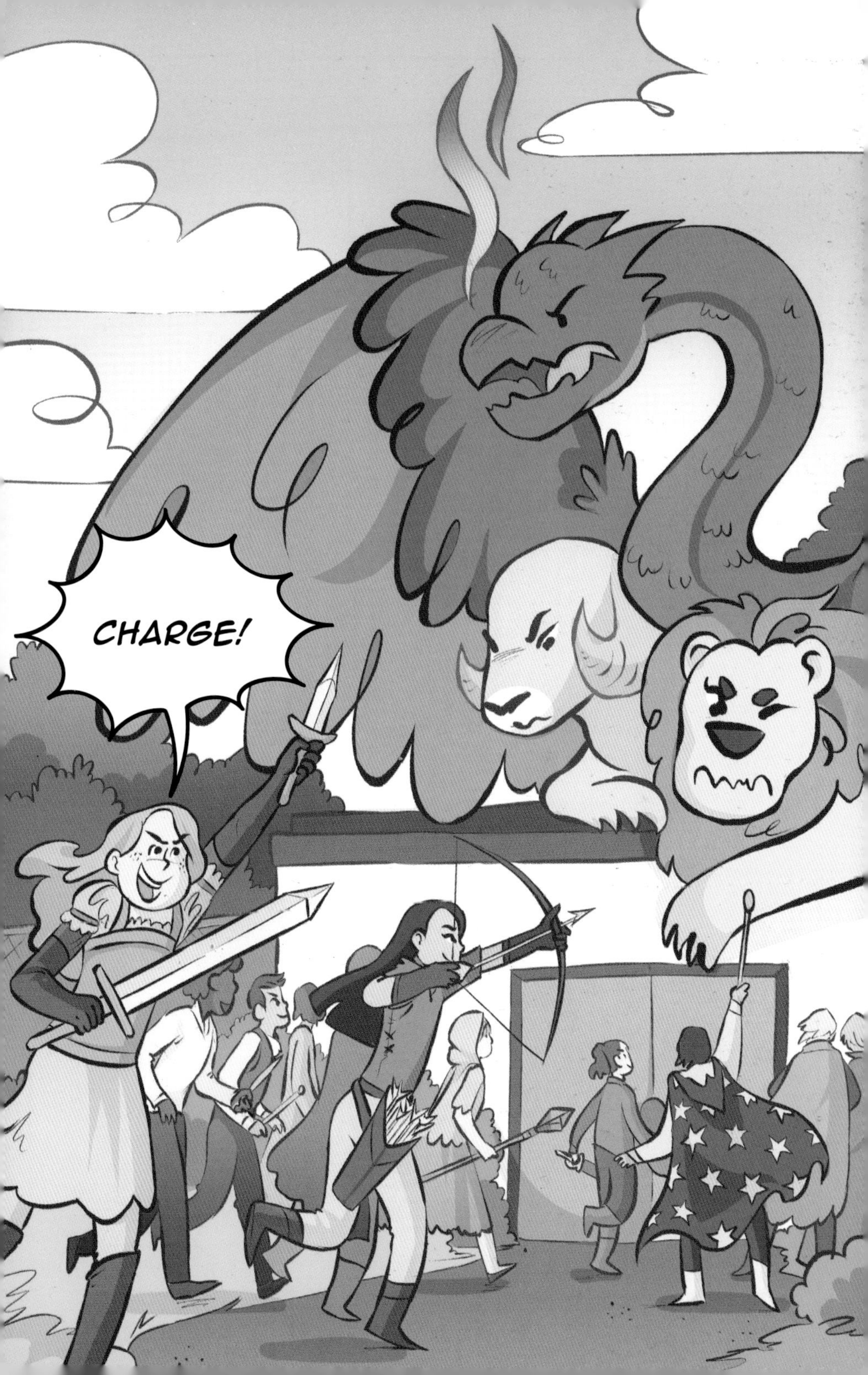
CHARGE!

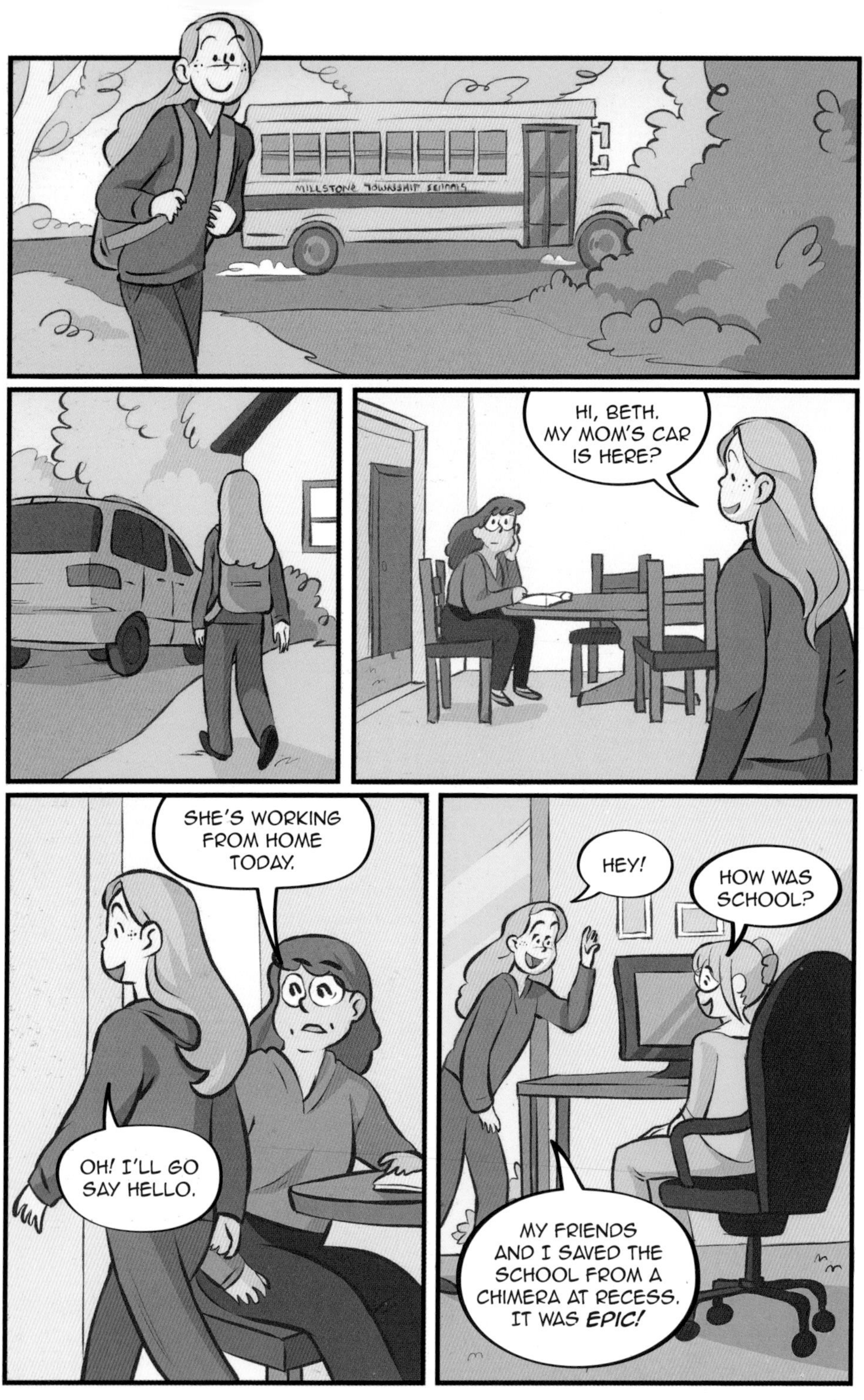
MILLSTONE TOWNSHIP SCHOOLS
HI, BETH. MY MOM'S CAR IS HERE?
SHE'S WORKING FROM HOME TODAY.
OH! I'LL GO SAY HELLO.
HEY!
HOW WAS SCHOOL?
MY FRIENDS AND I SAVED THE SCHOOL FROM A CHIMERA AT RECESS. IT WAS *EPIC!*

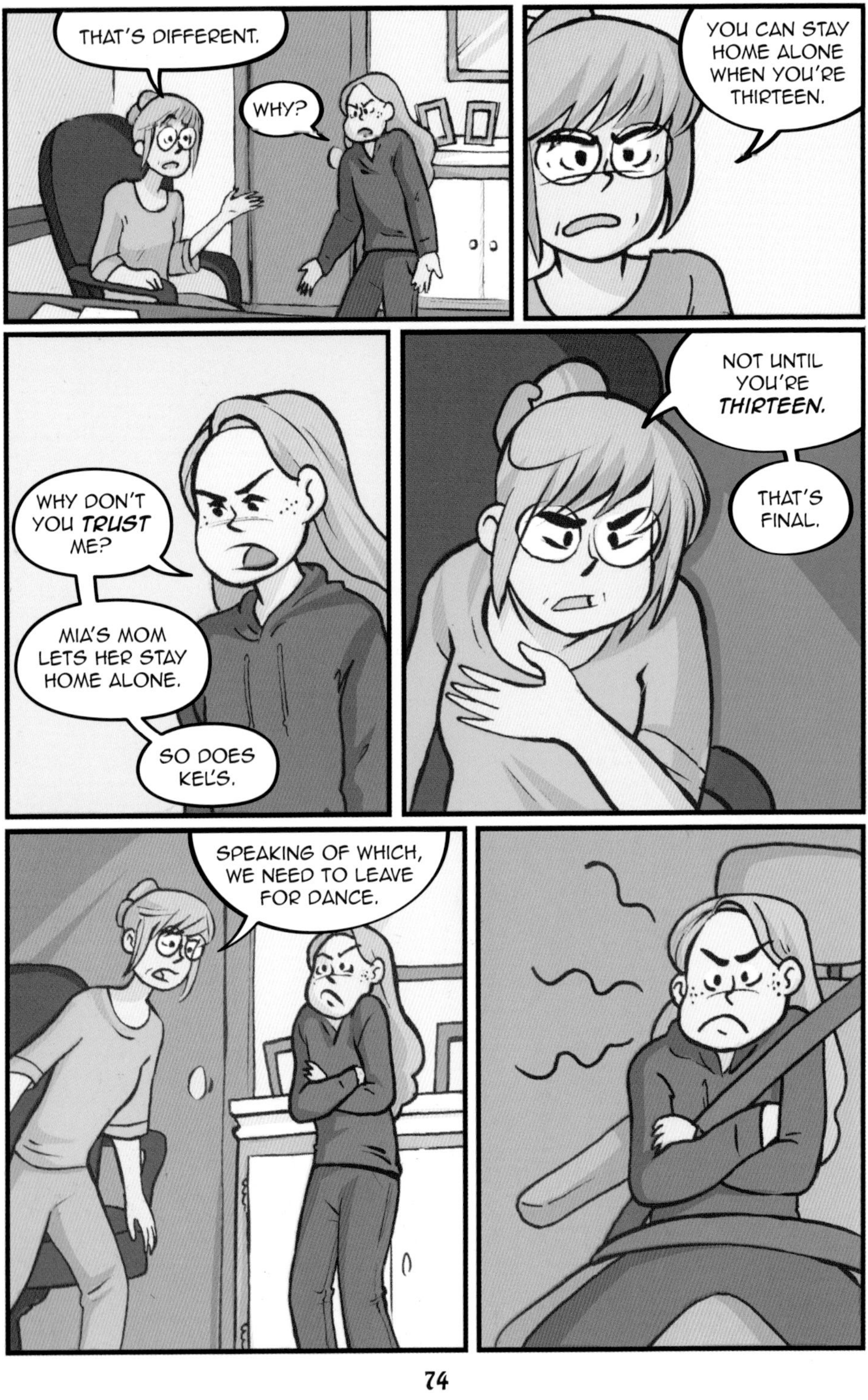
THAT'S DIFFERENT.
WHY?
YOU CAN STAY HOME ALONE WHEN YOU'RE THIRTEEN.
WHY DON'T YOU *TRUST* ME?
MIA'S MOM LETS HER STAY HOME ALONE.
SO DOES KEL'S.
NOT UNTIL YOU'RE ***THIRTEEN.***
THAT'S FINAL.
SPEAKING OF WHICH, WE NEED TO LEAVE FOR DANCE.

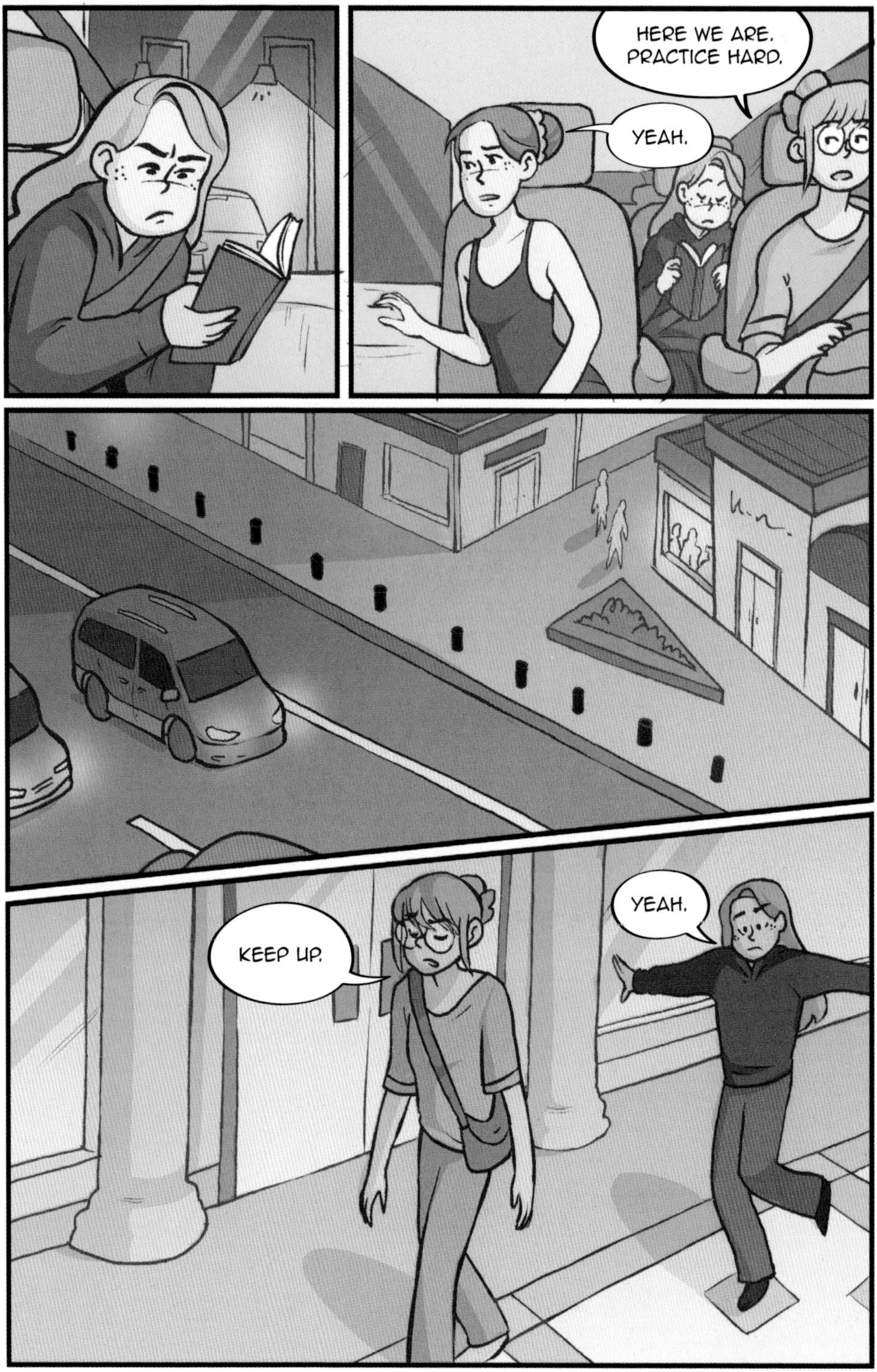
HERE WE ARE. PRACTICE HARD.
YEAH.
KEEP UP.
YEAH.

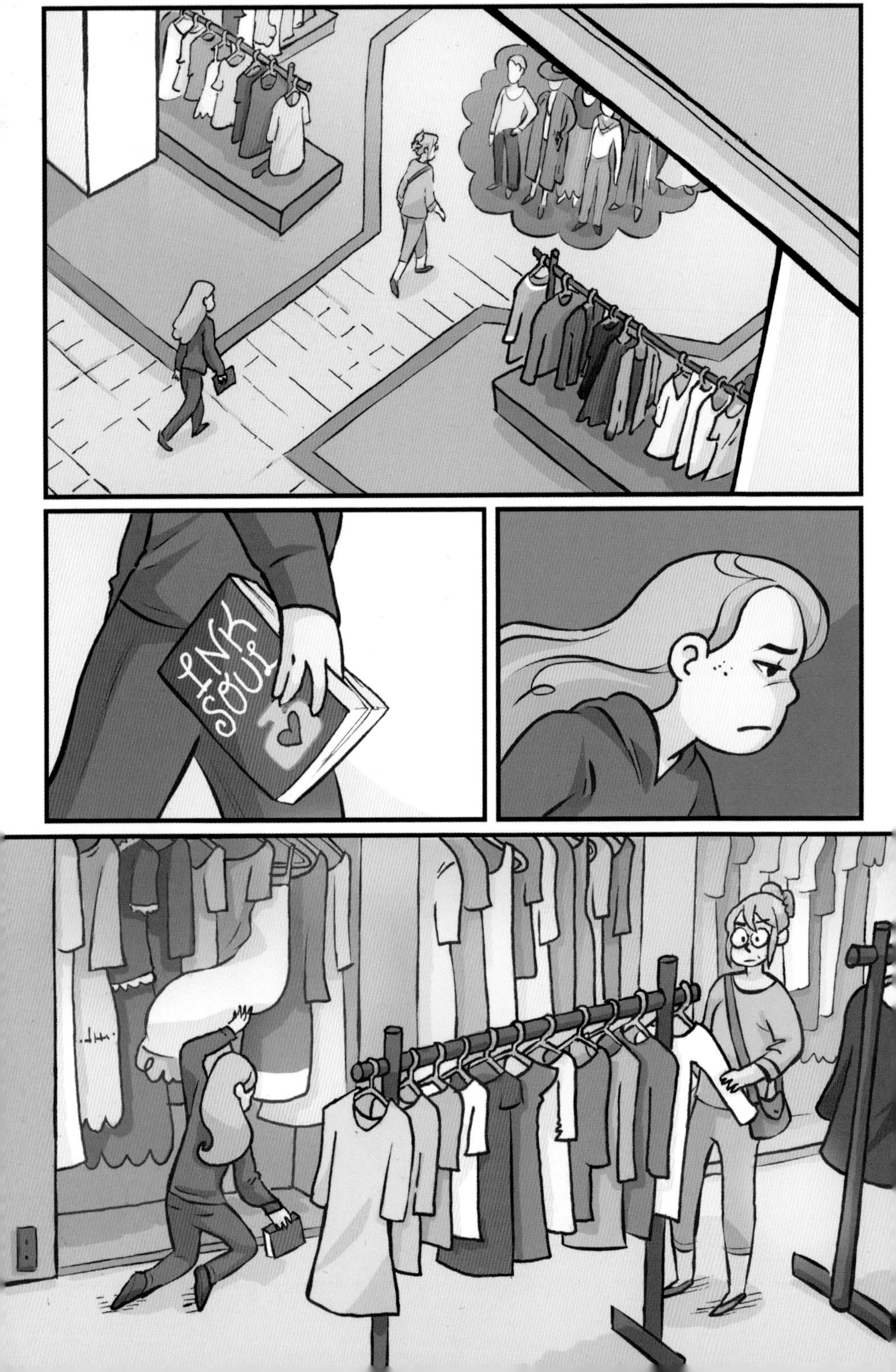
INK SOUL

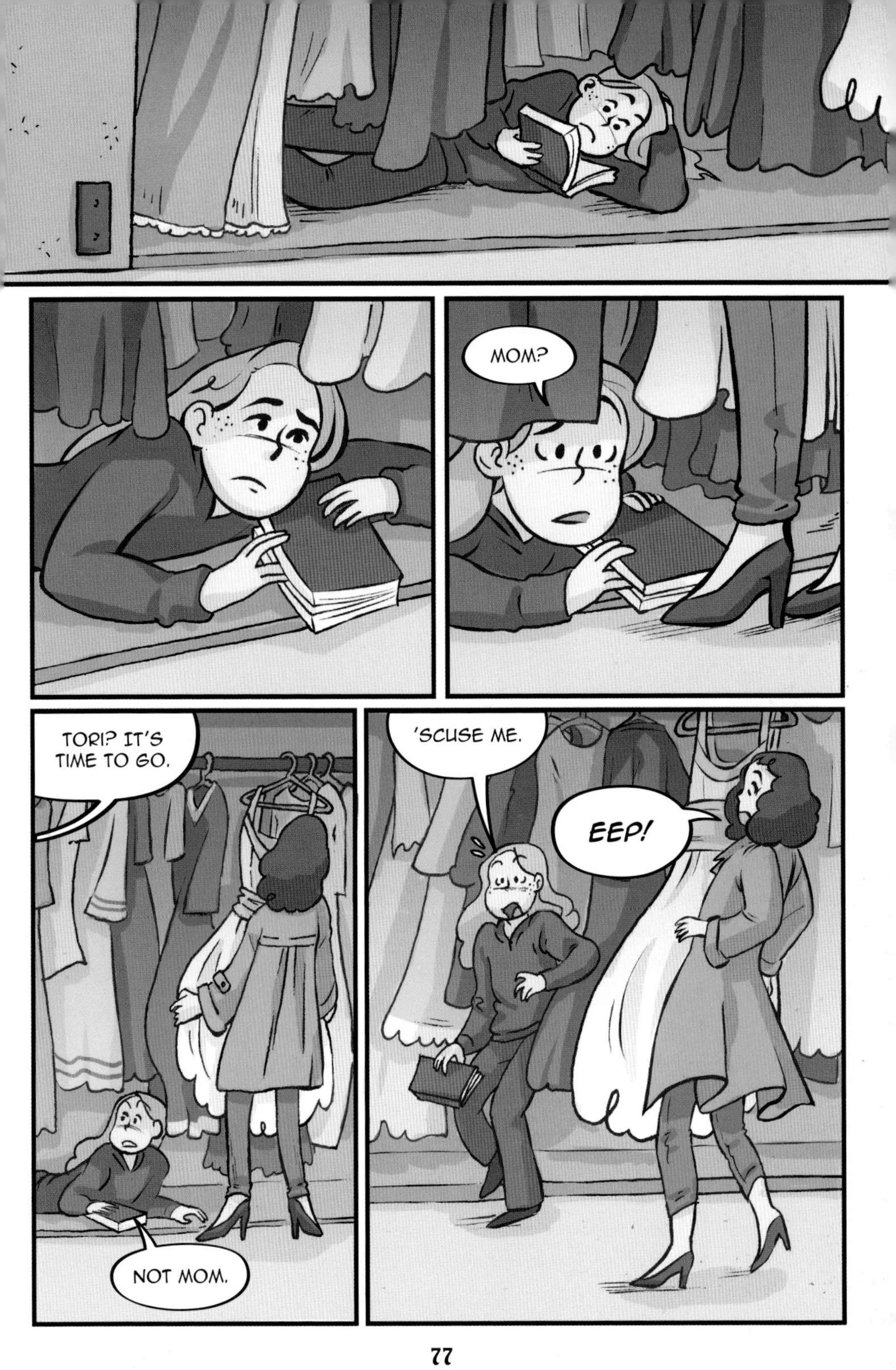
MOM?
TORI? IT'S TIME TO GO.
NOT MOM.
'SCUSE ME.
EEP!

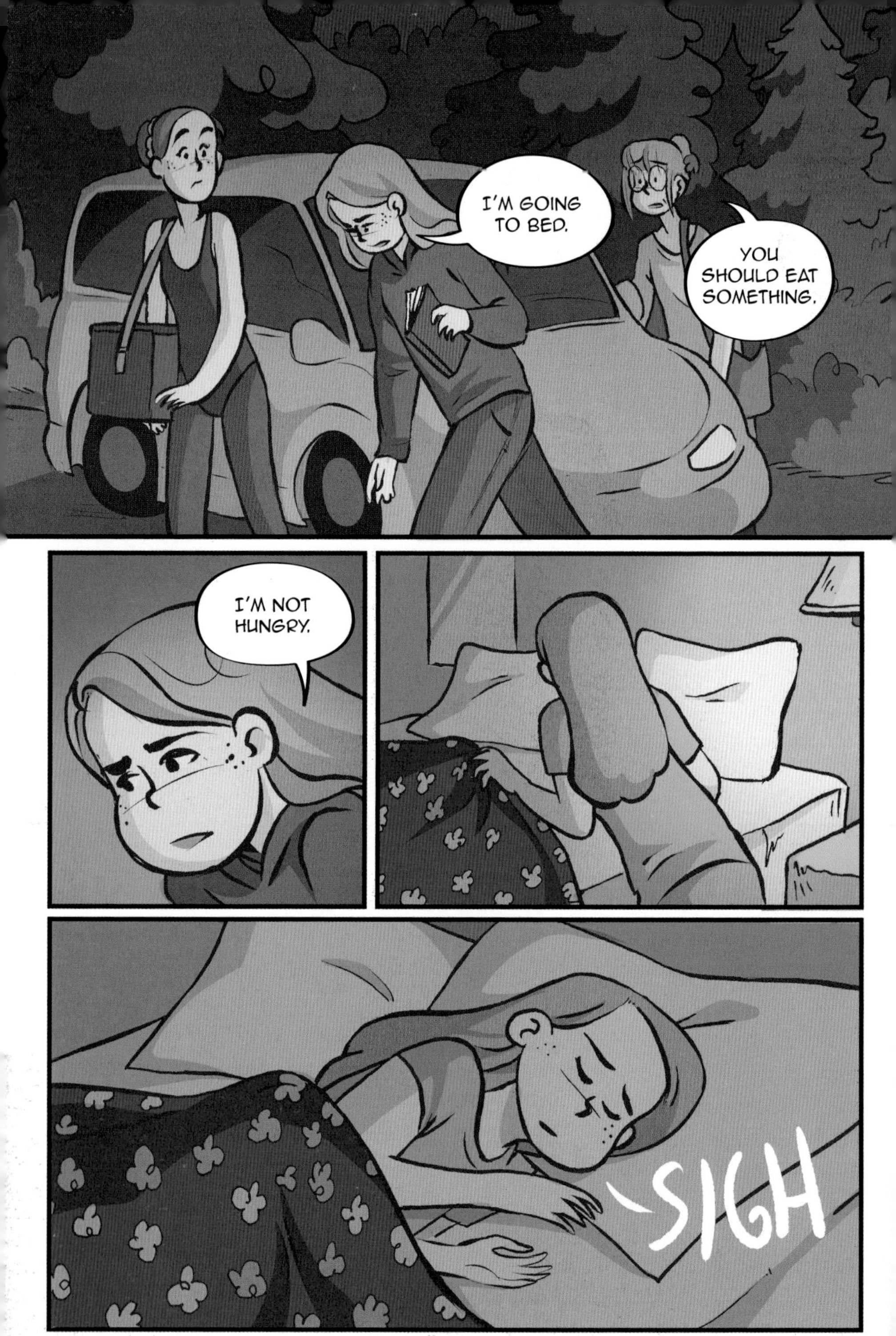
I'M GOING TO BED.
YOU SHOULD EAT SOMETHING.
I'M NOT HUNGRY.
SIGH

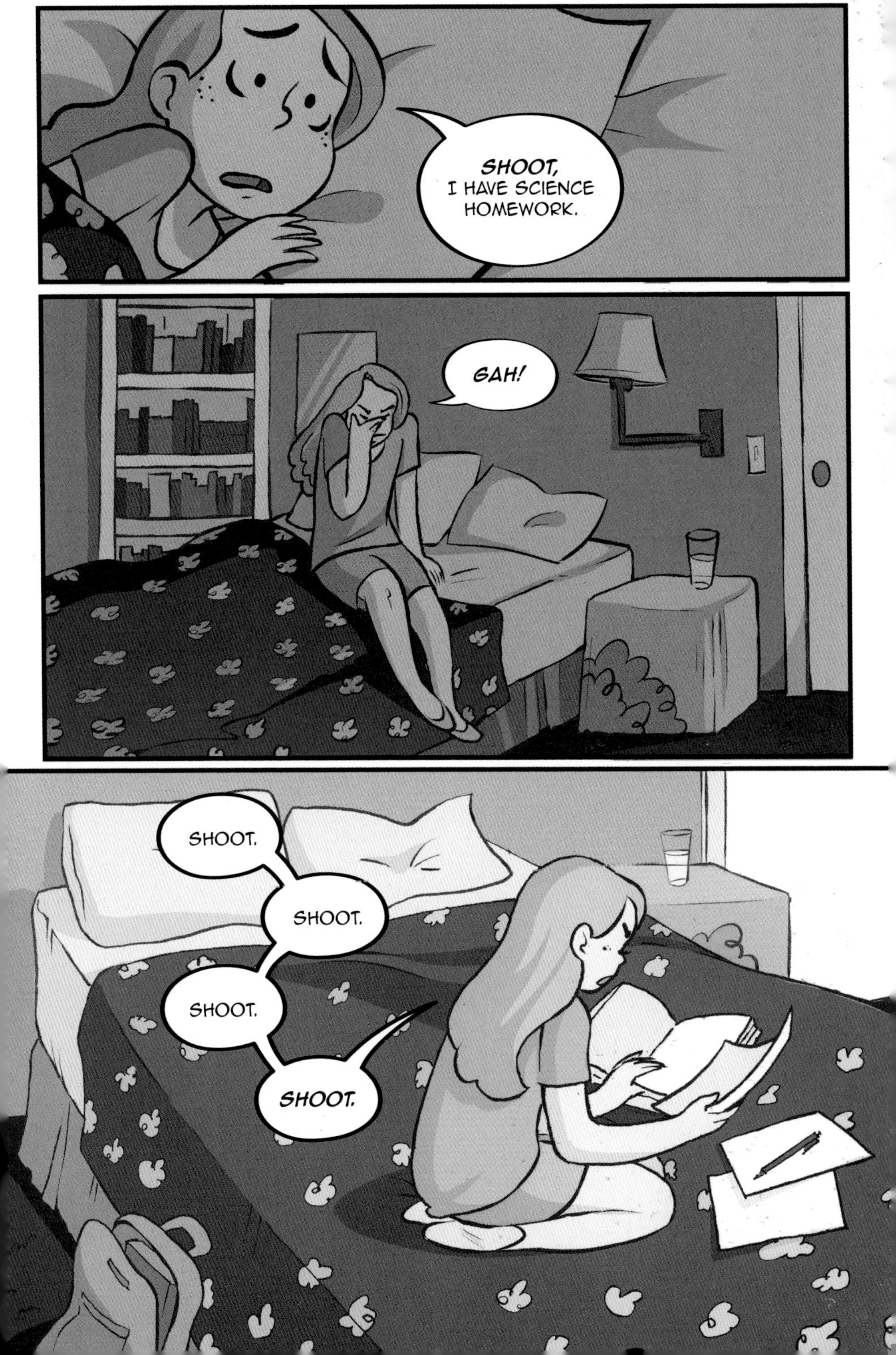
SHOOT, I HAVE SCIENCE HOMEWORK.
GAH!
SHOOT.
SHOOT.
SHOOT.
SHOOT.

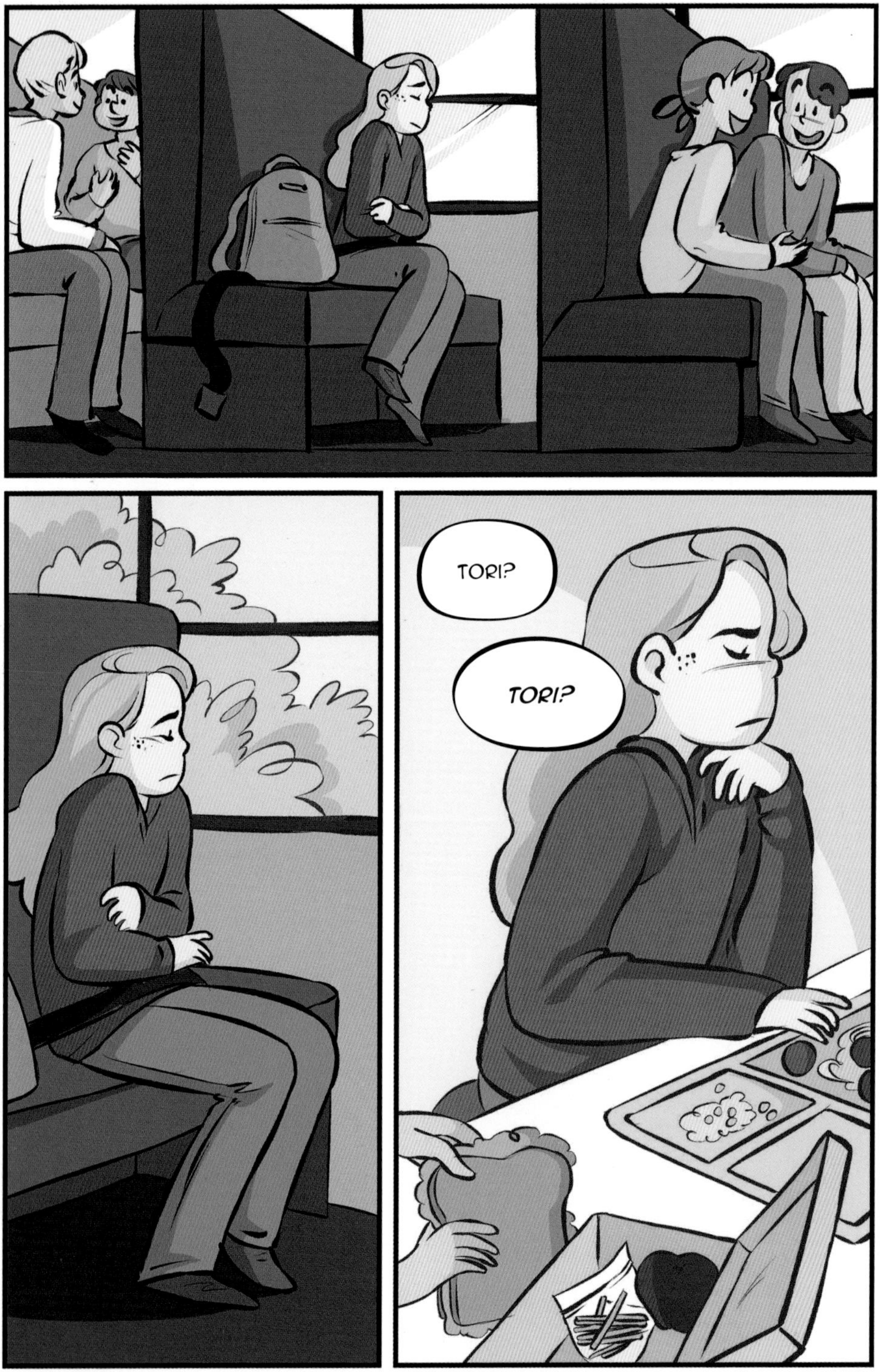
TORI?
TORI?

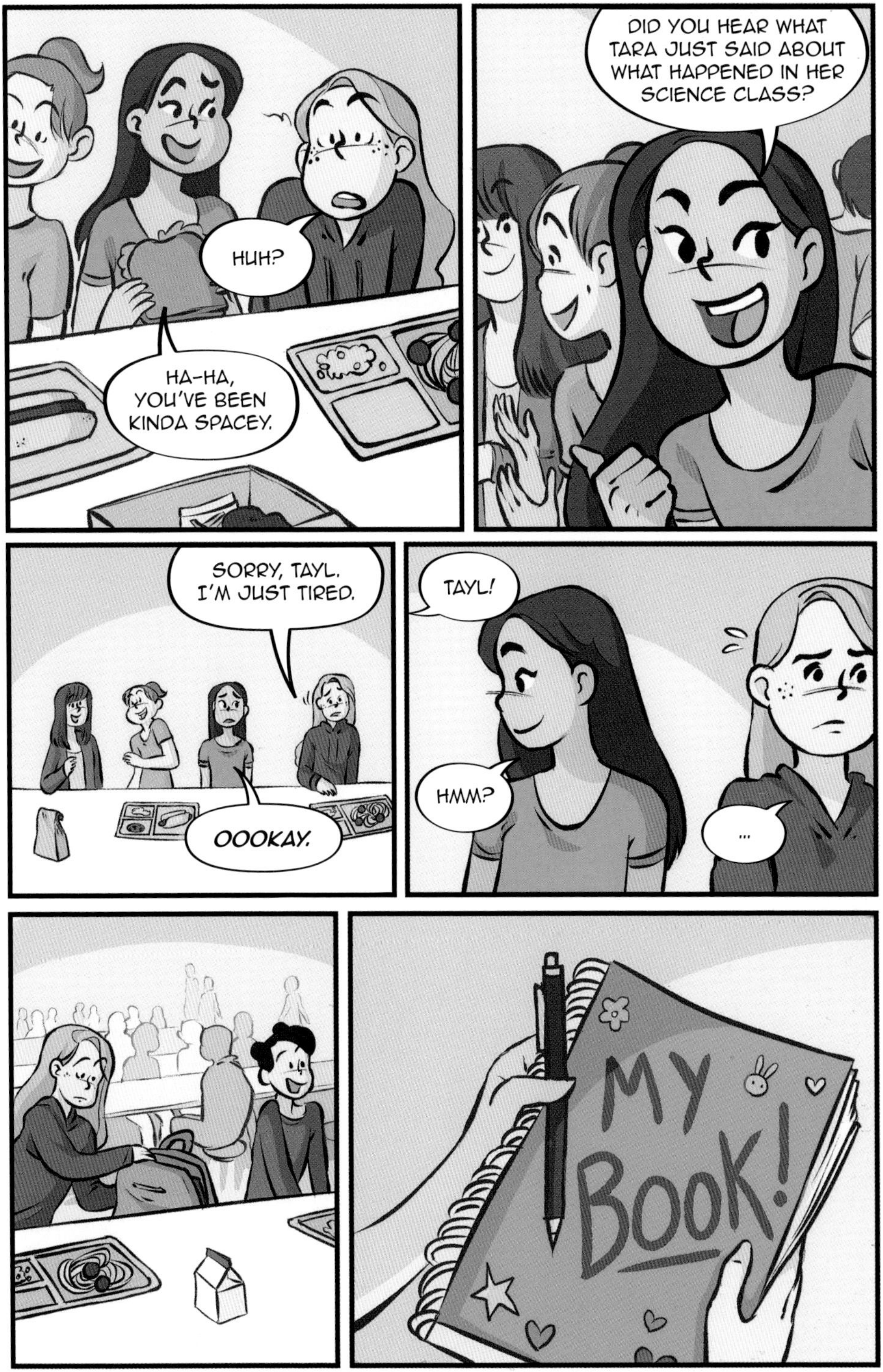
HUH?
HA-HA, YOU'VE BEEN KINDA SPACEY.
DID YOU HEAR WHAT TARA JUST SAID ABOUT WHAT HAPPENED IN HER SCIENCE CLASS?
SORRY, TAYL. I'M JUST TIRED.
OOOKAY.
TAYL!
HMM?
...
MY BOOK!

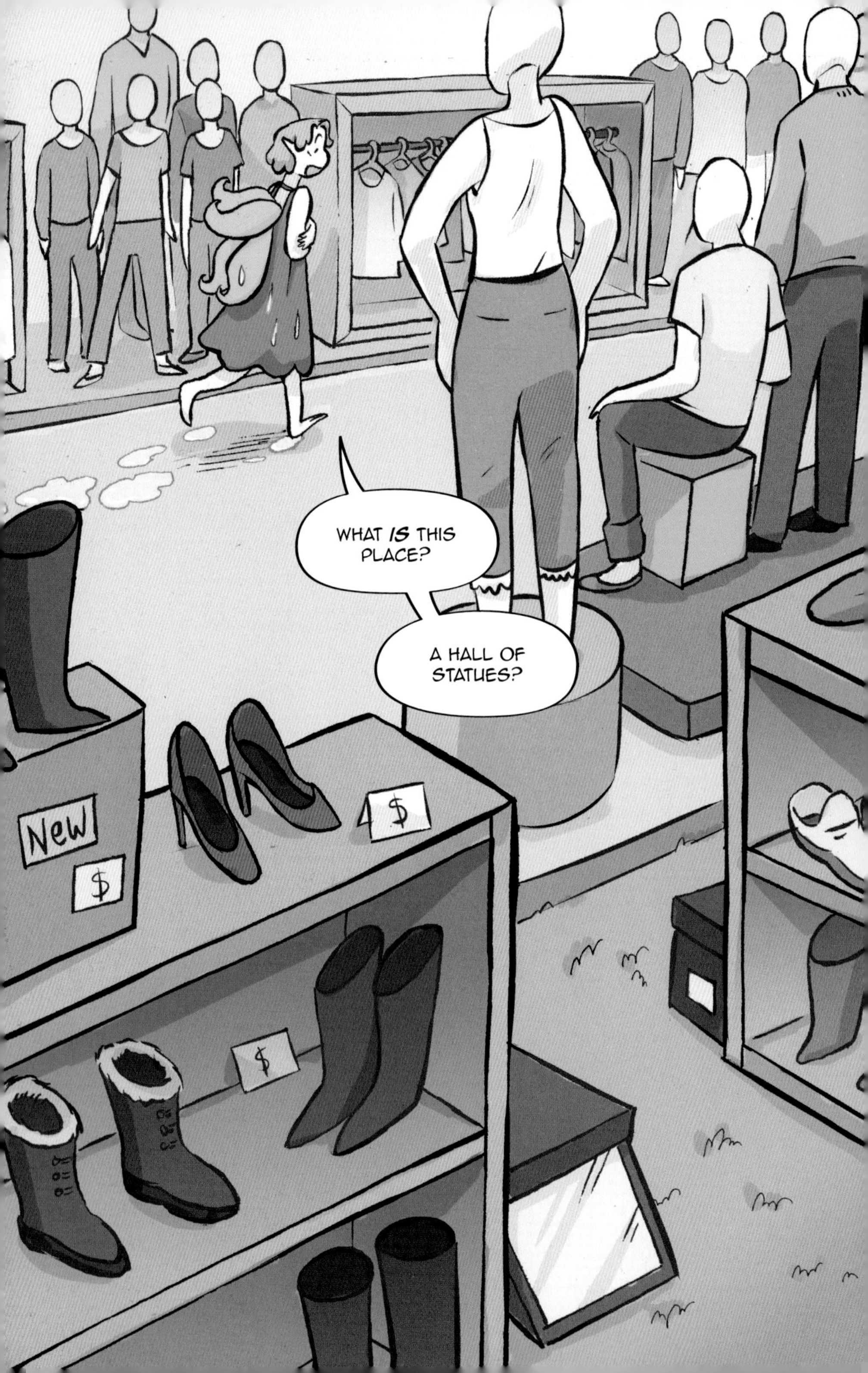
WHAT *IS* THIS PLACE?
A HALL OF STATUES?
New
$
$
$

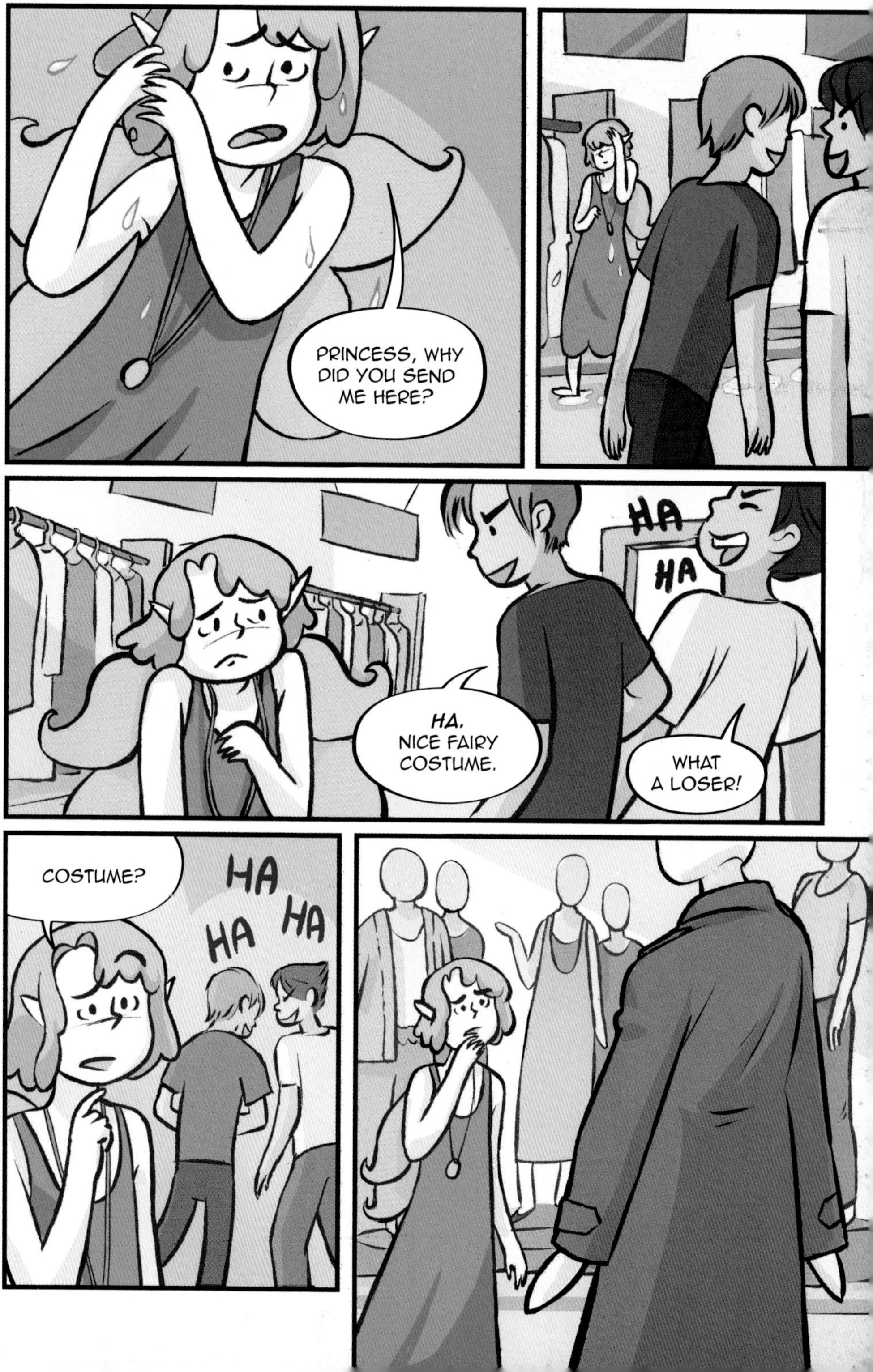
PRINCESS, WHY DID YOU SEND ME HERE?
HA HA
HA. NICE FAIRY COSTUME.
WHAT A LOSER!
COSTUME?
HA HA HA

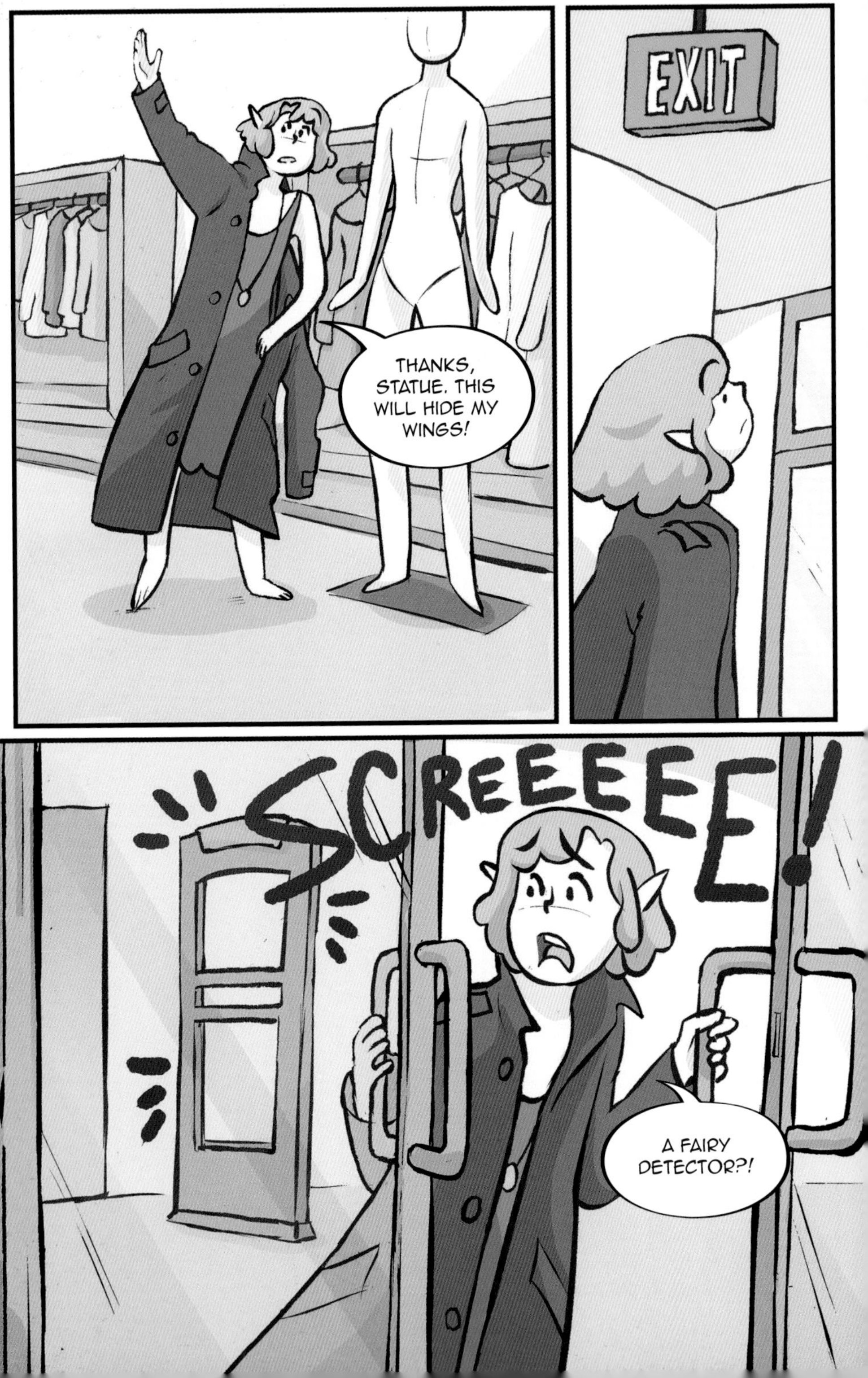
THANKS, STATUE. THIS WILL HIDE MY WINGS!
EXIT
SCREEEEE!
A FAIRY DETECTOR?!

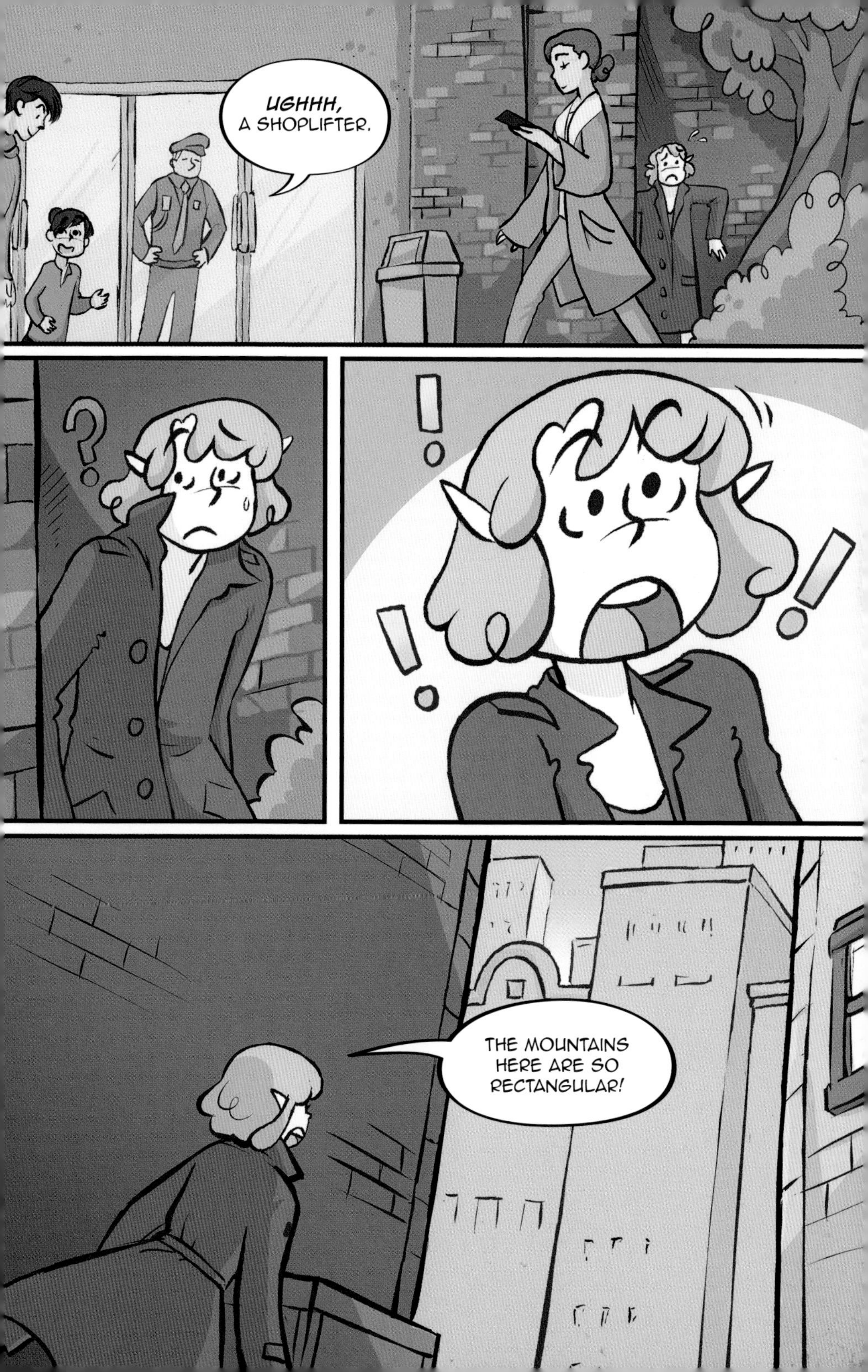
UGHHH, A SHOPLIFTER.
THE MOUNTAINS HERE ARE SO RECTANGULAR!

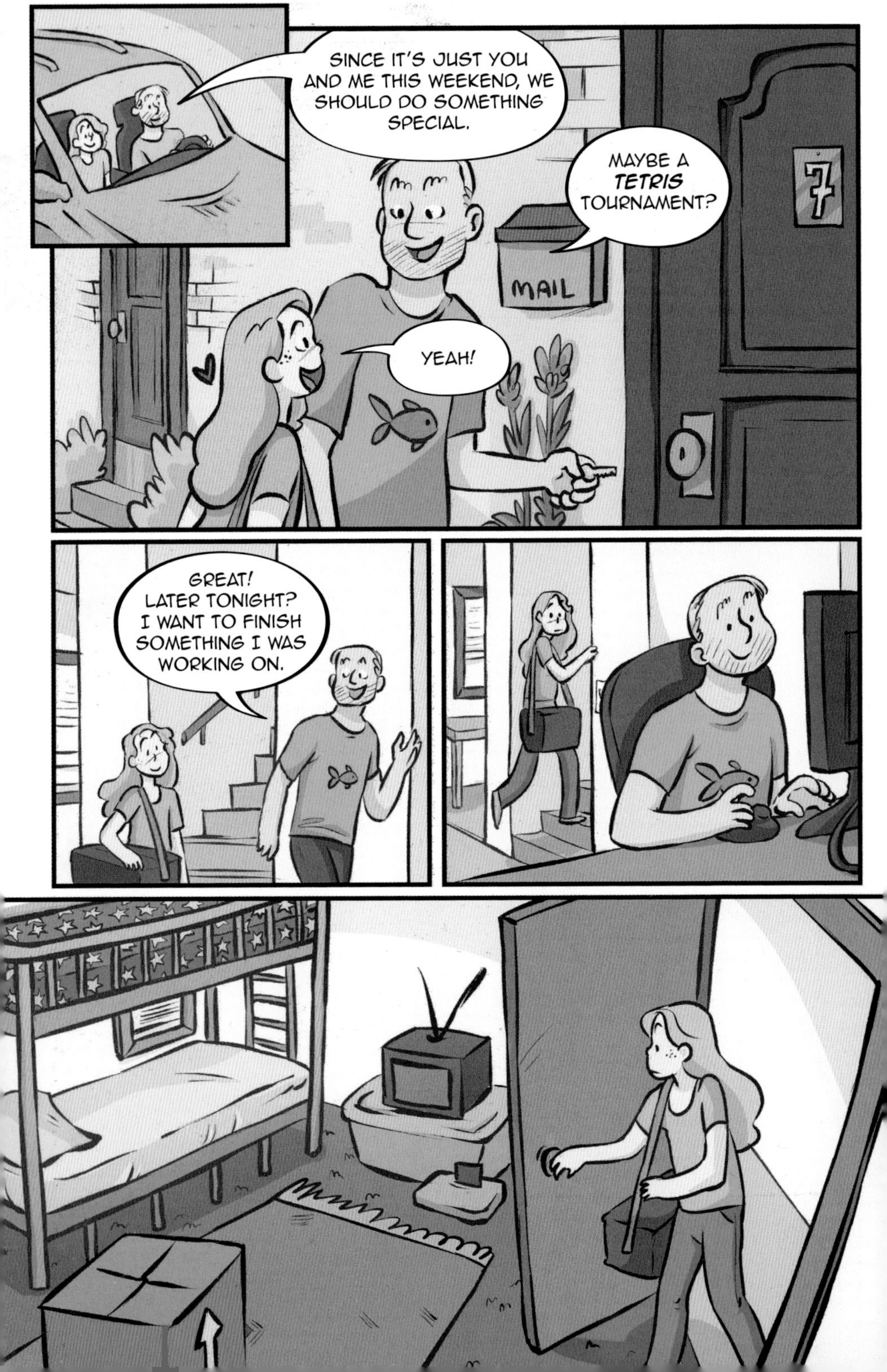
SINCE IT'S JUST YOU AND ME THIS WEEKEND, WE SHOULD DO SOMETHING SPECIAL.
MAYBE A TETRIS TOURNAMENT?
MAIL
7
YEAH!
GREAT! LATER TONIGHT? I WANT TO FINISH SOMETHING I WAS WORKING ON.

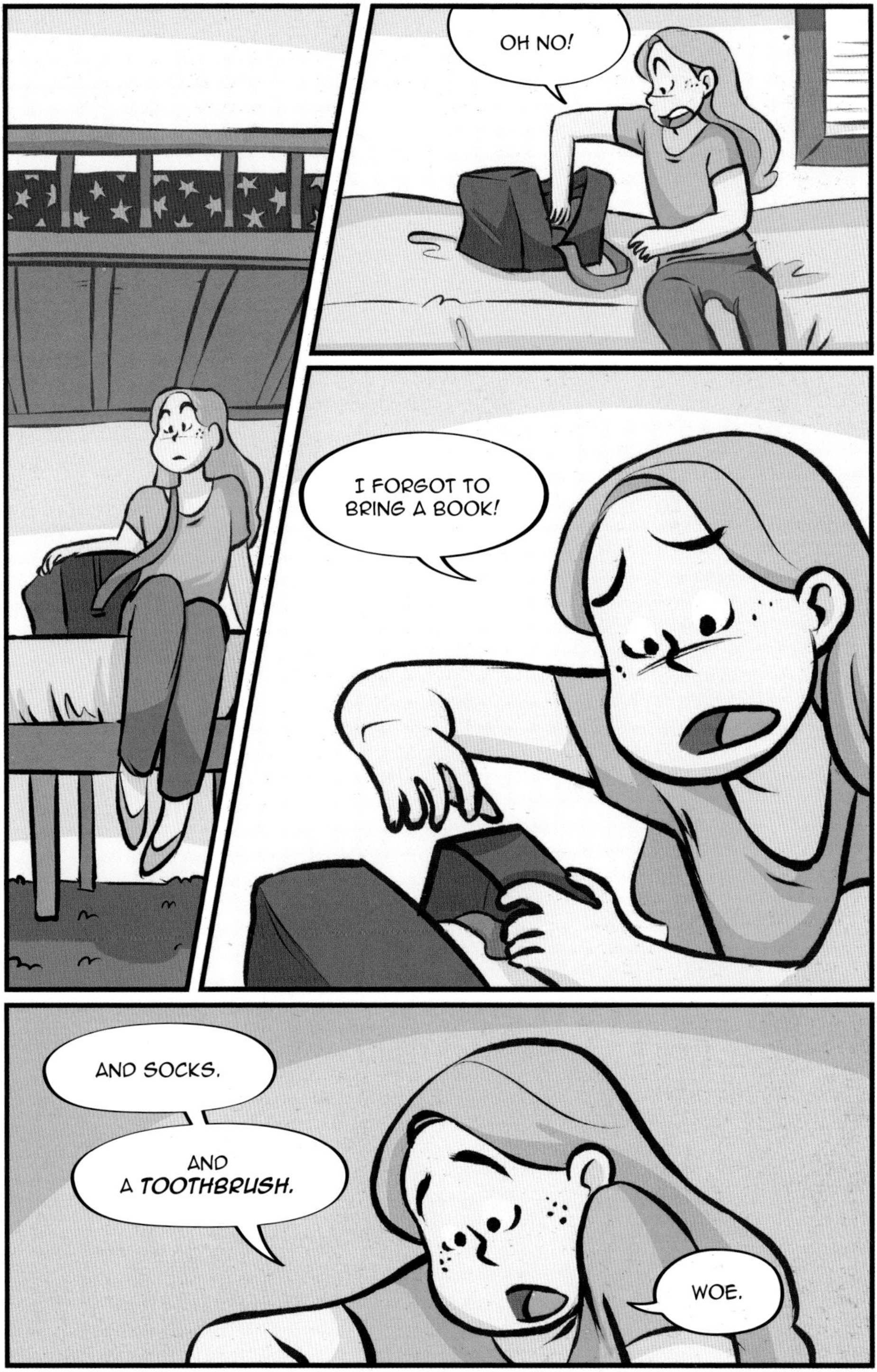
OH NO!
I FORGOT TO BRING A BOOK!
AND SOCKS.
AND A *TOOTHBRUSH.*
WOE.

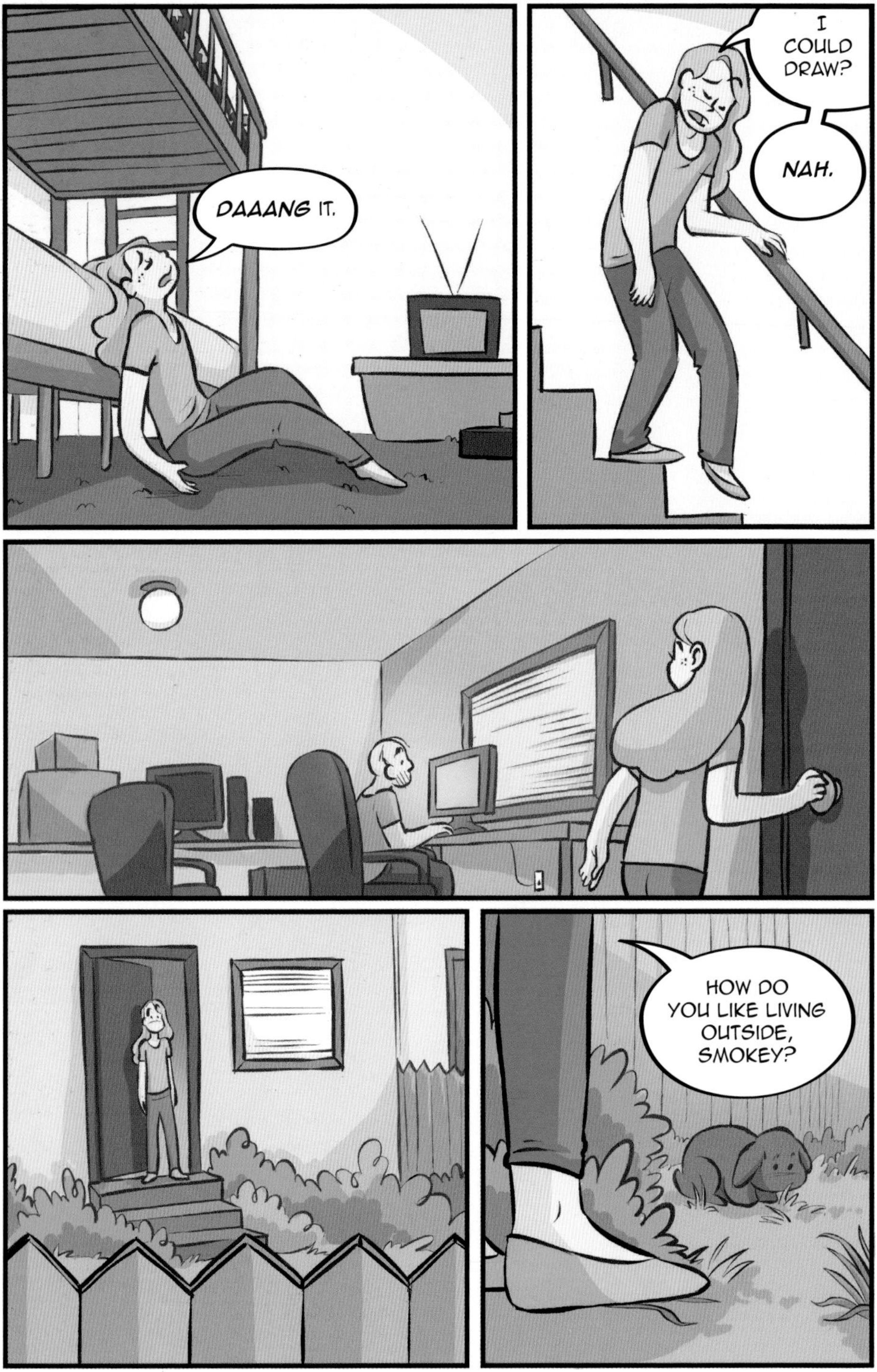
DAAANG IT.
I COULD DRAW?
NAH.
HOW DO YOU LIKE LIVING OUTSIDE, SMOKEY?

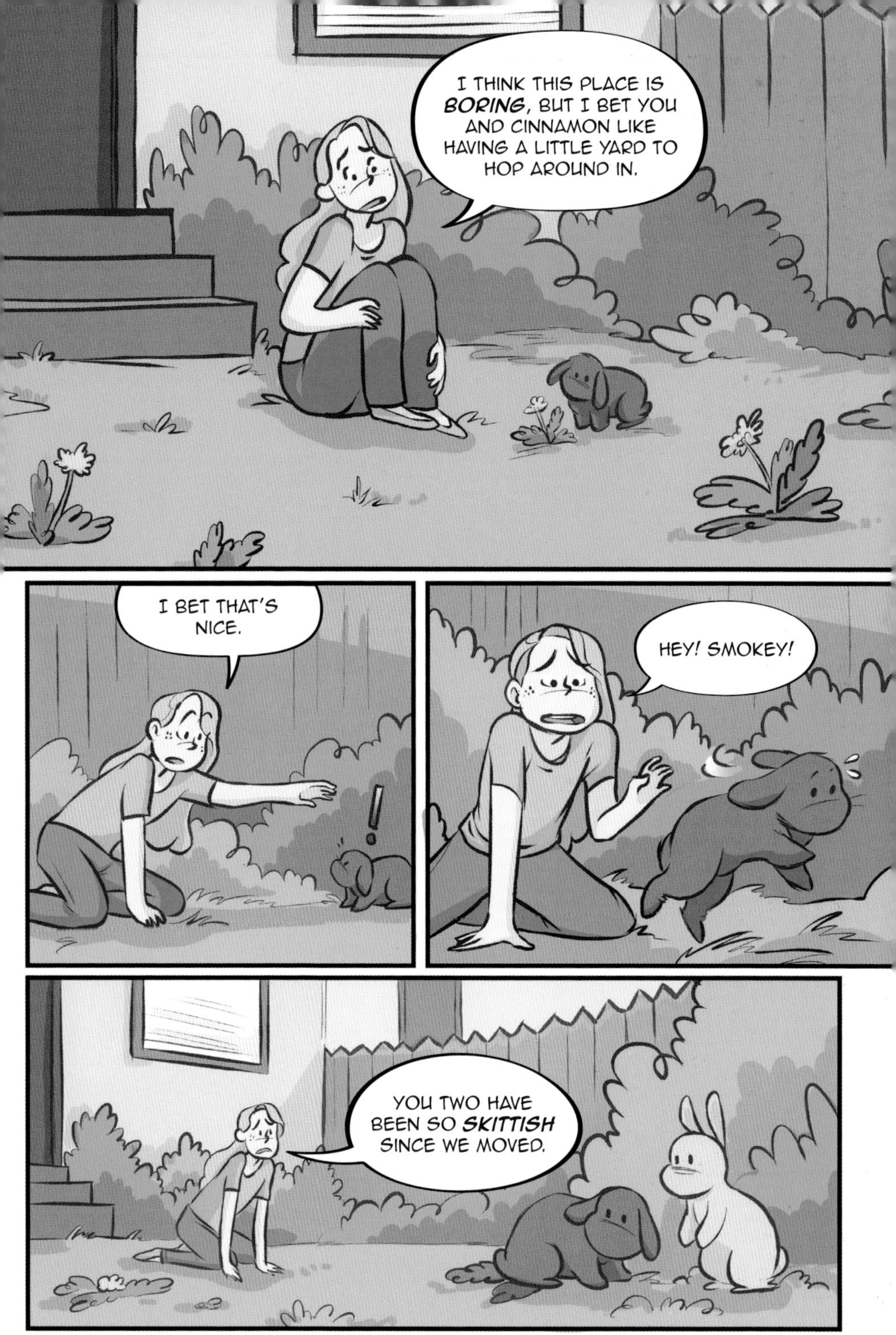
I THINK THIS PLACE IS *BORING*, BUT I BET YOU AND CINNAMON LIKE HAVING A LITTLE YARD TO HOP AROUND IN.
I BET THAT'S NICE.
!
HEY! SMOKEY!
YOU TWO HAVE BEEN SO *SKITTISH* SINCE WE MOVED.

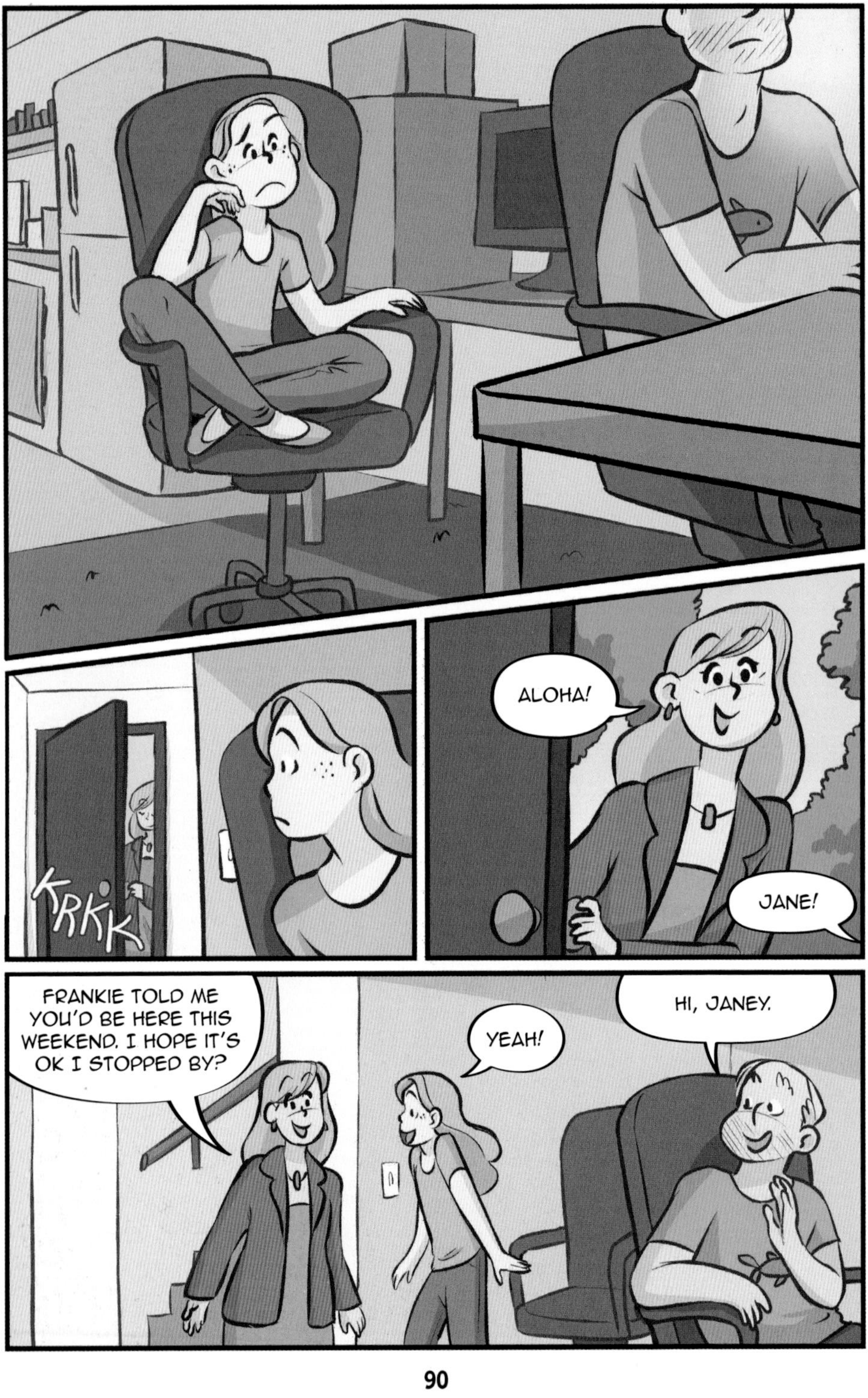
KRKK
ALOHA!
JANE!
FRANKIE TOLD ME YOU'D BE HERE THIS WEEKEND. I HOPE IT'S OK I STOPPED BY?
YEAH!
HI, JANEY.

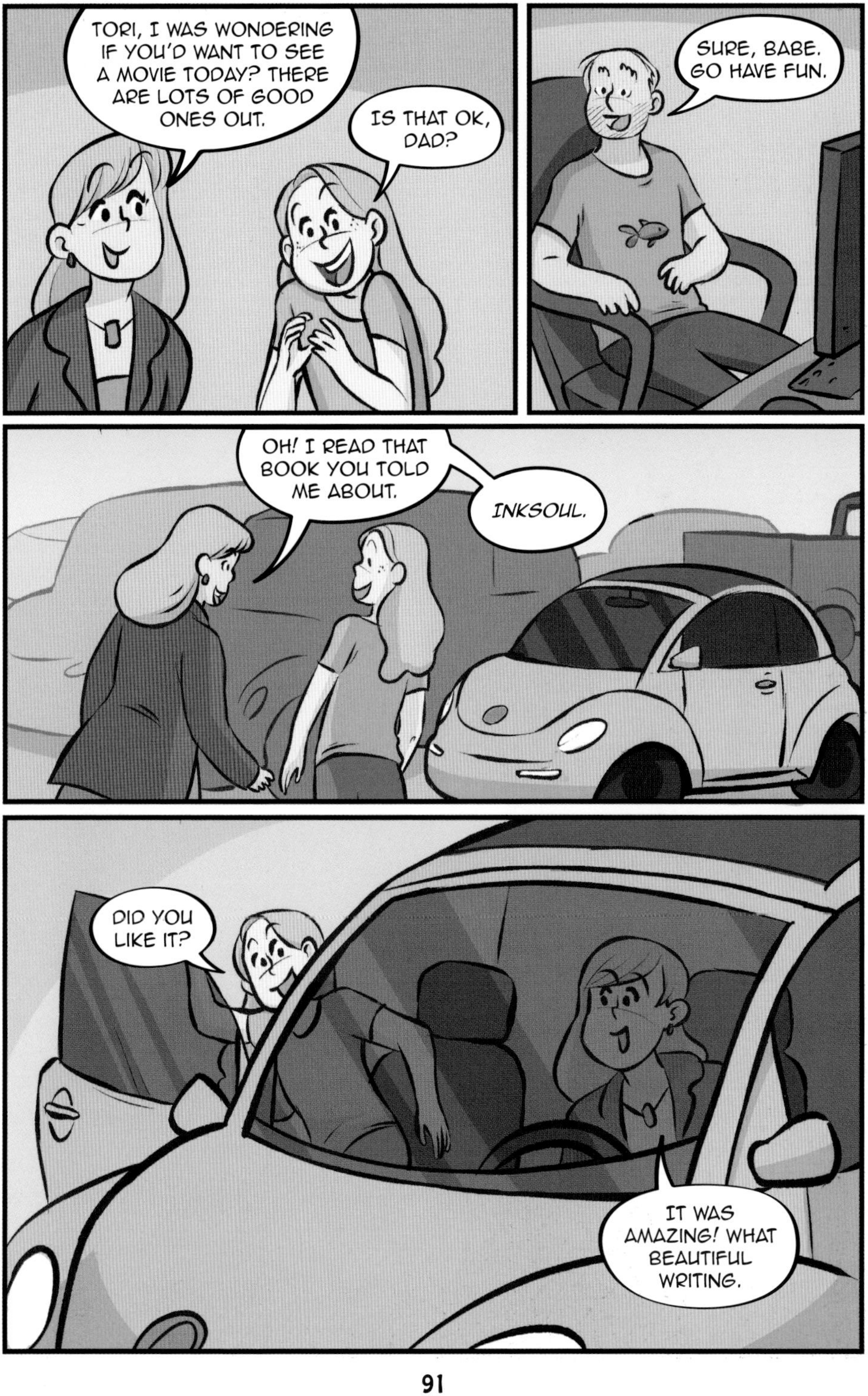
TORI, I WAS WONDERING IF YOU'D WANT TO SEE A MOVIE TODAY? THERE ARE LOTS OF GOOD ONES OUT.
IS THAT OK, DAD?
SURE, BABE. GO HAVE FUN.
OH! I READ THAT BOOK YOU TOLD ME ABOUT.
*INKSOUL.*
DID YOU LIKE IT?
IT WAS AMAZING! WHAT BEAUTIFUL WRITING.

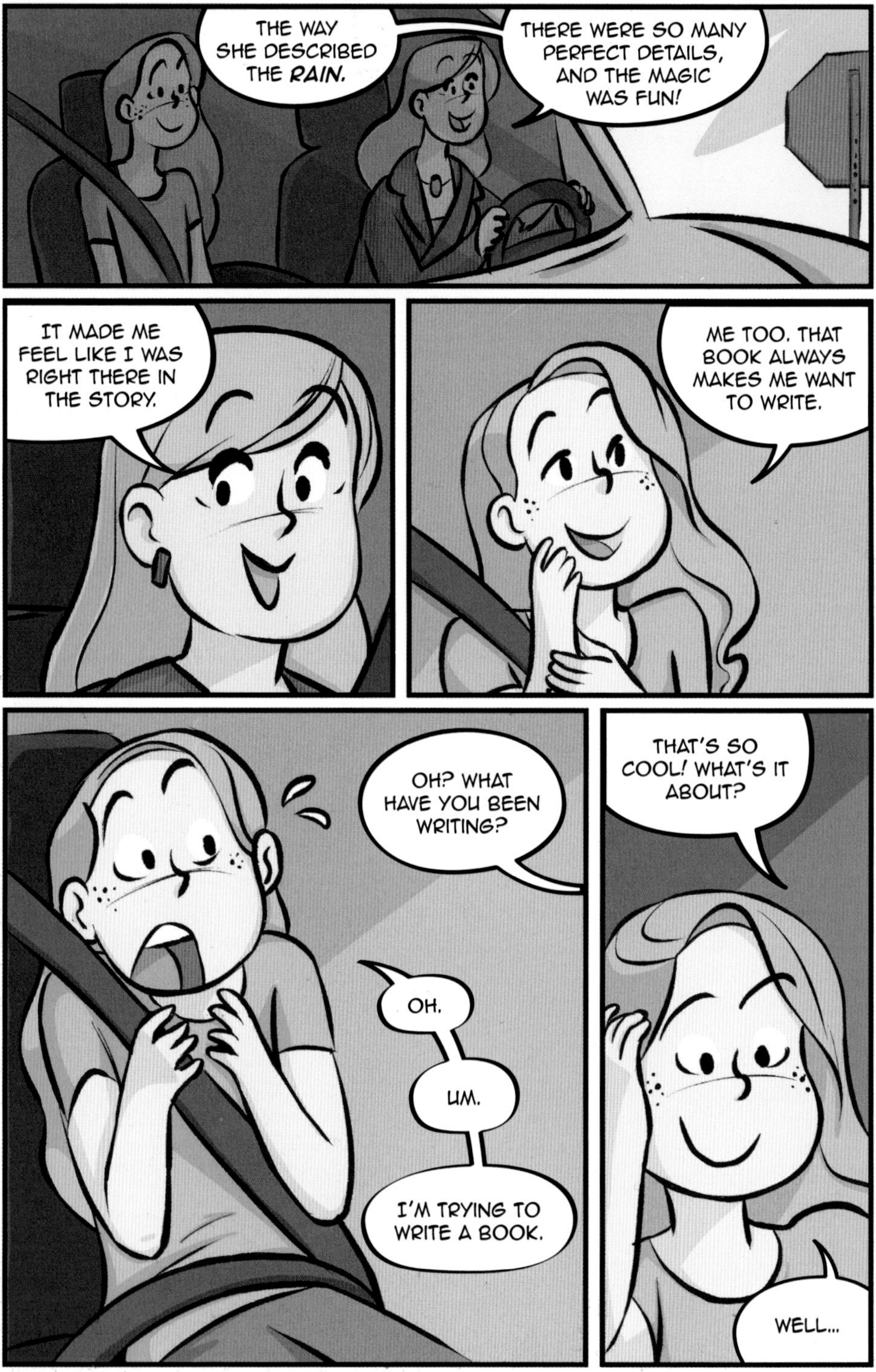
THE WAY SHE DESCRIBED THE *RAIN.*
THERE WERE SO MANY PERFECT DETAILS, AND THE MAGIC WAS FUN!
IT MADE ME FEEL LIKE I WAS RIGHT THERE IN THE STORY.
ME TOO. THAT BOOK ALWAYS MAKES ME WANT TO WRITE.
OH? WHAT HAVE YOU BEEN WRITING?
OH.
UM.
I'M TRYING TO WRITE A BOOK.
THAT'S SO COOL! WHAT'S IT ABOUT?
WELL...

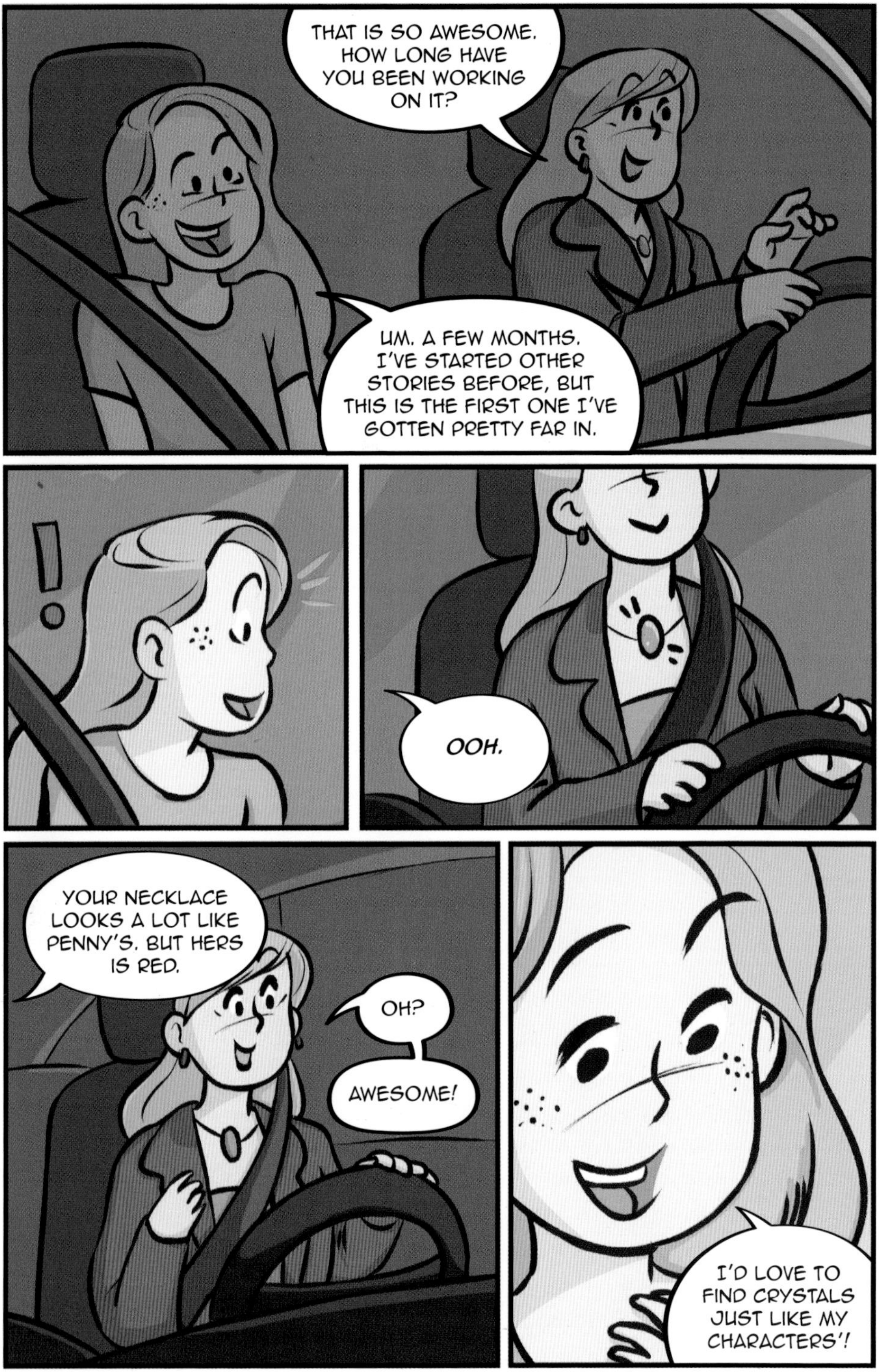
THAT IS SO AWESOME. HOW LONG HAVE YOU BEEN WORKING ON IT?
UM. A FEW MONTHS. I'VE STARTED OTHER STORIES BEFORE, BUT THIS IS THE FIRST ONE I'VE GOTTEN PRETTY FAR IN.
!
OOH.
YOUR NECKLACE LOOKS A LOT LIKE PENNY'S. BUT HERS IS RED.
OH?
AWESOME!
I'D LOVE TO FIND CRYSTALS JUST LIKE MY CHARACTERS'!

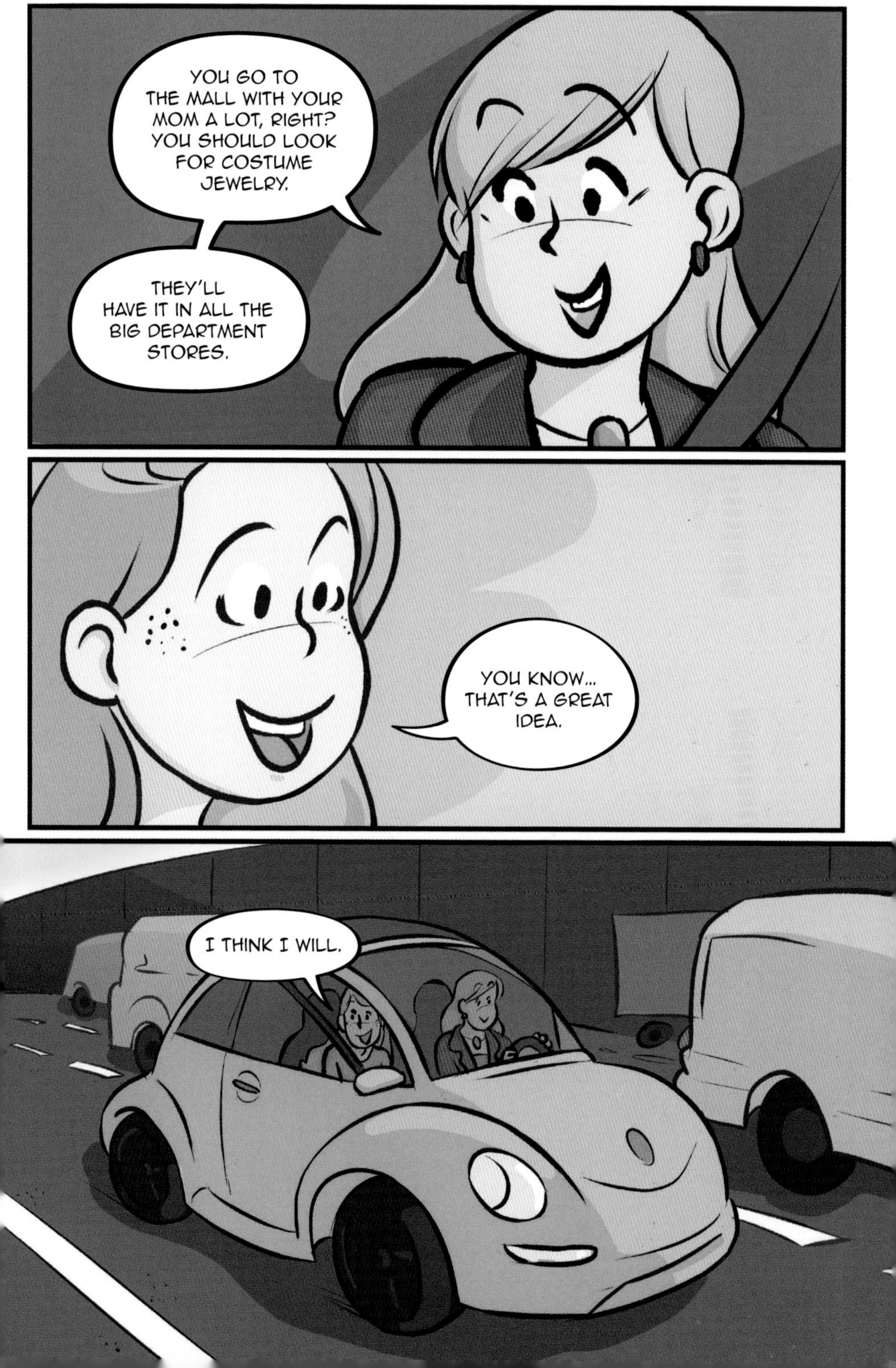
YOU GO TO THE MALL WITH YOUR MOM A LOT, RIGHT? YOU SHOULD LOOK FOR COSTUME JEWELRY.
THEY'LL HAVE IT IN ALL THE BIG DEPARTMENT STORES.
YOU KNOW... THAT'S A GREAT IDEA.
I THINK I WILL.

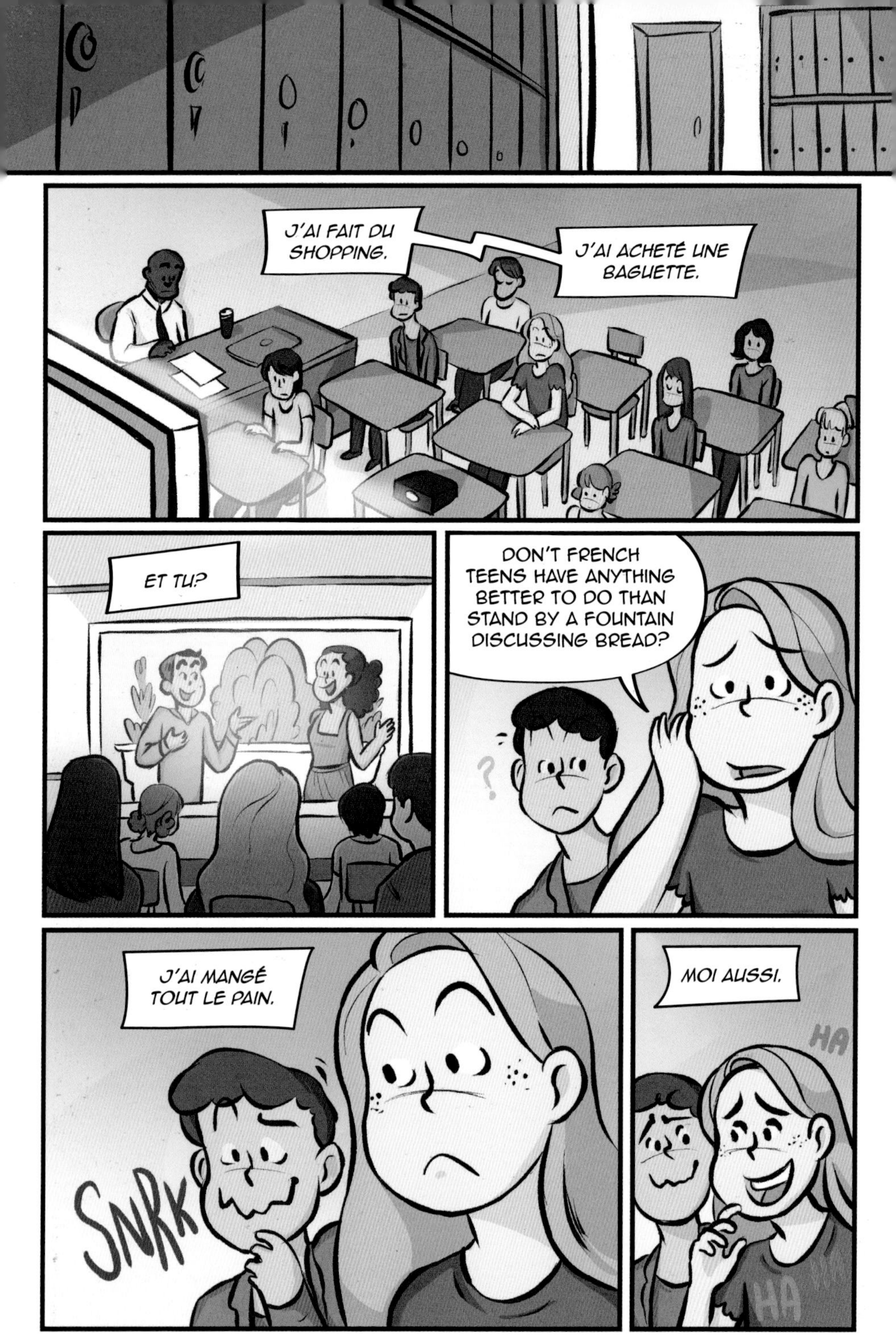
J'AI FAIT DU SHOPPING.
J'AI ACHETÉ UNE BAGUETTE.
ET TU?
DON'T FRENCH TEENS HAVE ANYTHING BETTER TO DO THAN STAND BY A FOUNTAIN DISCUSSING BREAD?
J'AI MANGÉ TOUT LE PAIN.
SNRK
MOI AUSSI.
HA
HA

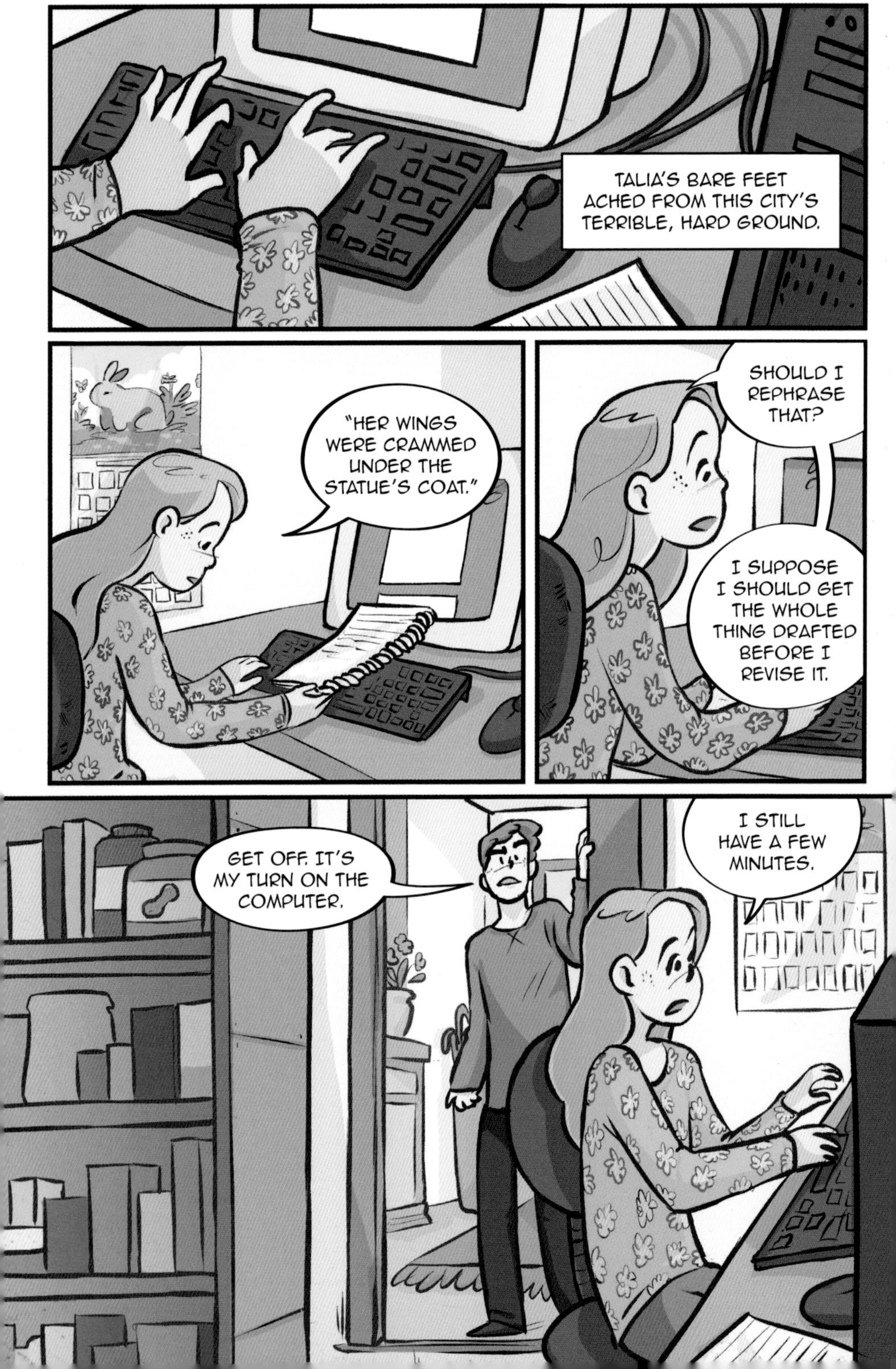
TALIA'S BARE FEET ACHED FROM THIS CITY'S TERRIBLE, HARD GROUND.
"HER WINGS WERE CRAMMED UNDER THE STATUE'S COAT."
SHOULD I REPHRASE THAT?
I SUPPOSE I SHOULD GET THE WHOLE THING DRAFTED BEFORE I REVISE IT.
GET OFF. IT'S MY TURN ON THE COMPUTER.
I STILL HAVE A FEW MINUTES.

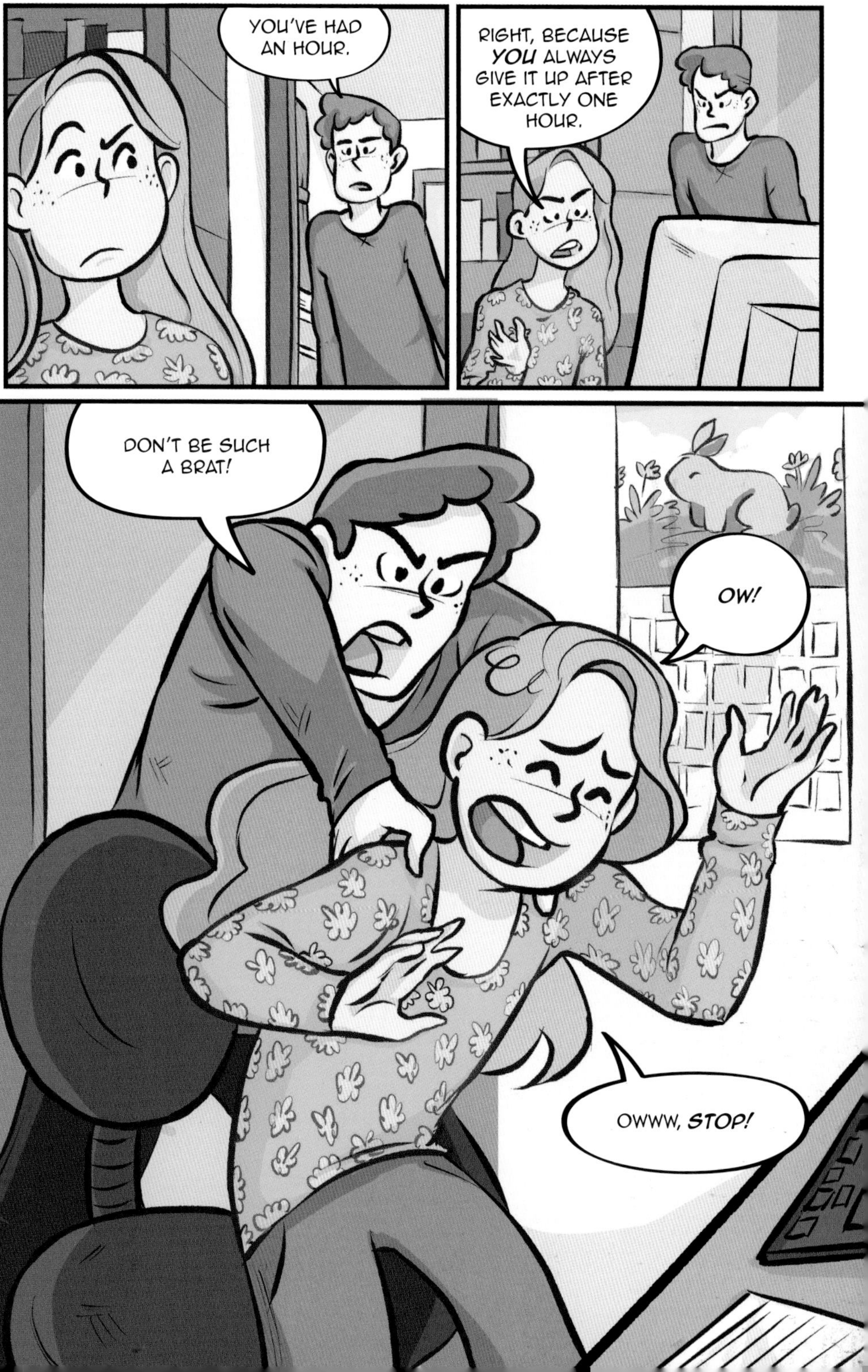

YOU'VE HAD AN HOUR.
RIGHT, BECAUSE *YOU* ALWAYS GIVE IT UP AFTER EXACTLY ONE HOUR.
DON'T BE SUCH A BRAT!
OW!
OWWW, *STOP!*

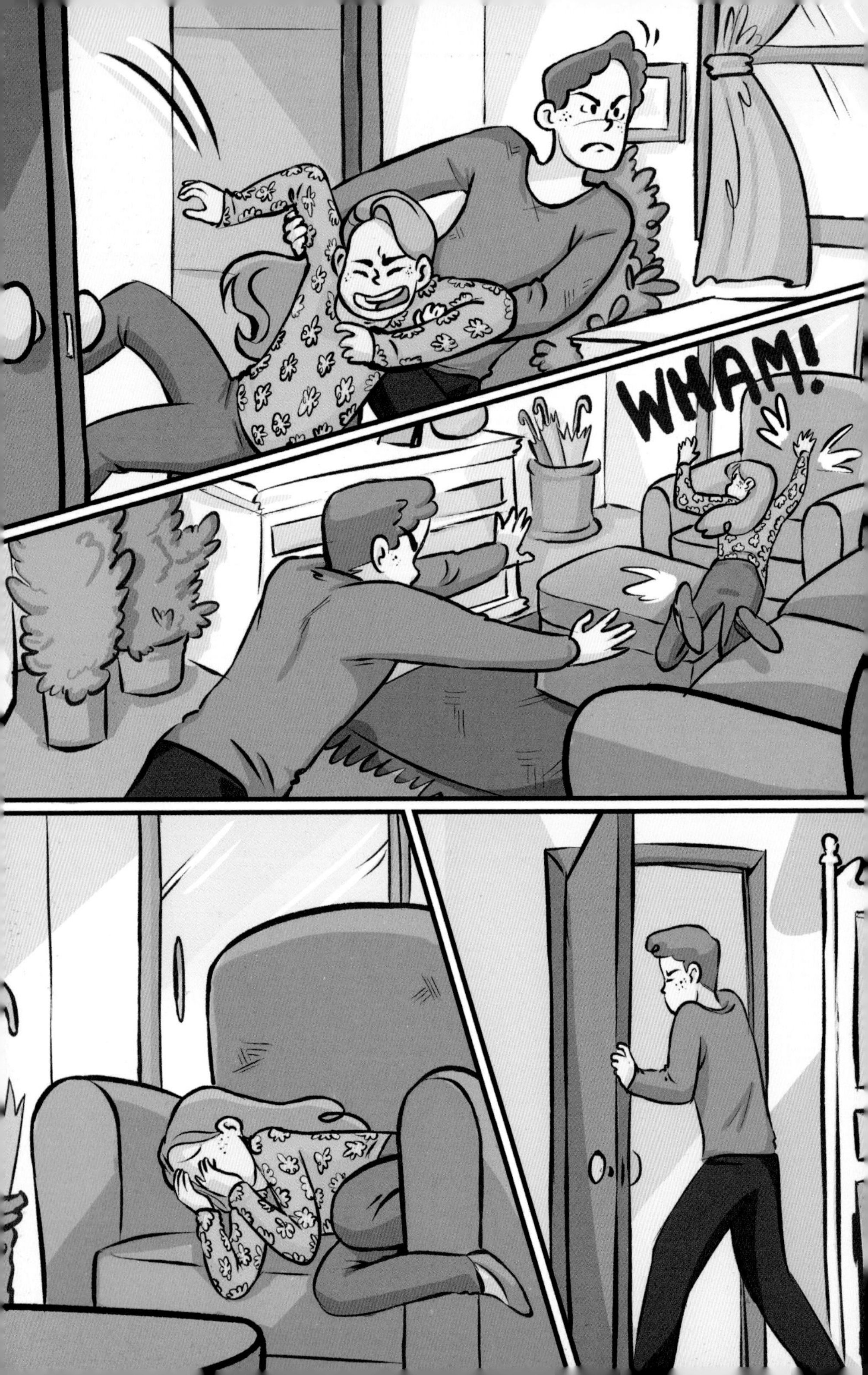
WHAM!

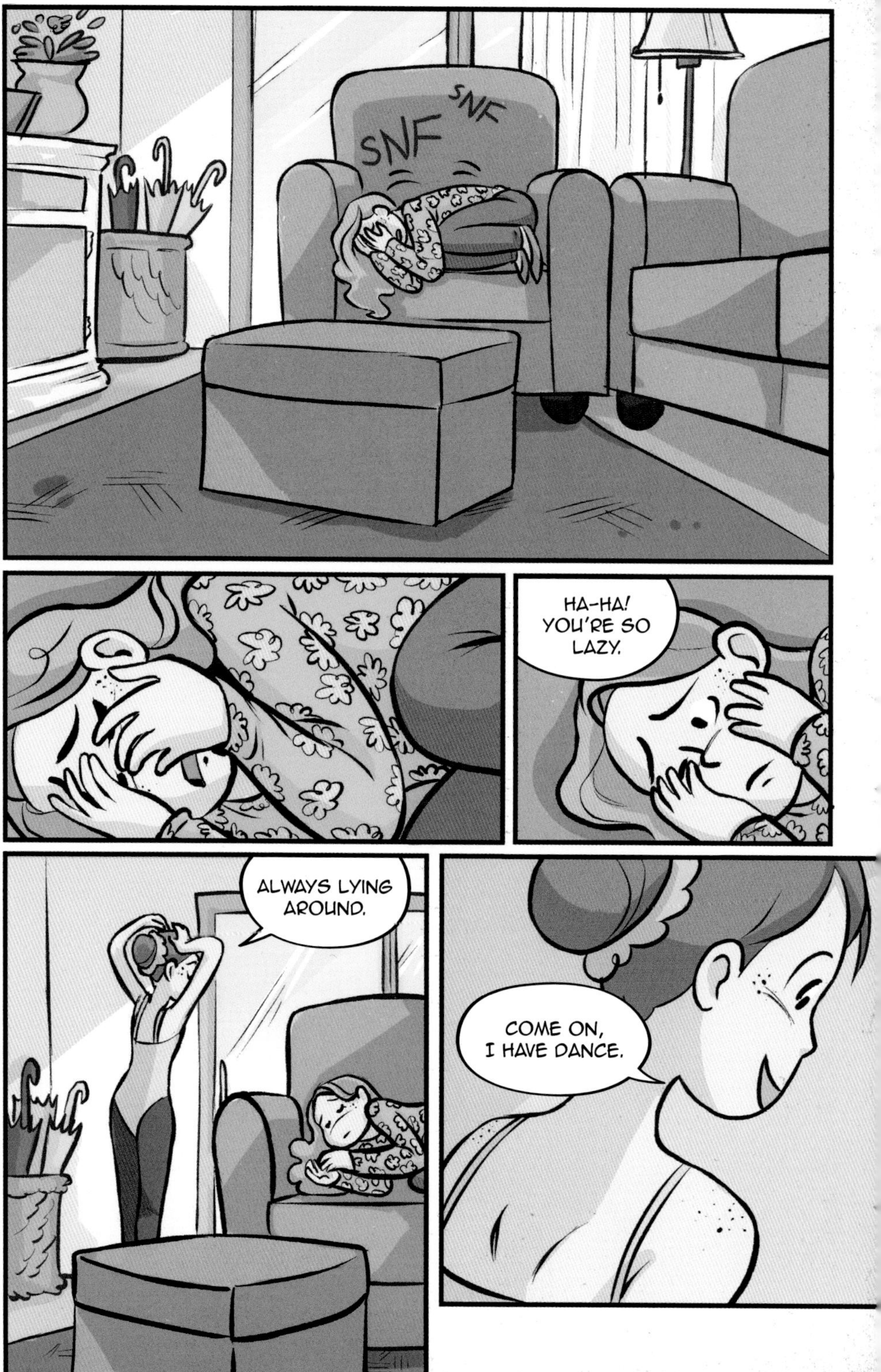
SNF
SNF
HA-HA! YOU'RE SO LAZY.
ALWAYS LYING AROUND.
COME ON, I HAVE DANCE.

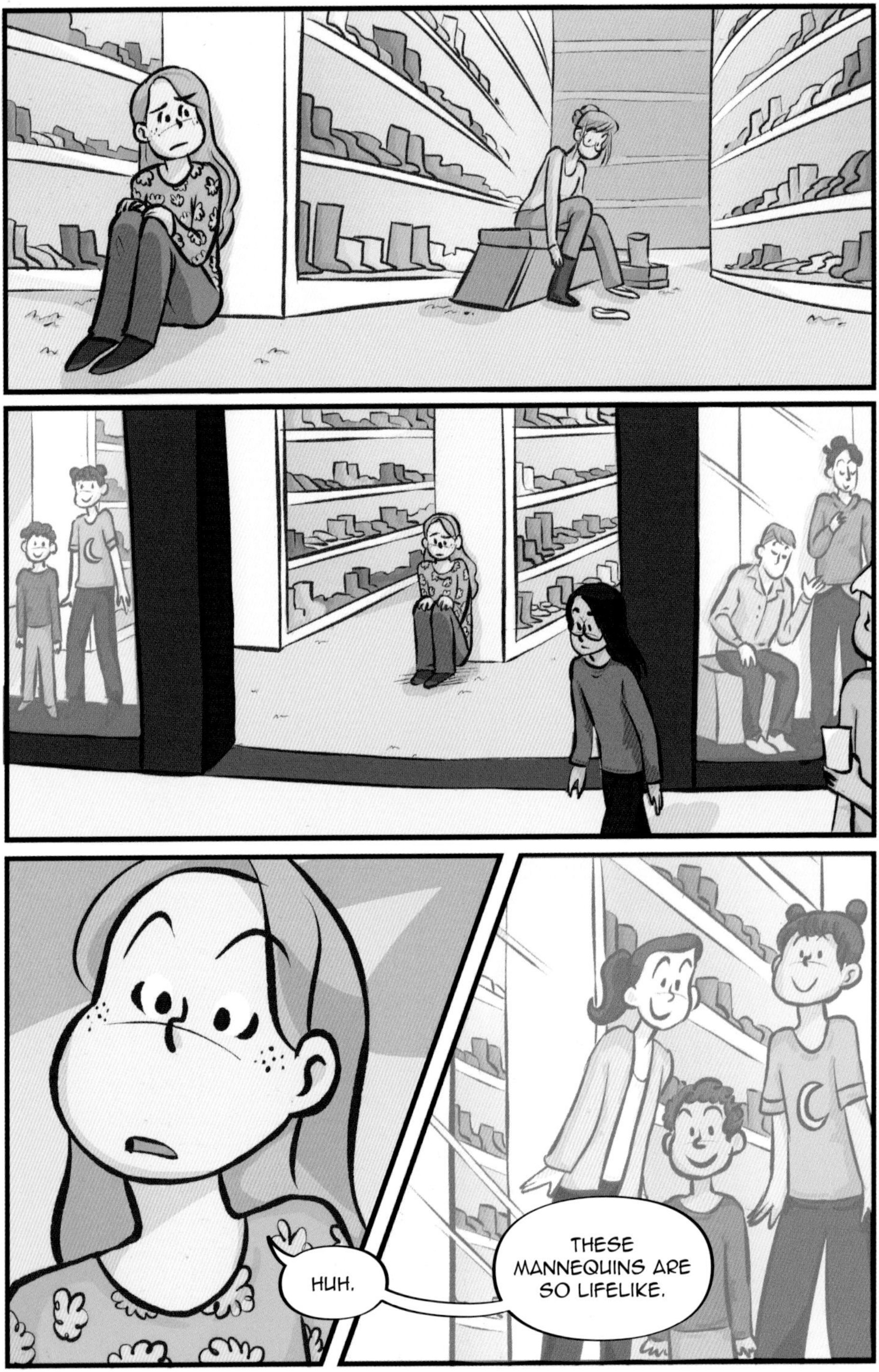
HUH.
THESE MANNEQUINS ARE SO LIFELIKE.

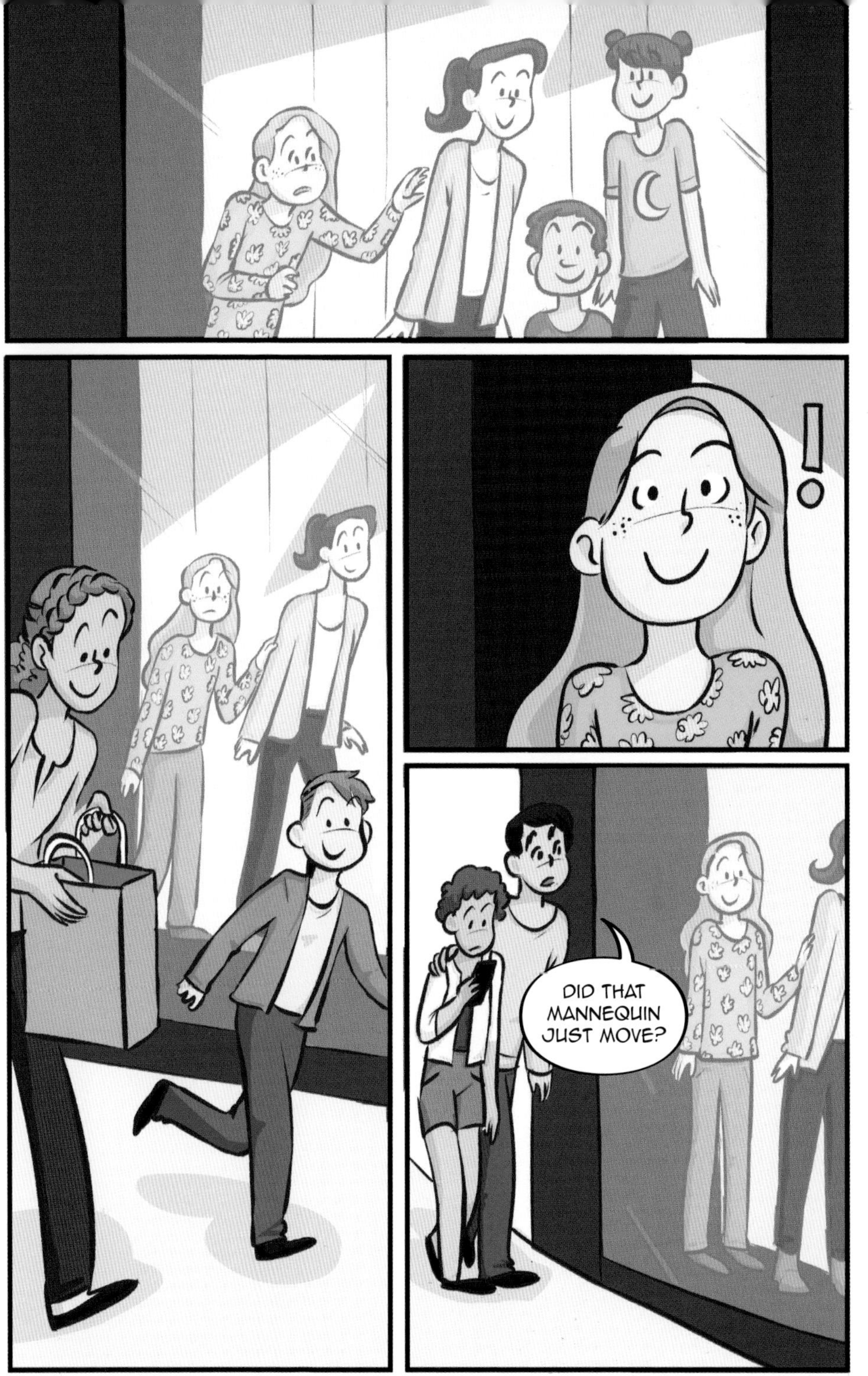
!
DID THAT MANNEQUIN JUST MOVE?

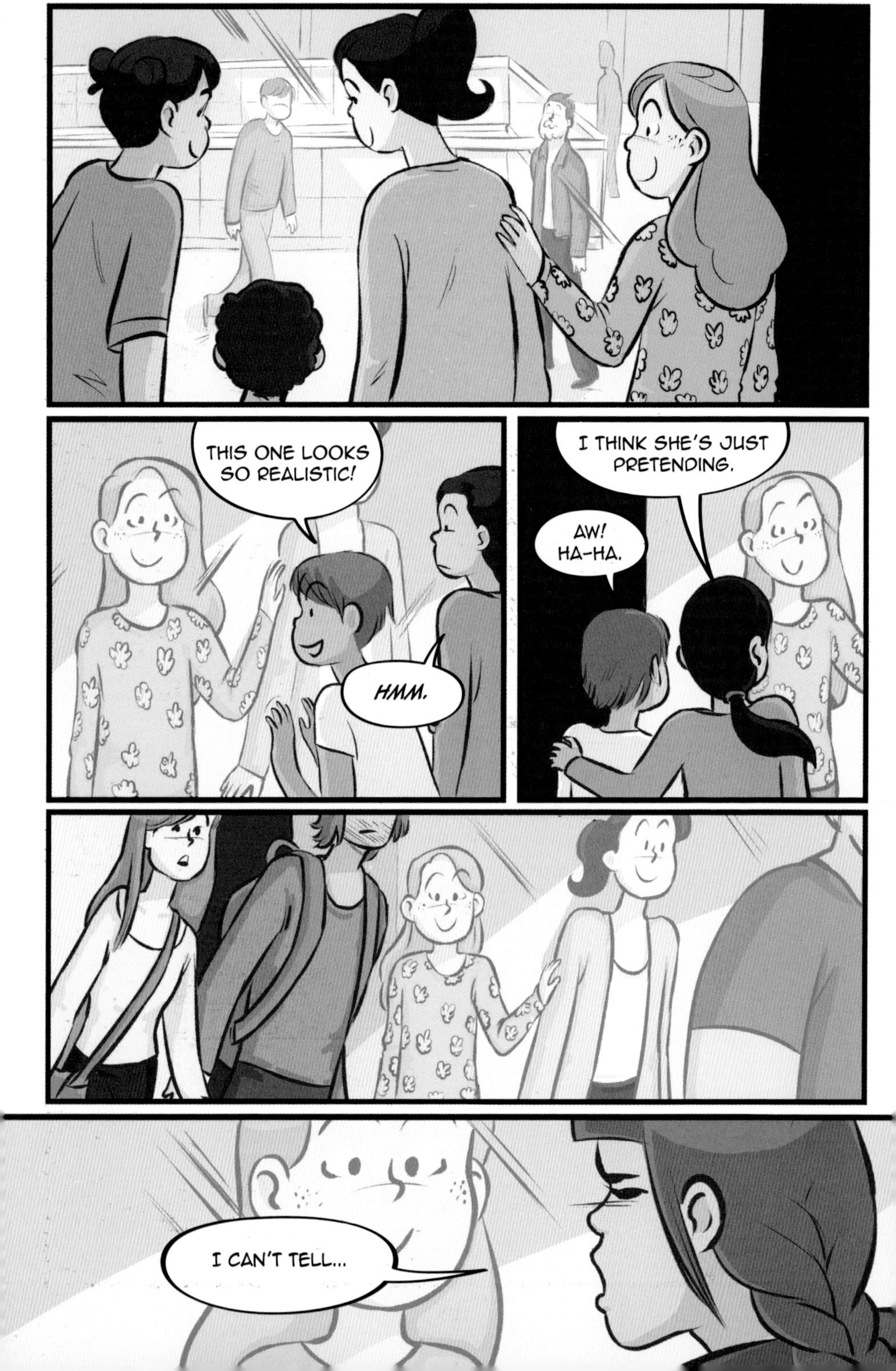
THIS ONE LOOKS SO REALISTIC!
HMM.
I THINK SHE'S JUST PRETENDING.
AW! HA-HA.
I CAN'T TELL...

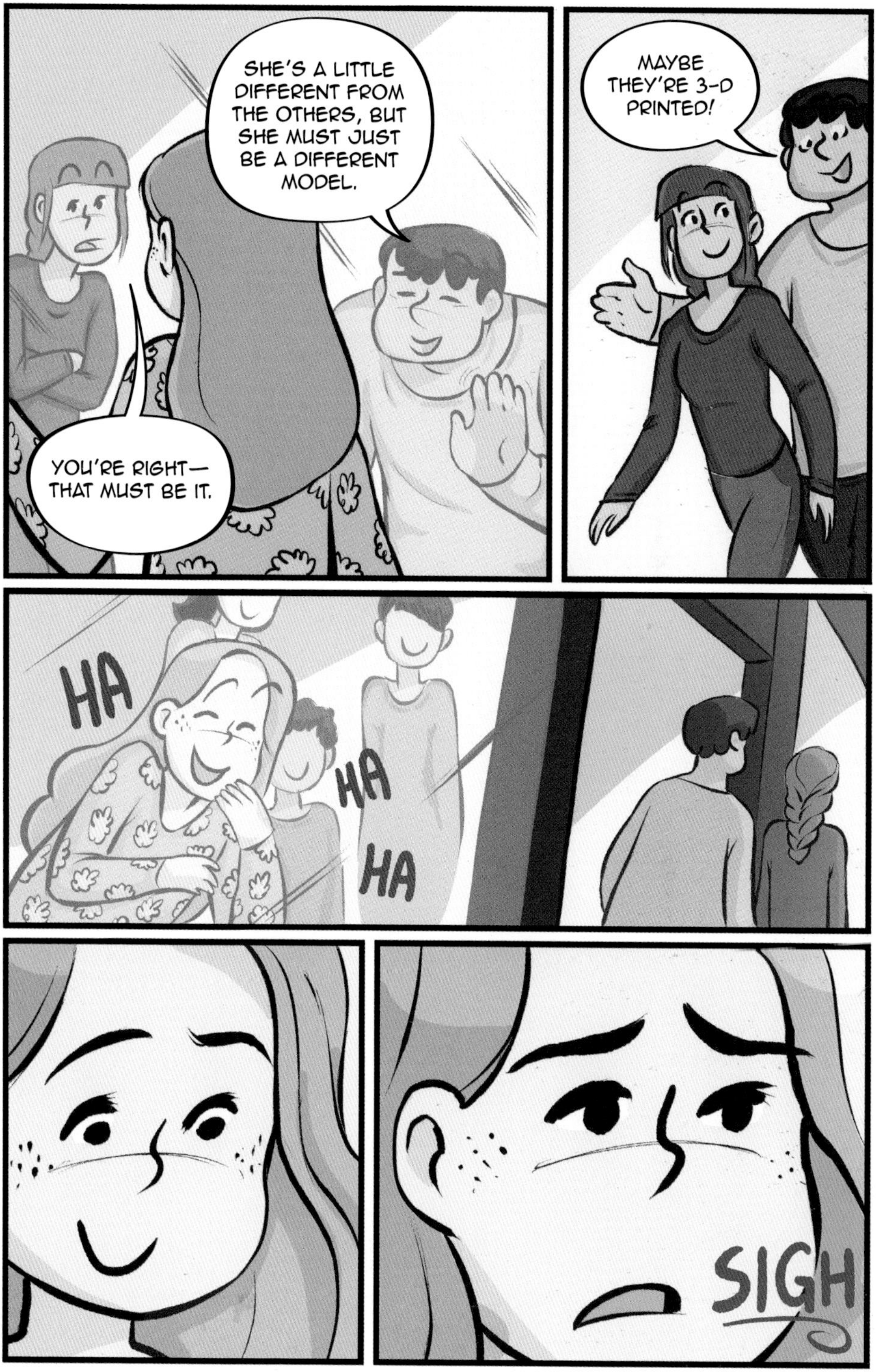
SHE'S A LITTLE DIFFERENT FROM THE OTHERS, BUT SHE MUST JUST BE A DIFFERENT MODEL.
YOU'RE RIGHT—THAT MUST BE IT.
MAYBE THEY'RE 3-D PRINTED!
HA
HA
HA
SIGH

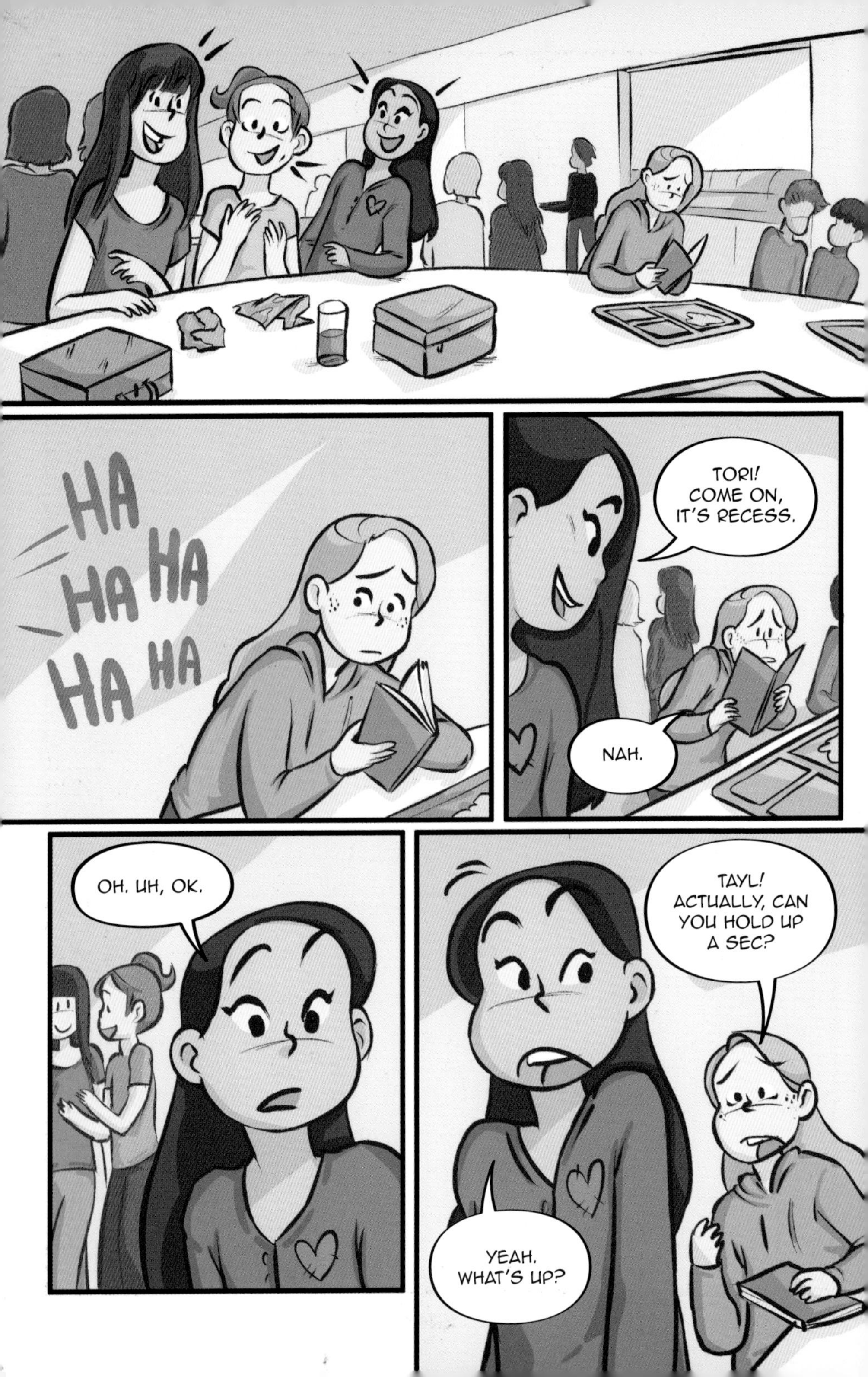
HA HA HA HA HA
TORI! COME ON, IT'S RECESS.
NAH.
OH. UH, OK.
TAYL! ACTUALLY, CAN YOU HOLD UP A SEC?
YEAH. WHAT'S UP?

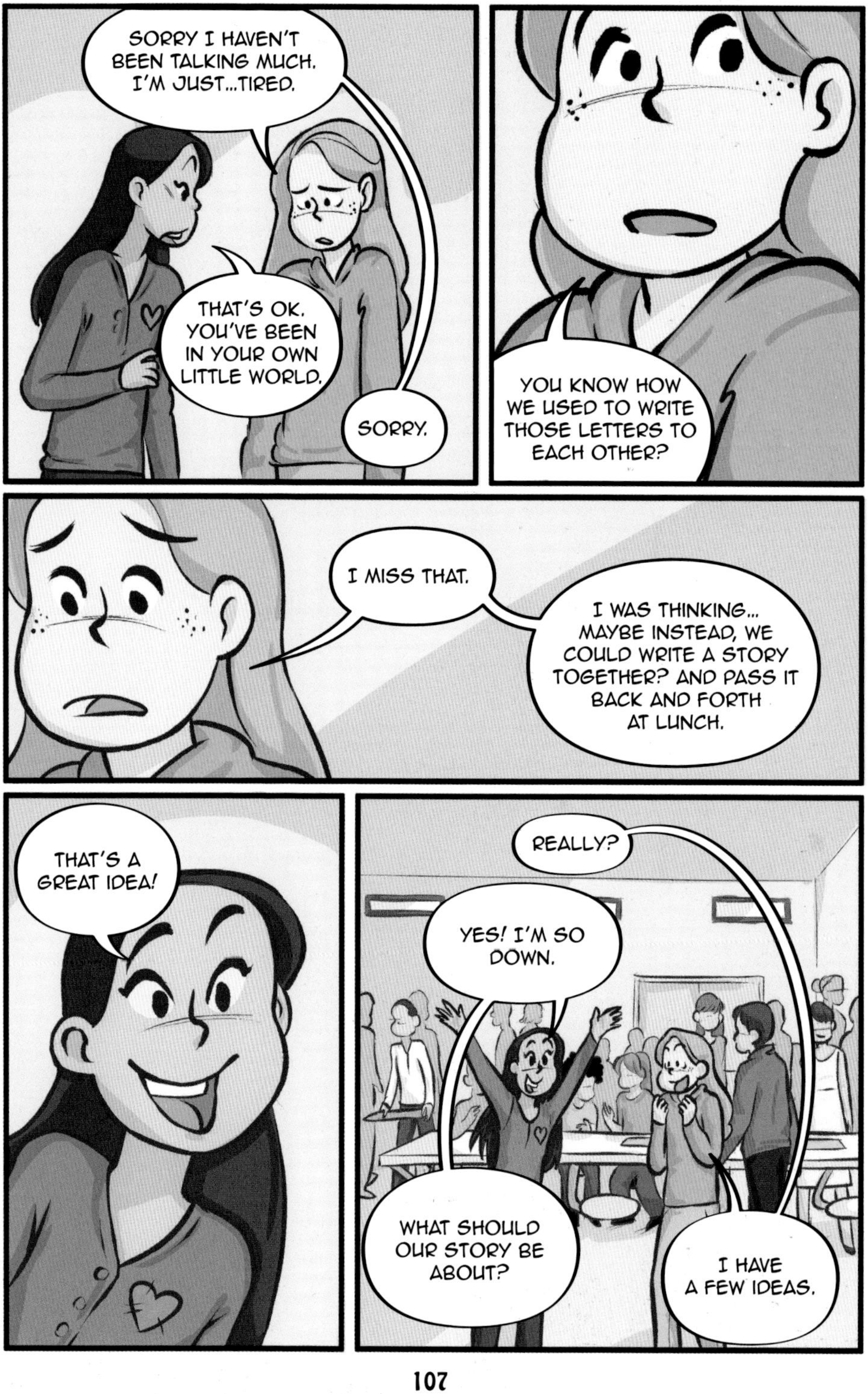
SORRY I HAVEN'T BEEN TALKING MUCH. I'M JUST...TIRED.
THAT'S OK. YOU'VE BEEN IN YOUR OWN LITTLE WORLD.
SORRY.
YOU KNOW HOW WE USED TO WRITE THOSE LETTERS TO EACH OTHER?
I MISS THAT.
I WAS THINKING... MAYBE INSTEAD, WE COULD WRITE A STORY TOGETHER? AND PASS IT BACK AND FORTH AT LUNCH.
THAT'S A GREAT IDEA!
REALLY?
YES! I'M SO DOWN.
WHAT SHOULD OUR STORY BE ABOUT?
I HAVE A FEW IDEAS.

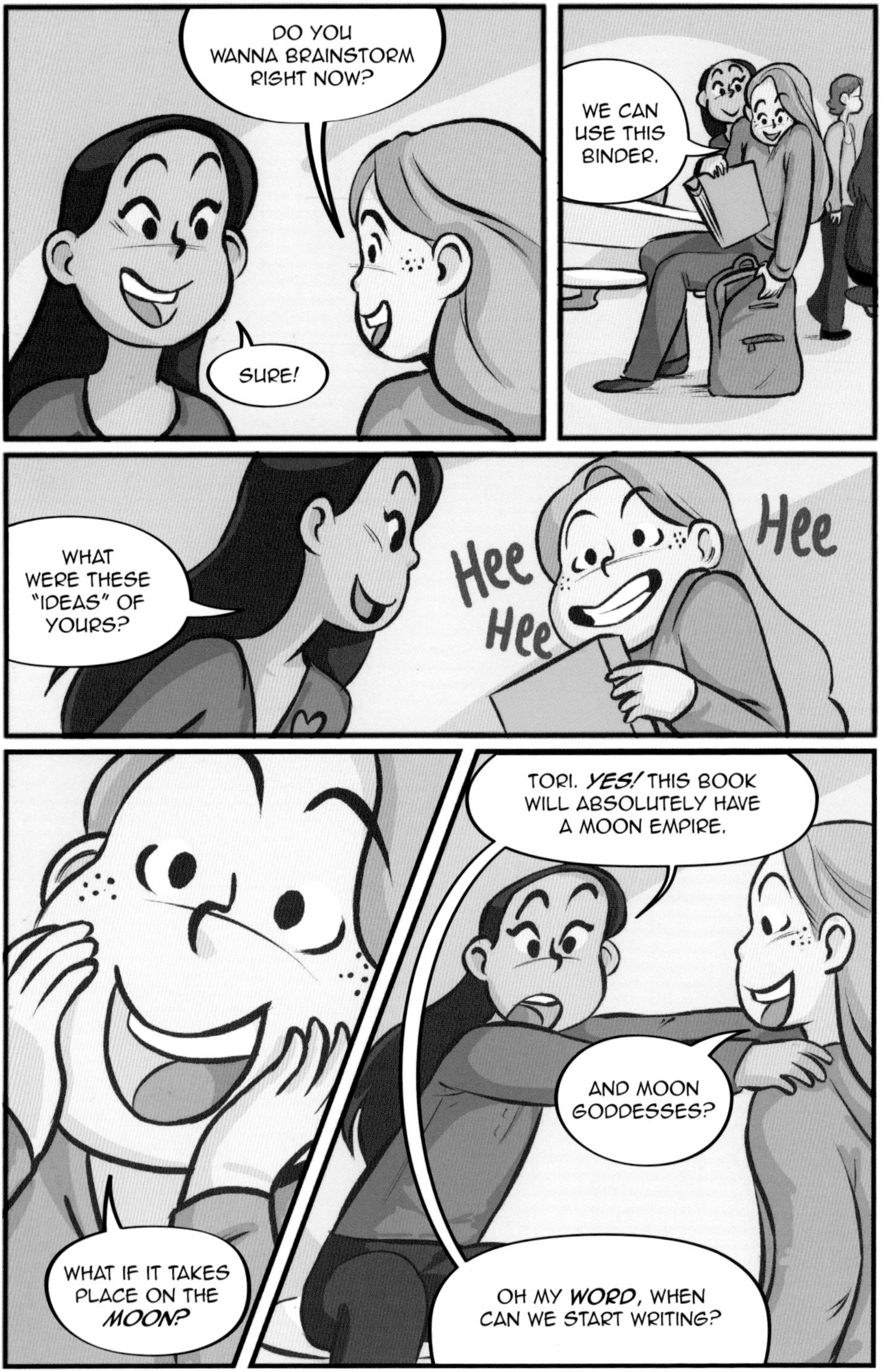
DO YOU WANNA BRAINSTORM RIGHT NOW?
SURE!
WE CAN USE THIS BINDER.
WHAT WERE THESE "IDEAS" OF YOURS?
Hee
Hee
Hee
WHAT IF IT TAKES PLACE ON THE *MOON*?
TORI. *YES!* THIS BOOK WILL ABSOLUTELY HAVE A MOON EMPIRE.
AND MOON GODDESSES?
OH MY *WORD*, WHEN CAN WE START WRITING?

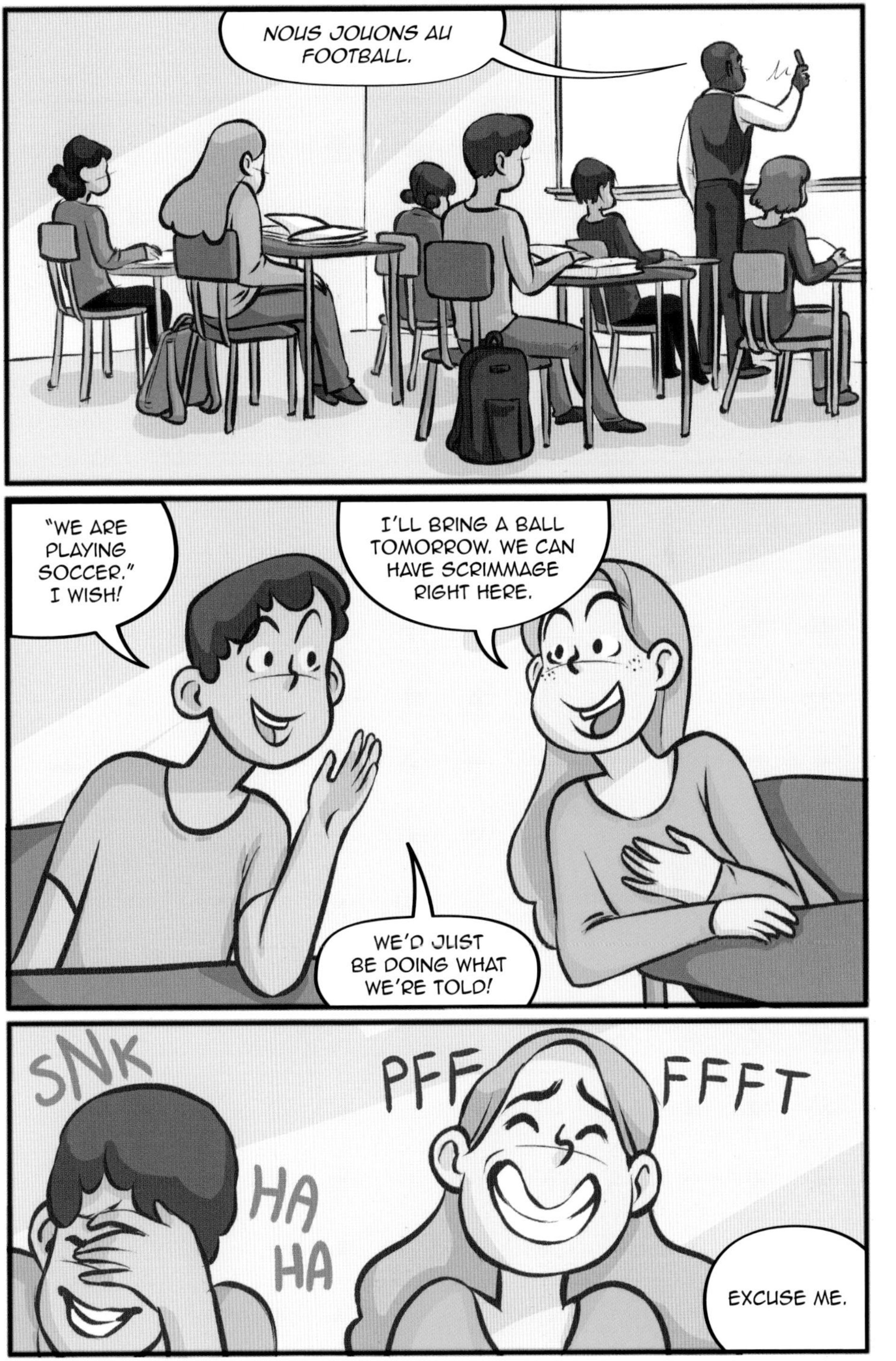
NOUS JOUONS AU FOOTBALL.
"WE ARE PLAYING SOCCER." I WISH!
I'LL BRING A BALL TOMORROW. WE CAN HAVE SCRIMMAGE RIGHT HERE.
WE'D JUST BE DOING WHAT WE'RE TOLD!
SNK
HA HA
PFF FFFT
EXCUSE ME.

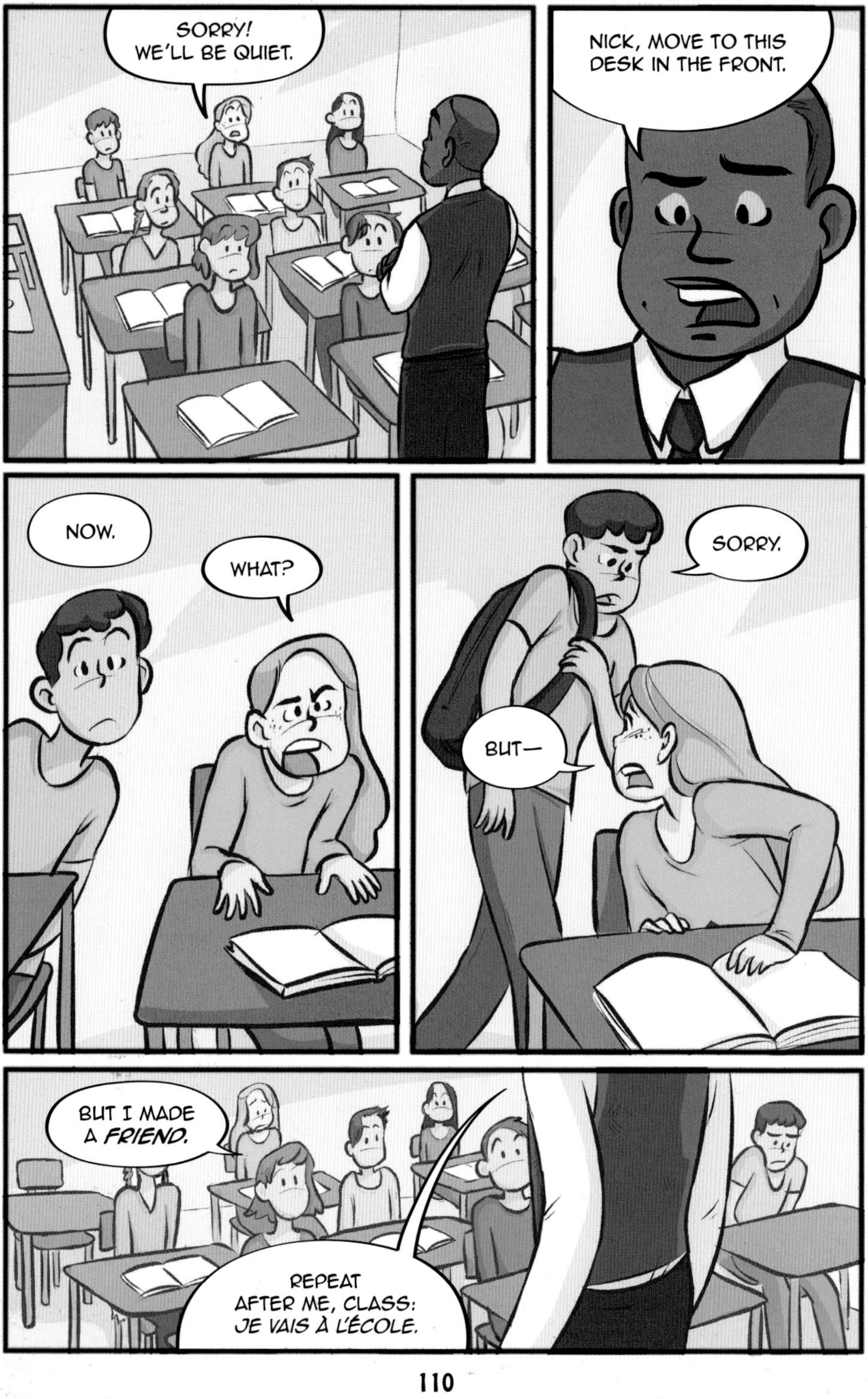
SORRY! WE'LL BE QUIET.
NICK, MOVE TO THIS DESK IN THE FRONT.
NOW.
WHAT?
SORRY.
BUT—
BUT I MADE A *FRIEND.*
REPEAT AFTER ME, CLASS: *JE VAIS À L'ÉCOLE.*

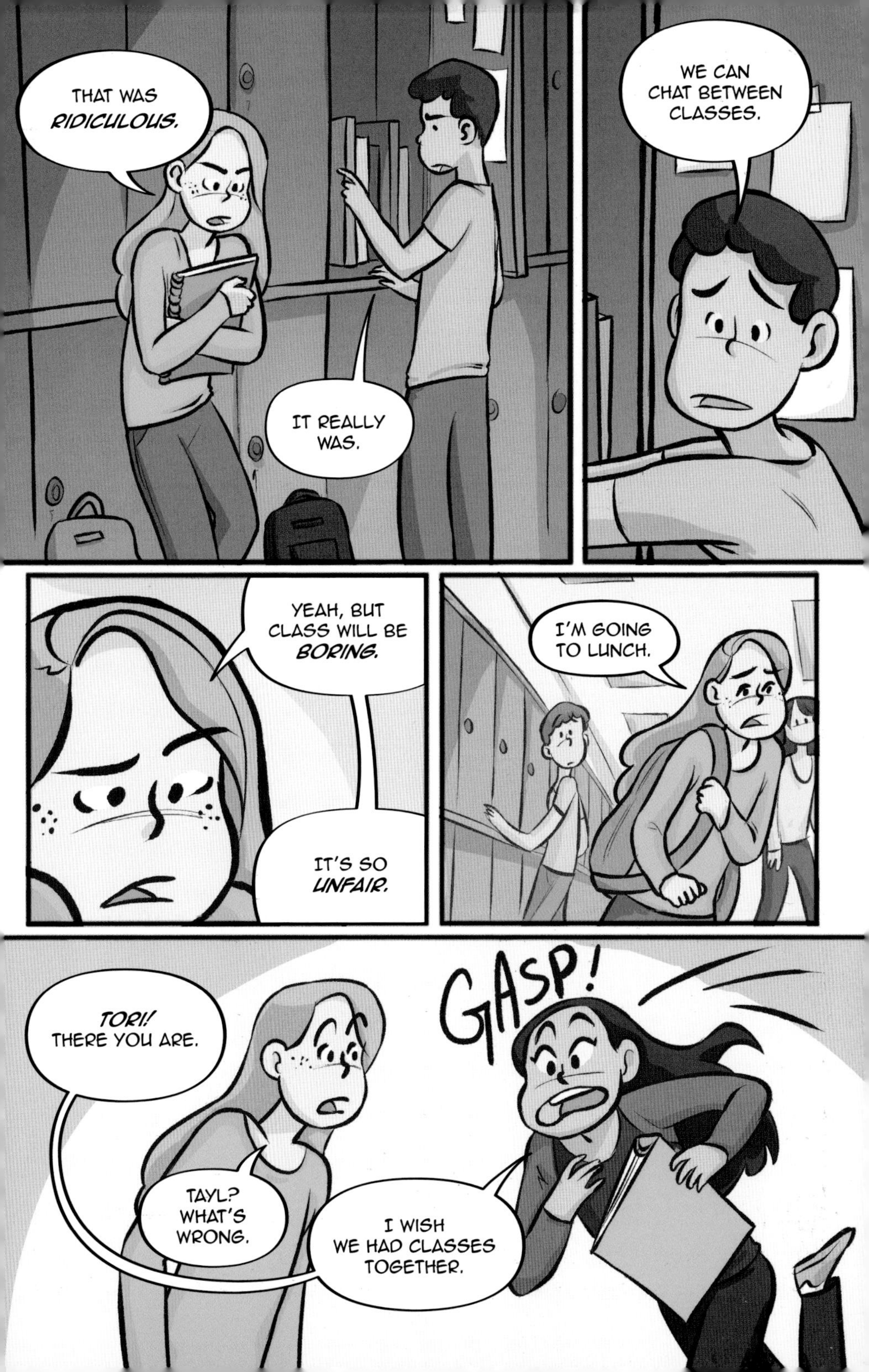
THAT WAS *RIDICULOUS.*
IT REALLY WAS.
WE CAN CHAT BETWEEN CLASSES.
YEAH, BUT CLASS WILL BE *BORING.*
IT'S SO *UNFAIR.*
I'M GOING TO LUNCH.
*TORI!* THERE YOU ARE.
GASP!
TAYL? WHAT'S WRONG.
I WISH WE HAD CLASSES TOGETHER.

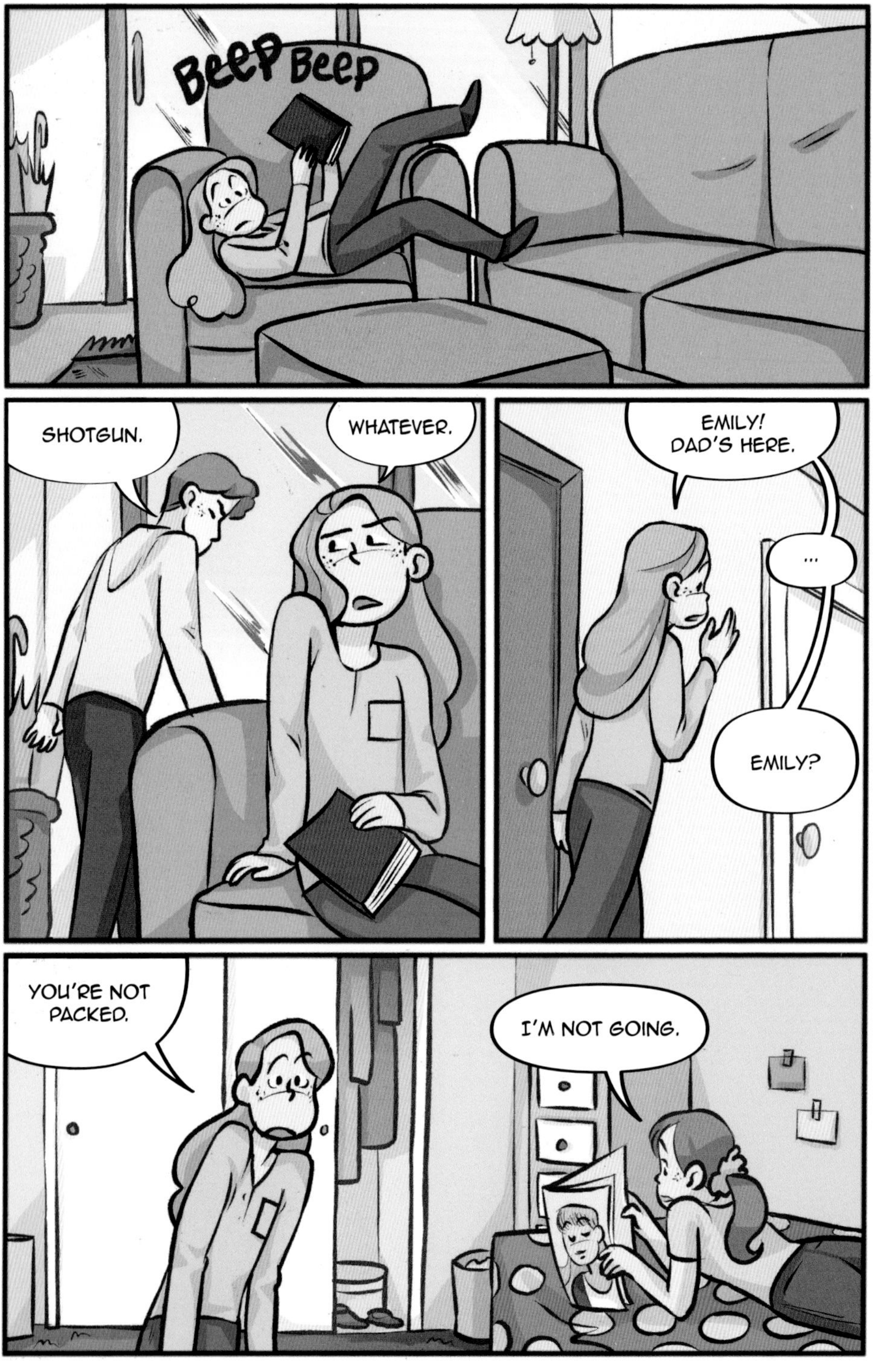
Beep Beep
SHOTGUN.
WHATEVER.
EMILY! DAD'S HERE.
...
EMILY?
YOU'RE NOT PACKED.
I'M NOT GOING.

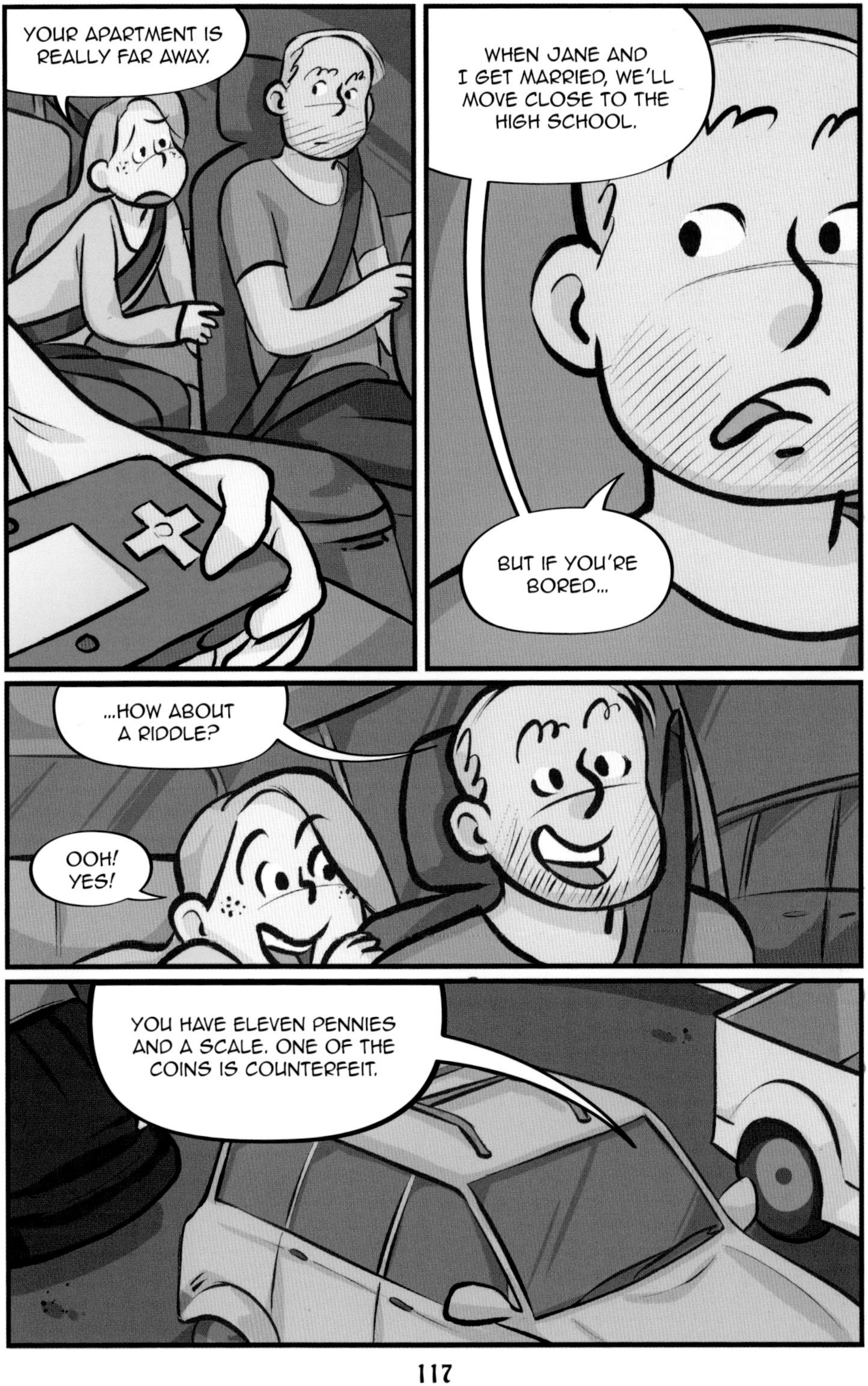
YOUR APARTMENT IS REALLY FAR AWAY.
WHEN JANE AND I GET MARRIED, WE'LL MOVE CLOSE TO THE HIGH SCHOOL.
BUT IF YOU'RE BORED...
...HOW ABOUT A RIDDLE?
OOH! YES!
YOU HAVE ELEVEN PENNIES AND A SCALE. ONE OF THE COINS IS COUNTERFEIT.

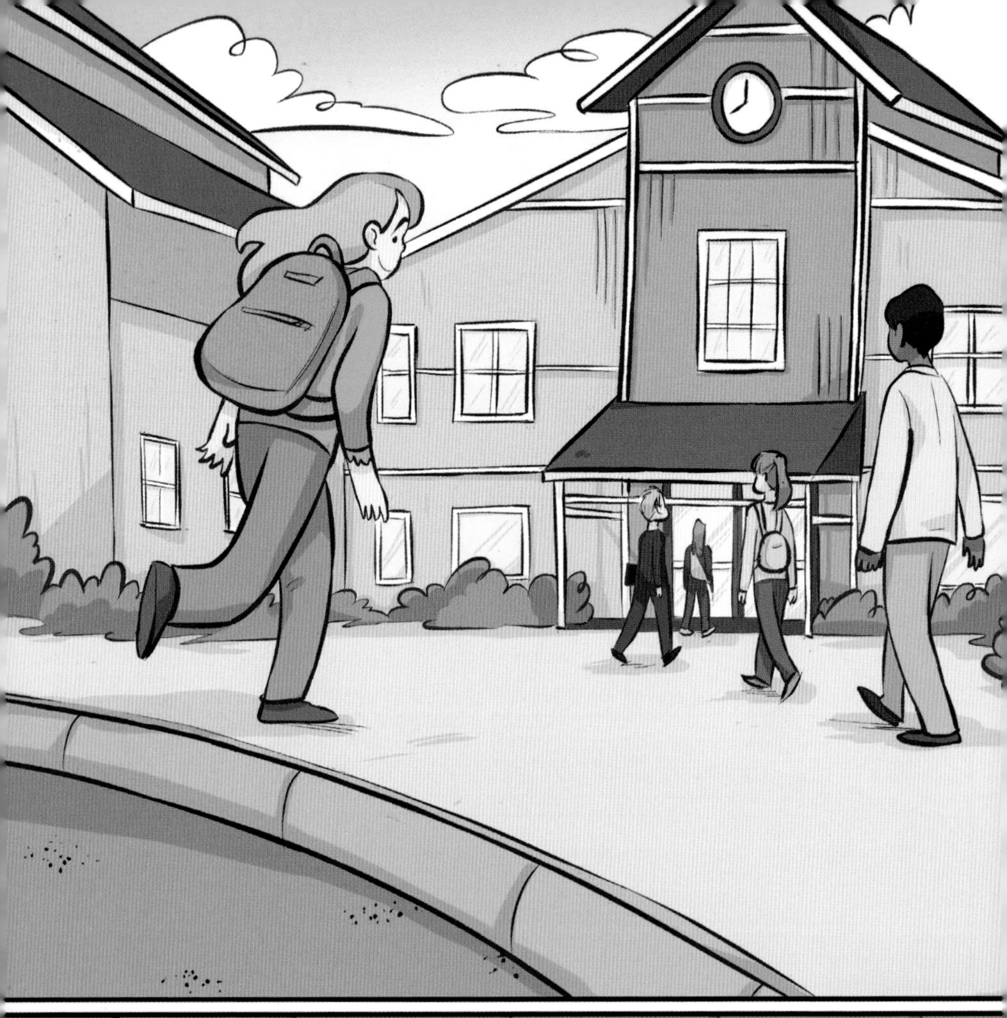
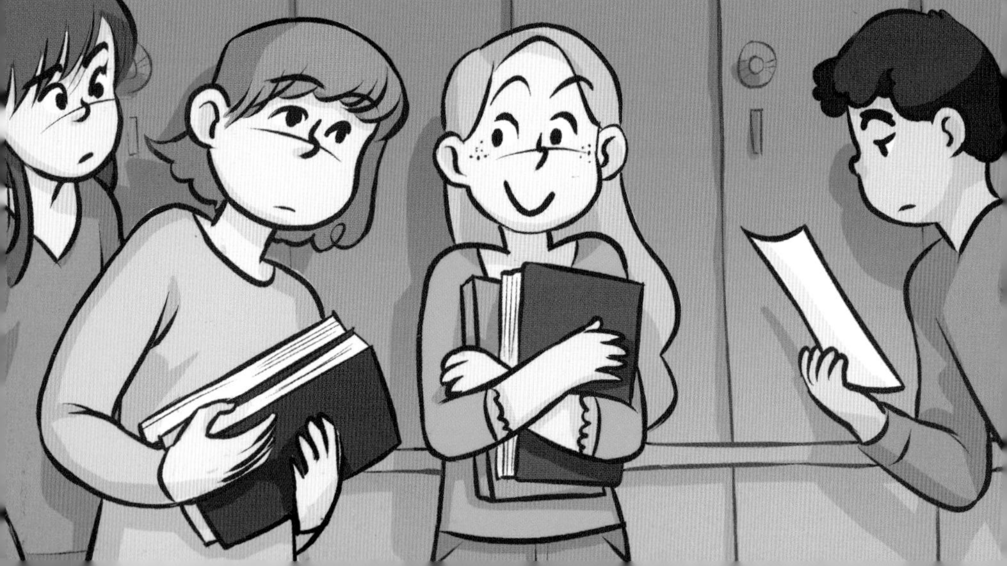

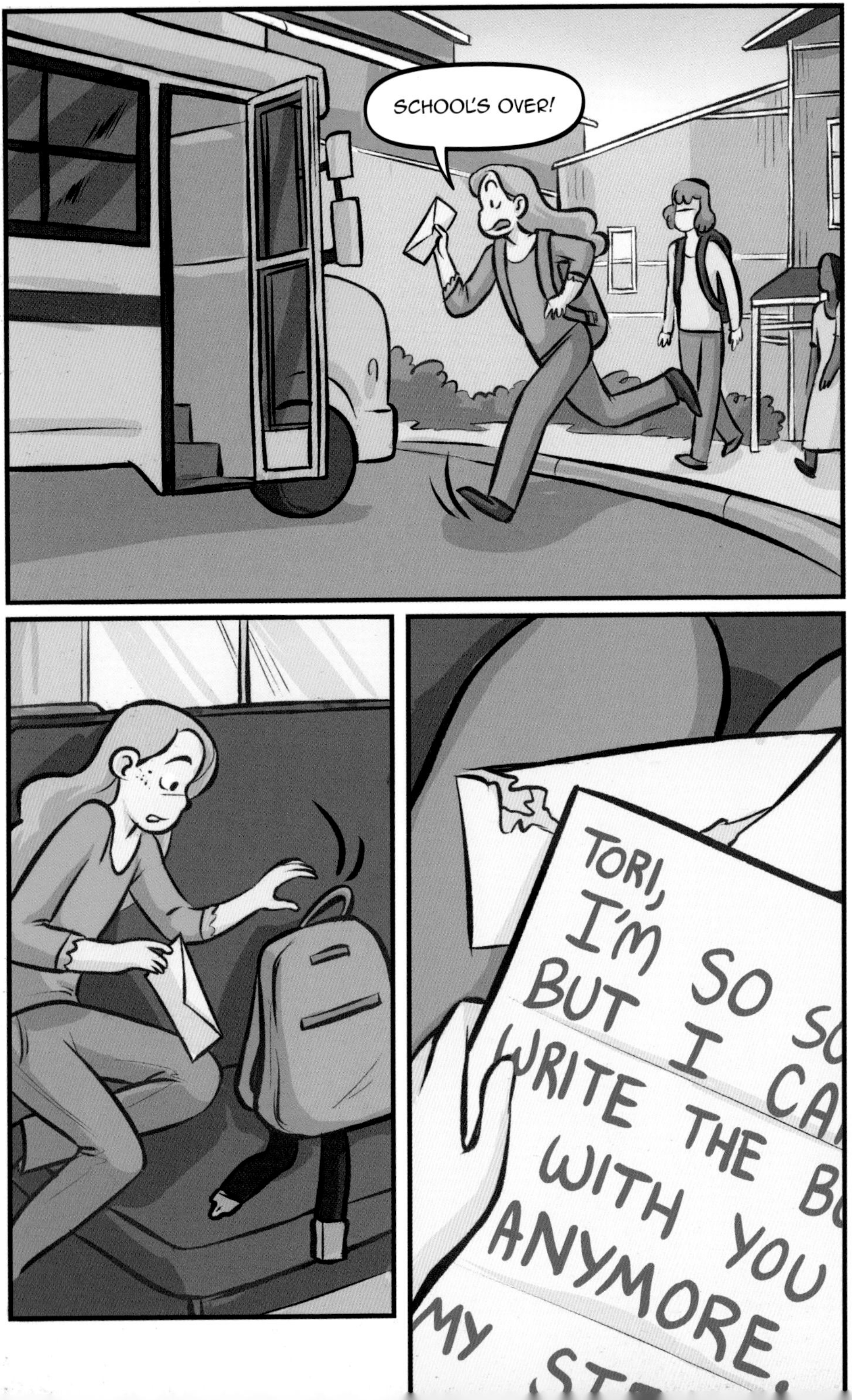
SCHOOL'S OVER!
TORI,
I'M SO
BUT I
WRITE THE
WITH YOU
ANYMORE.
MY

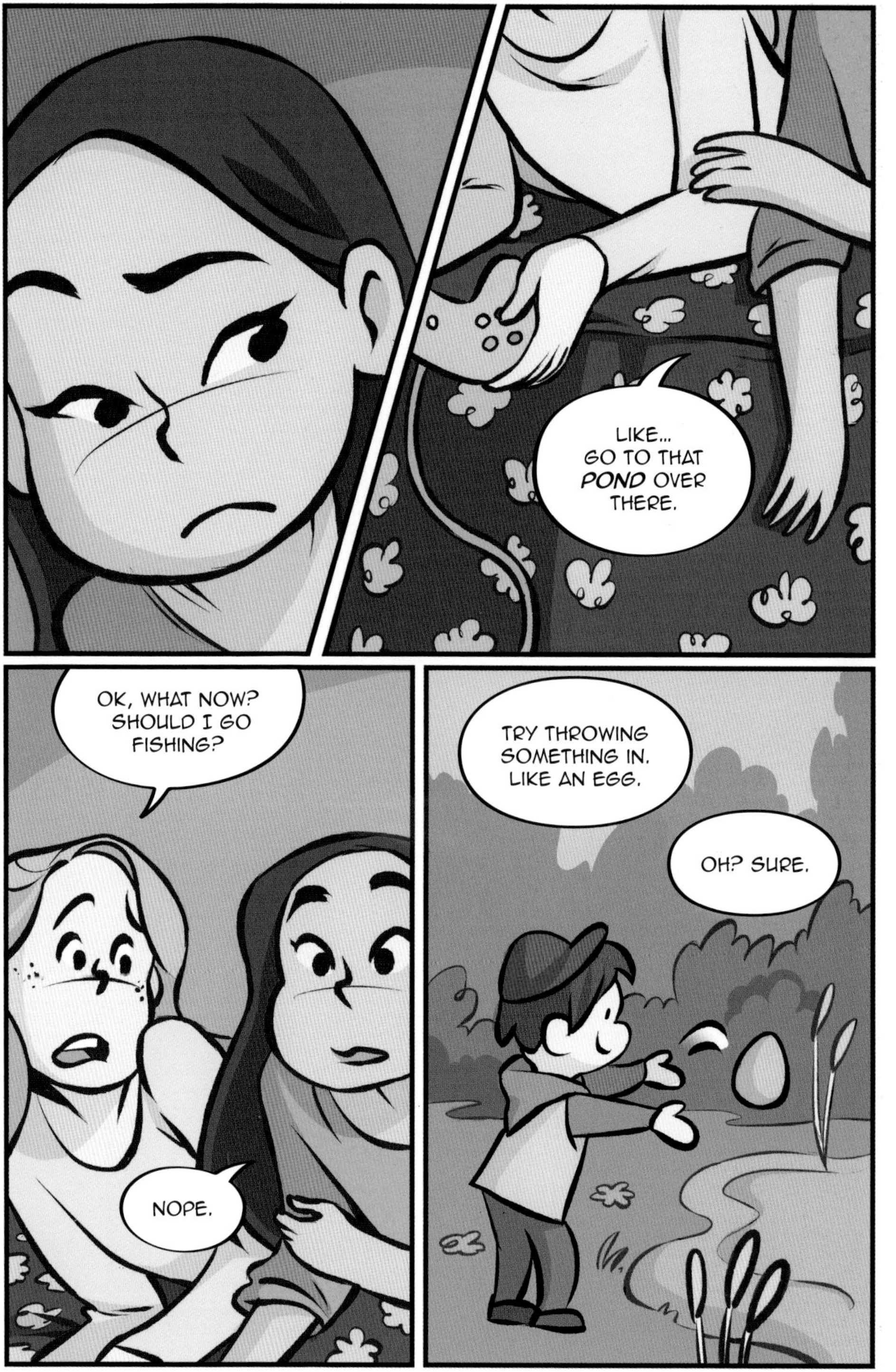
LIKE... GO TO THAT *POND* OVER THERE.
OK, WHAT NOW? SHOULD I GO FISHING?
NOPE.
TRY THROWING SOMETHING IN. LIKE AN EGG.
OH? SURE.

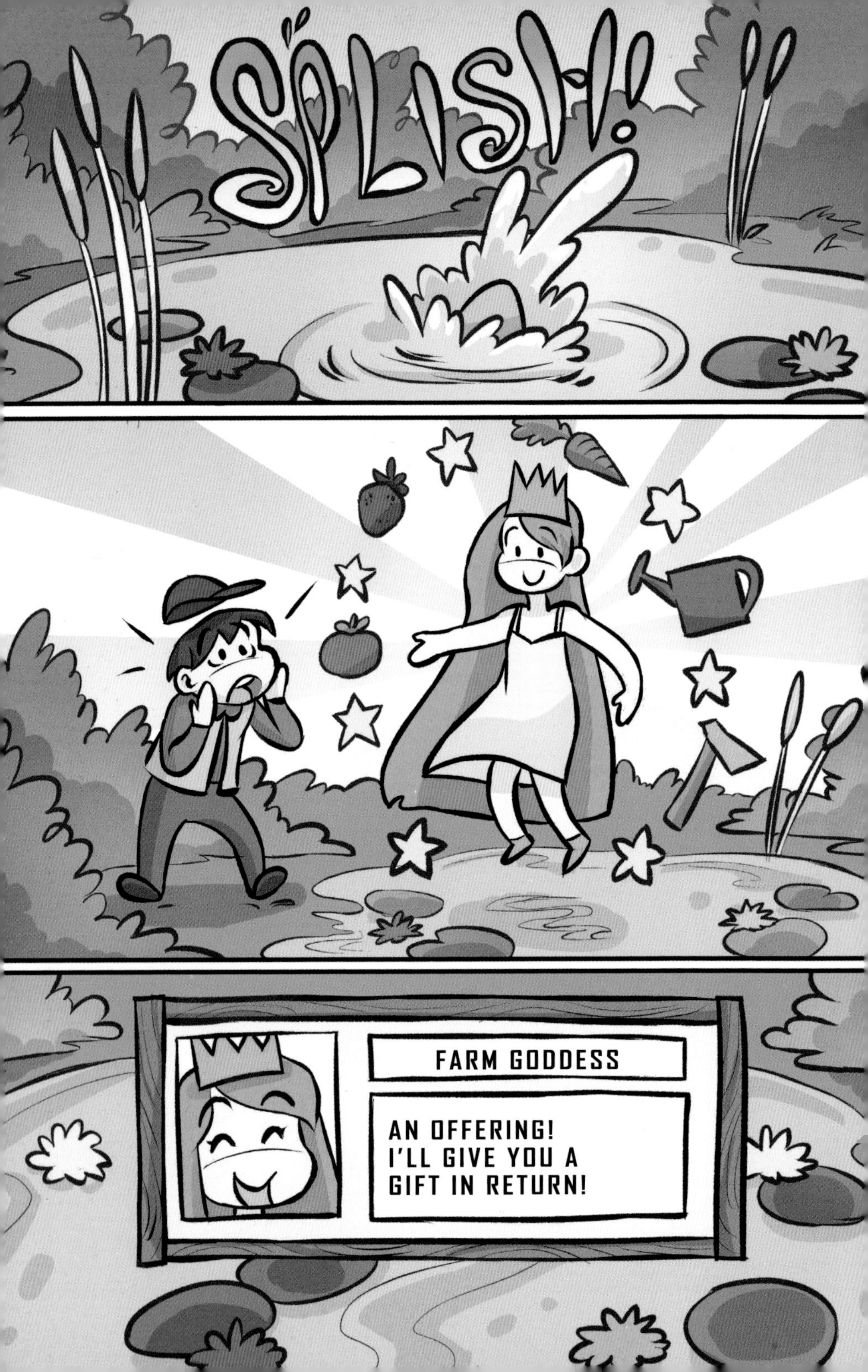
SPLASH!
FARM GODDESS
AN OFFERING!
I'LL GIVE YOU A
GIFT IN RETURN!

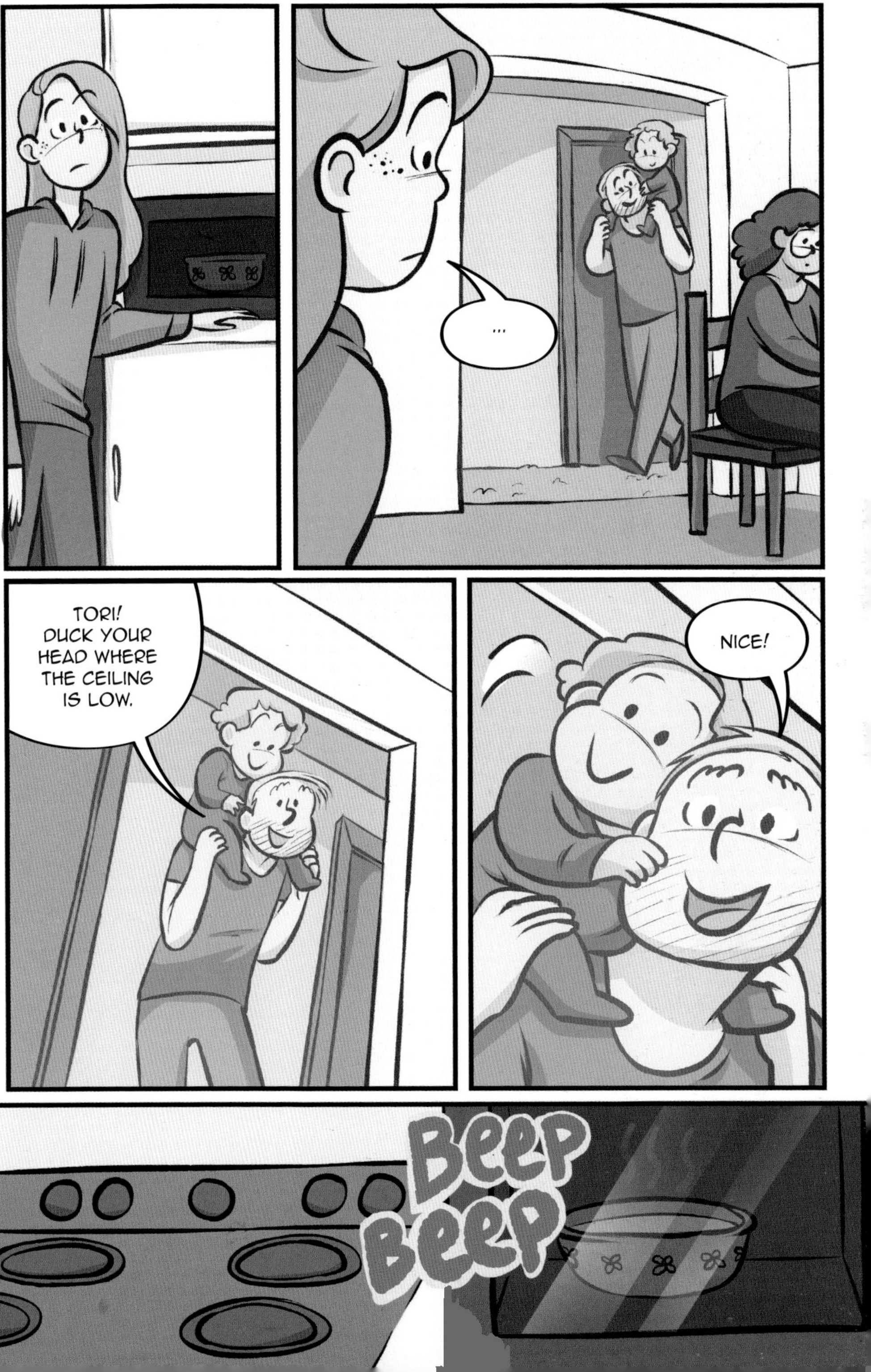
...
TORI! DUCK YOUR HEAD WHERE THE CEILING IS LOW.
NICE!
Beep Beep

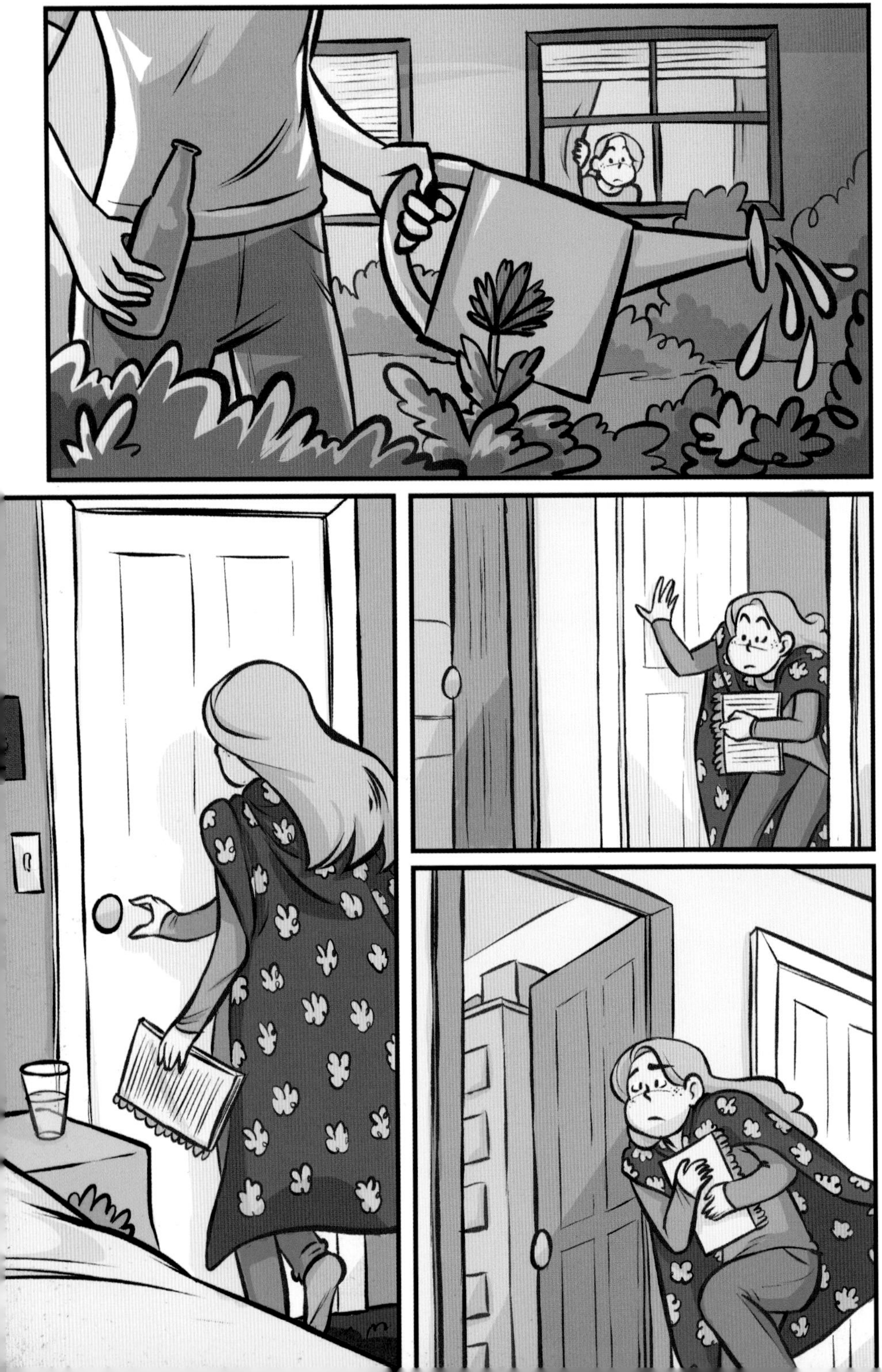

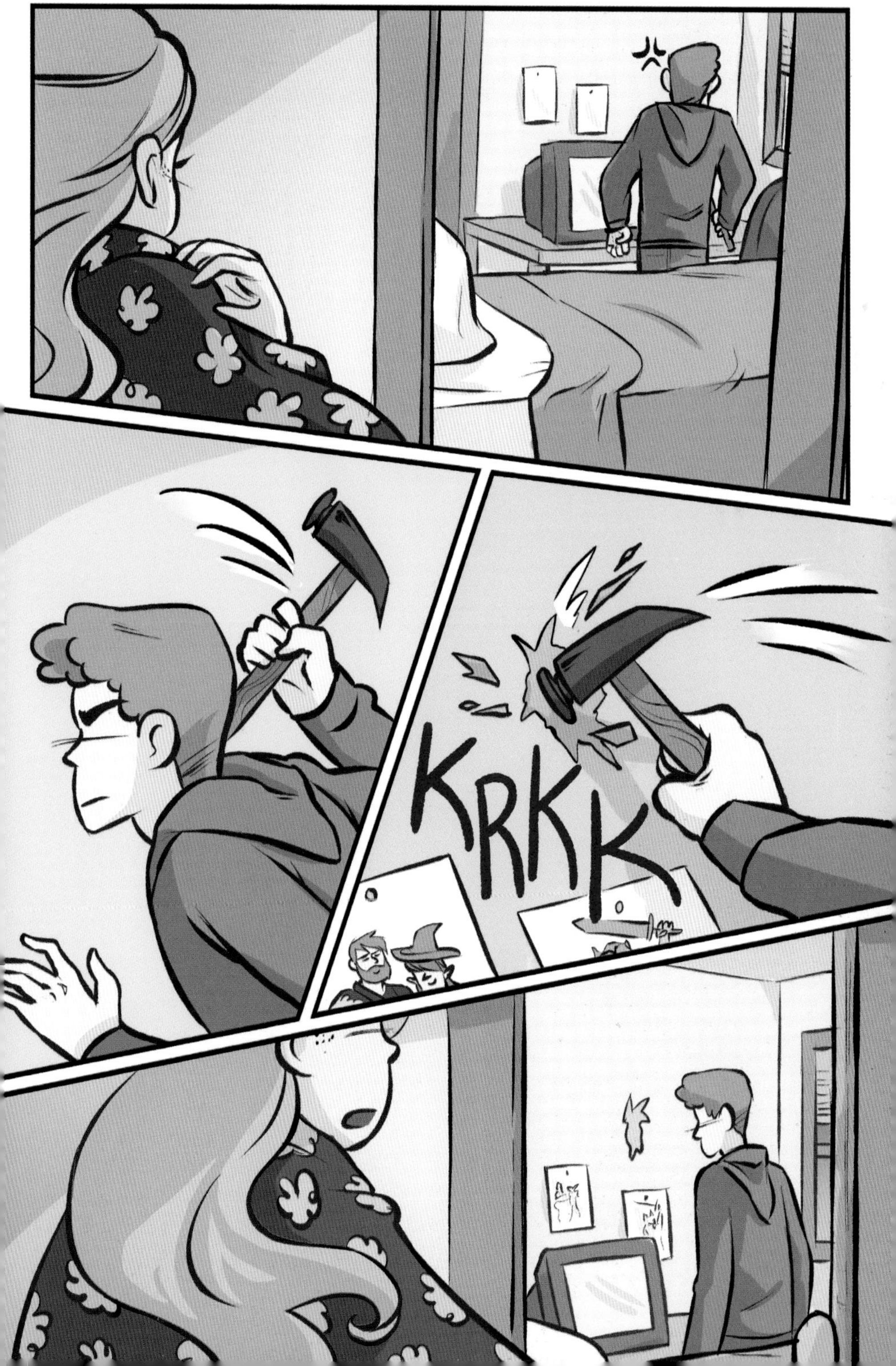
KRKK

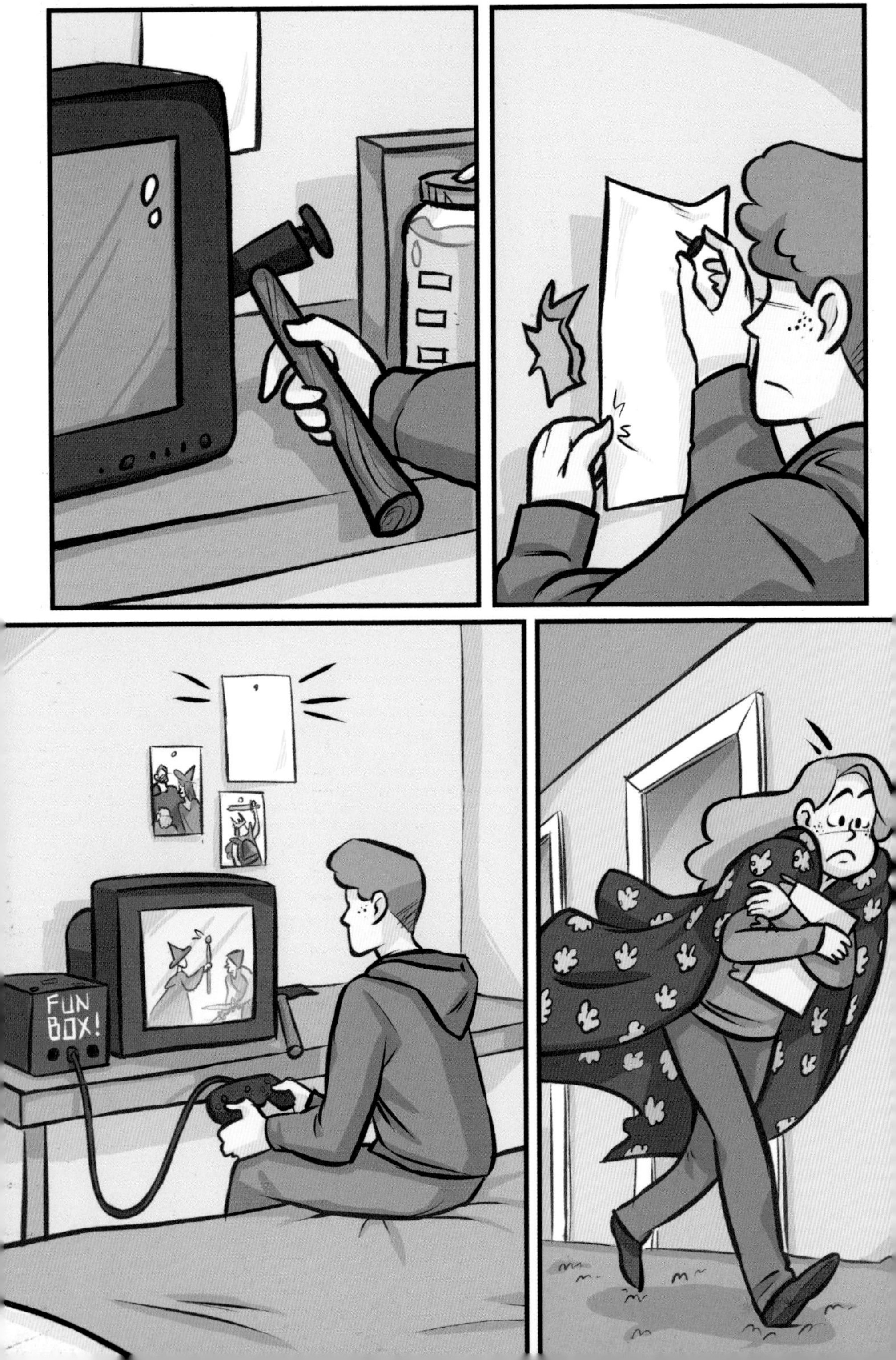
FUN BOX!

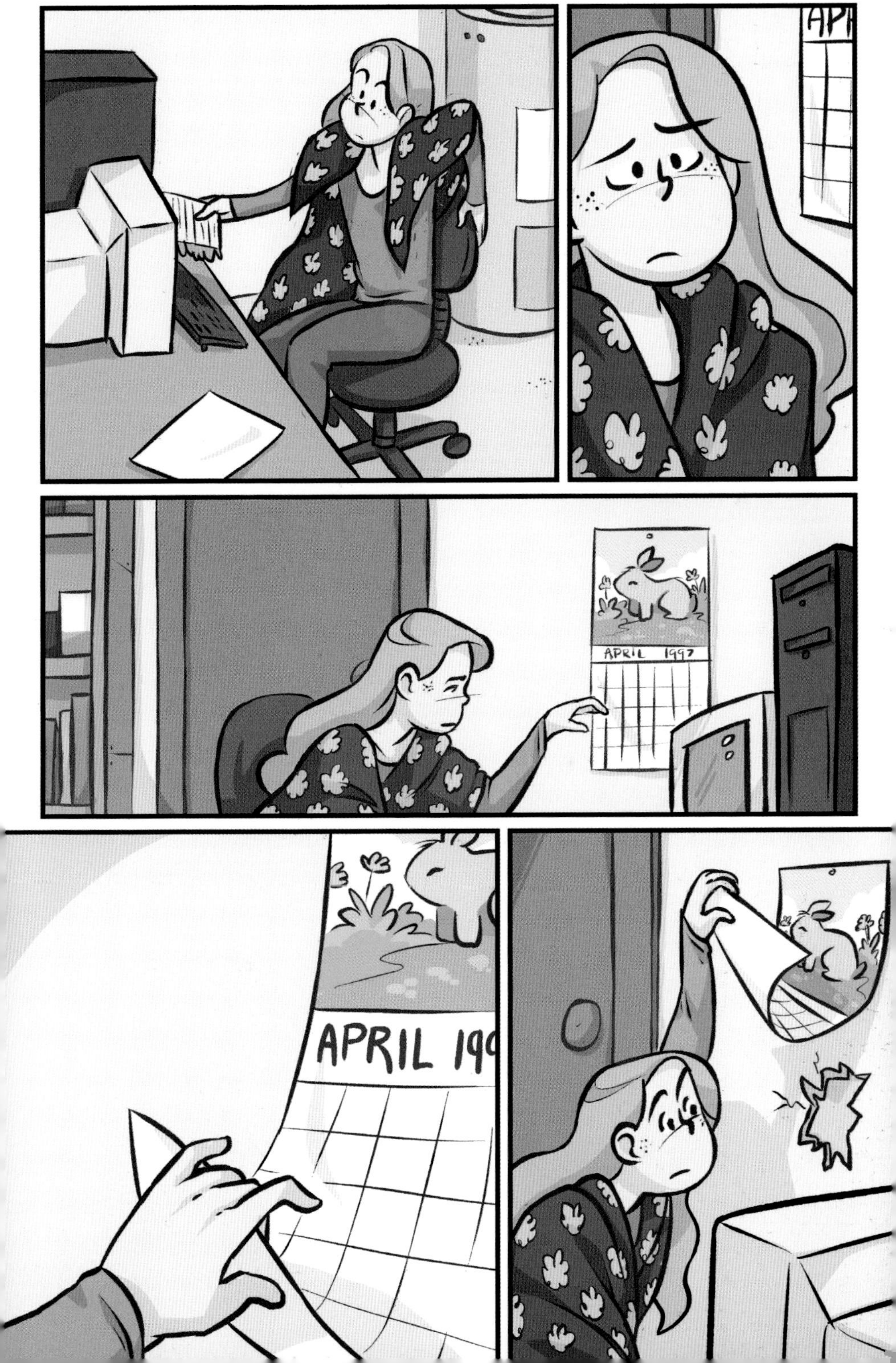
APRIL 1997
APRIL 199

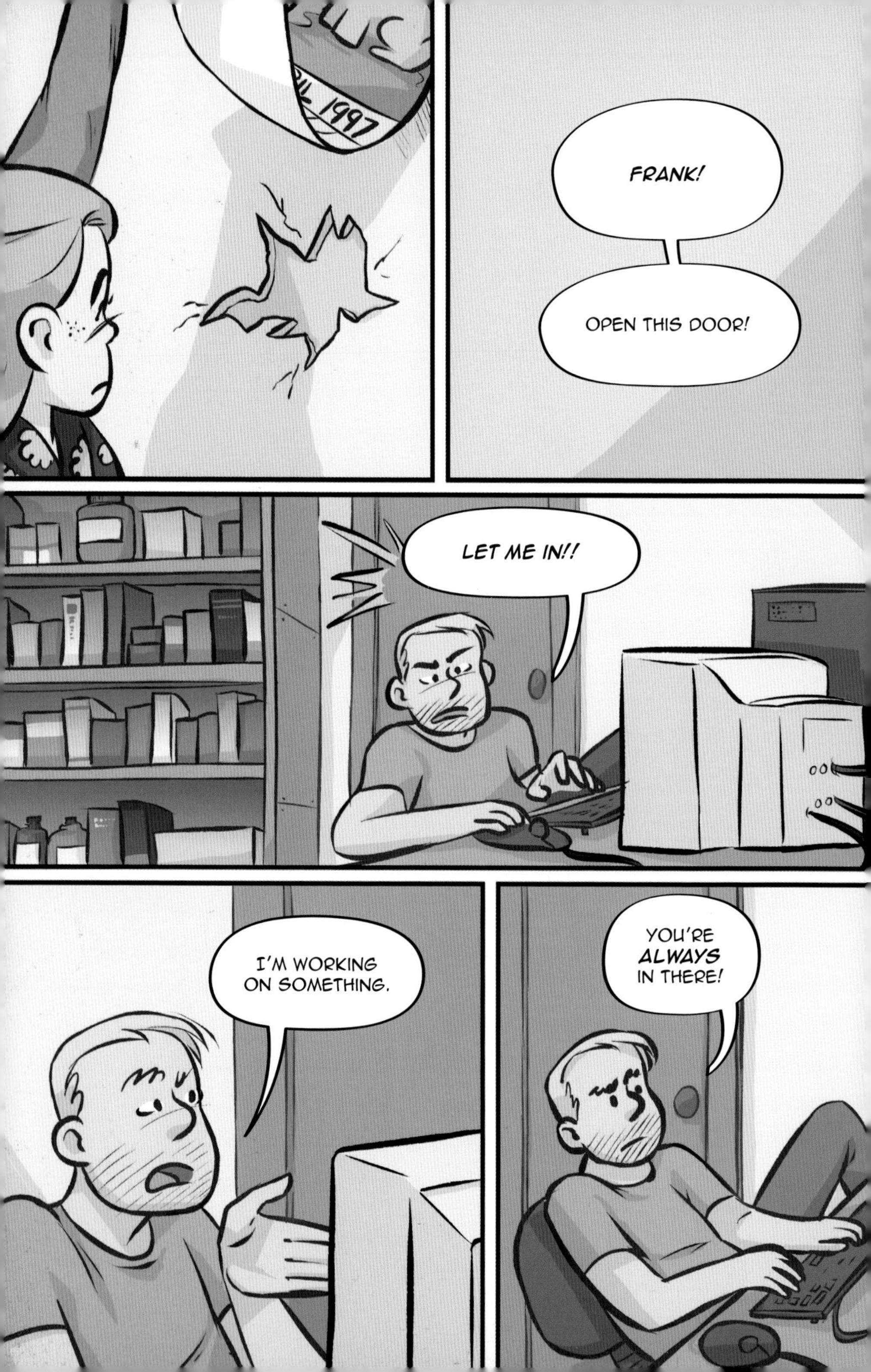
1997
FRANK!
OPEN THIS DOOR!
LET ME IN!!
I'M WORKING ON SOMETHING.
YOU'RE ***ALWAYS*** IN THERE!

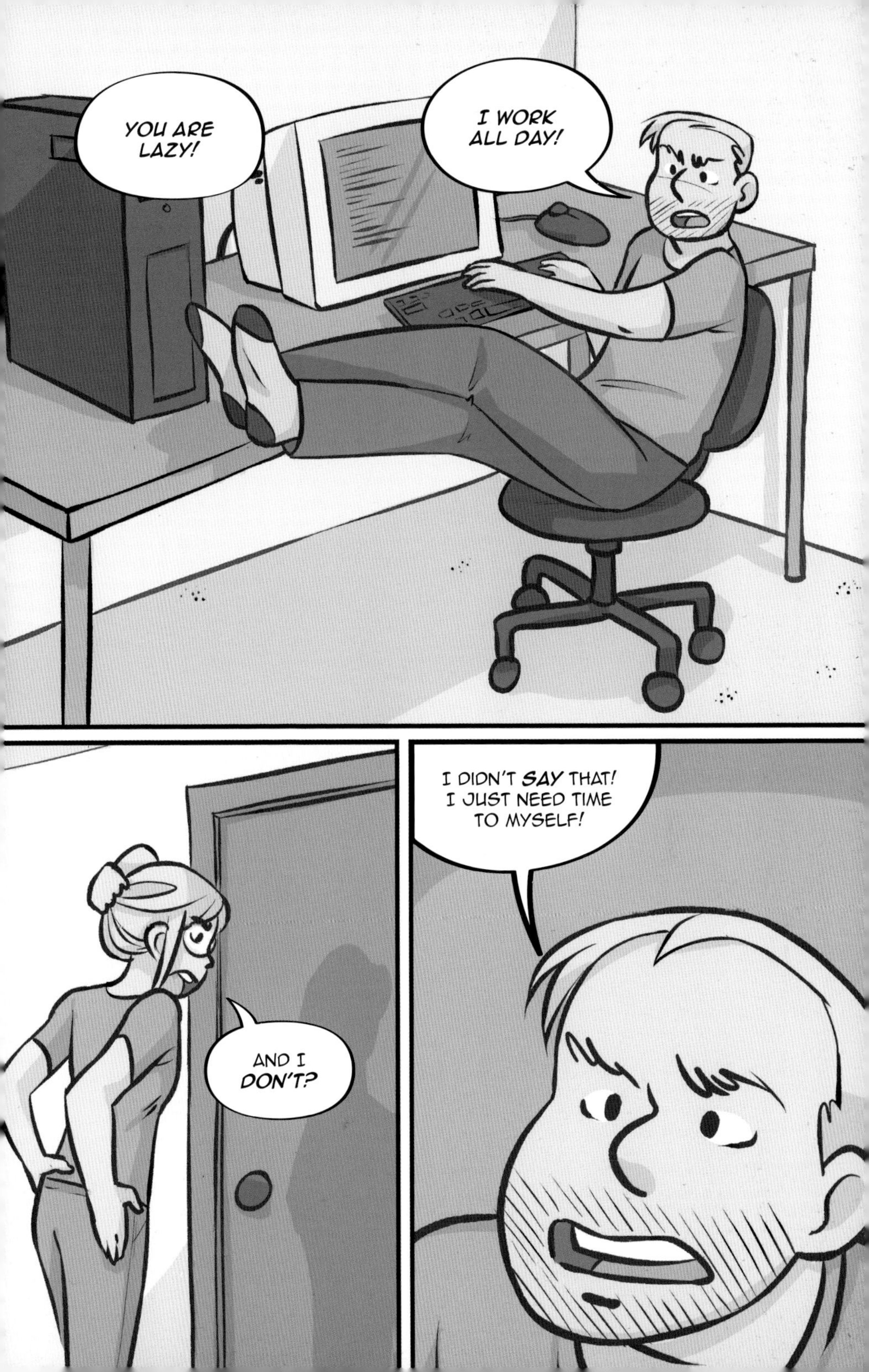
YOU ARE LAZY!
I WORK ALL DAY!
AND I DON'T?
I DIDN'T SAY THAT! I JUST NEED TIME TO MYSELF!

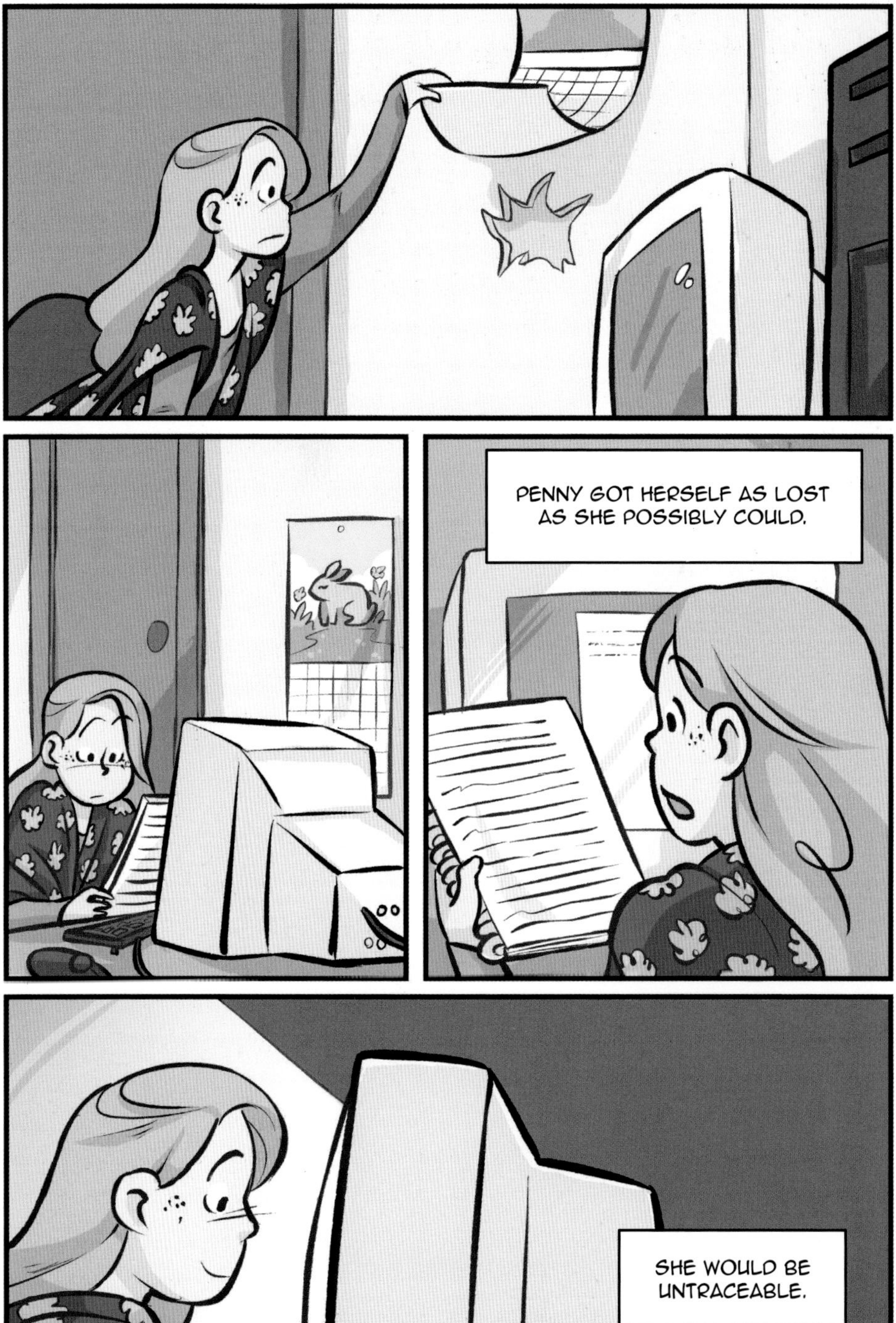
PENNY GOT HERSELF AS LOST AS SHE POSSIBLY COULD.
SHE WOULD BE UNTRACEABLE.

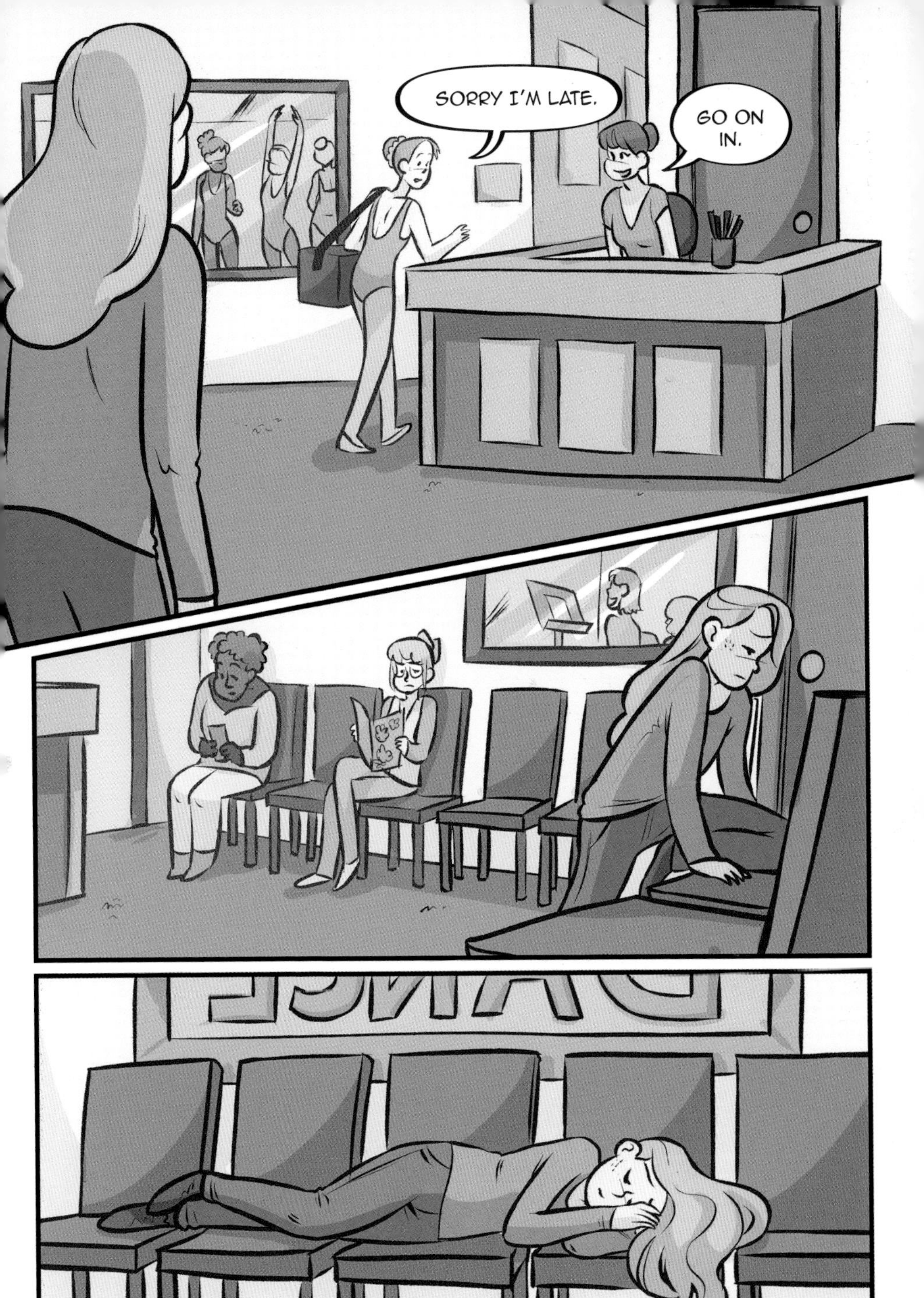
SORRY I'M LATE.
GO ON IN.

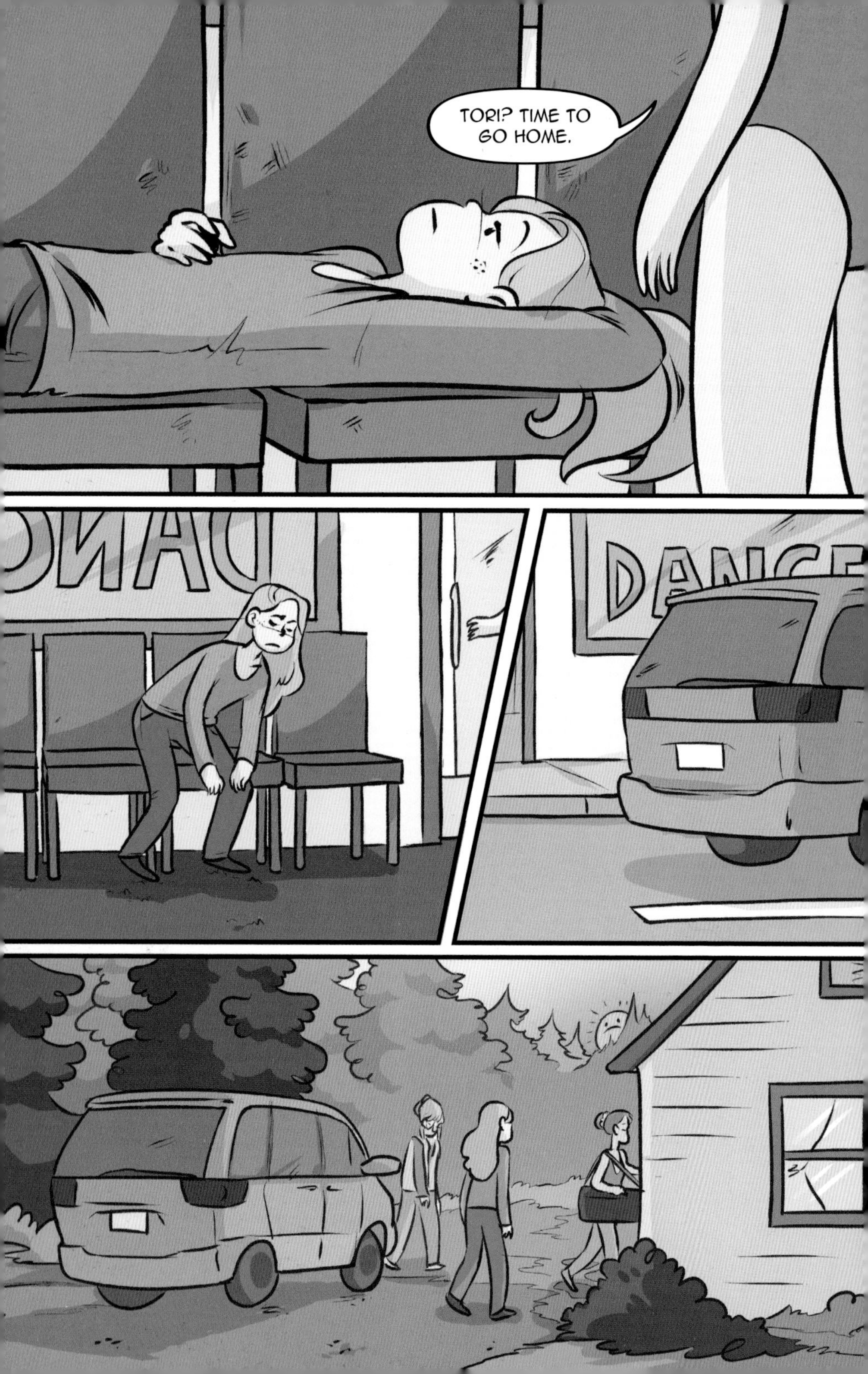
TORI? TIME TO GO HOME.

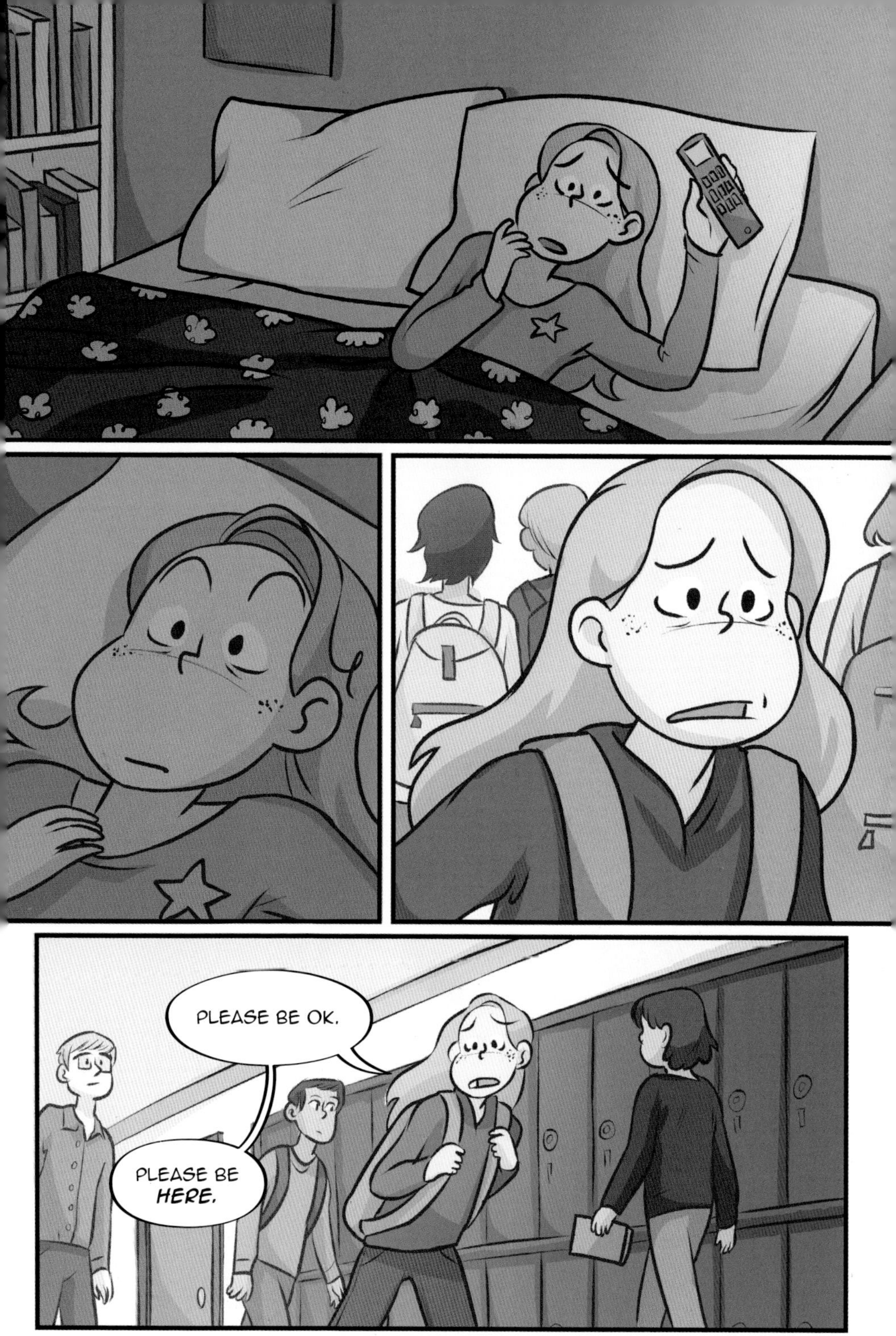

PLEASE BE OK.
PLEASE BE HERE.

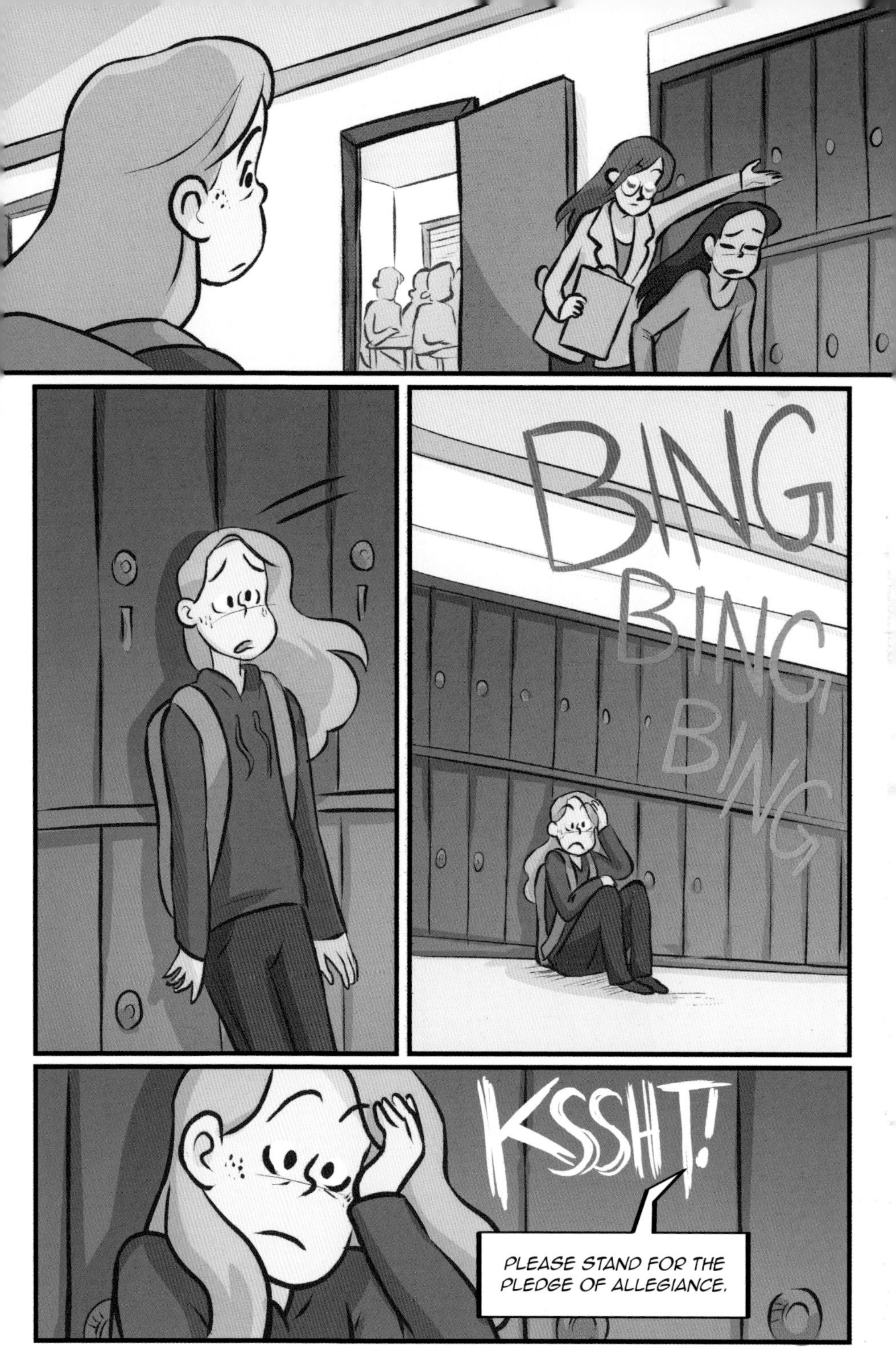
BING
BING
BING
BING
KSSHT!
PLEASE STAND FOR THE PLEDGE OF ALLEGIANCE.

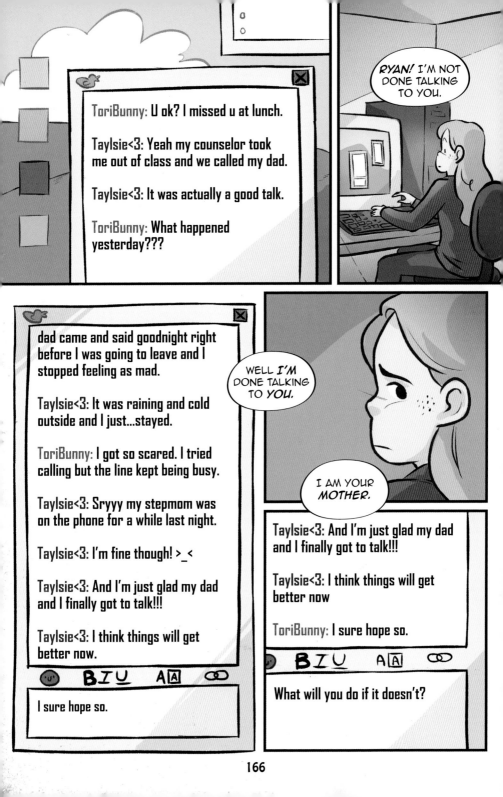

ToriBunny: U ok? I missed u at lunch.

Taylsie<3: Yeah my counselor took me out of class and we called my dad.

Taylsie<3: It was actually a good talk.

ToriBunny: What happened yesterday???

*RYAN!* I'M NOT DONE TALKING TO YOU.

dad came and said goodnight right before I was going to leave and I stopped feeling as mad.

Taylsie<3: It was raining and cold outside and I just...stayed.

ToriBunny: I got so scared. I tried calling but the line kept being busy.

Taylsie<3: Sryyy my stepmom was on the phone for a while last night.

Taylsie<3: I'm fine though! >_<

Taylsie<3: And I'm just glad my dad and I finally got to talk!!!

Taylsie<3: I think things will get better now.

B *I* U    A A    ∞

I sure hope so.

WELL *I'M* DONE TALKING TO *YOU.*

I AM YOUR *MOTHER.*

Taylsie<3: And I'm just glad my dad and I finally got to talk!!!

Taylsie<3: I think things will get better now

ToriBunny: I sure hope so.

B *I* U    A A    ∞

What will you do if it doesn't?

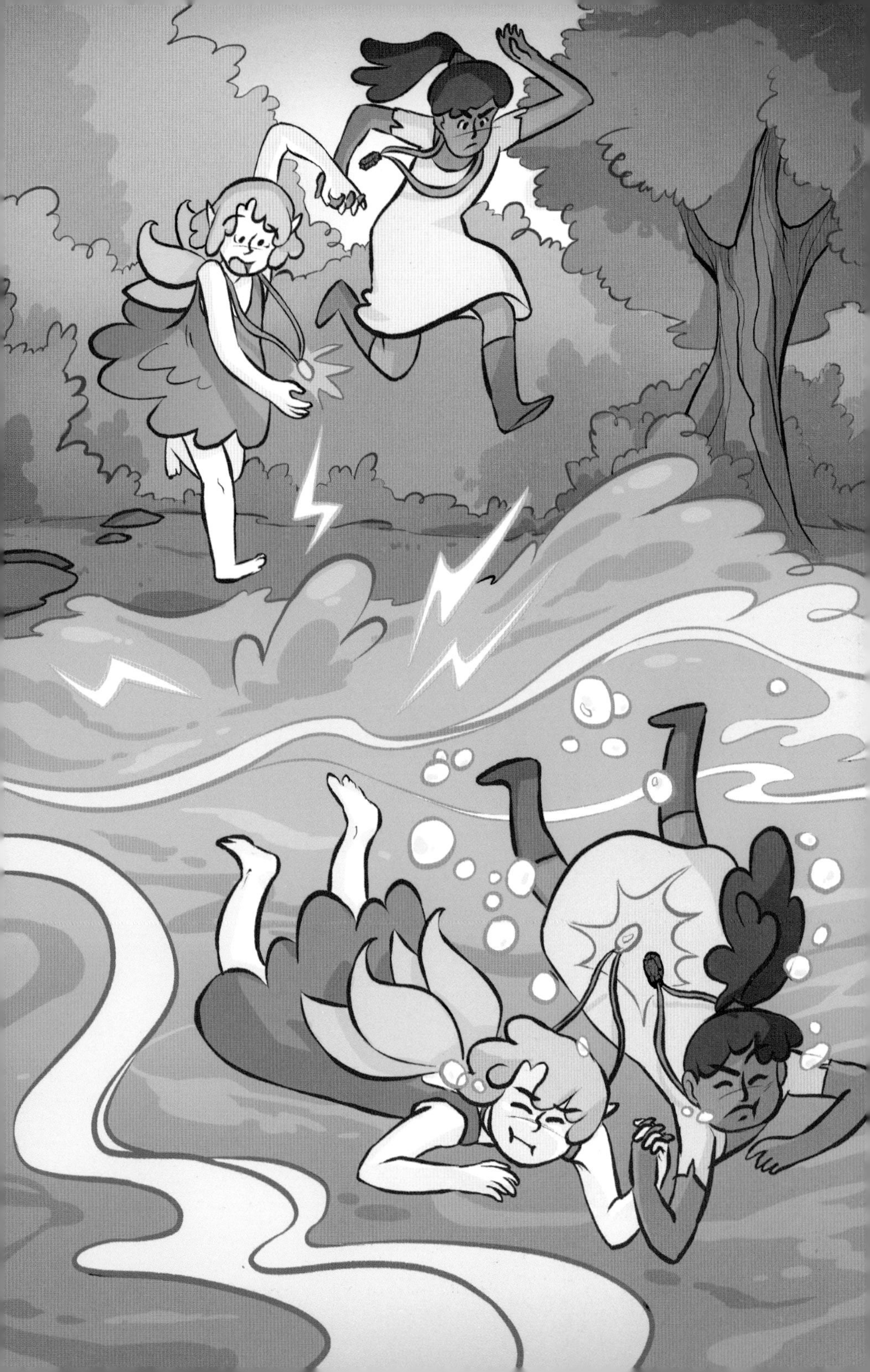

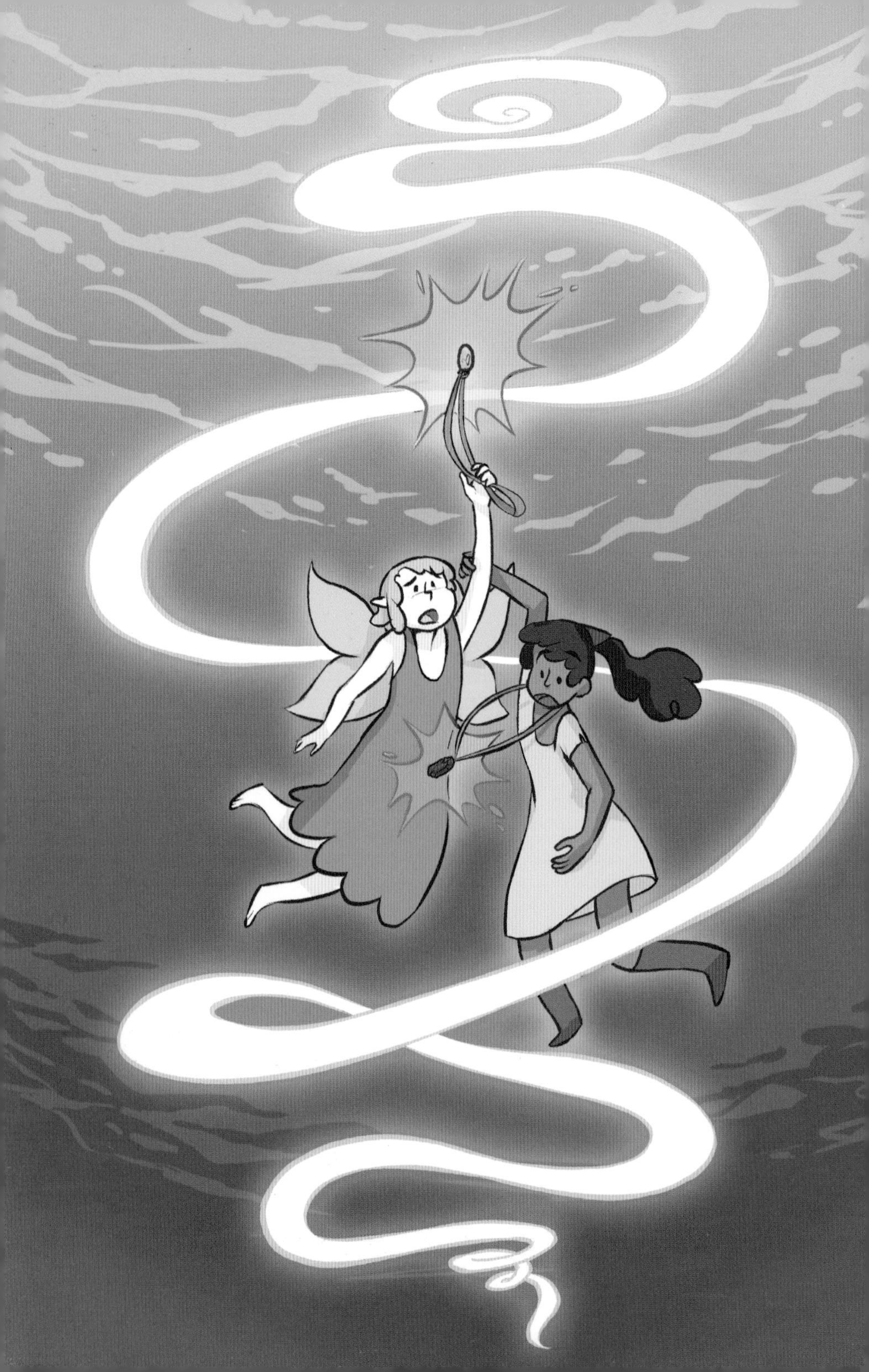

173

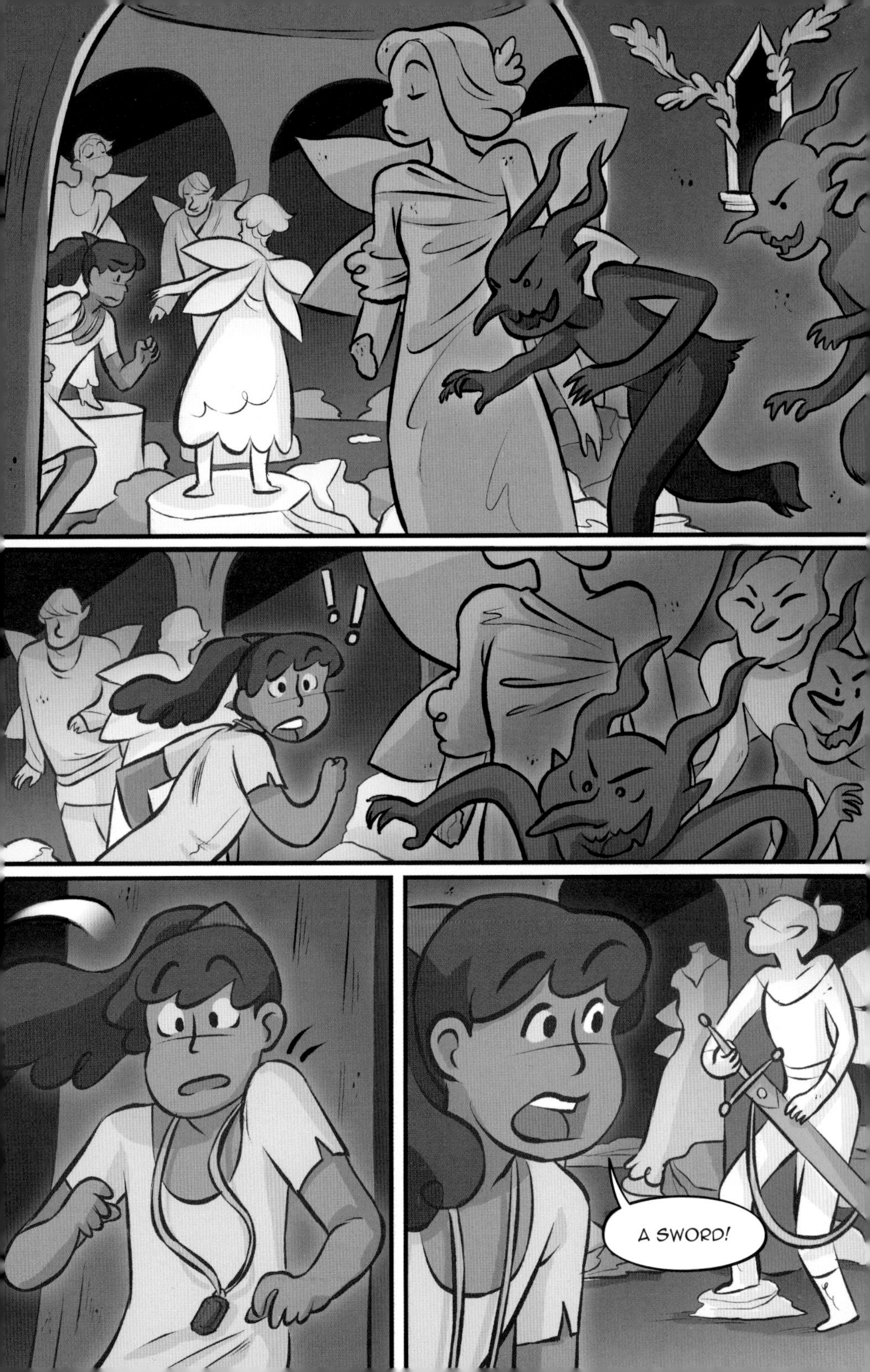
A SWORD!

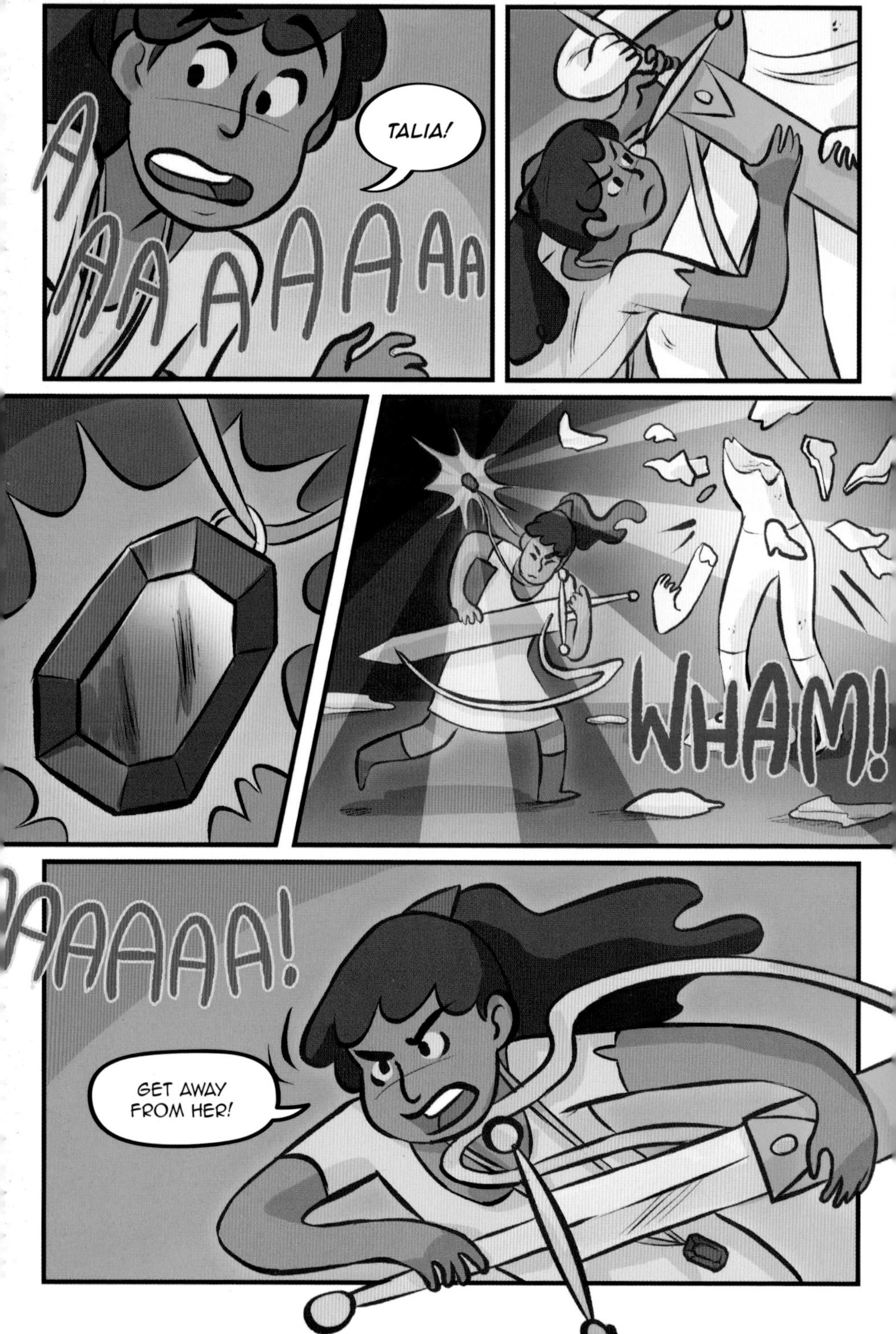

TALIA!
AAAAAAAAA
WHAM!
AAAAAA!
GET AWAY FROM HER!

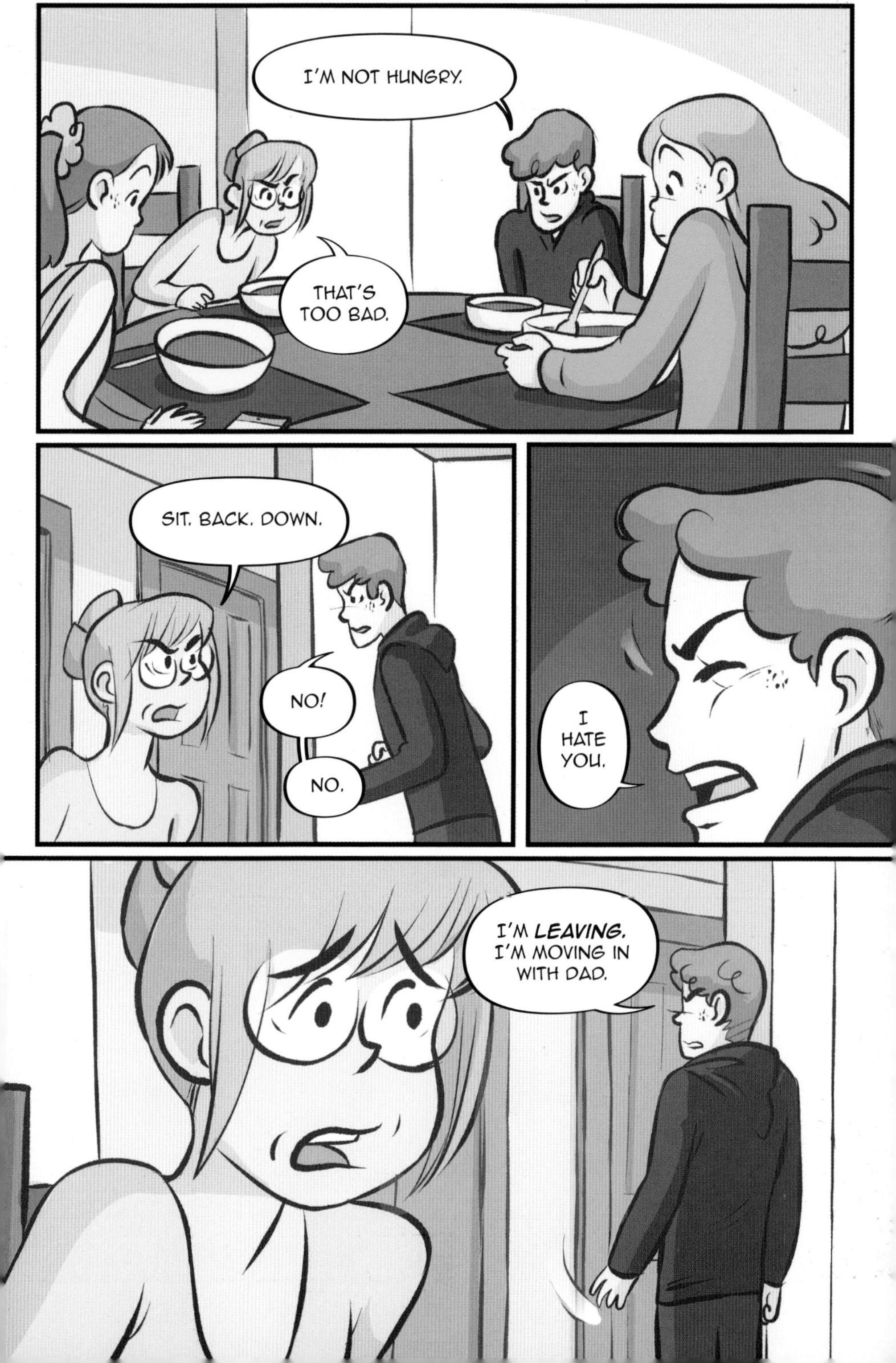
I'M NOT HUNGRY.
THAT'S TOO BAD.
SIT. BACK. DOWN.
NO!
NO.
I HATE YOU.
I'M LEAVING. I'M MOVING IN WITH DAD.

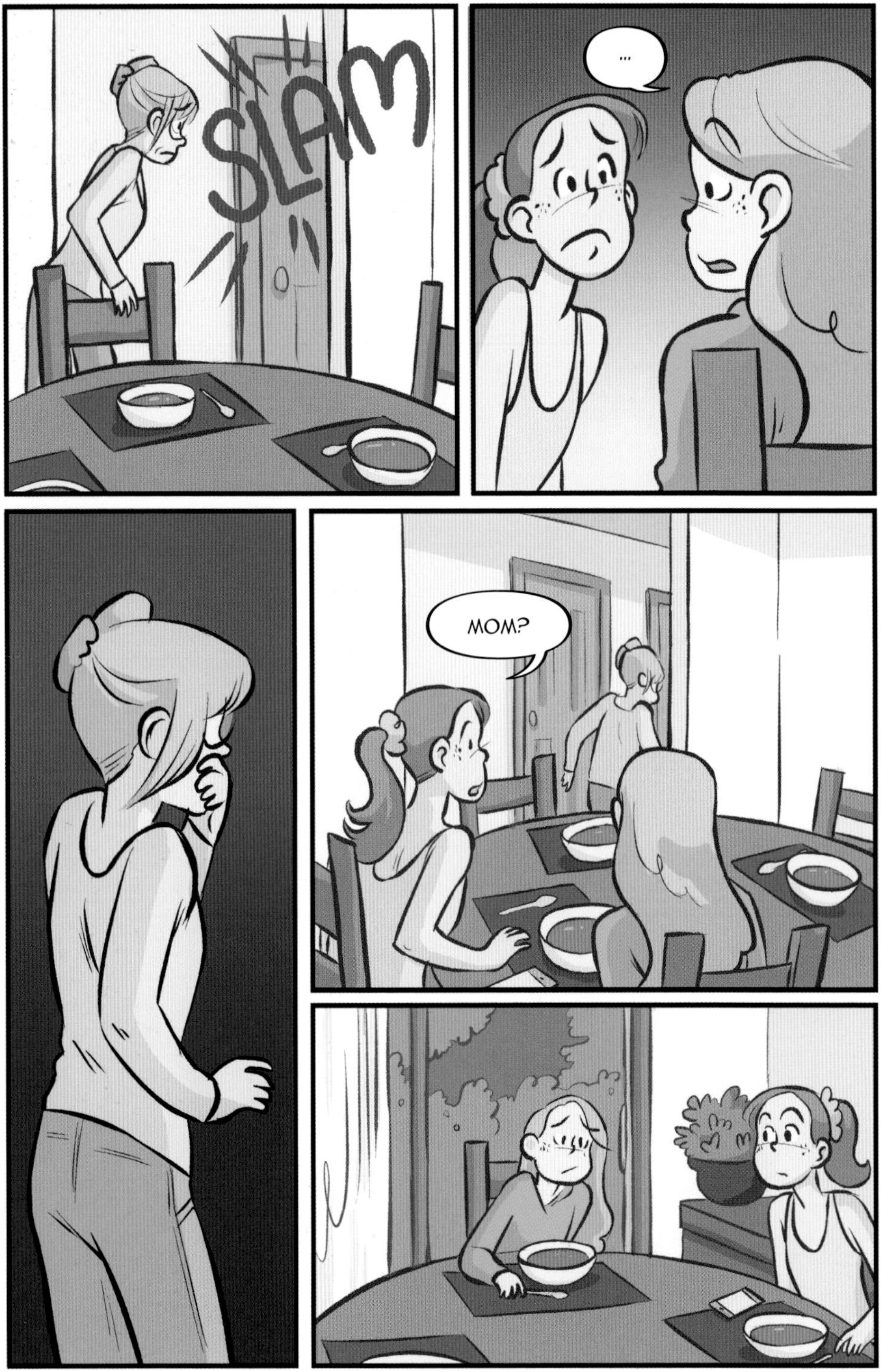
SLAM
...
MOM?

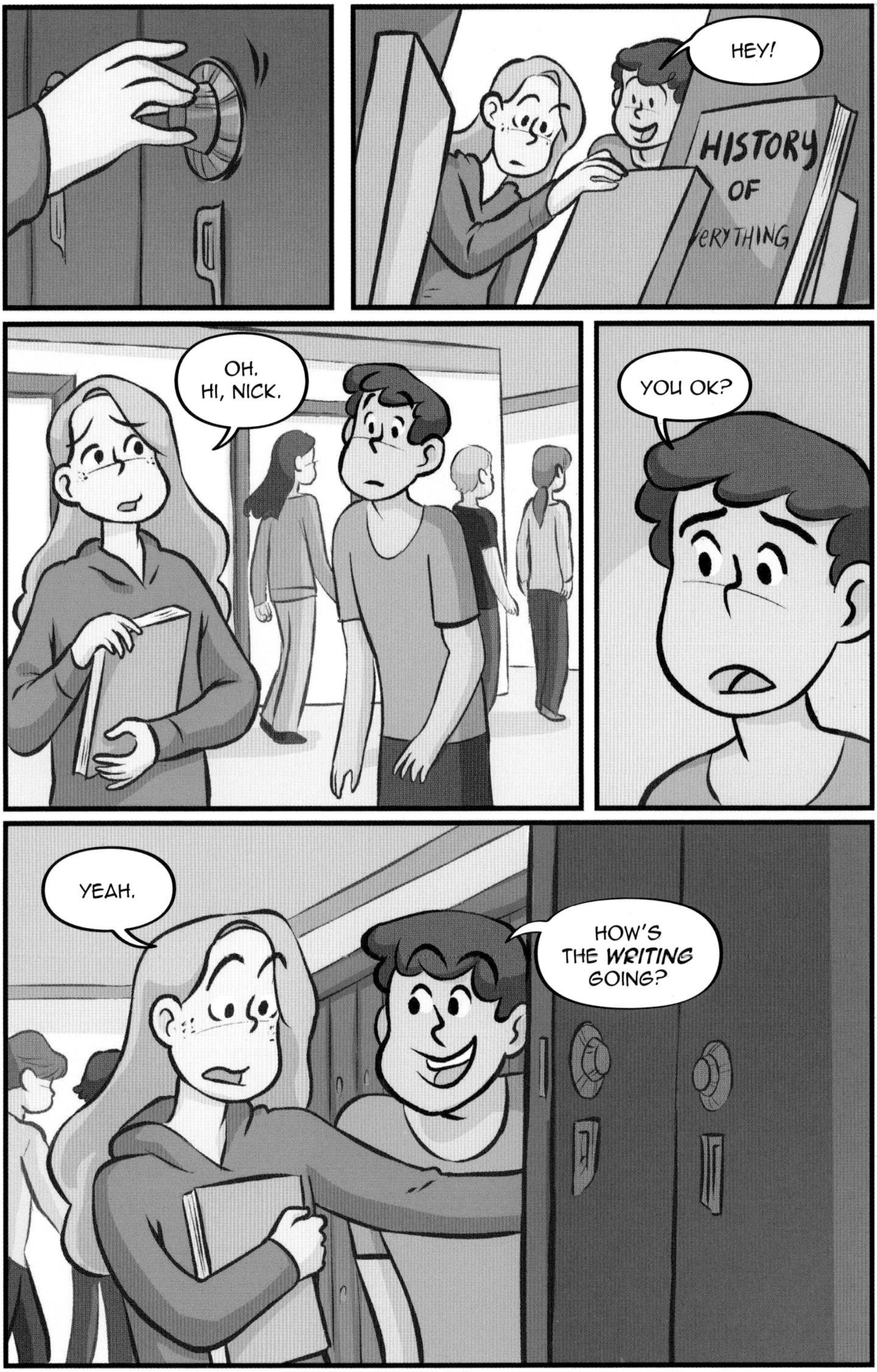
HEY!
HISTORY OF
ERYTHING
OH. HI, NICK.
YOU OK?
YEAH.
HOW'S THE *WRITING* GOING?

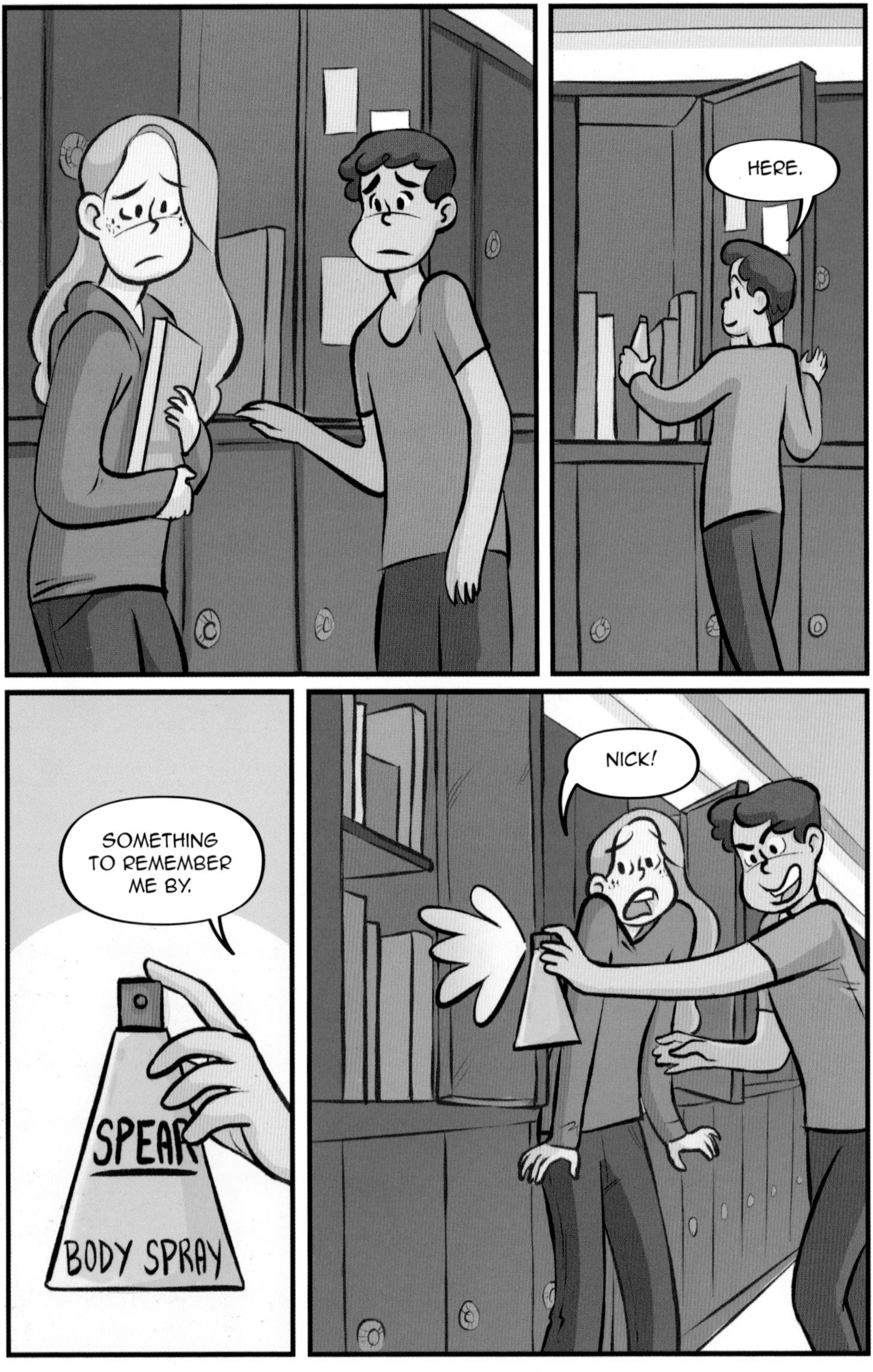
HERE.
SOMETHING TO REMEMBER ME BY.
SPEAR
BODY SPRAY
NICK!

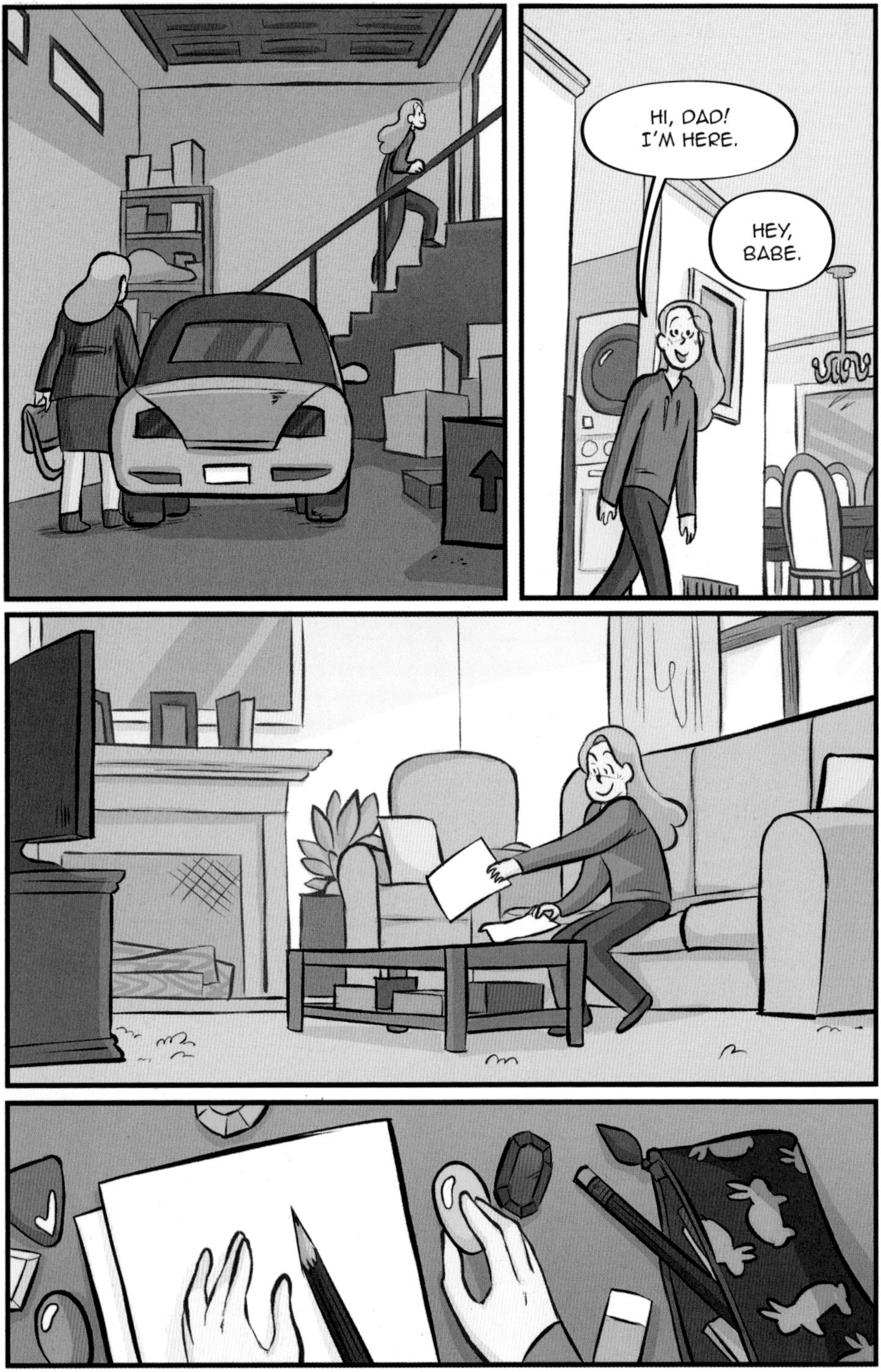
HI, DAD!
I'M HERE.
HEY,
BABE.

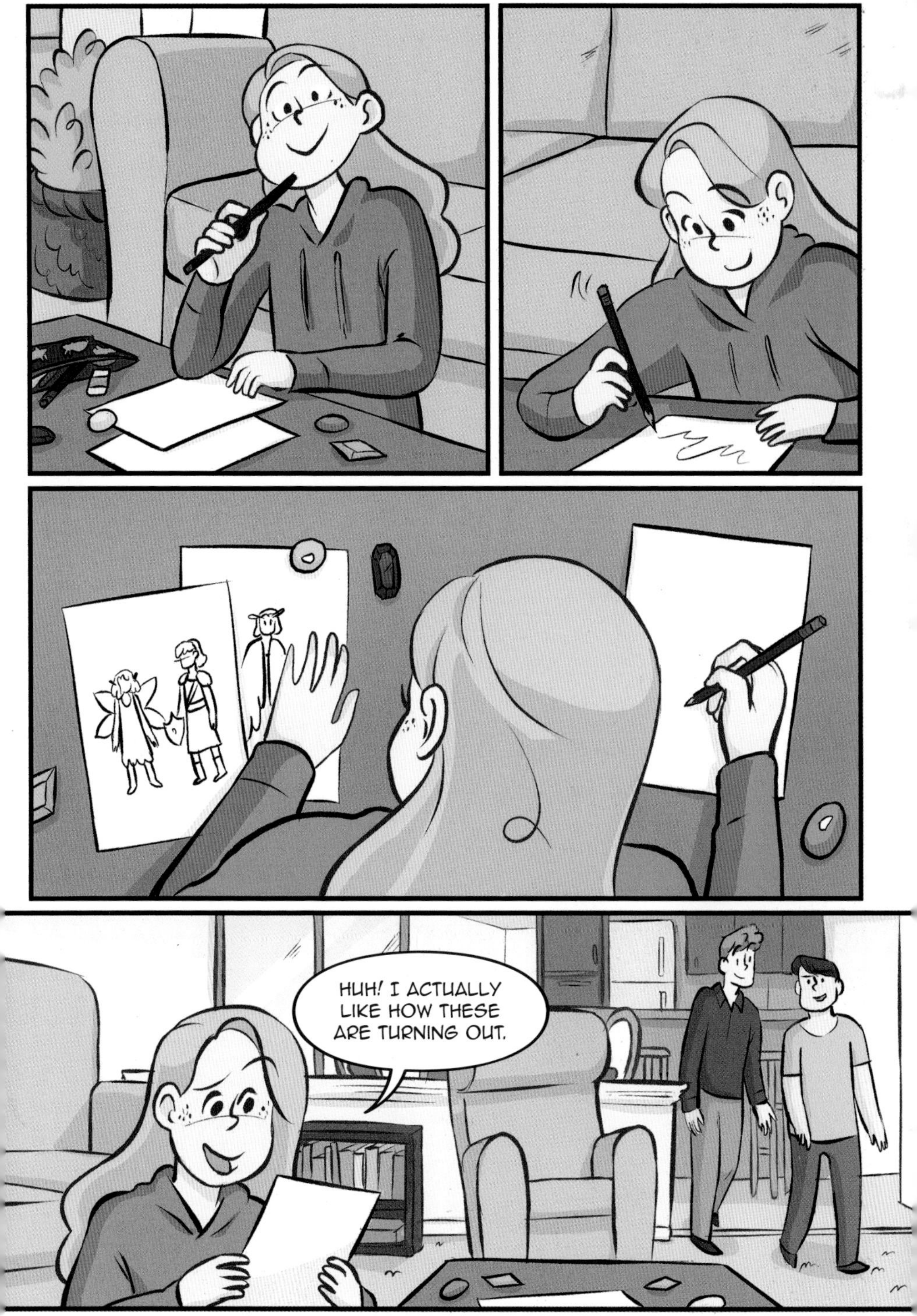
HUH! I ACTUALLY LIKE HOW THESE ARE TURNING OUT.

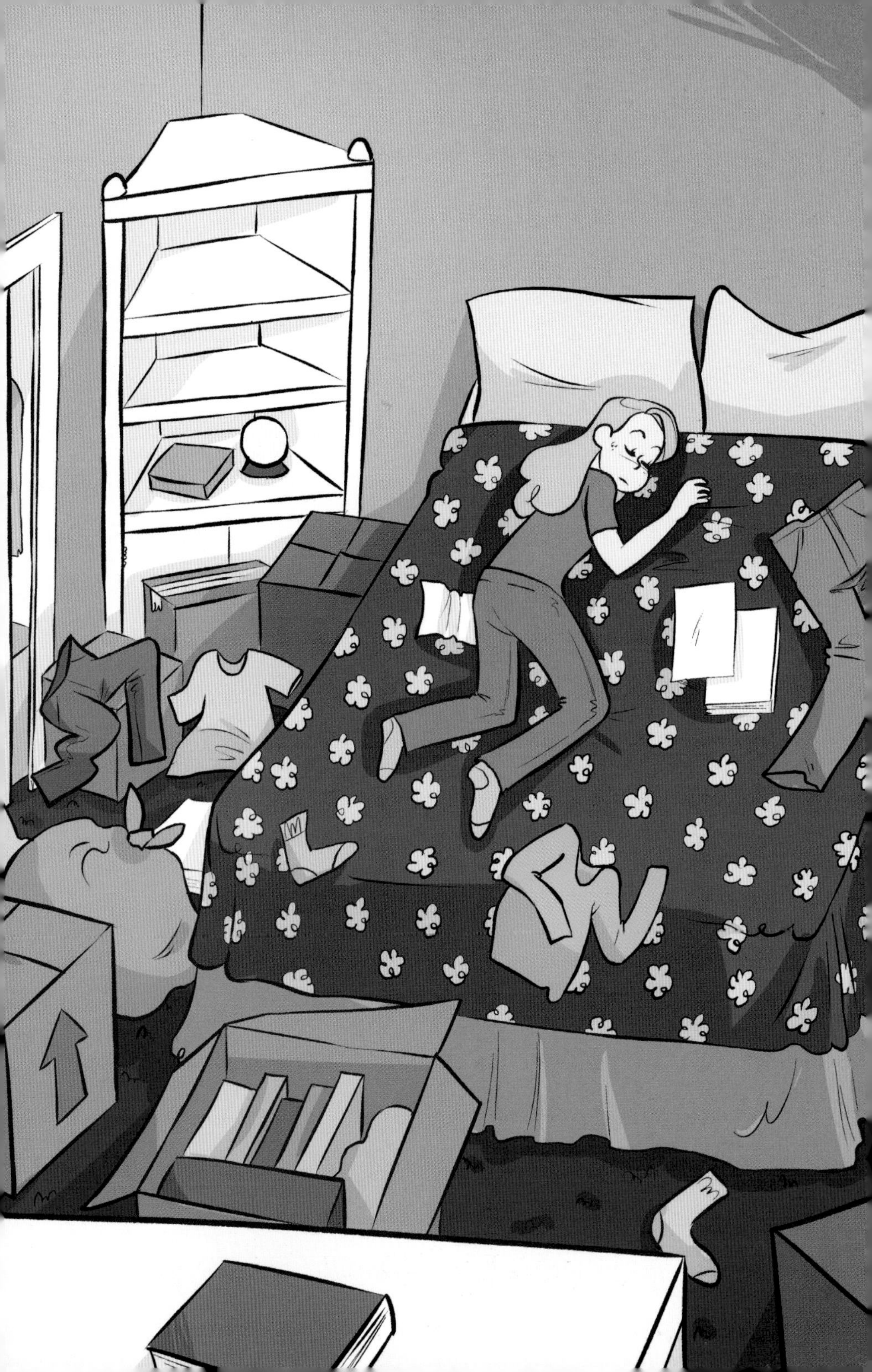

211

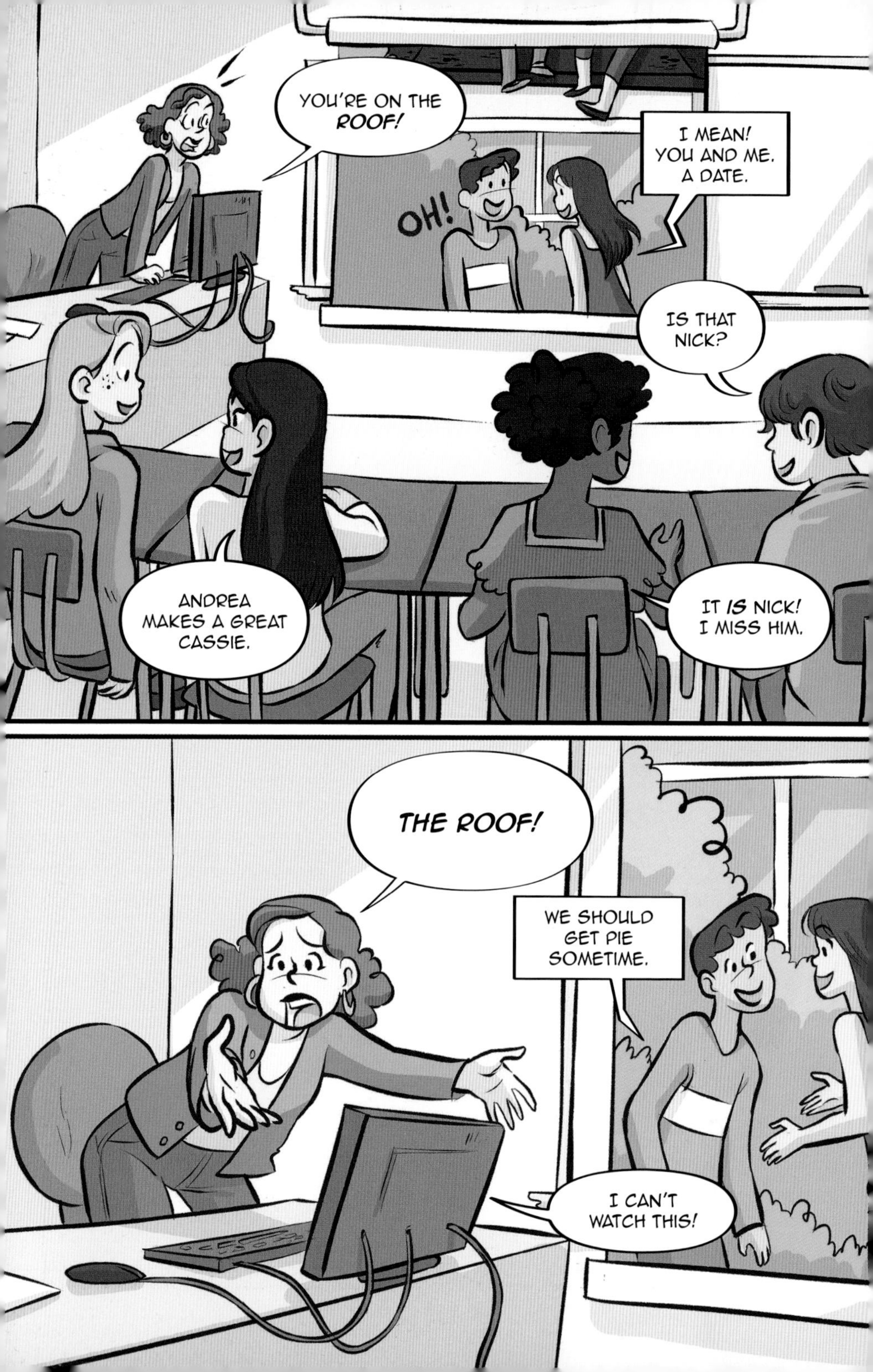
YOU'RE ON THE *ROOF!*
OH!
I MEAN! YOU AND ME. A DATE.
IS THAT NICK?
ANDREA MAKES A GREAT CASSIE.
IT *IS* NICK! I MISS HIM.
*THE ROOF!*
WE SHOULD GET PIE SOMETIME.
I CAN'T WATCH THIS!

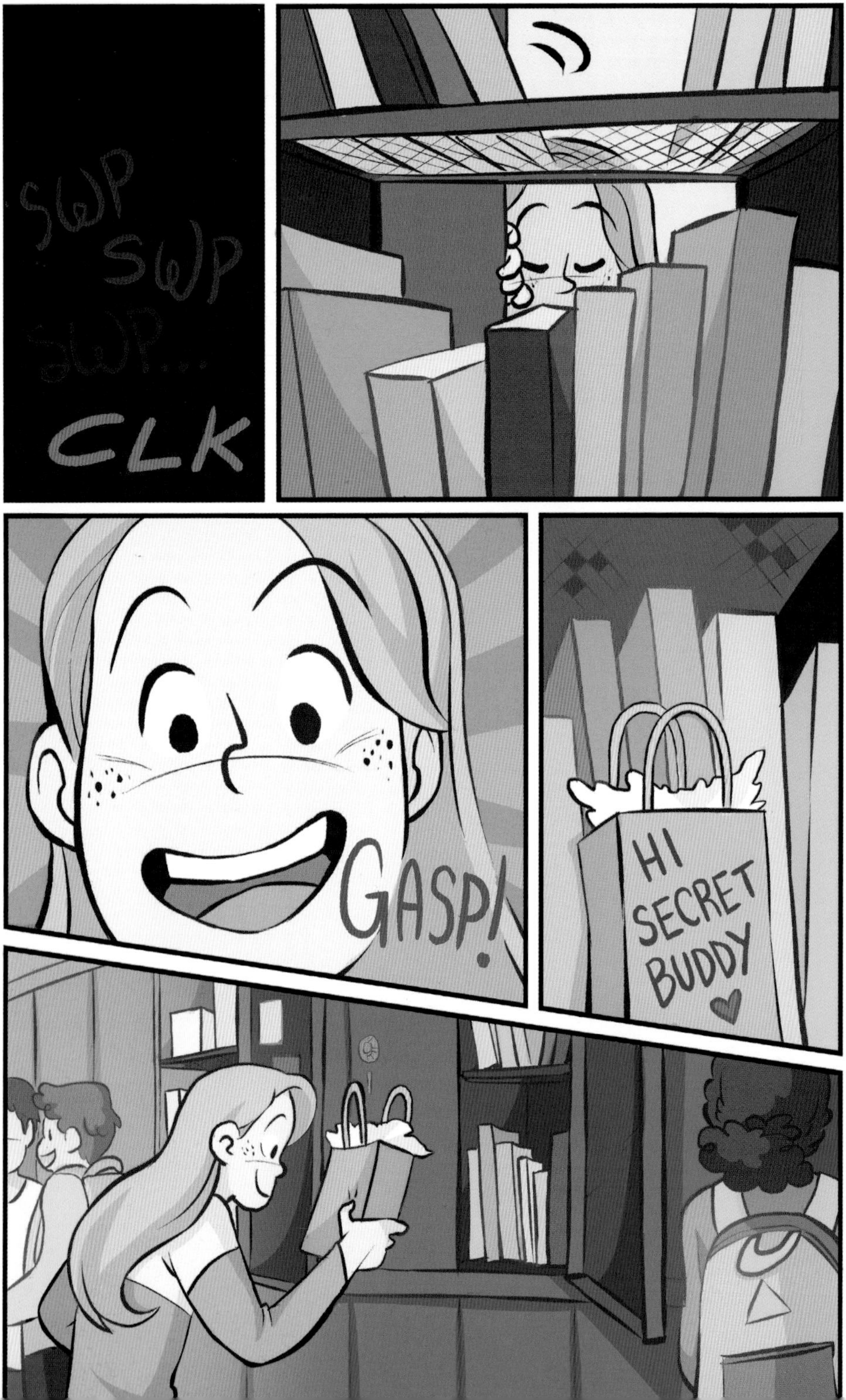
SWP
SWP
SWP...
CLK
GASP!
HI SECRET BUDDY

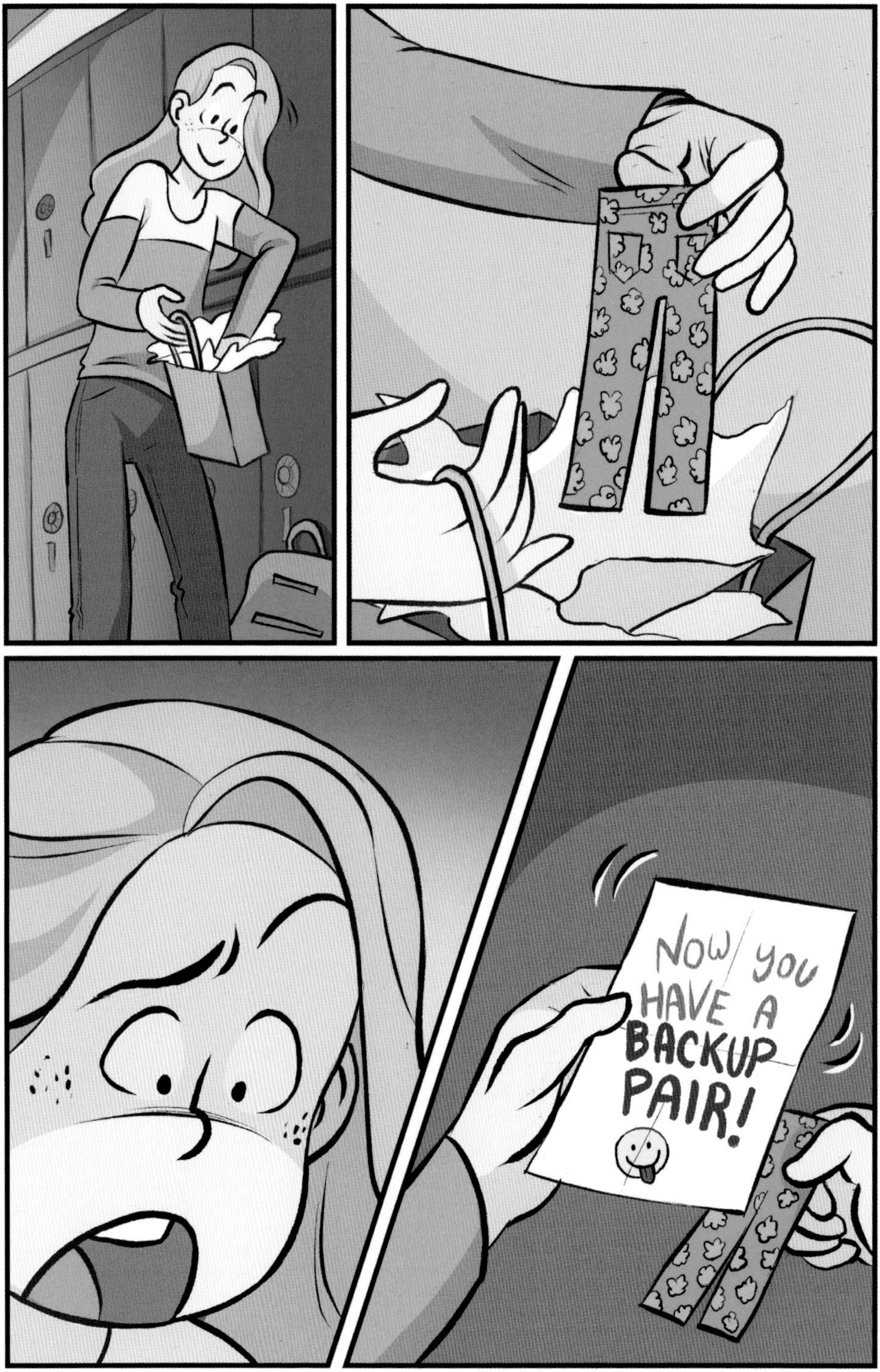
NOW YOU HAVE A BACKUP PAIR!

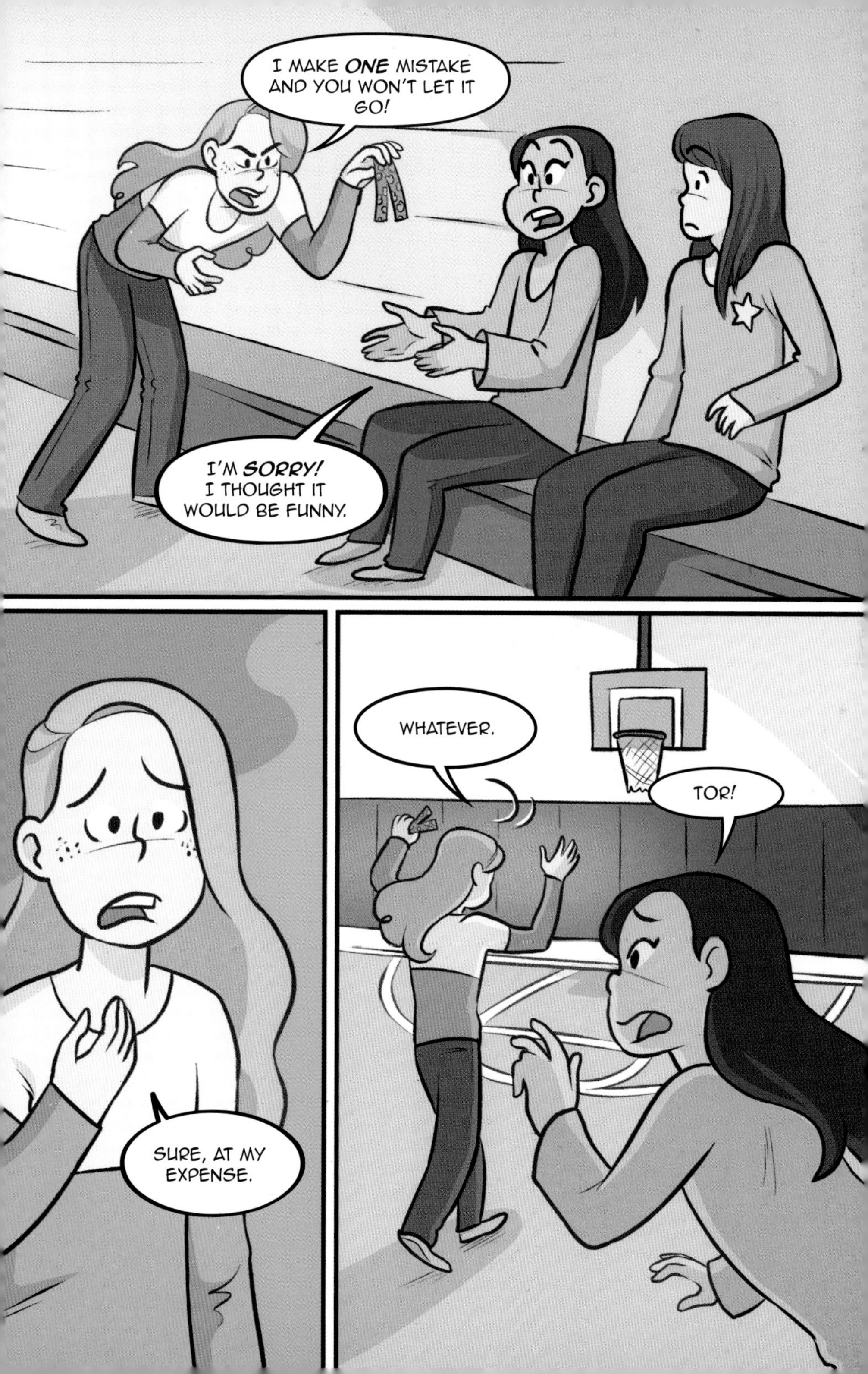
I MAKE ONE MISTAKE AND YOU WON'T LET IT GO!
I'M SORRY! I THOUGHT IT WOULD BE FUNNY.
SURE, AT MY EXPENSE.
WHATEVER.
TOR!

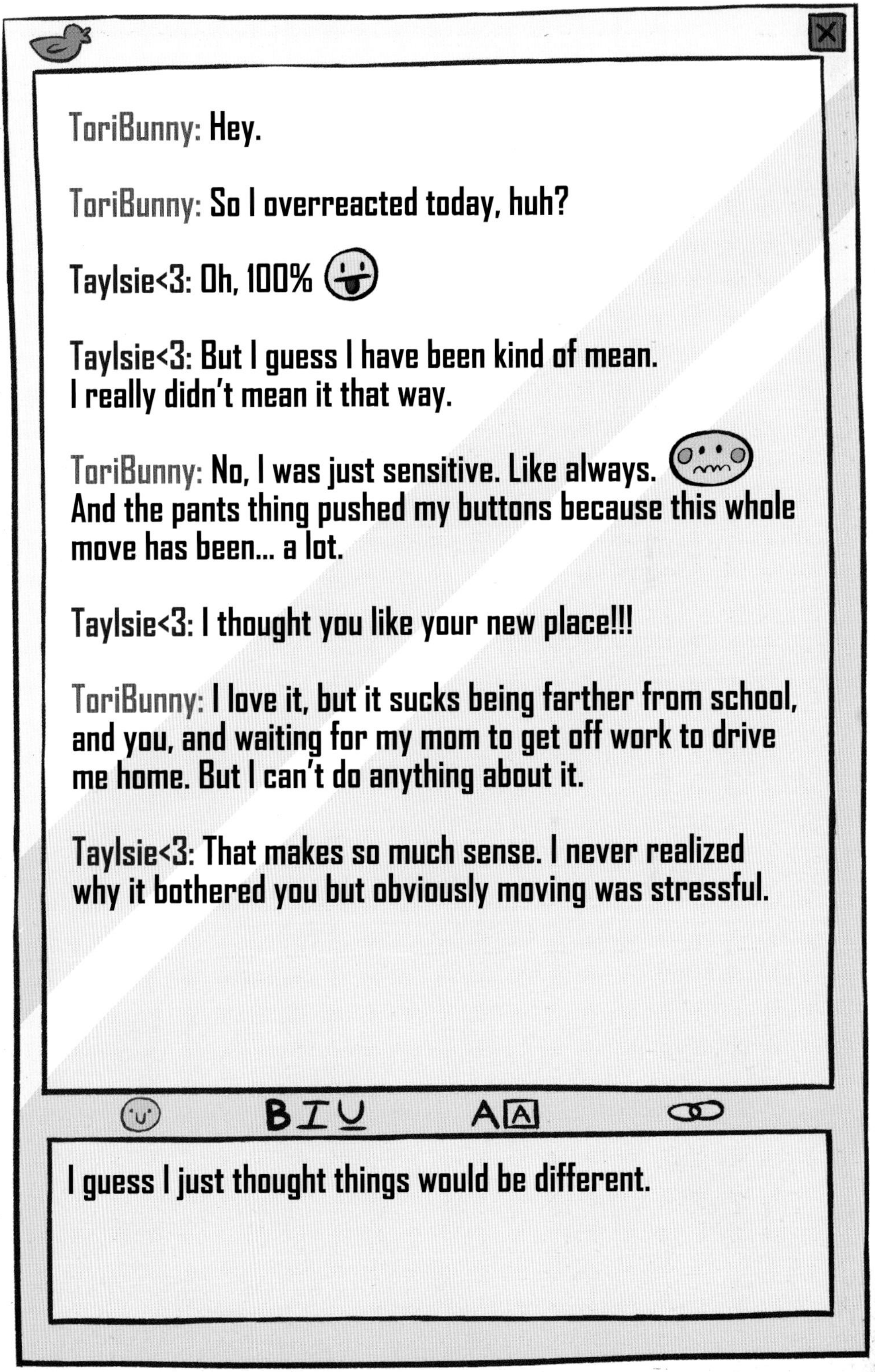
ToriBunny: Hey.
ToriBunny: So I overreacted today, huh?
Taylsie<3: Oh, 100%
Taylsie<3: But I guess I have been kind of mean. I really didn't mean it that way.
ToriBunny: No, I was just sensitive. Like always. And the pants thing pushed my buttons because this whole move has been... a lot.
Taylsie<3: I thought you like your new place!!!
ToriBunny: I love it, but it sucks being farther from school, and you, and waiting for my mom to get off work to drive me home. But I can't do anything about it.
Taylsie<3: That makes so much sense. I never realized why it bothered you but obviously moving was stressful.
B I U
A A
I guess I just thought things would be different.

233

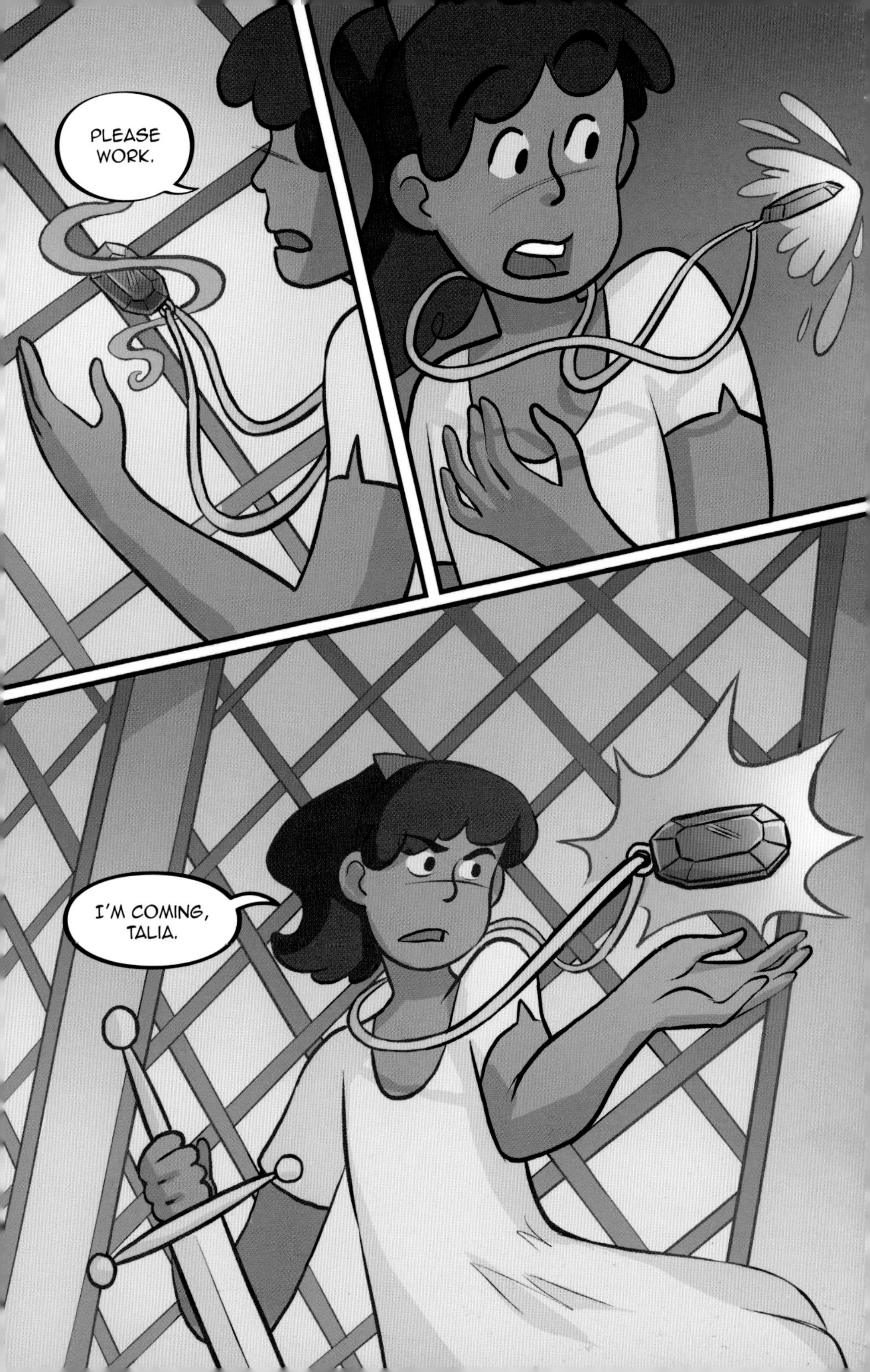
PLEASE WORK.
I'M COMING, TALIA.

238

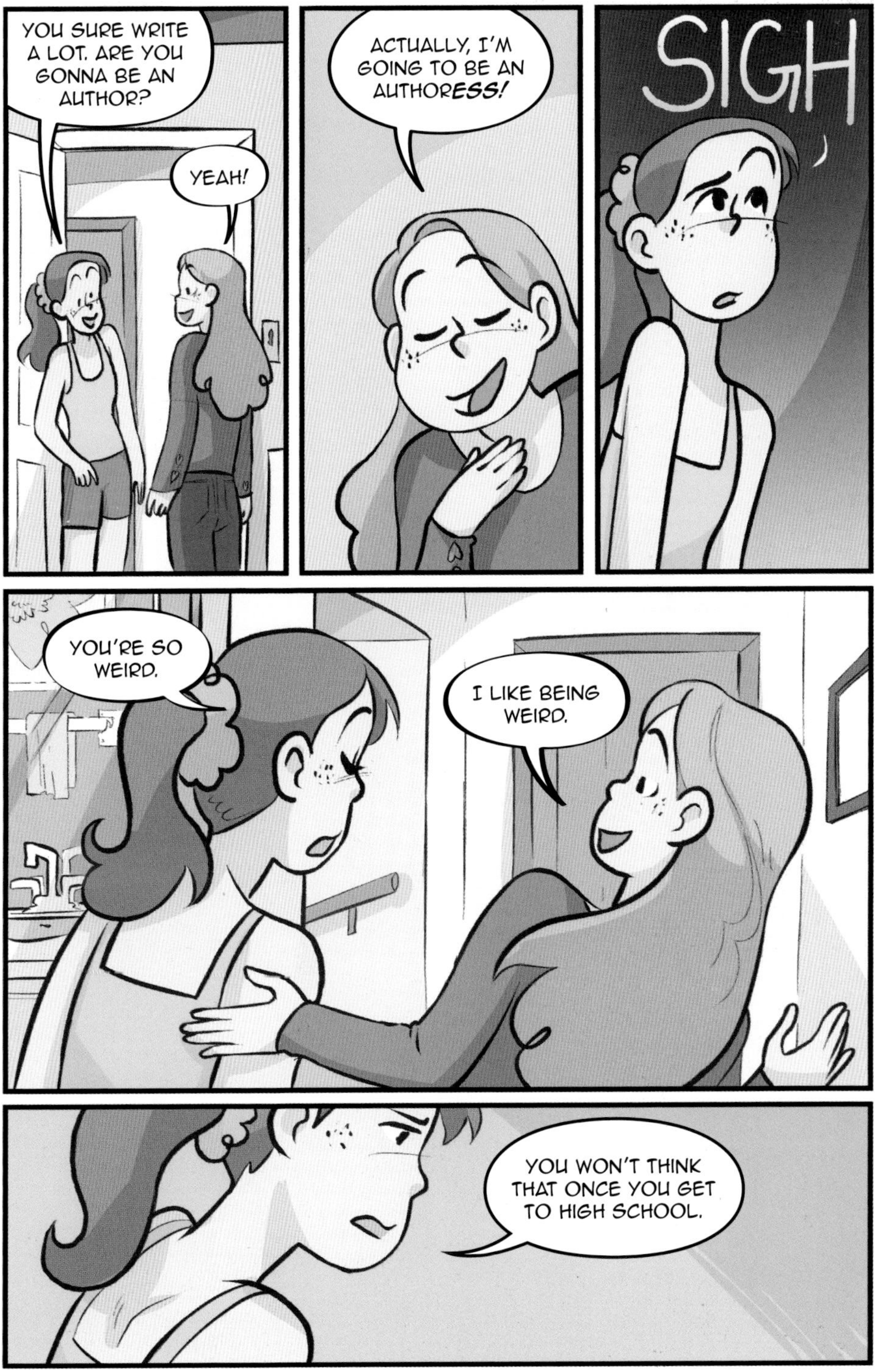
YOU SURE WRITE A LOT. ARE YOU GONNA BE AN AUTHOR?
YEAH!
ACTUALLY, I'M GOING TO BE AN AUTHOR*ESS!*
SIGH
YOU'RE SO WEIRD.
I LIKE BEING WEIRD.
YOU WON'T THINK THAT ONCE YOU GET TO HIGH SCHOOL.

251

252

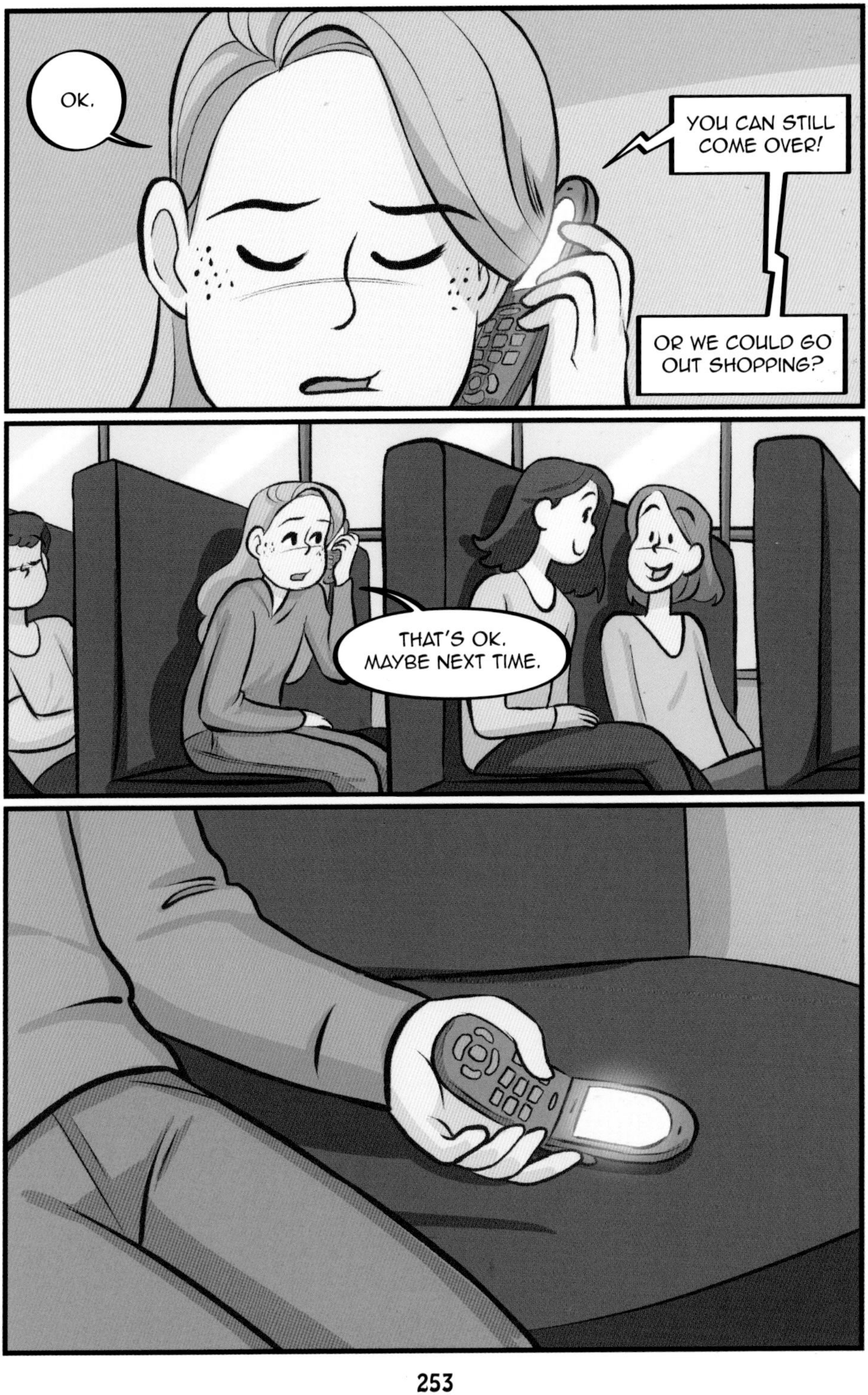
OK.
YOU CAN STILL COME OVER!
OR WE COULD GO OUT SHOPPING?
THAT'S OK. MAYBE NEXT TIME.

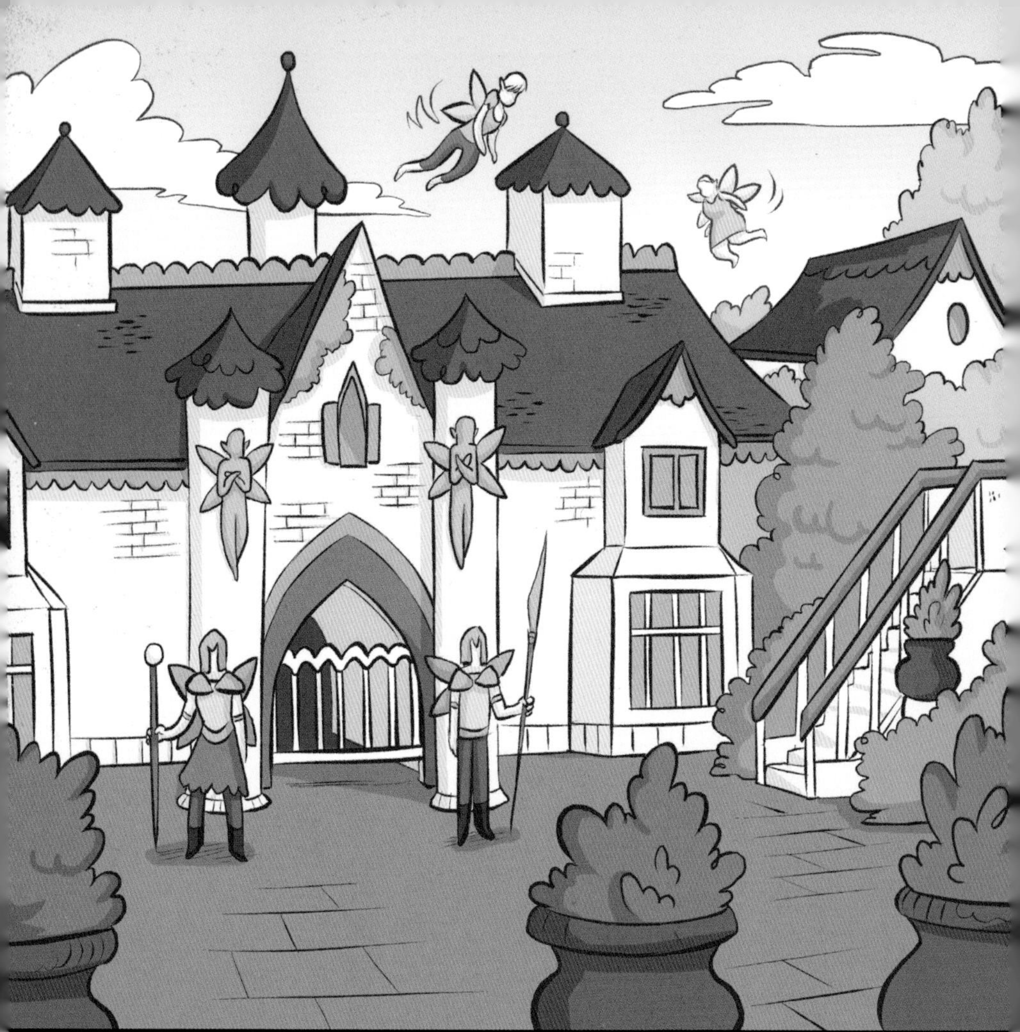

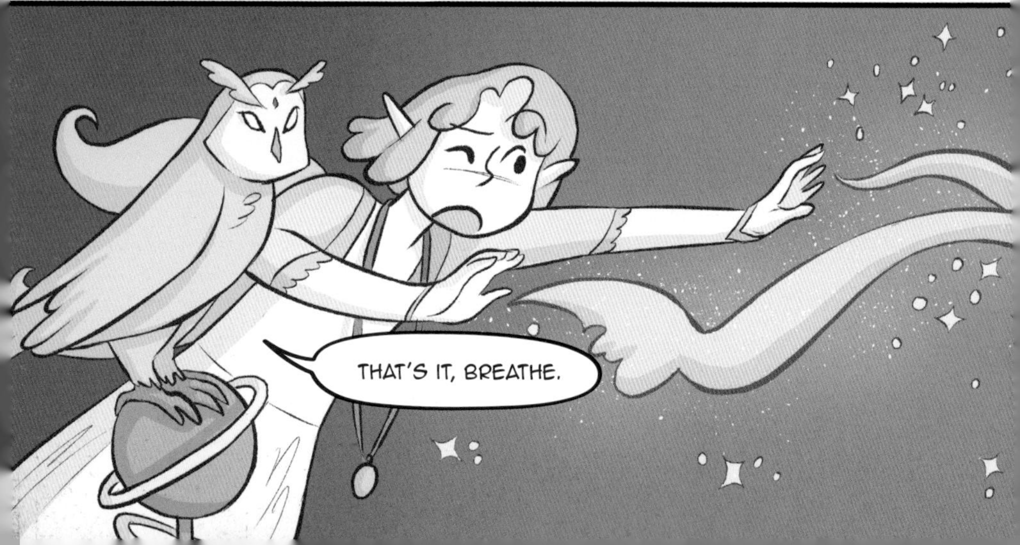
THAT'S IT, BREATHE.

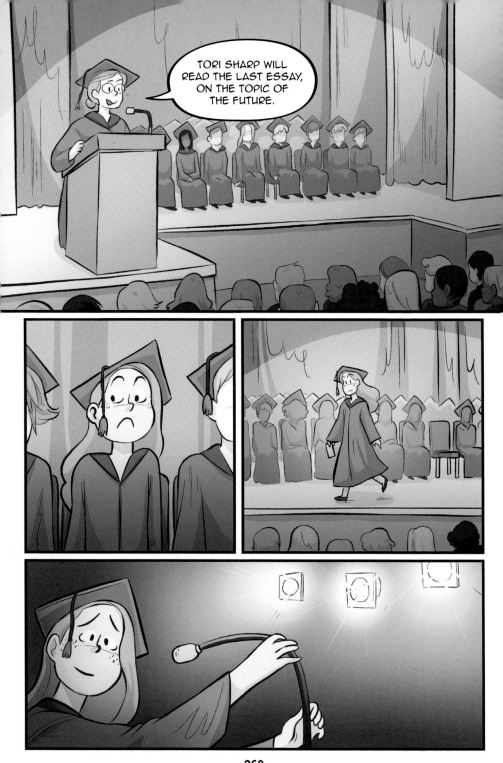

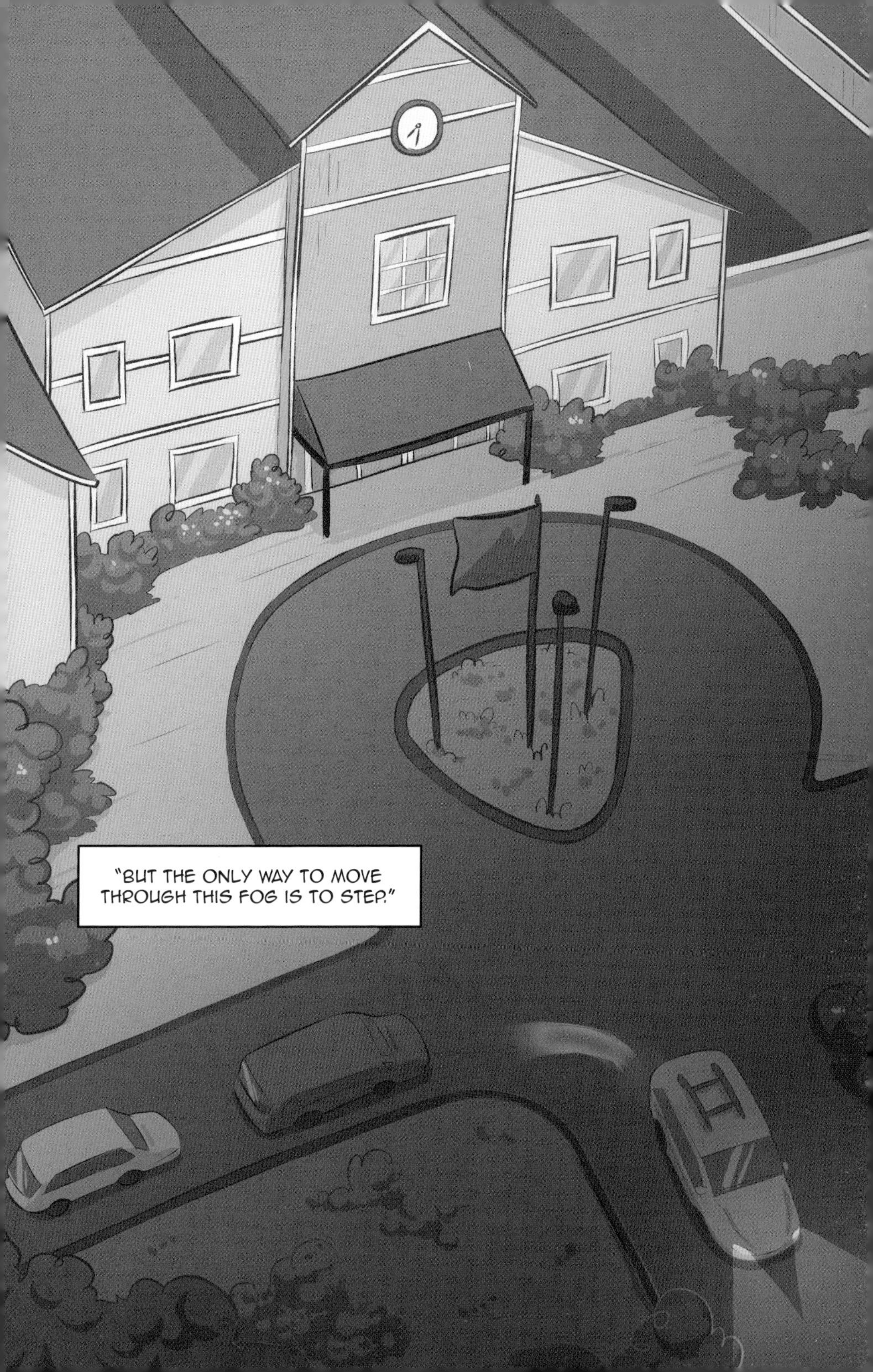
"BUT THE ONLY WAY TO MOVE THROUGH THIS FOG IS TO STEP."

267

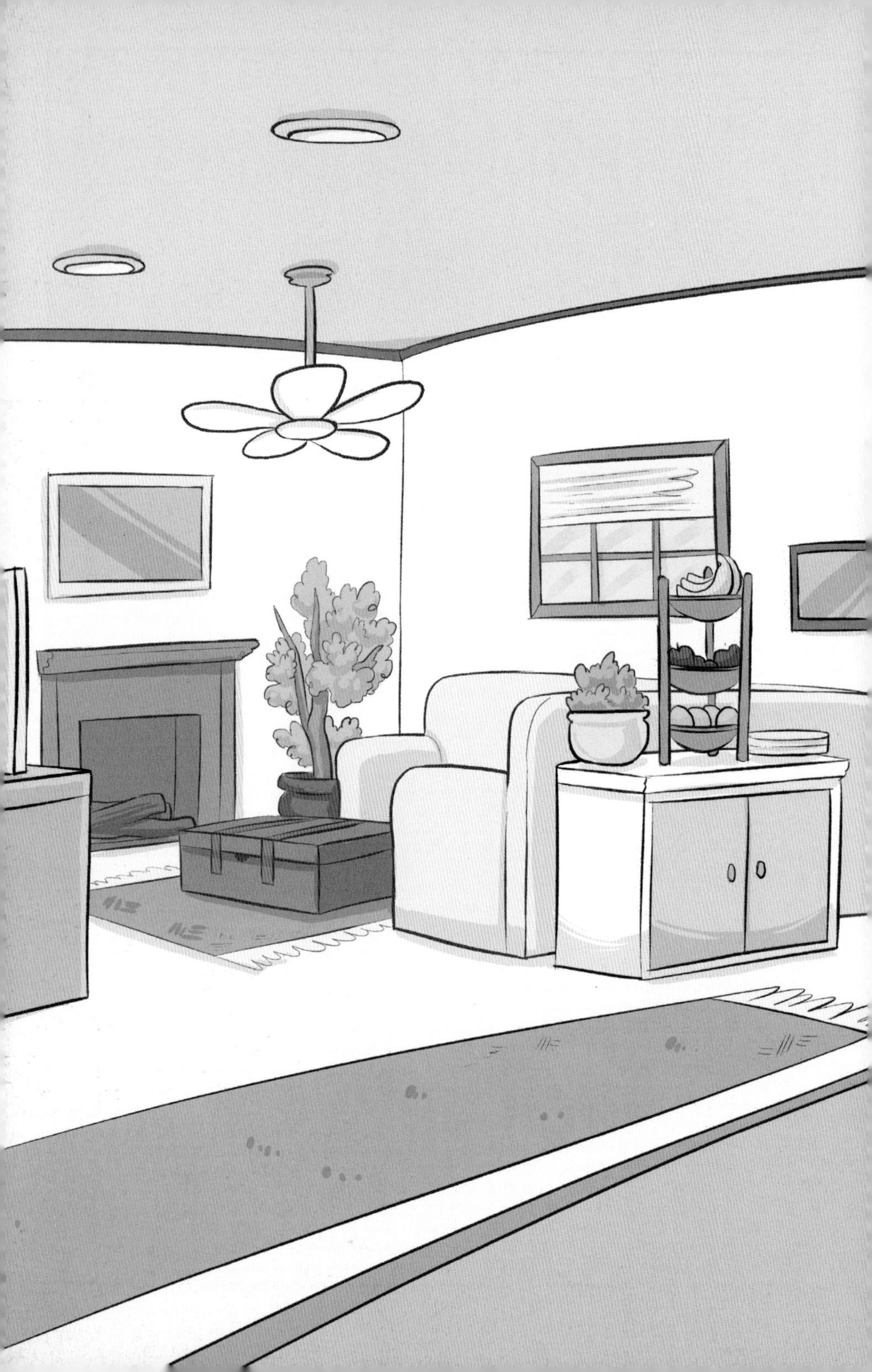

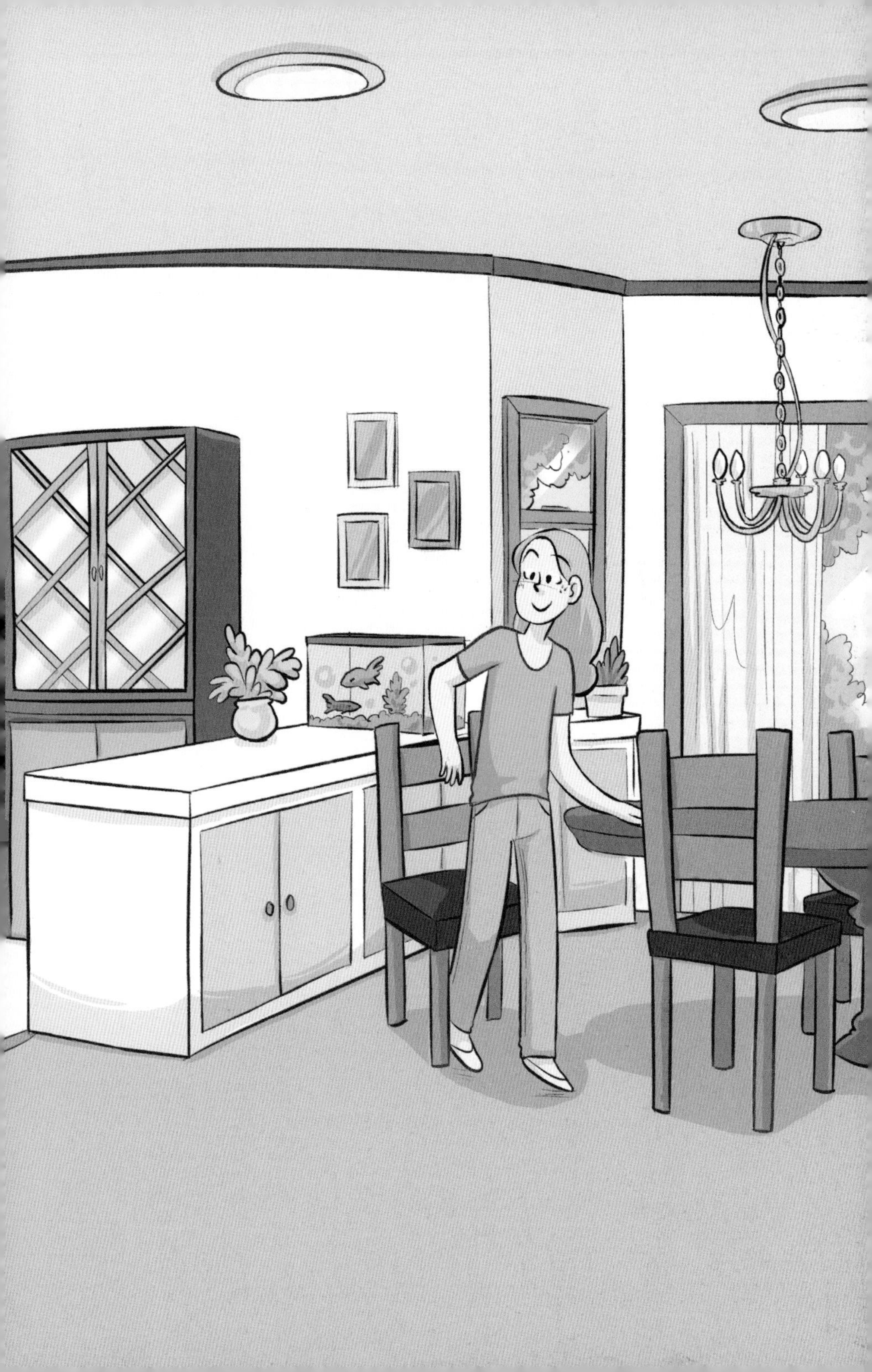

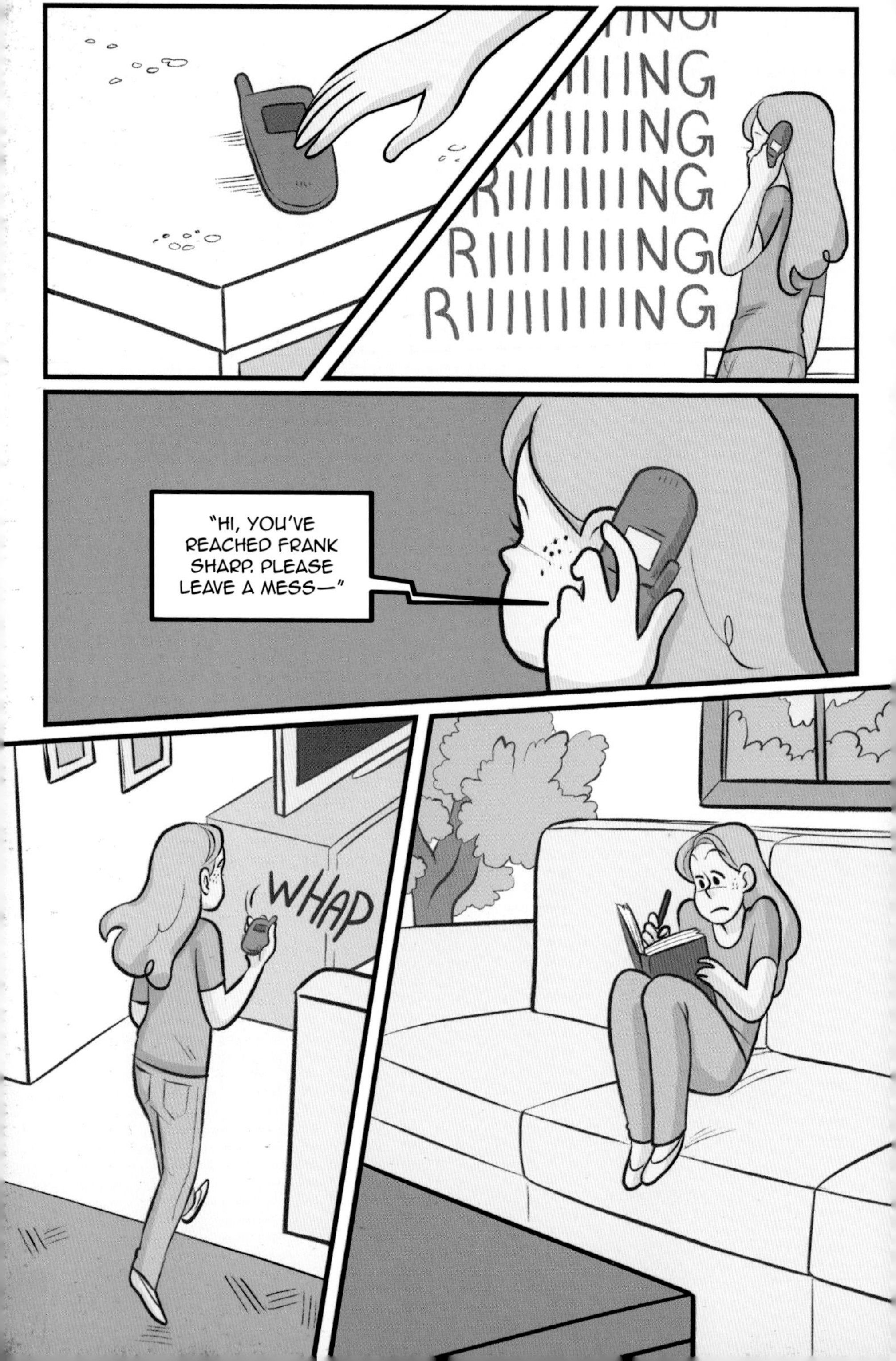
RIIIIING
RIIIIIING
RIIIIIIING
RIIIIIIIING
"HI, YOU'VE REACHED FRANK SHARP. PLEASE LEAVE A MESS—"
WHAP

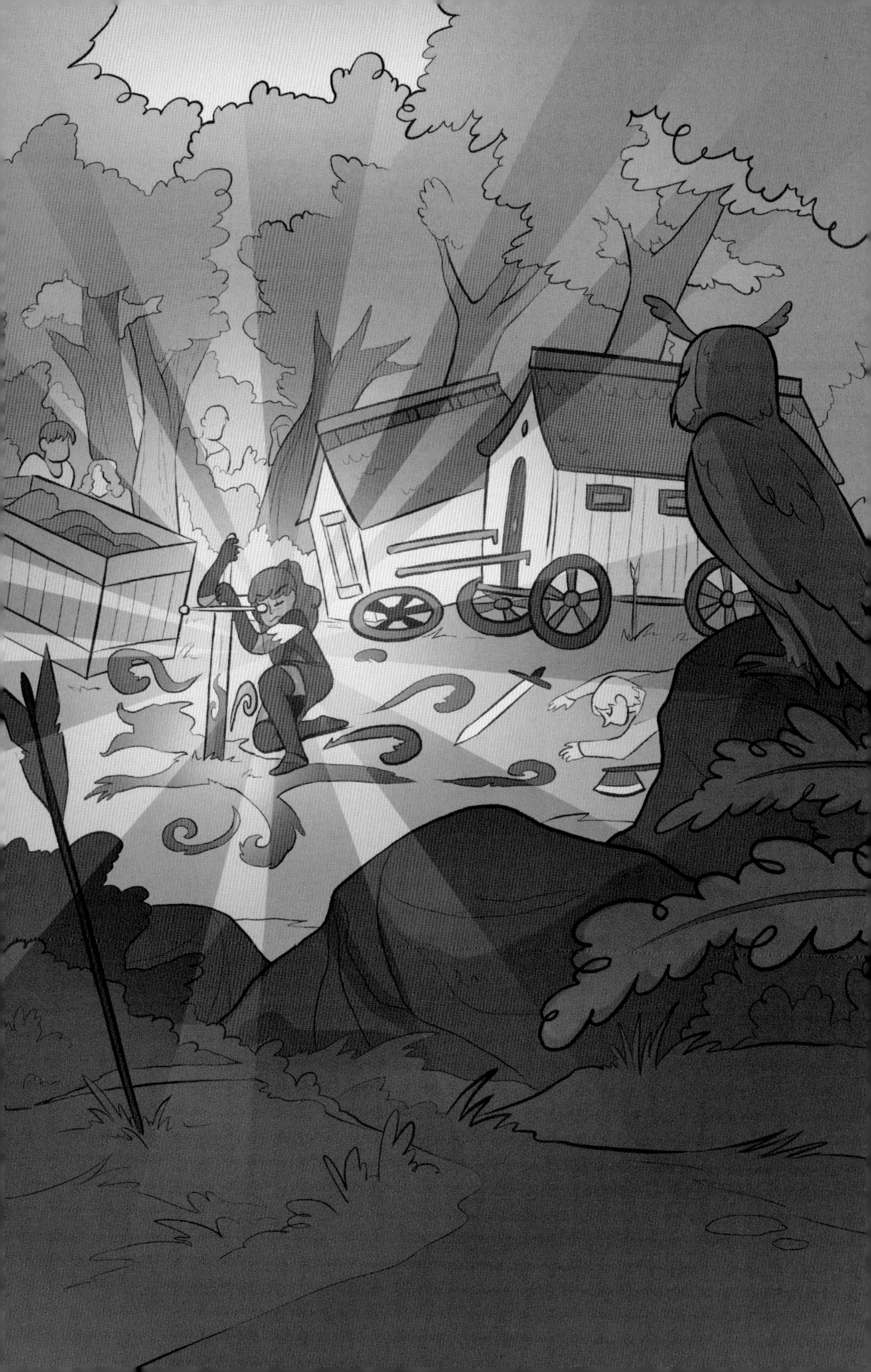

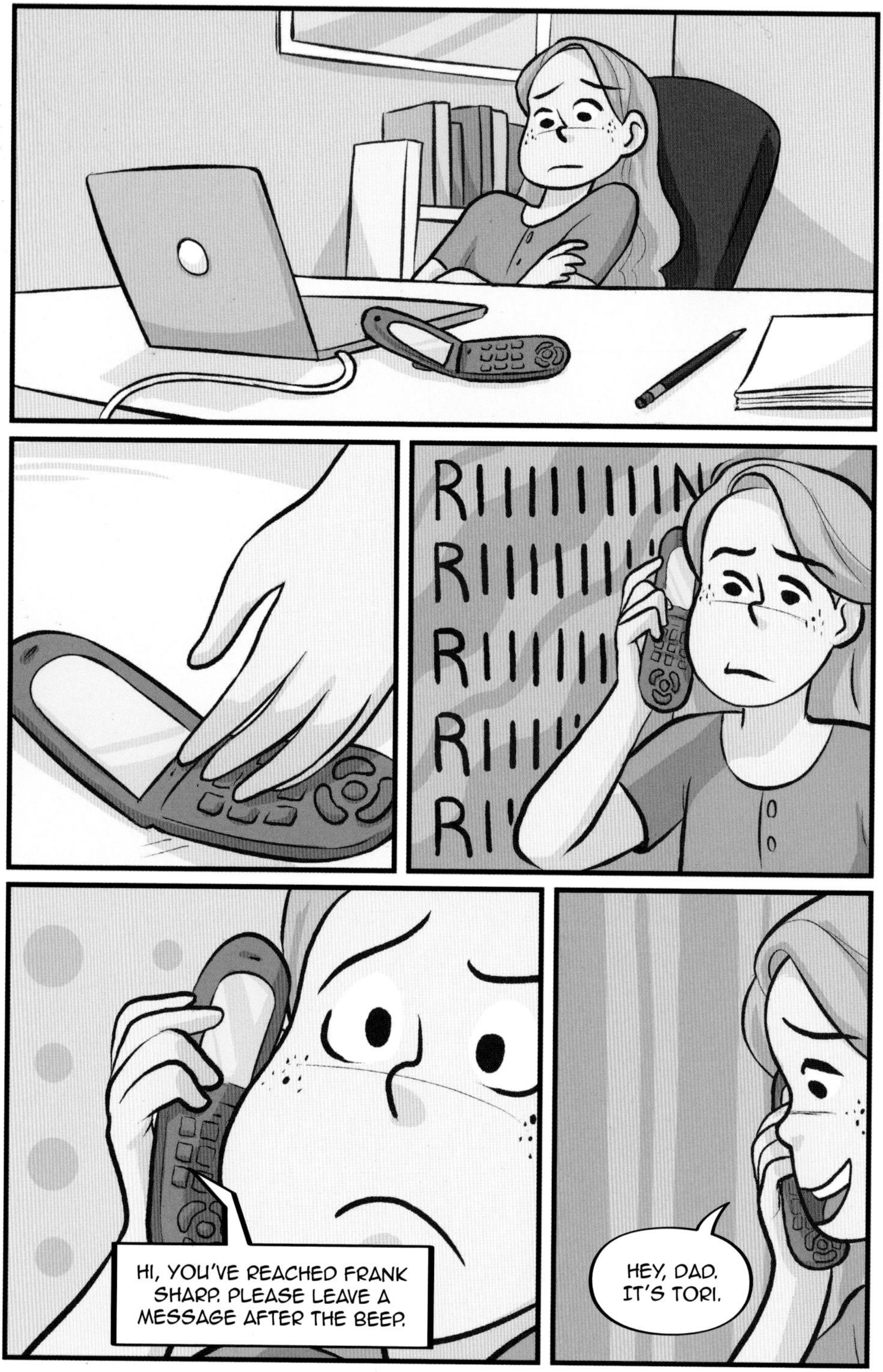
RIIIIIIIN
RIIIIIII
RIIIIIII
RIIII
RII
HI, YOU'VE REACHED FRANK SHARP. PLEASE LEAVE A MESSAGE AFTER THE BEEP.
HEY, DAD. IT'S TORI.

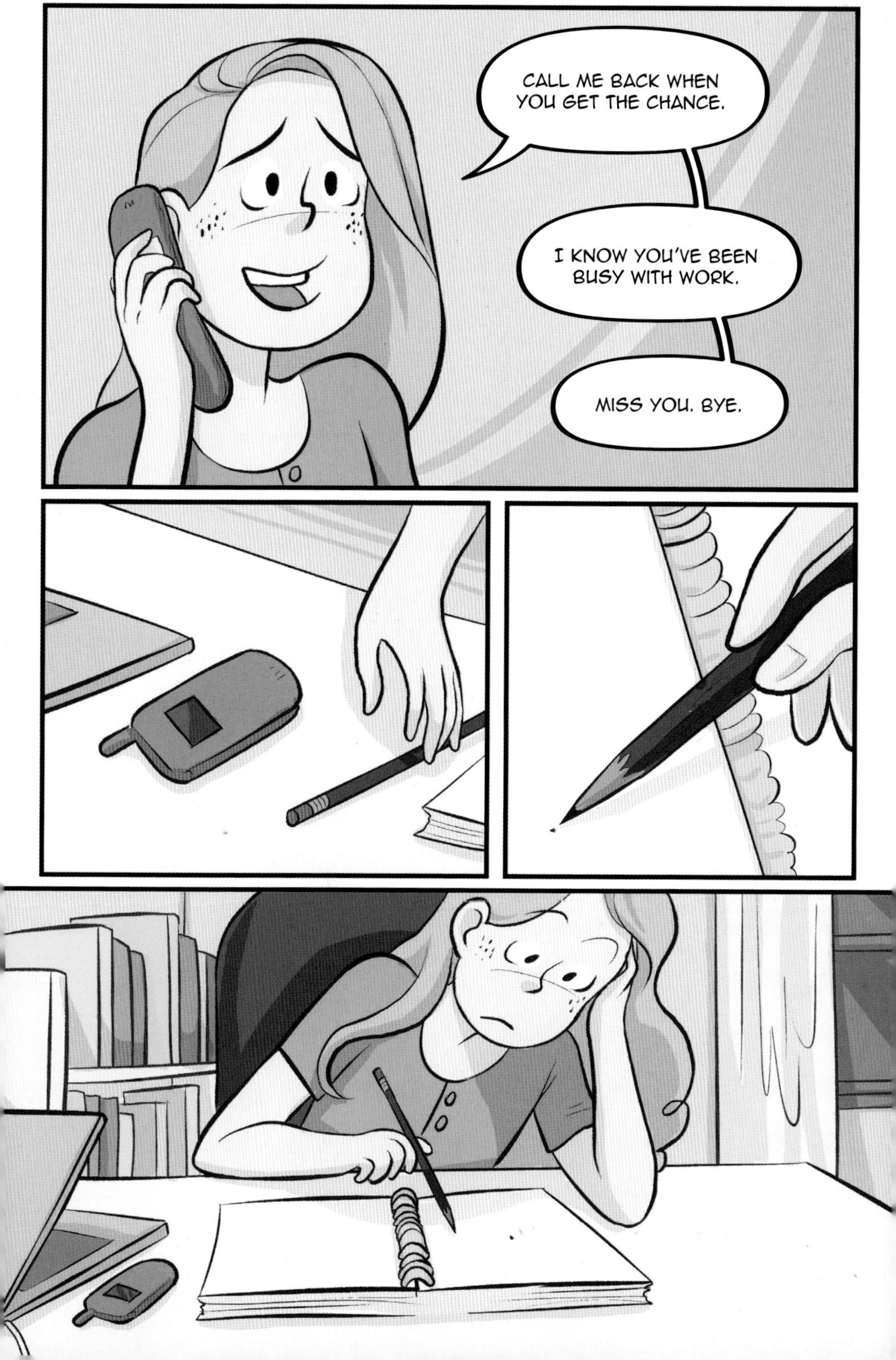
CALL ME BACK WHEN YOU GET THE CHANCE.
I KNOW YOU'VE BEEN BUSY WITH WORK.
MISS YOU. BYE.

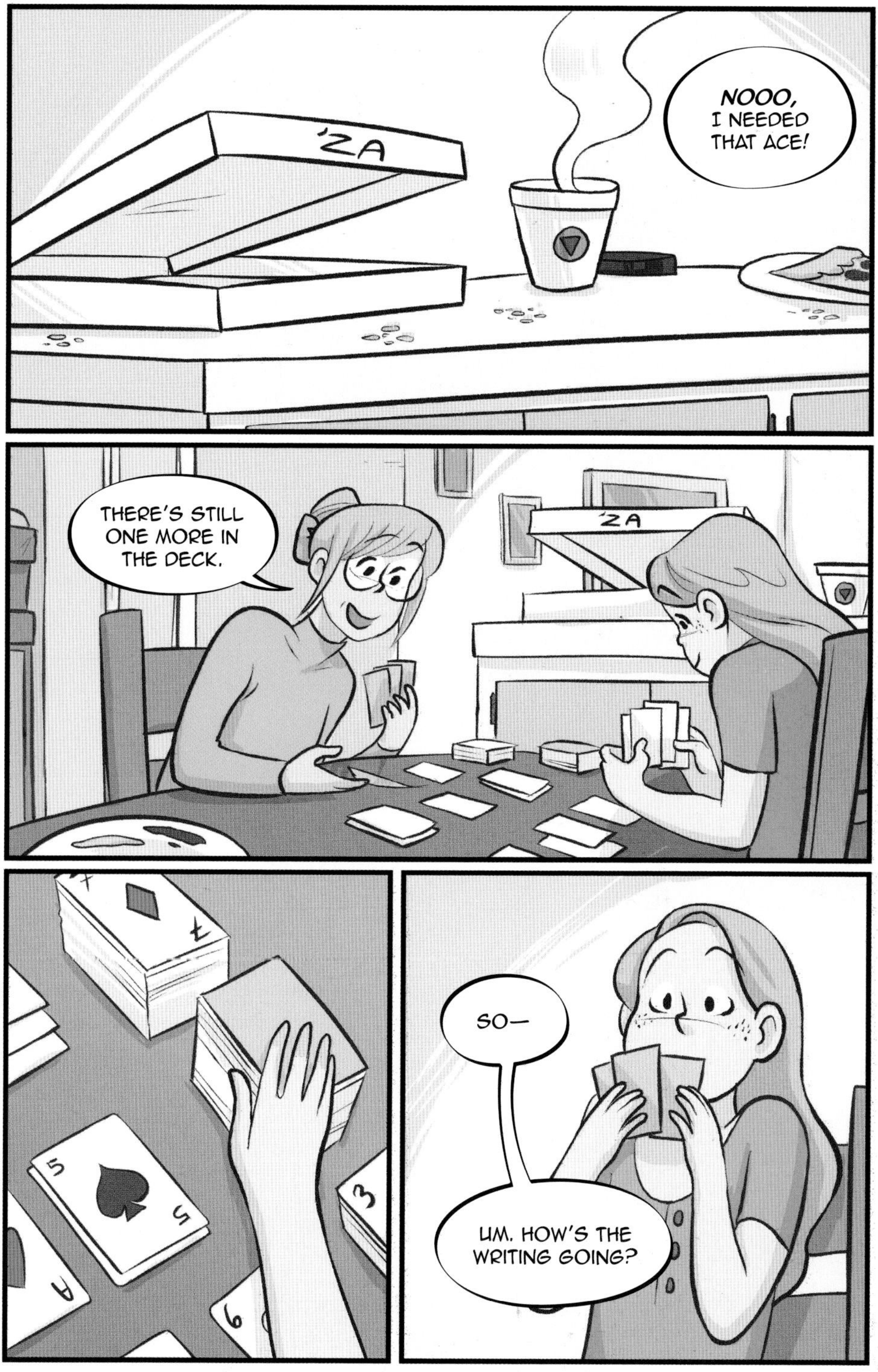
'ZA
NOOO, I NEEDED THAT ACE!
'ZA
THERE'S STILL ONE MORE IN THE DECK.
SO—
UM. HOW'S THE WRITING GOING?

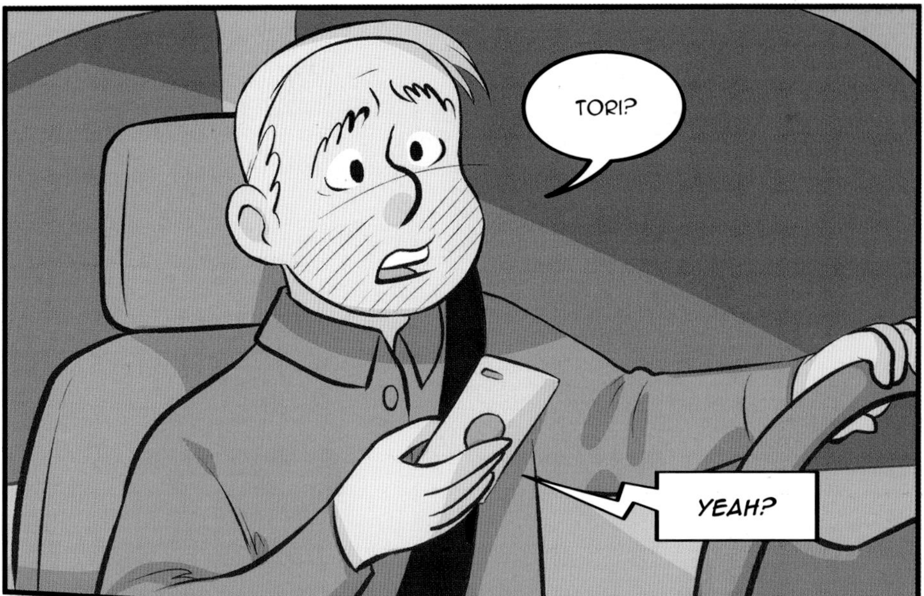
TORI?
YEAH?

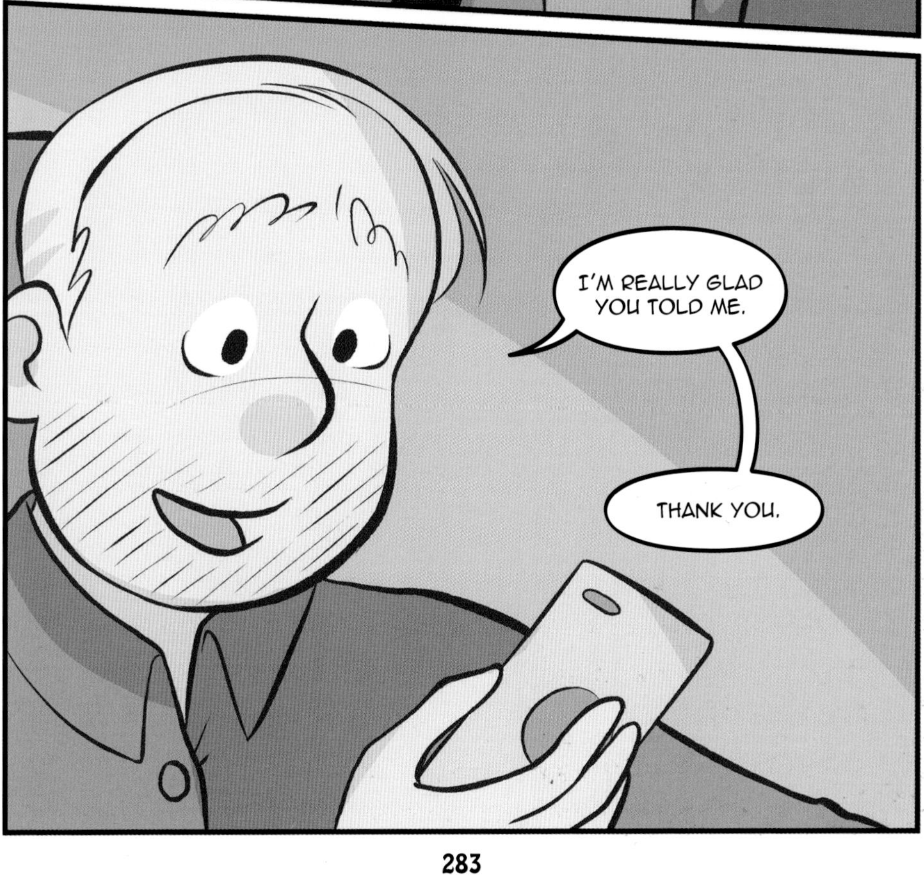
I'M REALLY GLAD YOU TOLD ME.
THANK YOU.

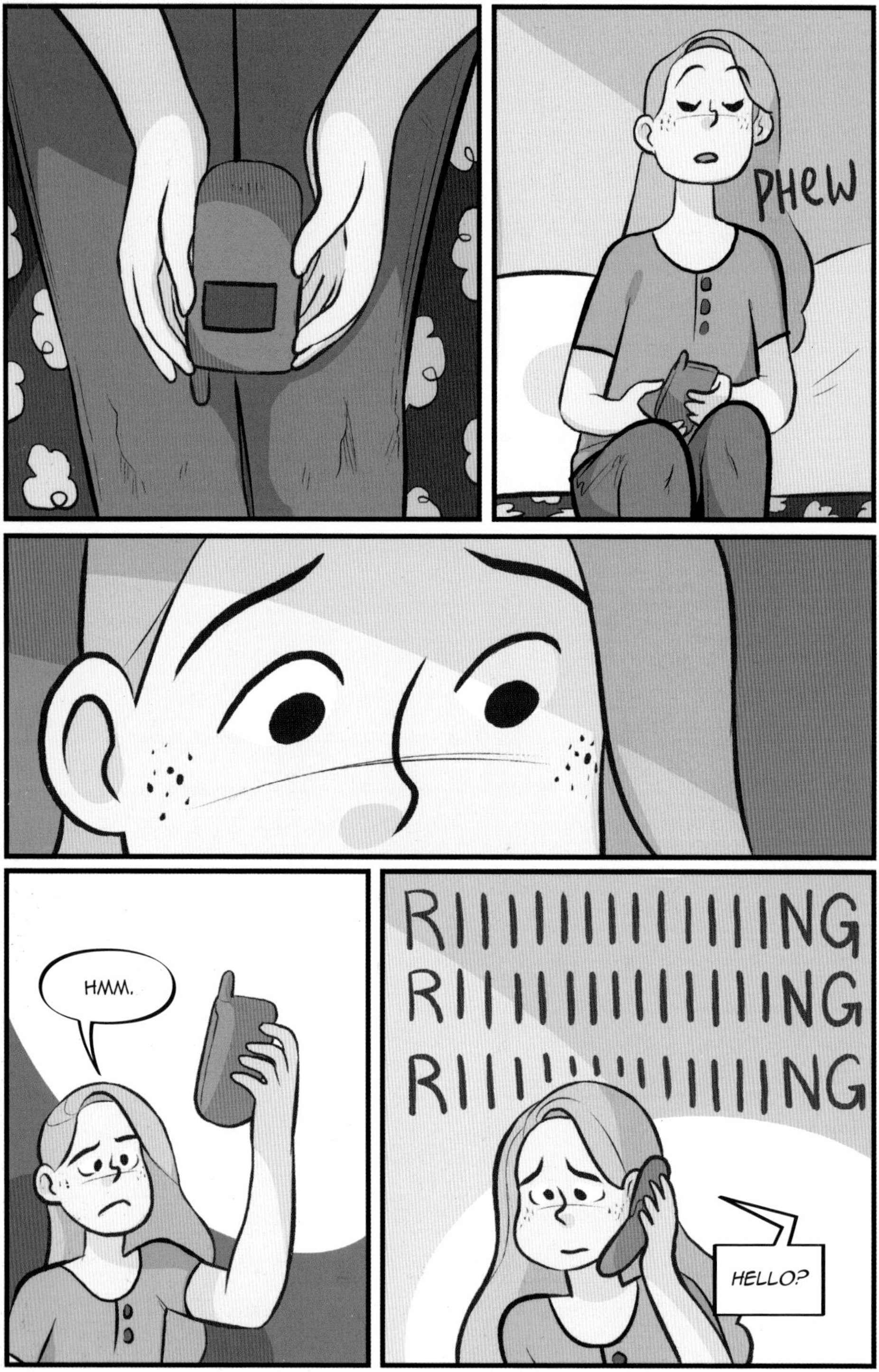
PHEW
HMM.
RIIIIIIIIIIIING
RIIIIIIIIIIIING
RIIIIIIIIIIIING
HELLO?

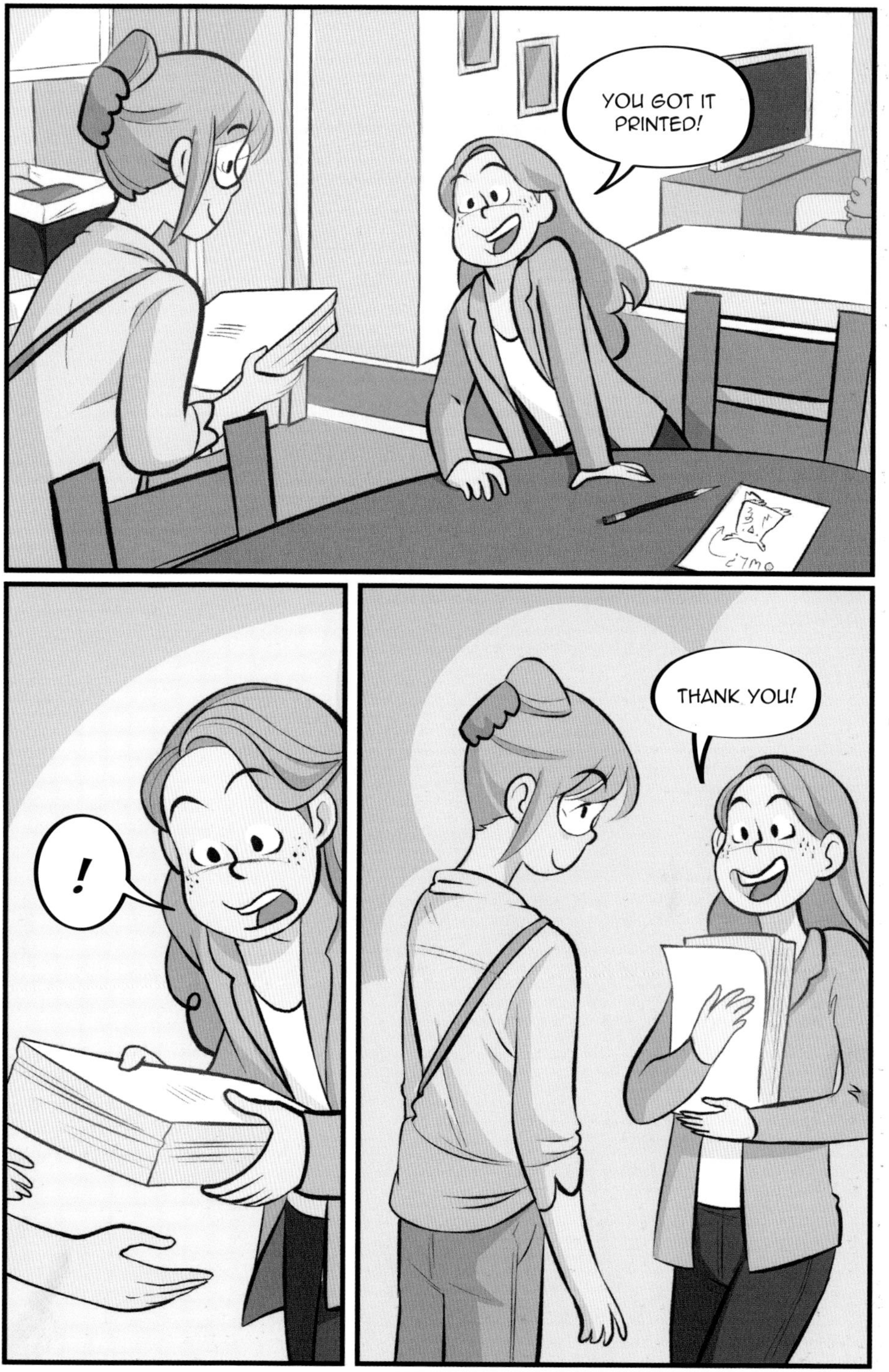
YOU GOT IT PRINTED!
!
THANK YOU!

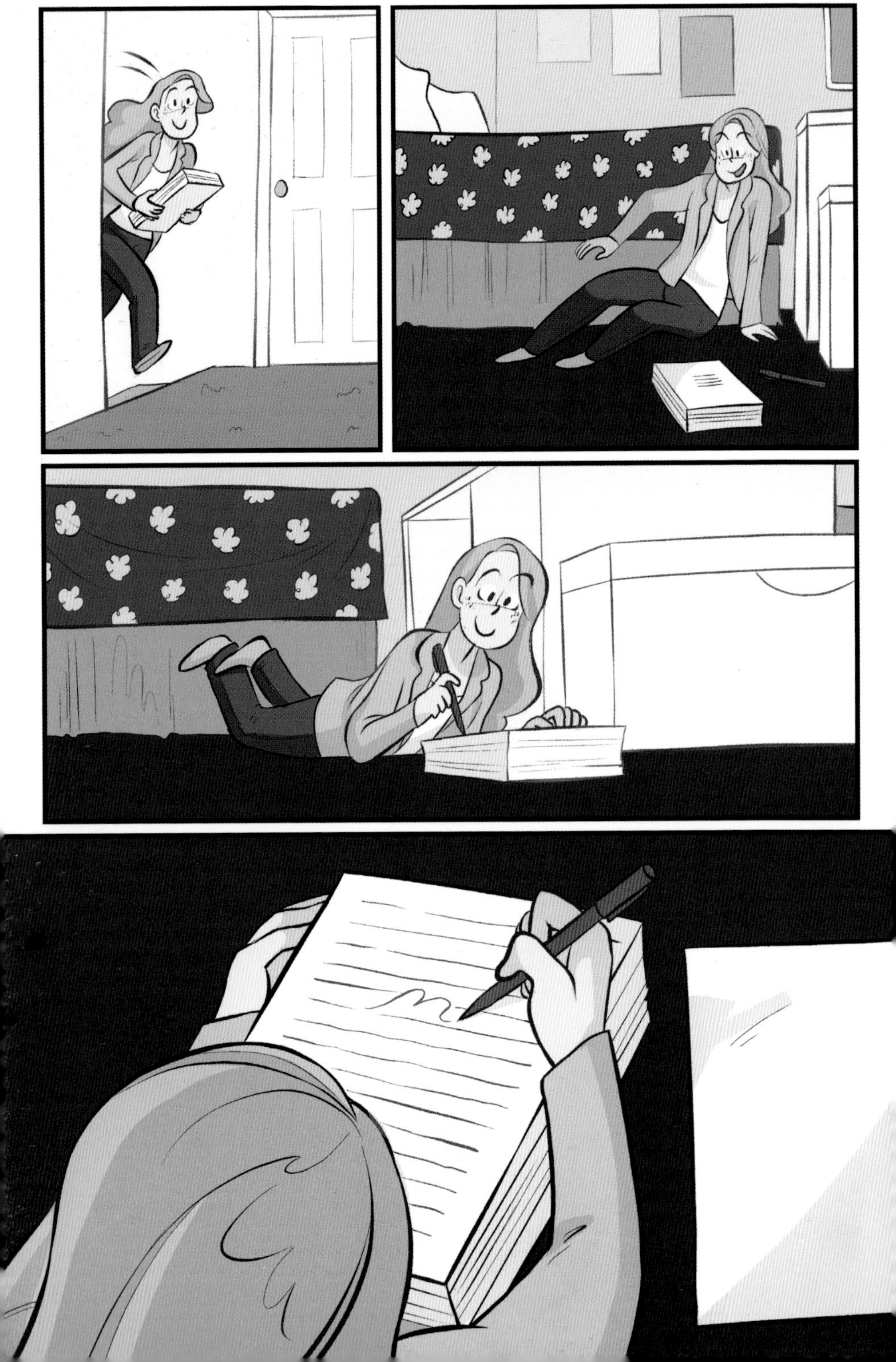

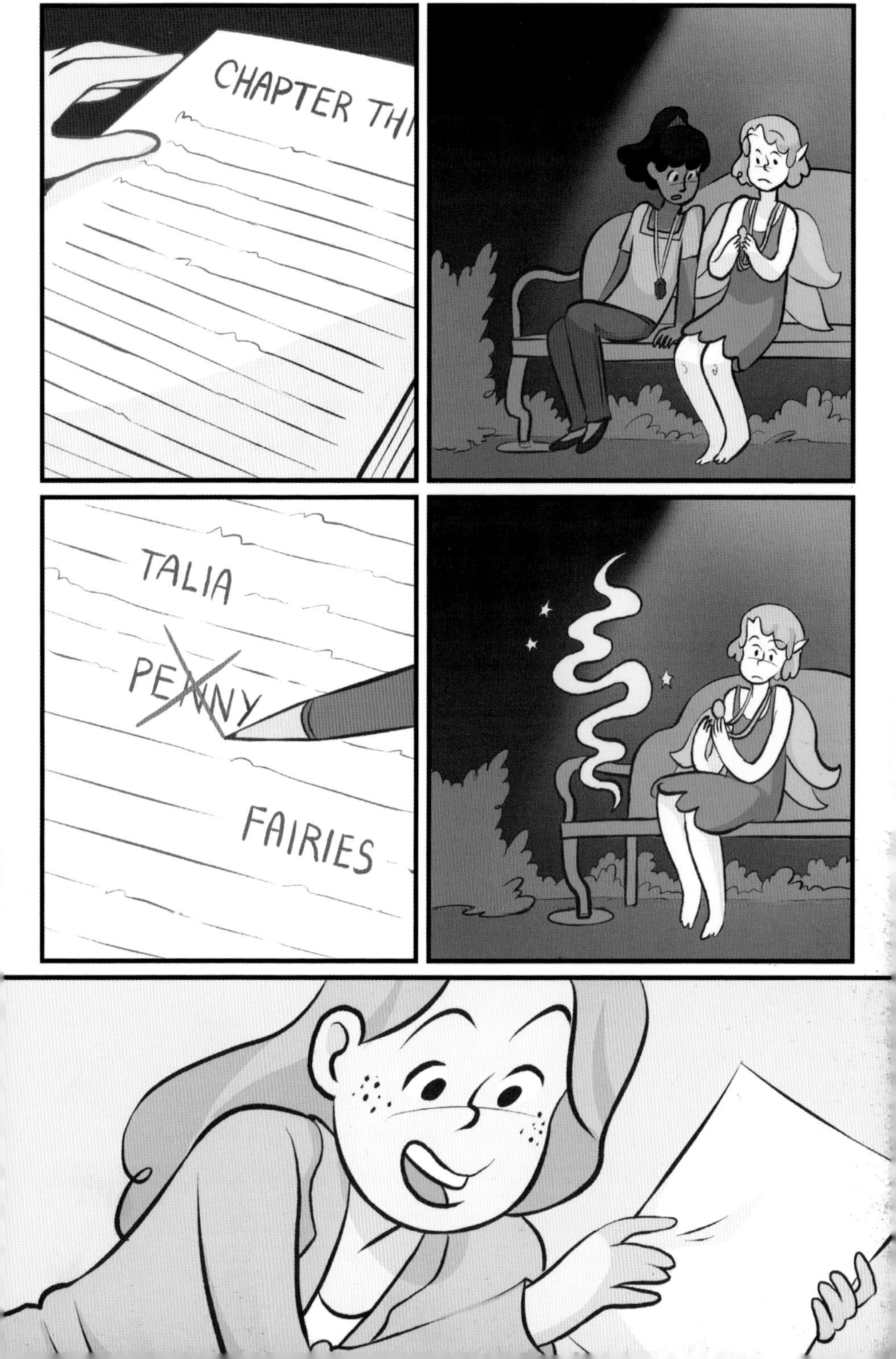
CHAPTER THI
TALIA
PENNY
FAIRIES

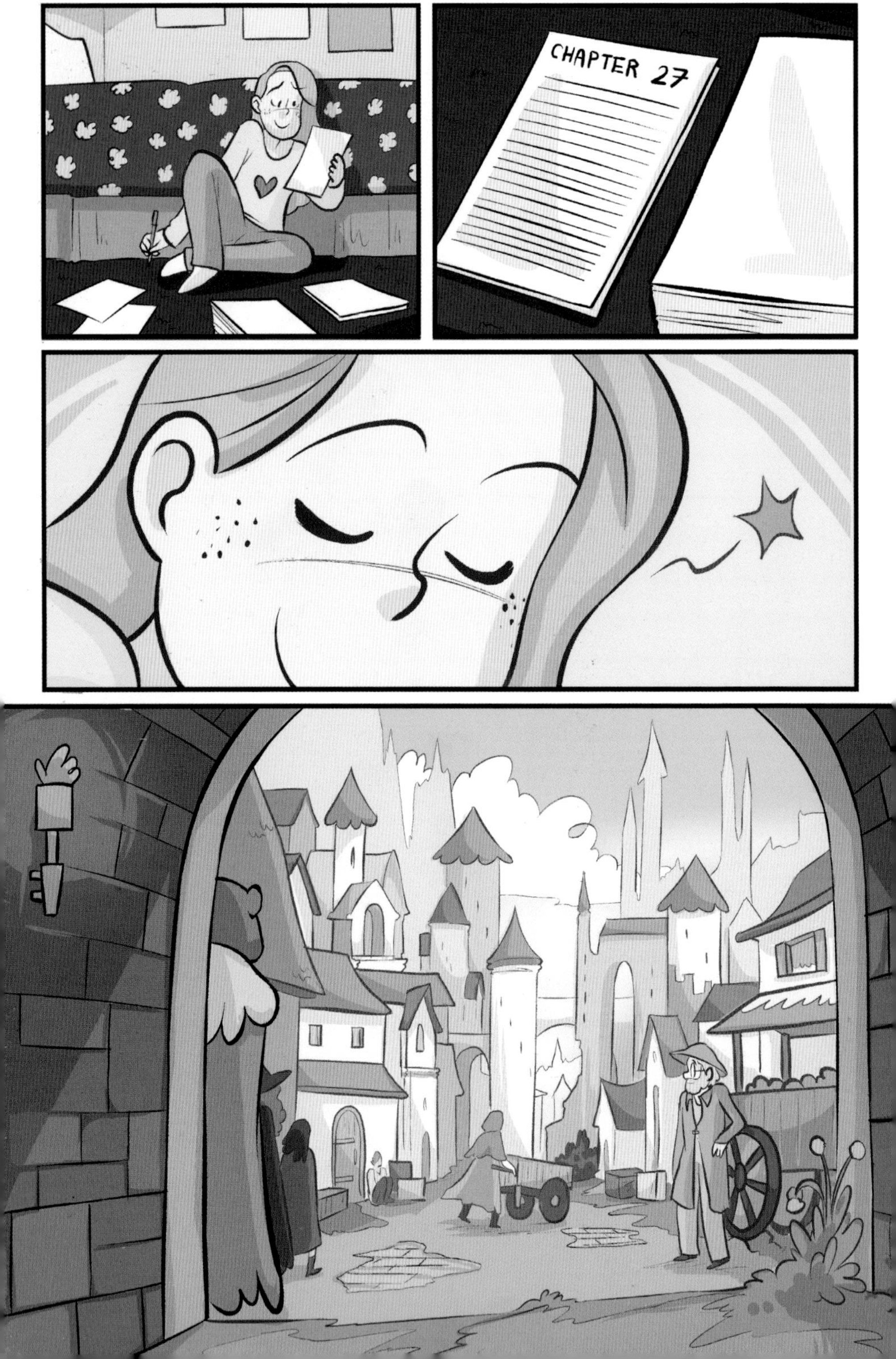
CHAPTER 27

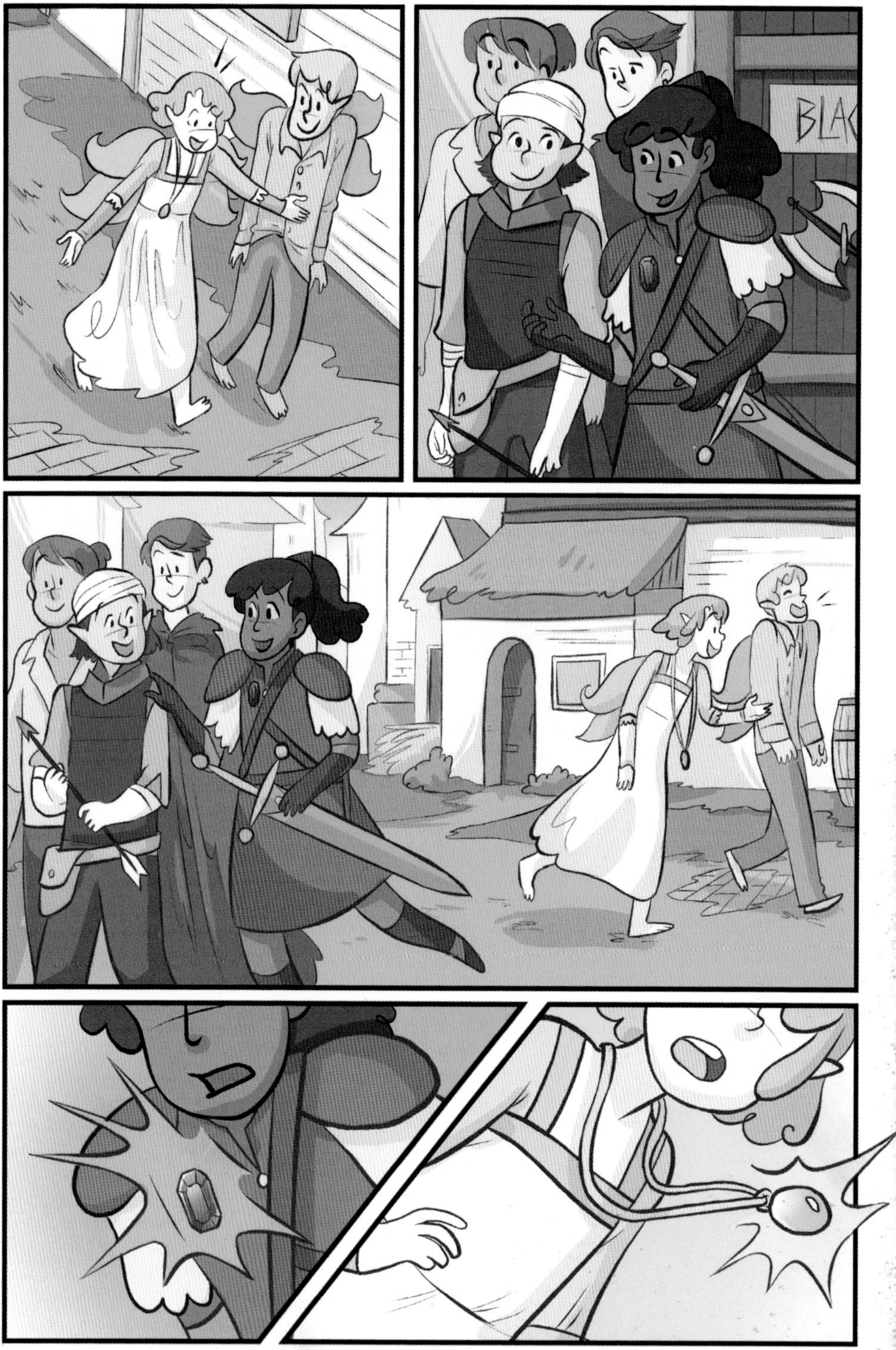
BLAC

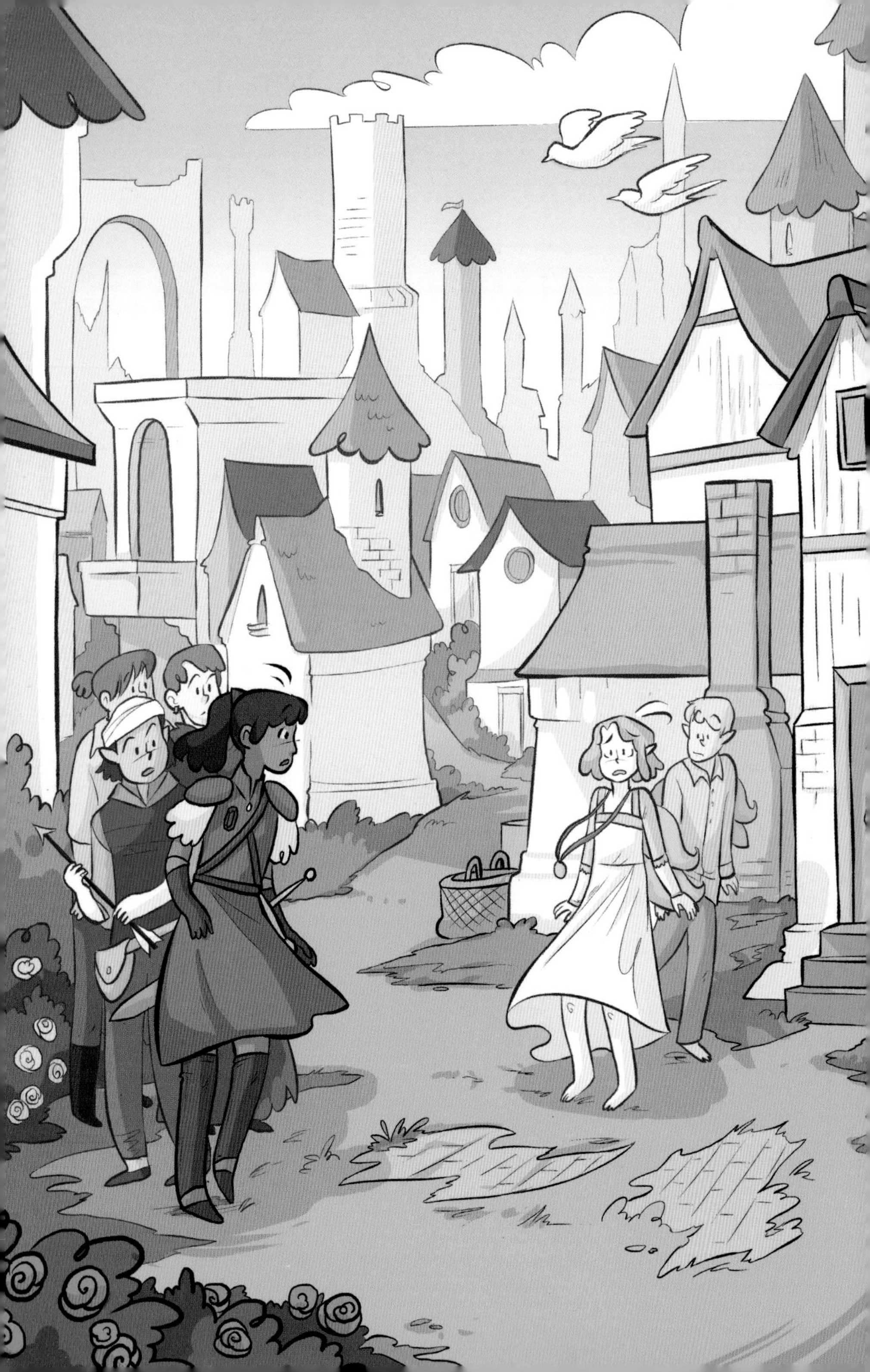

**W**RITING ABOUT YOUR LIFE IS A WILD, FUN, AND SCARY THING TO DO. This is a true story, which means it's a *story*. I tried to be as accurate as possible, but as the narrator, I got to decide how to tell it and which details to include. My family and friends will certainly remember these events differently.

This is a true story, but it's also about things that *aren't* real—what I imagined, hoped for, and wrote. I tried to be honest about what all of it *felt* like, but these events happened fifteen years ago, and I hope you'll forgive any inaccuracies. The only "lie" in these pages is how tidy my bedroom looks. I was more of a "messy artist" type of kid, but I didn't feel like drawing laundry and art supplies strewn across my floor in every panel. I am much tidier as an adult!

There are two events I could not have been present for but became family legends: the times my dad and Ryan broke holes in the walls of my mom's first house. I drew those how I *imagine* they must have happened. I remember Ryan trying to patch those holes with a can of plaster. I remember the blank sheet of paper he pinned over the hole and the outdated calendar covering my dad's footprint by the computer. What seemed like a big deal became trivial in the end. That house is gone now, so what do those holes matter? Sometimes the best way to erase a hole is to tear down the wall. Sometimes that's how you move forward.

Speaking of Ryan, I'd like to take a moment to brag about him: Ryan is one of the most supportive people about my art, and I love him very much. Growing up, we had a lot of reasons to dislike each other, but eventually we became friends. Now we play board games and talk about fantasy books. He's the coolest big brother!

I love my siblings, parents, and friends, and it's been a privilege to spend the past year drawing these stories about us. Since stories center on conflicts, a memoir tends to highlight the complexities and drama of personal relationships, skipping over most of the quiet, happy moments (since they would simply be less entertaining to read). A single book, no matter how thick, can't begin to capture a whole messy, complicated life or the nuances of a fractured family. Please think of this story as a single sentence in an even larger book. By the time I got the whole comic down on paper, I felt removed from my own story, as if I'd drawn someone else's life. Memory is funny like that; it changes all the time based on your new perceptions. Turning your childhood into a pile of cartoons changes how you remember it. So does growing up!

# CHARACTER DESIGN

To design the characters, I thought about what makes each of these people distinctive.

It was hardest to design Emily because she and I look so similar in real life! When we were teenagers, my friends would get us mixed up sometimes. My face is rounder (in the art and real life!), and I put her hair up, so you can't see that we have matching cowlicks. She resembles our dad, so I gave them both short tufts of hair on one side of their faces.

My dad's design came to me very quickly. I think he's secretly always been a cartoon.

I considered giving Ryan longer curls, since he wore his hair long in high school, but I ended up feeling like it looked too "flat" or exaggerated in this style of cartooning.

Taylor's hair was hard to get right because I wanted it to have some nice curves and movement but still look straight and glossy.

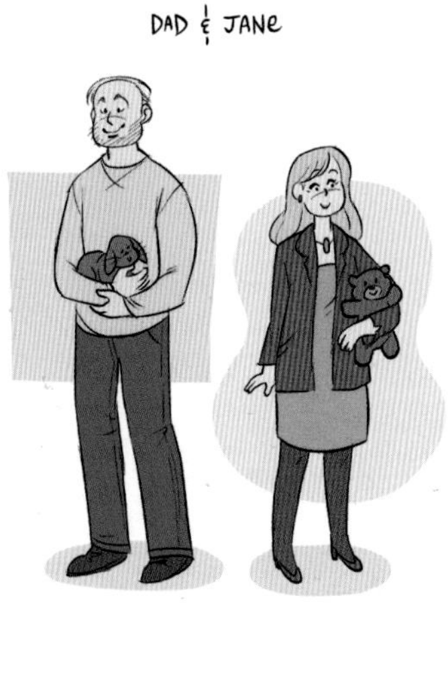
DAD & JANE

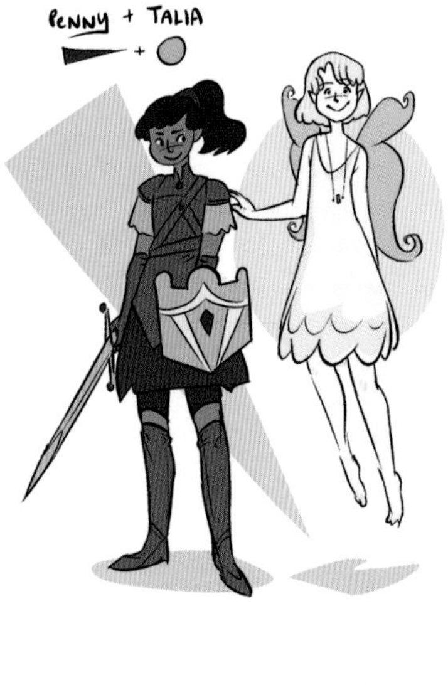
PENNY + TALIA

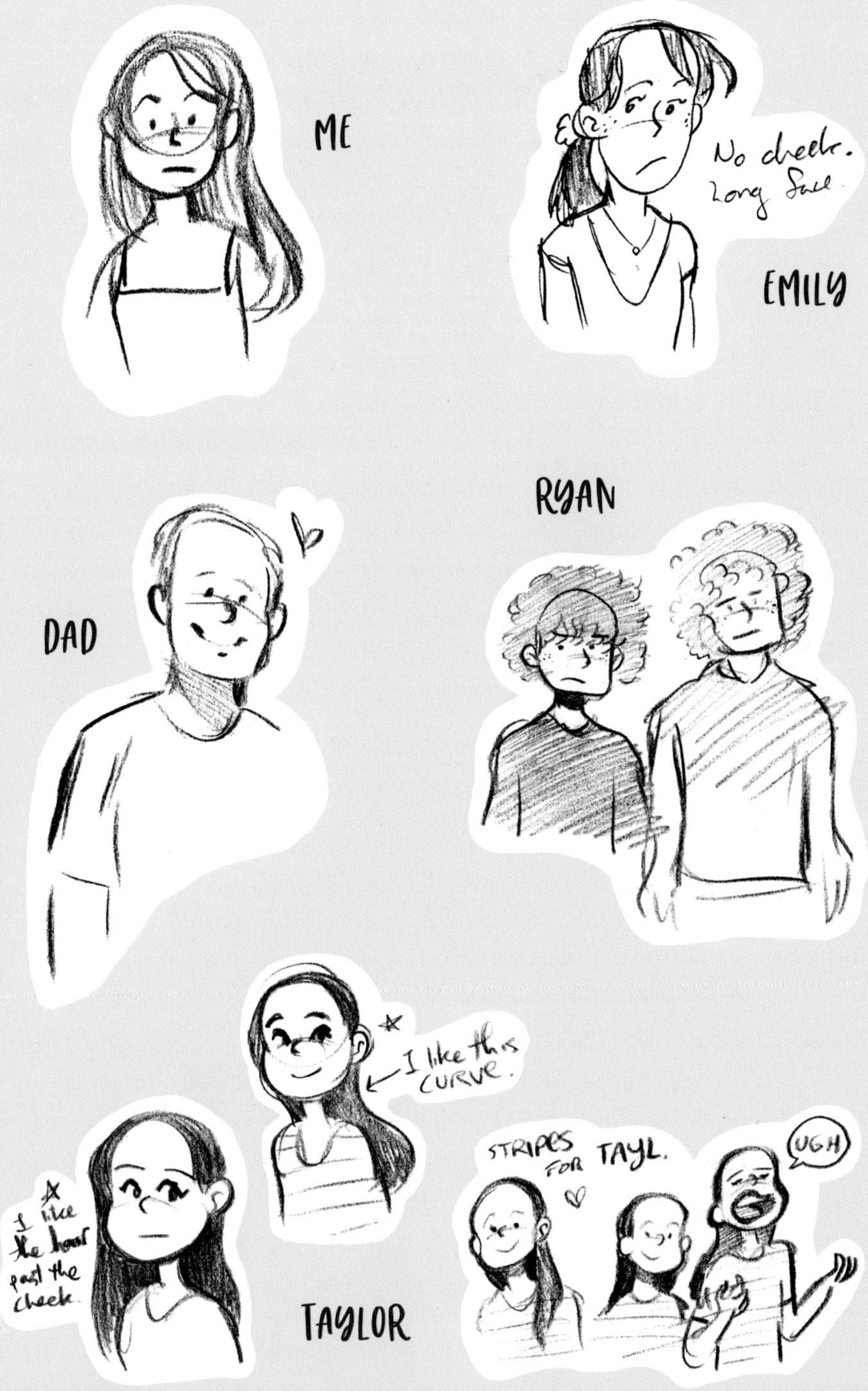
ME
EMILY
No cheek. Long face
DAD
RYAN
I like this CURVE.
I like the hair past the cheek
TAYLOR
STRIPES FOR TAYL.
UGH

# MATERIALS

When I first start designing a character, I draw them again and again very quickly. I take what I like in each sketch and apply it to the next one while also trying new things until I land on a design that feels right. Little, tiny features—like the size of a character's ears and how thick their eyebrows are—can change a character design so much!

At first, I used a pad of newsprint paper and a tool called a china marker to draw the characters over and over and over, not spending too long on each sketch. China markers are also called grease pencils, apparently. I'm not sure which name is more common. Professors at the Savannah College of Art and Design—where I went to college—called them china markers because you can use them to write on hard, nonporous materials like porcelain...or china!

China markers aren't typical "markers." They're waxy like crayons, but very smooth and good for gesture drawing—quick sketches that capture (and often exaggerate) the energy of a pose or expression. I like these markers because, unlike pencils, they don't smudge much, and you can't erase; you have to keep moving forward and try again!

I also used ballpoint or felt-tip pens to do some messy, flowy sketches. Switching tools gives you a new kind of line quality, so it can help you notice different things about your designs and make you really think about the choices you're making while you draw. I love to doodle in pen.

Then, once I had a better idea of what the characters would look like, I did some tighter drawings in pencil and took notes about what was working in the designs. I also went "shopping" for them; I dressed them up in clothes they'd wear.

Finally, I did some clean digital drawings of the characters with a focus on each one's shape and color language.

Giving each character a basic shape gave me something to fall back on when I wasn't sure why they didn't look quite right in a panel. If Penny looked off, I tried to incorporate isosceles triangles, and if Ryan looked off, I tried to make his head shape and pose look more like trapezoids.

# PAGE PROCESS

Each page went through four phases: roughs, pencils, inks, and colors.

Roughs are quick, messy layouts. I try not to take more than 20-30 minutes roughing out a page, unless there's going to be an intricate background and I want to use reference photos.

My roughs are pretty detailed compared to what many artists do! Some comic artists do a "thumbnail" stage before the roughs that's even messier and squigglier, using stick figures to show where the characters are. Whatever works! I feel like my characters' body language and expressions are so important to the storytelling that I really need to see them during this stage.

Pencils are more refined than roughs, and inks are the final line art. Even though they're called "pencils" and "inks," I drew most of them digitally on my laptop, using a Wacom Intuos Pro medium drawing tablet and Clip Studio Paint Pro. The amazing thing about comics, though, is that you don't need special tools. You can draw comics with just paper and pencil, crayons or sidewalk chalk, or sticky notes. I used to draw comics on lined notebook paper on my music stand in band class!

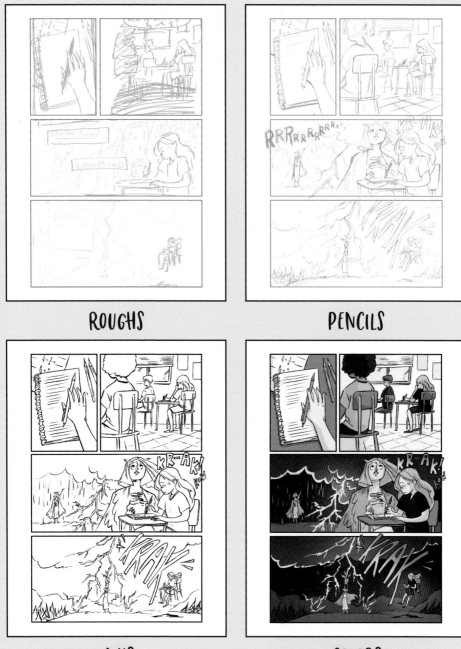

ROUGHS

PENCILS

INKS

COLORS

# ACKNOWLEDGMENTS

This book simply wouldn't exist without my agent, Brent Taylor. Thank you for pushing me to write this memoir when I was tangled up in a few different story ideas. Thank you for your masterful pep talks and tireless dedication. You saw the spark in my messy first draft of *Just Pretend* and helped me see it, too. Sometimes you see the statue inside the marble before I've even started carving, like only the very best agents can.

Thank you to Andrea Colvin, my magnificent, brilliant editor, for helping me see straight into the heart of my own book. I feel lucky every day that you, specifically, acquired *Just Pretend*.

Thank you to the entire team at LBYR and to the colorists and letterers who lent their expertise to this comic and made it shine. Putting together a book like this takes a tremendous amount of work, and the fingerprints of so many people hide all over these pages.

Thank you to the many teachers who impacted me, among them Brad Nicklas, Ellen Jacko, Brian Ralph, John Larison, and Kit Seaton.

Many hugs to my critique partners and friends: Chelsea Crane, Hannah Golden, Gabrielle Stern, Ragon Dickard, Zach Turcich, Jeana Coppa, Carly Racklin, Sydnie Long, Rachel Lynn Solomon, Alec Marsh, and Karin de Weille.

A special thank you to Kel Lyle, my amazing friend and critique partner who patiently reads every scrap of writing I push at her (and who's always down to watch cartoons), and to Aimee Meester, a kindred spirit, for being my virtual coworker and Dungeon Master while I drew this book. I'm proud of you, too.

Thanks to Roseanne Wells, my mentor while I queried agents and worked on the proposal for *Just Pretend*, and to Jennifer De Chiara for the apprenticeship that followed. I have learned so much from both of you and the whole team at JDLA about the world of books and what makes good writing.

I owe enormous thanks to my friends and family members who encouraged me to tell this story. Thank you to my sister, one of the very first people I told when I decided to write a memoir, and to my dad, who knew I was a writer before I did.

Although I had many wonderful friends in middle school, this story—about writing and family—kept circling back to my friendship with Taylor. Thank you, Tayl, for being my first writing partner and for reminiscing with me for hours while I collected memories for this book. Here's to twenty more years of friendship and many more after that.

**TORI SHARP** is a Seattle-based author-illustrator and a swing and blues dancer with a BFA in sequential art from SCAD. You can find her online at noveltori.com and on Twitter @noveltori. This is her debut graphic novel.